Carving the CCA Circus

Presented by the Caricature Carvers of America

FOX BOOKS
Fox Chapel Publishing Co Inc.

Fox Chapel Publishing Co., Inc.
1970 Broad Street
East Petersburg, PA 17520

Publisher: Alan Giagnocavo
Project Editor: Ayleen Stellhorn
Desktop Specialist: Robert Altland, Altland Design
Photography: Bob Polett, VMI Productions
CCA Project Editor: Bob Travis
CCA Publication Committee: Bob Travis
Dave Stetson
Dave Dunham
Desiree Hajny

ISBN # 1-56523-094-9

To order your copy of this book,
please send check or money order
for $19.95 plus $2.50 to:
Fox Chapel Book Orders
1970 Broad Street
East Petersburg, PA 17520

Try your favorite book supplier first!

TABLE OF CONTENTS

An Introduction To This Book

This book is about a circus, and it is about woodcarving, but most of all it is about creativity. As you read the following pages, note how each carver approaches the creative process. The circus brings back wonderful memories from childhood for most adults. Because of this, many of the contributors to this book initiated the creative process by remembering circuses that they had attended at an earlier time. After that though, the approach varies for different people. Take note of how they develop an initial idea. Some just sketch it on a piece of basswood and begin carving. Some draw extensively. Others use mannequins. Still others work the idea out in clay before beginning the carving process. However, in spite of the variation in approaches, there is one common element in this book: In every case the creative process leads to an original carving.

The pieces featured here are the individual efforts of twenty-three carvers representing every geographical region of the United States. Each is a member of a carving group called the Caricature Carvers of America. There was some communication among contributors, but in most cases any one member did not know what the others were doing. CCA members did have a clearing house for ideas so that carvings would not be duplicated. But as expected, not everyone cleared their ideas with the committee. Rather, they just carved what they thought should be in a circus. Knowing that, it might seem surprising that such a diverse group of carvers could come together with such an all-encompassing project. Indeed, it might seem surprising to most people, but not to us. Well, in truth, maybe we were a little surprised. But we accomplished the same result with the *Full Moon Saloon*, our first joint carving project, and we were confident that we could repeat it with the circus.

We would like to leave you with one final thought. We hope that you will use this book to enhance your own creativity. We have included patterns for many of the major carvings in the circus. If you are a novice carver, feel free to carve any, or all, of the pieces in this book. If you are an intermediate carver, try using the figures in different scenes or modifying the patterns to fit your needs. For example, try carving some of these characters in other positions or engaged in different activities. Finally, if you are an accomplished carver, we hope that this book will in some way stimulate your interest in enhancing your own creative abilities.

The Caricature Carvers of America

The Caricature Carvers of America

Seven years have passed since a group of ten wood carvers with the common goal of promoting the art of caricature carving met in the back room of the Paxton Lumber Company in Ft. Worth, Texas, to discuss the formation of a national organization to further that goal. From that meeting came the Caricature Carvers of America (CCA). The founding group consisted of fifteen nationally recognized carvers representing a broad geographical distribution and diverse styles of caricature carving. Since the inception of the CCA, two members have resigned, one has moved to emeritus status, and twelve new members have been elected, bringing the 1997 active membership to 24. The newly formed organization made no claims as being "the best," although many of the members are readily recognized as being among the elite in the carving community.

The purpose of the CCA is two-fold: 1) to promote and elevate the appreciation of caricature woodcarving within both the woodcarving community and the general public, and 2) to provide a non-competitive environment that will encourage growth in skill, creativity and excellence among its members and the carving public. To achieve these goals the members of the CCA have embarked on an ambitious schedule of activities, which includes exhibitions of their work, group-taught seminars and the publication of trend-setting books on caricature carving.

Their premier exhibit was held at the National Museum of Woodcarving in Custer, South Dakota, during the summer of 1991. That exhibit, consisting of 40–50 original carvings, has returned to Custer each year. Other exhibits have been presented on several occasions. The annual meeting always includes a public reception during which recent carvings are exhibited by members in attendance. The annual meeting is held in different geographical regions of the United States each year to make the exhibits accessible to the maximum number of people.

To enhance their professional growth, CCA members take every opportunity to learn from each other. A "creativity day" is scheduled with each annual meeting. The creativity day at the 1994 meeting in Ft. Worth, Texas, was utilized to assemble the *Full Moon Saloon,* and in 1996 it was used to set up the CCA *Circus*. In addition, the meetings typically include a program that focuses on creativity in caricature carving for local woodcarvers.

The CCA membership is strongly committed to education in woodcarving. A group-taught seminar series was initiated in Ft. Worth, Texas, in 1992. Since the inception of this program, the CCA has presented yearly seminars in California, and in 1996, the schedule was expanded to include sessions in Iowa and New York. These seminars utilize the talents of several CCA instructors, each teaching one- and two-day classes over a three- or four-day weekend. In addition, all members provide seminar instruction on a regular basis.

Their first book, *Carving the Full Moon Saloon* was published by Fox Chapel in 1995. That book, featuring the work of 21 CCA members, includes over 150 color photographs, substantial text concerning the creative aspect of caricature carving and patterns for each of the principal carvings in the saloon.

The Origin of the CCA Circus

The CCA *Full Moon Saloon* scene and book were very well received and seemed to be a big step toward achieving our goal of making the public aware of the art of woodcarving in general and caricature carving in particular. There was a quiet consensus among the group that we should create a sequel to the saloon, but what would it be?

At the International Congress of Woodcarving in Davenport, Iowa, June 1995, several members were brainstorming possibilities for a new project. Many ideas were proposed, but when a circus was suggested, eyes lit up and wheels began turning. There were so many possibilities: clowns in all manner of situations, animals, wagons, high wire artists, the ringmaster, cotton candy vendors, members of the audience....

The decision on any new project was set to be made during the CCA annual meeting in Albuquerque, New Mexico, October 1995. A committee was set up to build a circus mock up with cardboard characters and present it for approval at the October meeting.

When the order of business in Albuquerque came around to new projects, a western street scene was suggested as a logical follow-up to the *Full Moon Saloon*. This suggestion received considerable support, but we were concerned that another western scene would stigmatize us as "cowboy carvers." Many of us do focus primarily on western humor, but we carve other things as well. Then, when the circus was proposed there was immediate acceptance, and the project was adopted unanimously by those present.

A committee was appointed to construct the base and tent and to receive the carvings as they were submitted. Their charge was to present the circus at the 1996 meeting in Minneapolis. One year to complete such a project was a very ambitious undertaking, but there was so much enthusiasm displayed that it seemed possible.

Each member pledged to contribute a minimum of three carvings with due dates of January 15, February 15 and March 15, 1996. We wanted to ensure that

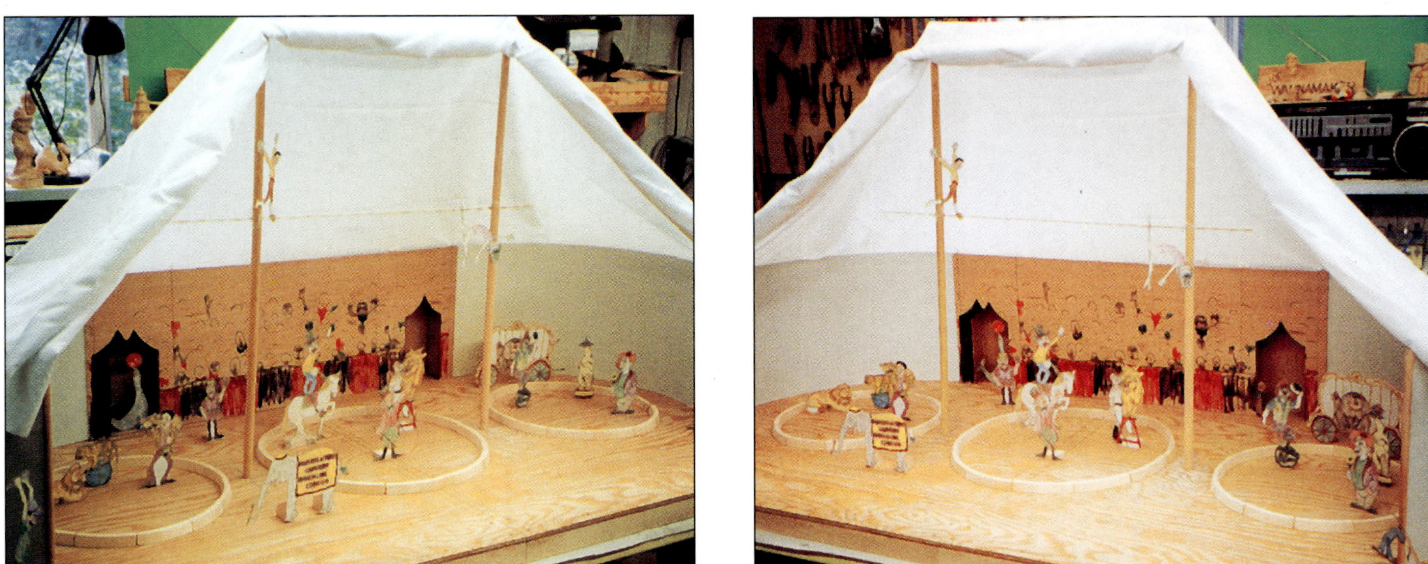

The original plan for the CCA Circus *called for three rings under the big top as shown here in this cardboard mock-up. However, due to space restrictions and scale requirements, a two-ring circus was developed instead.*

most basic subject matter pertinent to a circus would be included, so each member was assigned one specific carving. These were drawn out of a hat at the Albuquerque meeting. The other two carvings were to be original pieces designed by the carver. To avoid duplication, all ideas were to be cleared with the committee. The scale for the circus was set at 0.7 inches to the foot in order to accommodate everything on a 4' x 8' base. Bingo! Now all we had to do was make it happen.

And happen it did! We arrived in Minneapolis on Thursday, October 17, to find the circus in several packages and boxes. Our first order of business was to set up the base and tent and to place the carvings where we thought they should go. Once again, we had managed to pull off a complicated project, contributed to by 23 members, even though we were spread all over the United States and Canada. With a little paint added to the base, a few signs to liven up the show and a recognized need for a few more carvings, we were off and running.

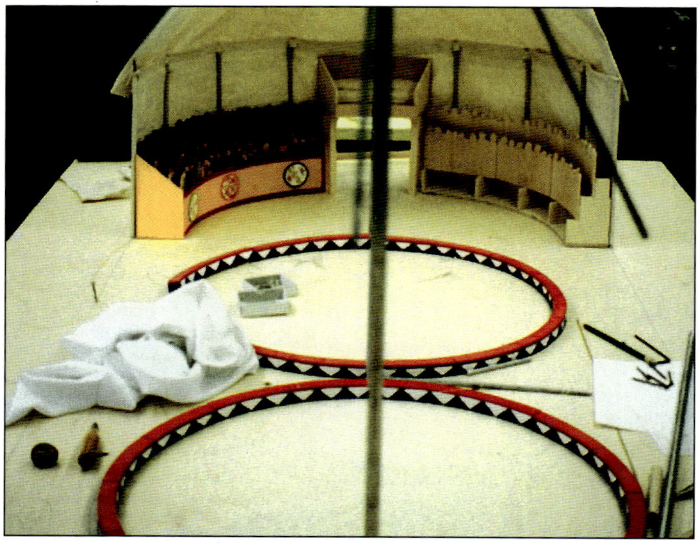

The rings were cut in four-inch segments, painted and doweled to the base.

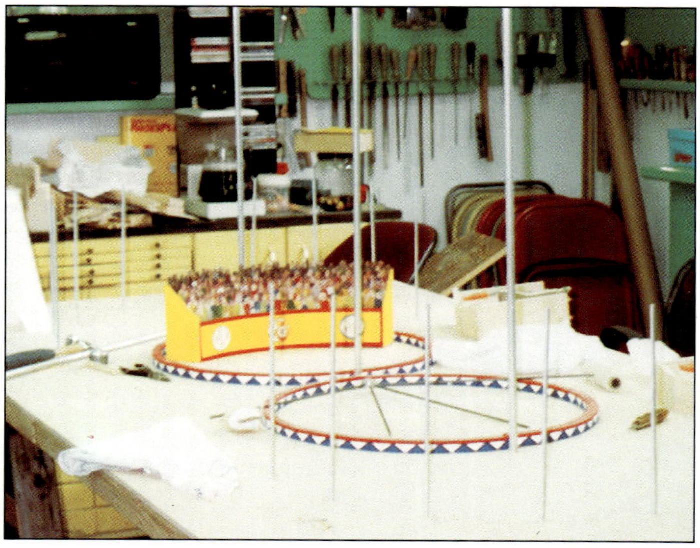

Supports for the tent were fashioned from metal rods.

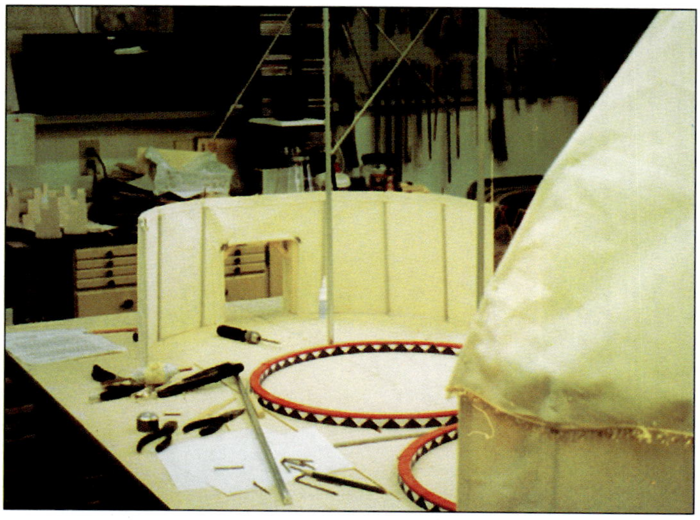

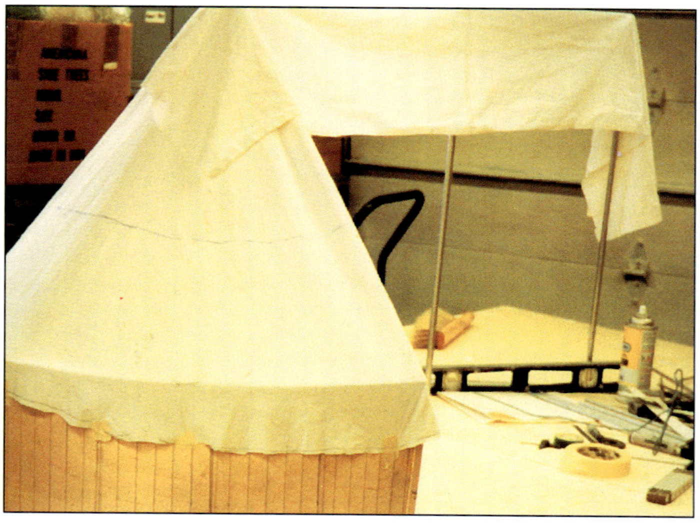

Redesigned as a two-ring circus, these photos show the construction of the actual circus. The tenting is still temporary at this point.

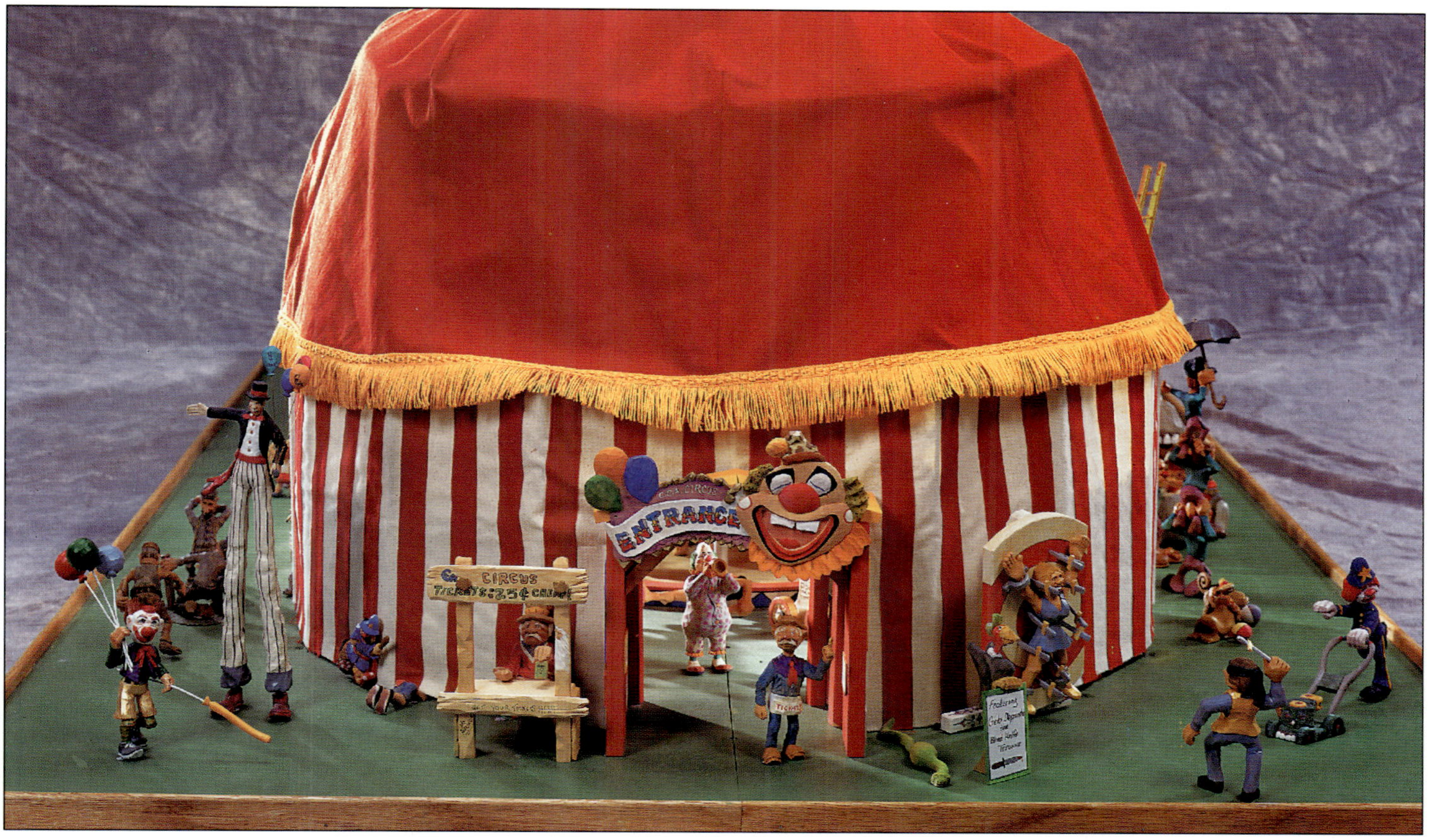

Twenty-five cents admits you to the show, no matter which entrance you choose.

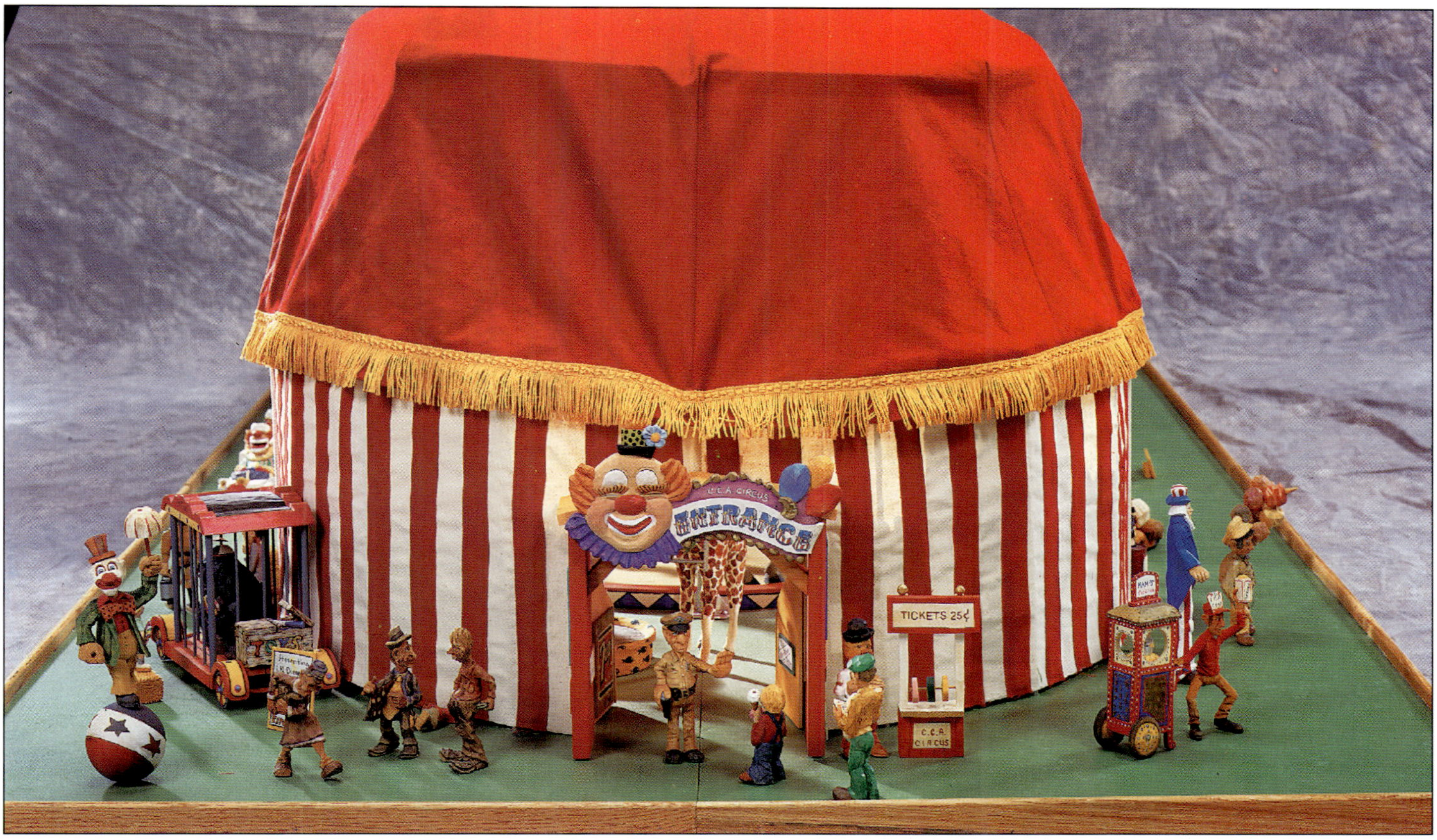

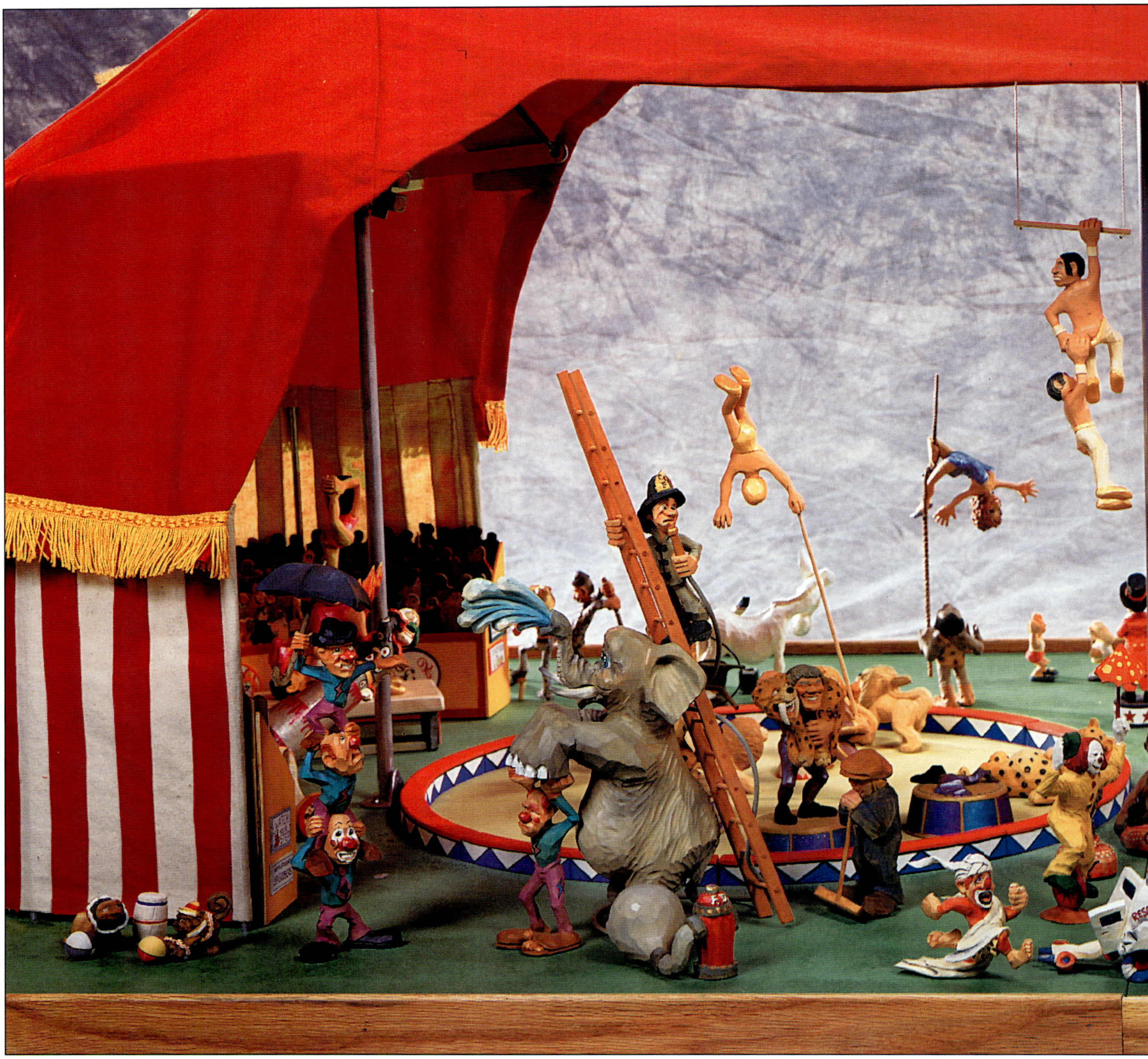

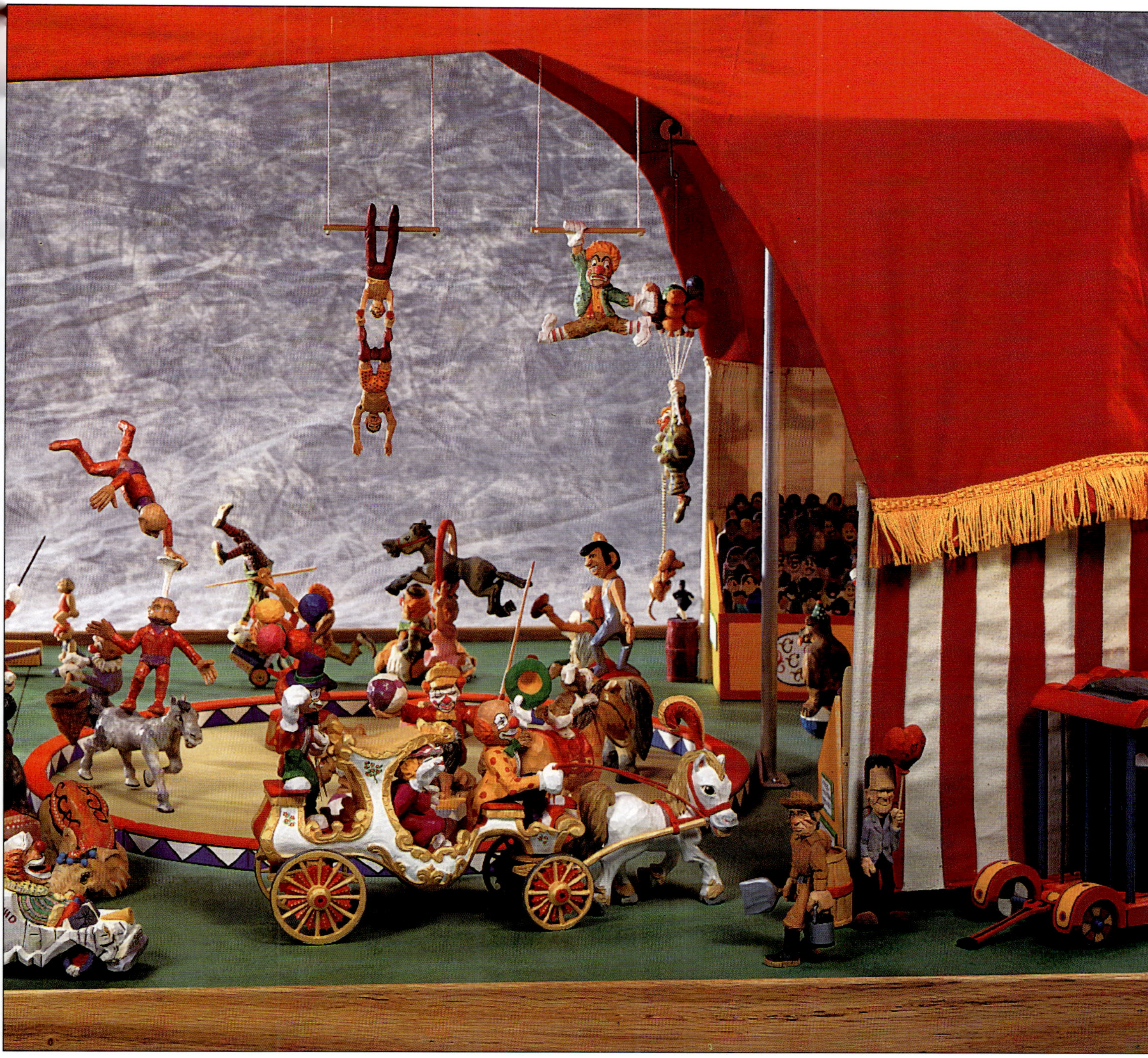

Twenty-three carvers from the United States and Canada collaborated to create the CCA Circus. The Circus features acts of all kinds—from fire-fighting elephants to unicycle-riding clowns to daring trapeze artists—nearly 120 pieces in all.

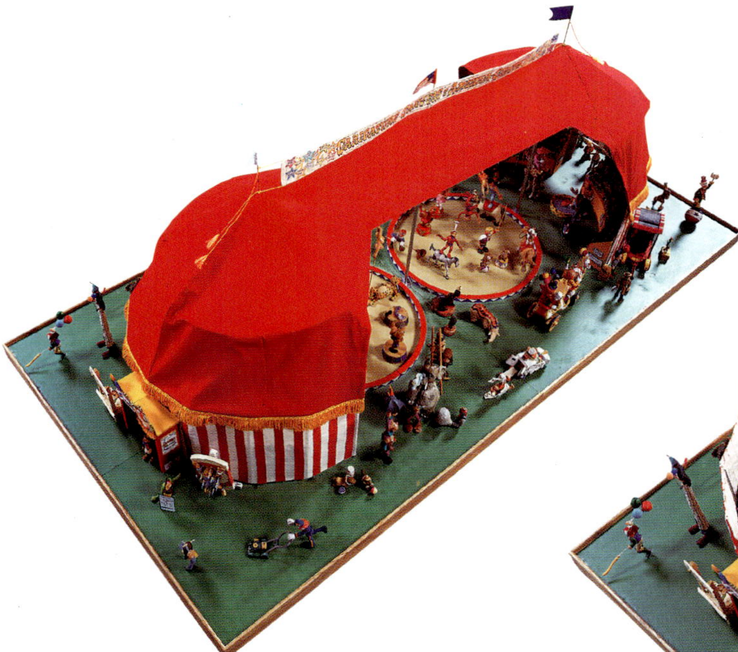

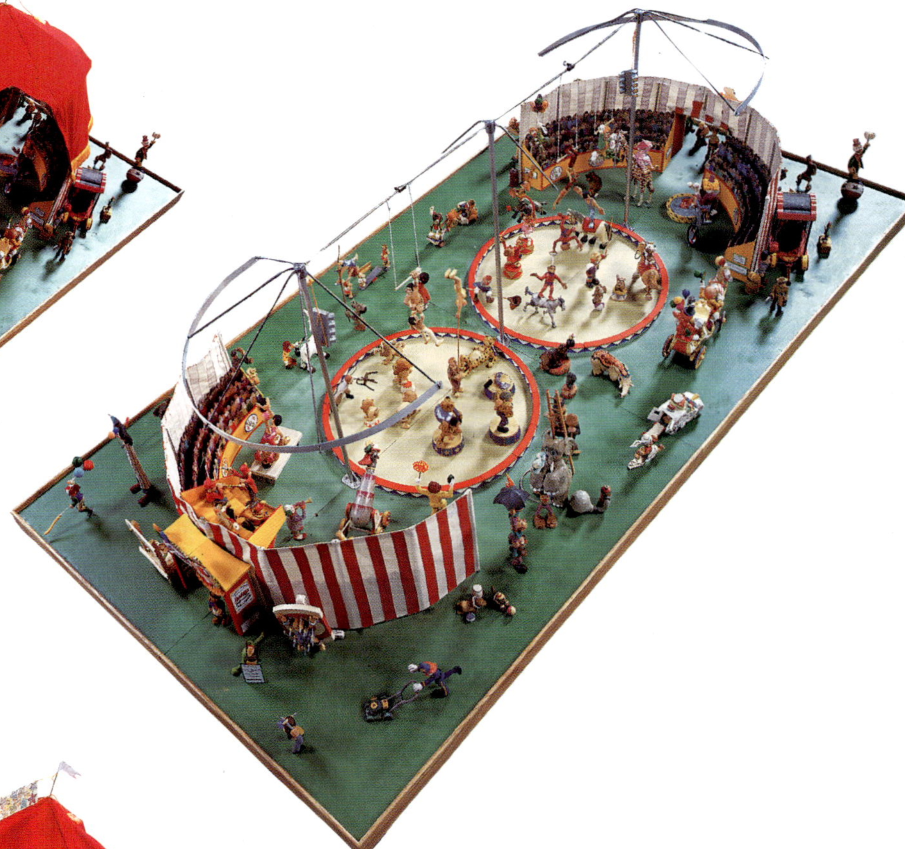

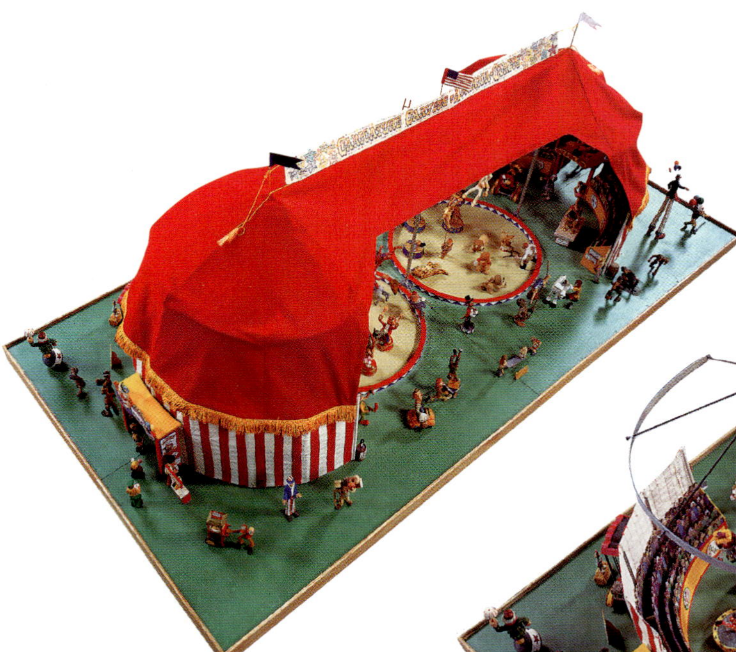

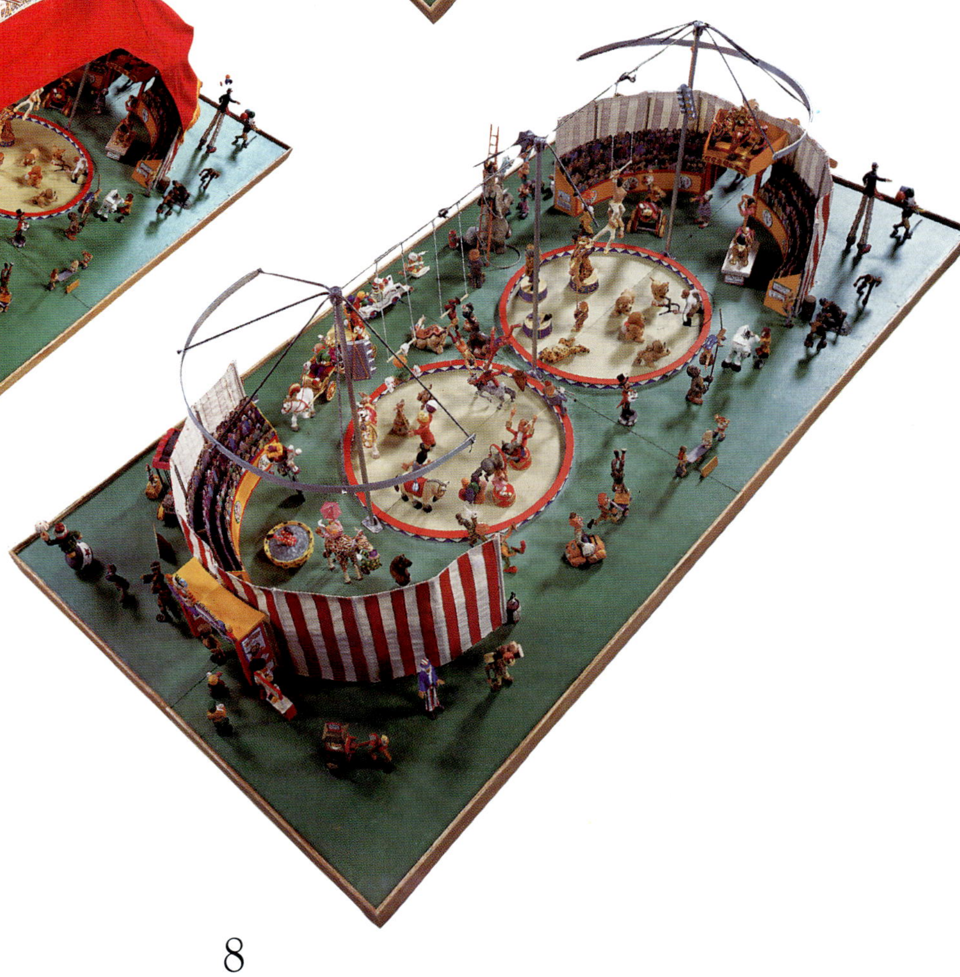

CLOWNS

That's Some Zebra by Gary Batte

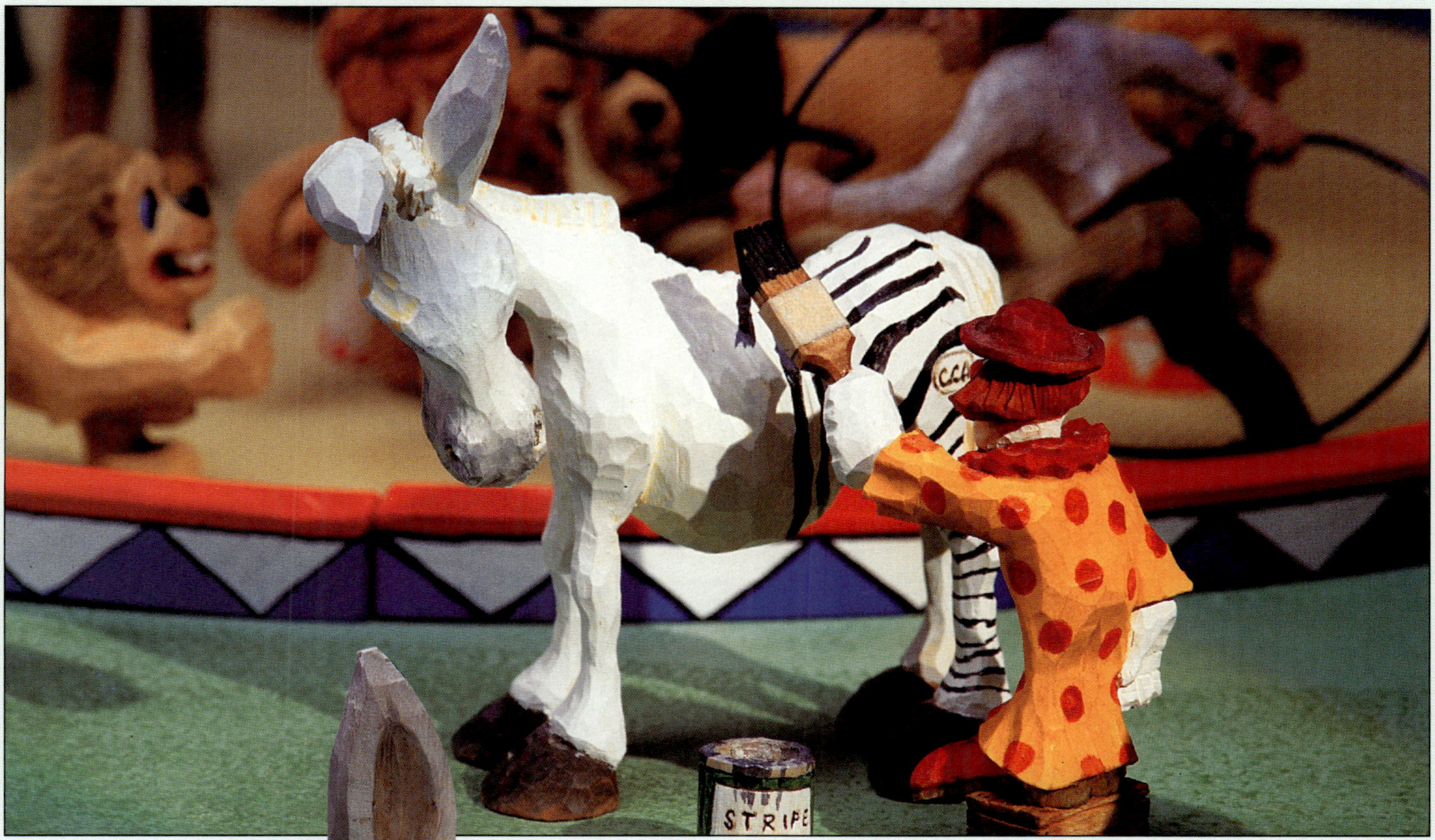

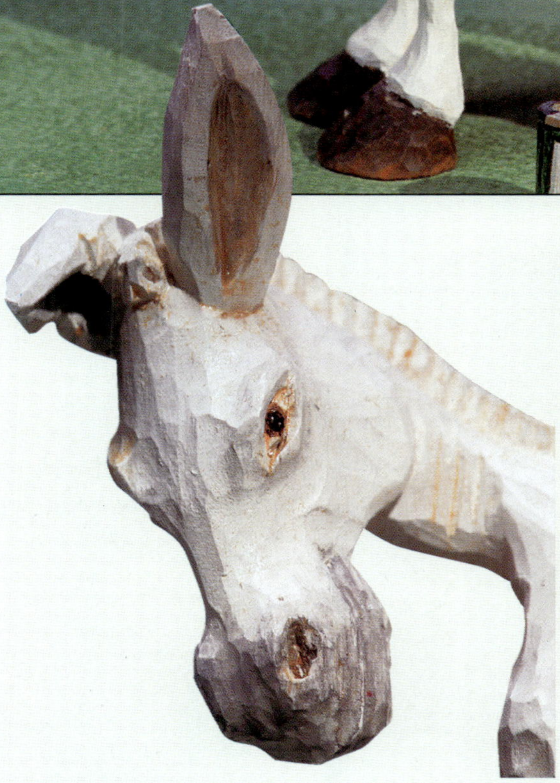

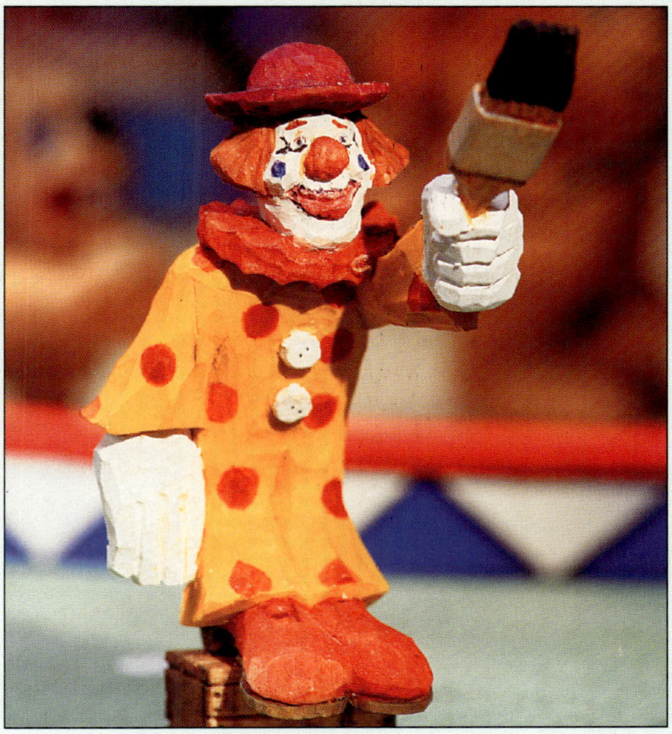

Gary Batte's clown is concentrating on methodically turning this ordinary circus mule into an extraordinary circus zebra. The mule was carved from one piece of wood, with extra wood left around the head so the mule could turn to look at the clown.

Hang Tight by Bob Travis

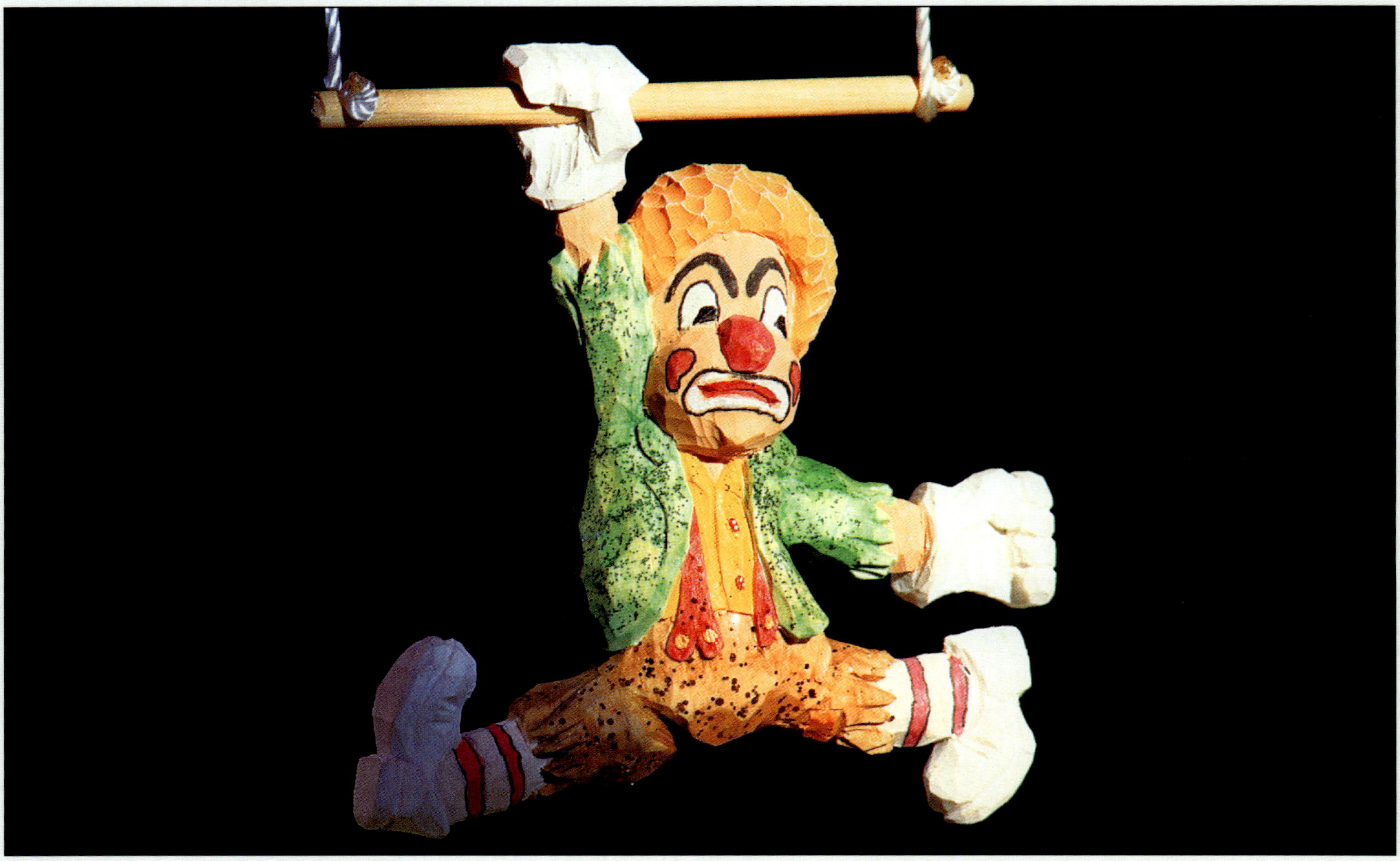

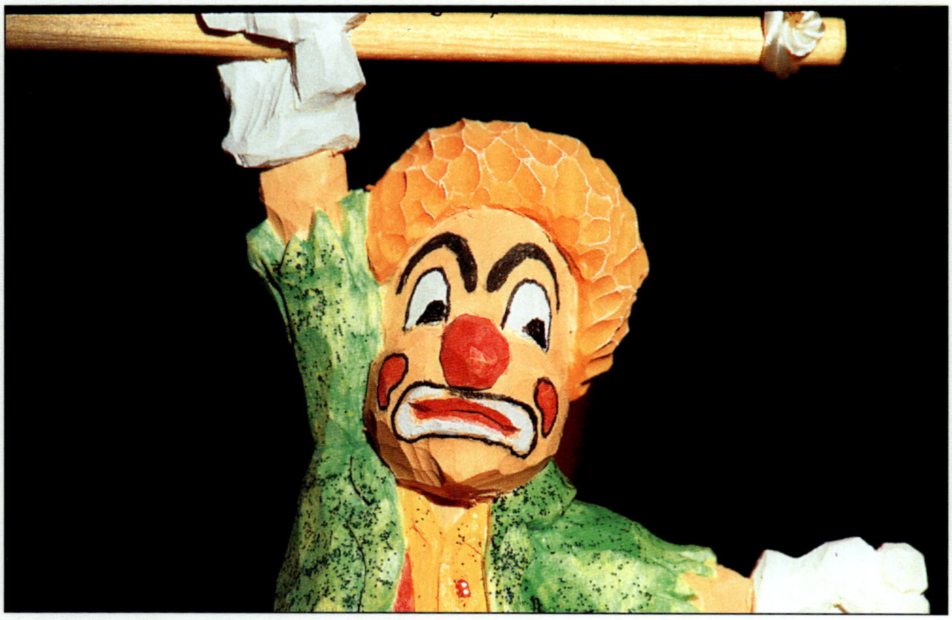

Hanging from a trapeze high above the circus floor, this clown by Bob Travis appears to be on the verge of falling. The clown is carved from one piece of basswood and painted with acrylics. Bob omitted the final antiquing finish to keep the colors bright. The clown's right hand was carved so the trapeze bar, fashioned from a dowel, could slide through his fingers.

Caught by Harley Schmitgen

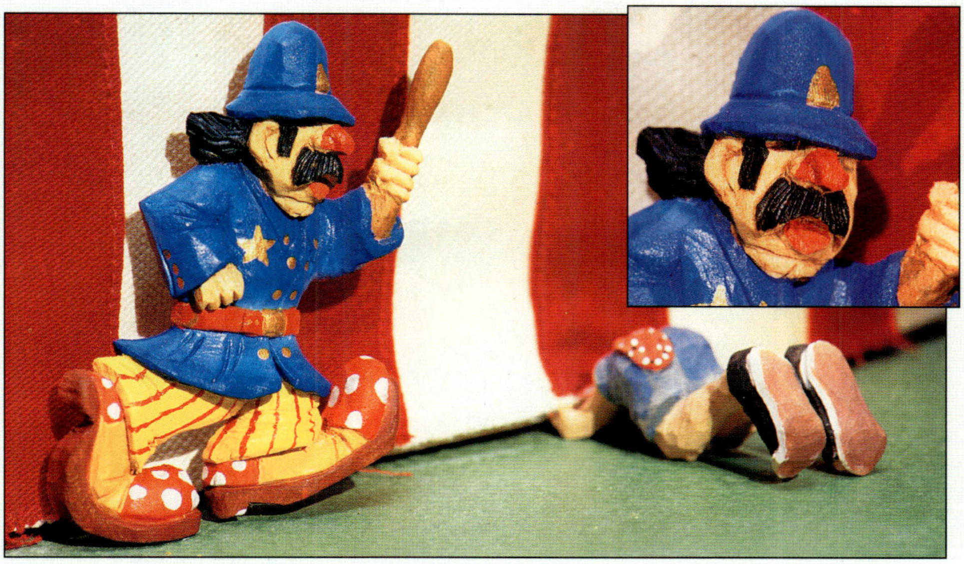

This is one spectator who won't be seeing too much more of the circus for free. The policeman, a flat relief carving by Harley Schmitgen, is only about 1/4" thick. The side of the carving against the tent is flat; the front is carved in the round.

Safety Net by Cleve Taylor

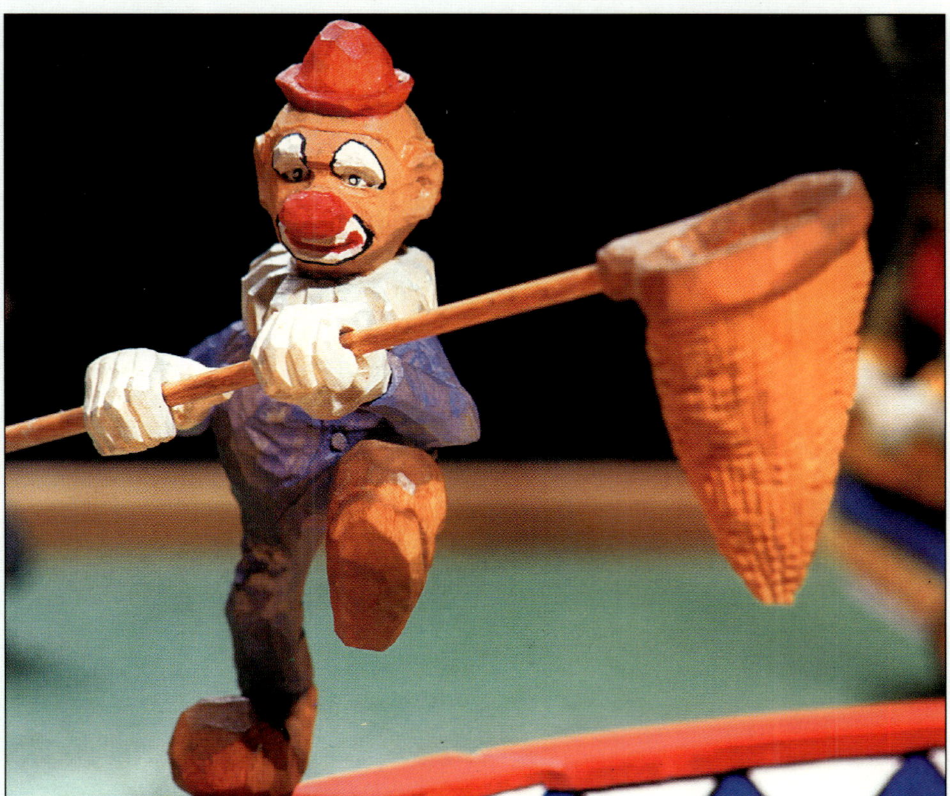

This little clown by Cleve Taylor has the all-important job of catching unfortunate acrobats in the event of a fall. The net was hollowed out with a power tool, attached to a dowel, and then inserted into the clown's hands.

Harley Schmitgen

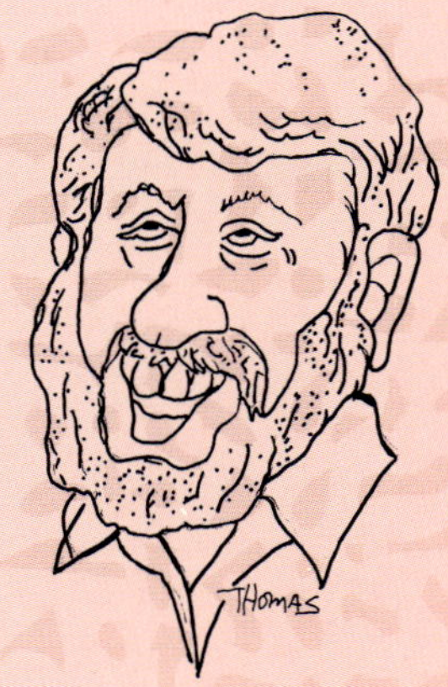

Harley has been a woodcarver for nearly 25 years. A self-taught artist and enthusiastic instructor from Blue Earth, Minnesota, Harley enjoys flat relief carving. With this technique, the finished carving is very thin, sometimes only 1/4" thick. The back of the piece is flat and only the front is carved in the wood.

Harley's contributions to the CCA Circus appear on pages 11, 36, 69, 72, 73 and 74.

Harley has won top honors at many shows, including the International Woodcarvers Congress, the Silver Dollar City Showcase, the Upper Midwest Woodcarvers' Exhibition, and the Vesterheim in Decorah, Iowa. He is recognized as a master carver and is one of the founders and coordinators of the Upper Midwest Woodcarvers Exhibition.

Harley belongs to several carving organizations including the Central Minnesota Woodcarvers Association, the California Carvers Guild, the Minnesota Woodcarvers Association, the National Woodcarvers Association, and the Affiliated Woodcarvers, Ltd.

The Juggler by Claude Bolton

Claude Bolton

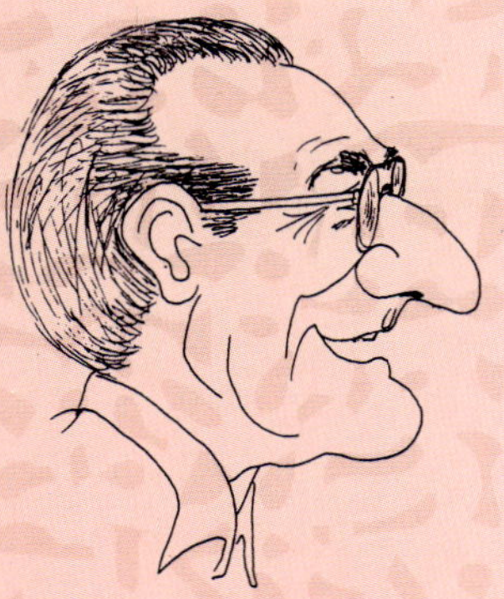

Claude is a retired Texas educator from Fort Worth, Texas. His interest in carving has grown steadily since he took his first carving class at a local museum in 1974. Claude generally carves cowboys, with an occasional deviation such as the clowns he carved for the CCA Circus. In keeping with caricature style, his carvings show exaggerated features and actions.

Claude's contributions to the CCA Circus *appear on pages 12, 13 and 42.*

Claude has written three books on caricature carving: Carving Cowboy Faces, Carving Cowboys, *and* Heads, Hats and Hair. *He has conducted nearly 100 seminars in 20 states and has been an instructor at the War Eagle, Arkansas, summer seminar for several years.*

Claude organized the Fort Worth Woodcarvers in 1975 and is a founding member of CCA. He is a member of the North Texas Woodcarvers, the Texas Wildfowl Carvers and the California Carvers Guild.

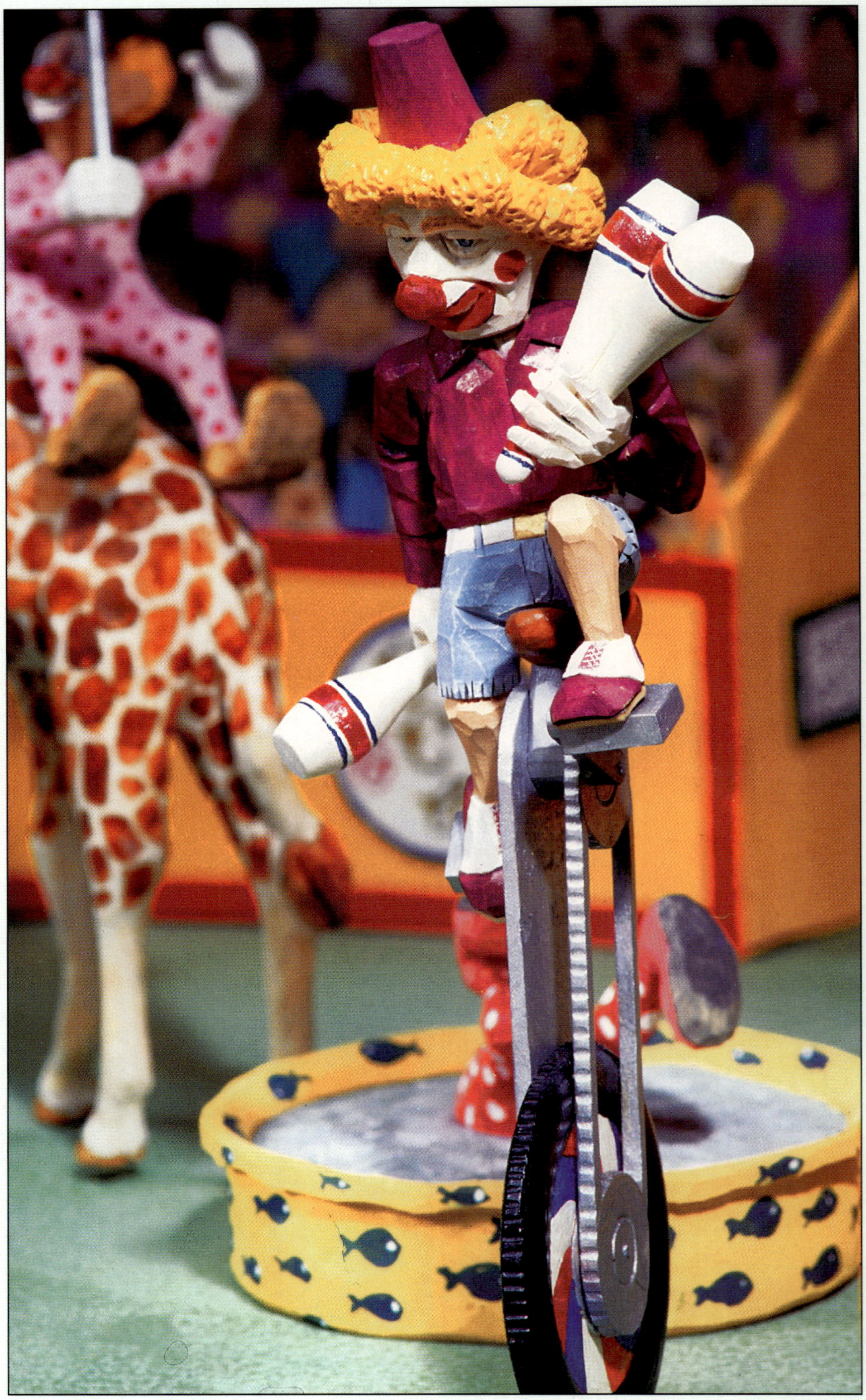

Claude Bolton carved a unicycle-riding clown for the CCA Circus. Carving the figure so he appeared to be balancing precariously proved to be a challenge. The clown, the unicycle, the wheel, the peddles and the bowling pins were all carved separately.

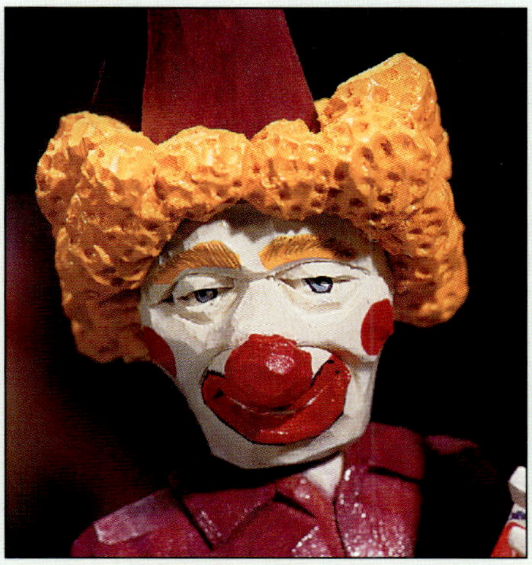

Balloons by Claude Bolton

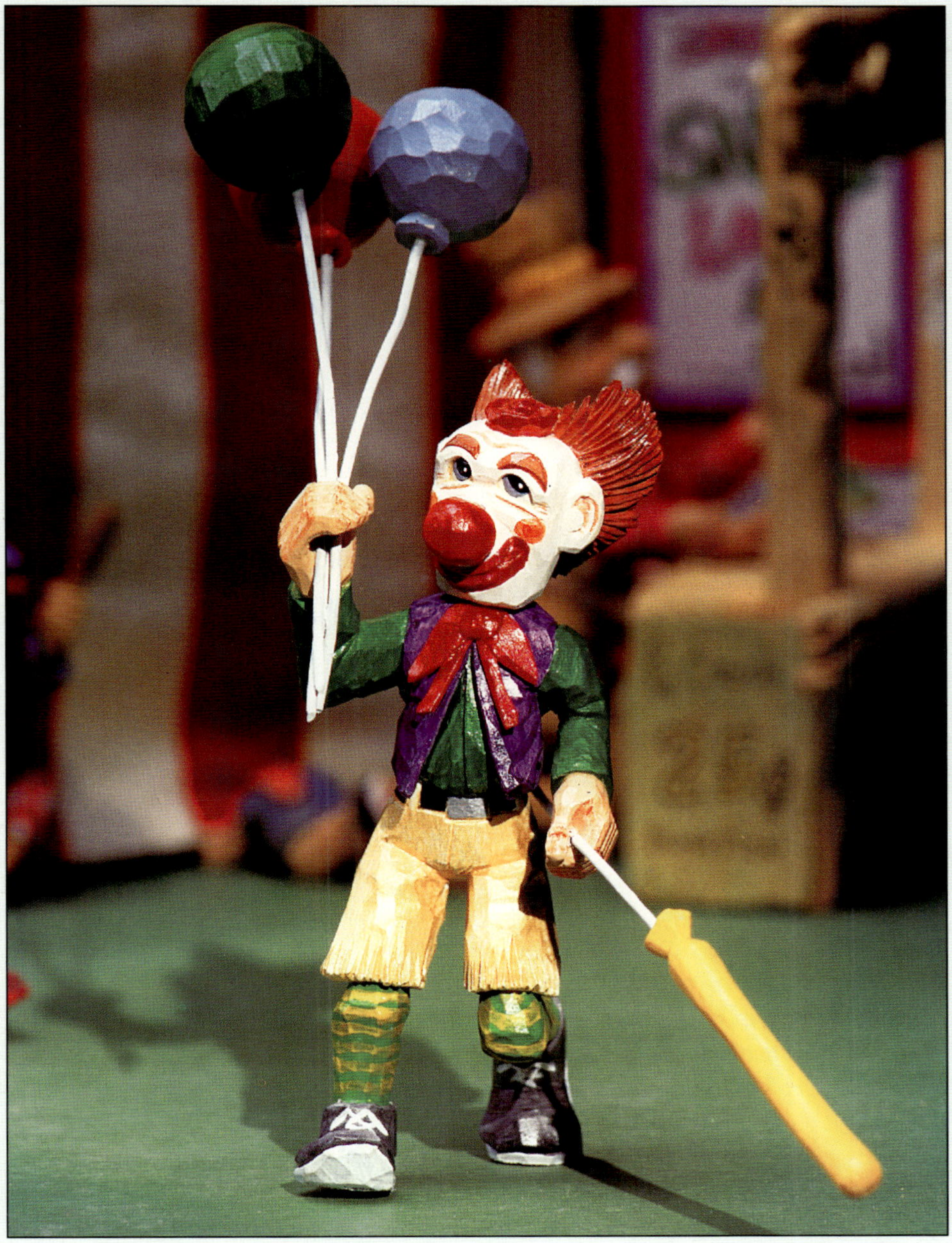

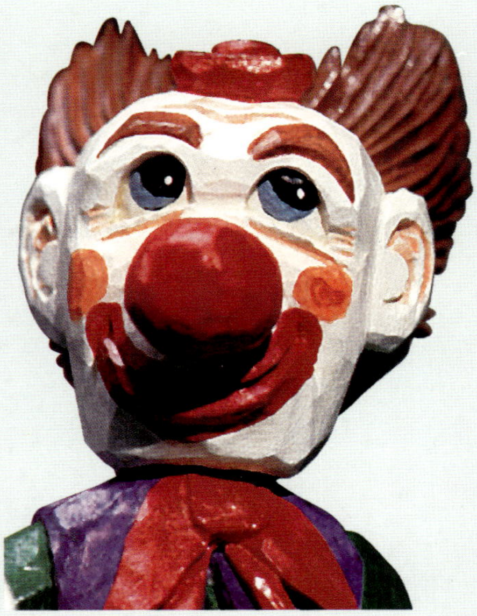

A handful of brightly colored balloons adds an extra touch of color to Claude Bolton's second carving for the CCA Circus. The balloons are carved from basswood and the strings were fashioned from copper wire painted white.

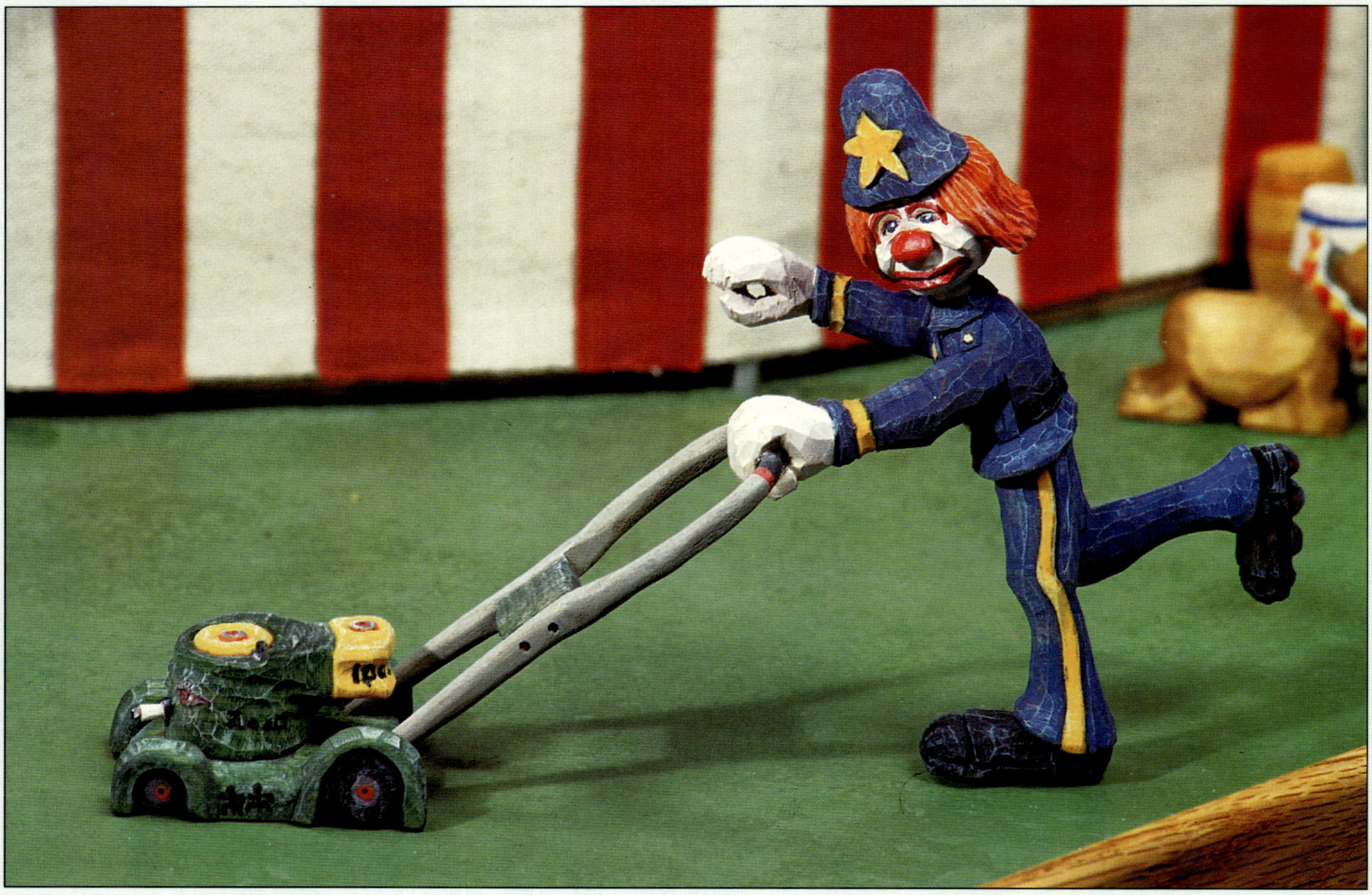

Free-Wheeling Willy by Tom Brown

In October, 1995, I spent a very anxious day waiting for Dave Dunham to call and let me know if I would have the honor of joining CCA. The call finally came, and at that time I was invited to participate in the circus project. My first assignment was to come up with a few ideas, and being eager (like most new kids on the block), I compiled a list a foot long. Once I got my list down to a few do-able projects of particular interest to me, I was ready to start.

This piece, which I call "Free-Wheeling Willy," came from a lawnmower commercial that I saw on television. I developed an idea of a clown on a set of roller blades with a self-propelled lawnmower. At first glance you might think he is chasing the mower, which has a caricature face on it. But upon closer inspection, you realize the clown is being pulled by a runaway mower.

Because my drawing skills are limited, I rely on stick figures, pipe cleaners and armatures with movable joints that can be twisted and bent. I started this project with balled-up aluminum foil and aluminum clothesline wire, and wrapped clay around them in thin layers. This technique allows me to bake the clay for a shorter period of time, and it gives me the flexibility to change the pattern before baking. Using my clay figure as a guide, I outlined the design on a basswood block and then made a cut-out on my bandsaw.

My biggest challenge was to obtain the proper balance for this project without using a base. The clown rests on one foot, which is on roller blades, so the mower would have to help support him. After I worked out the correct angles, I needed more weight in the mower to balance the piece, so I drilled out the bottom and added lead fish sinkers.

I used a knife and a #3 gouge to rough out the project. The rest of the work was done with the knife and a set of palm tools.

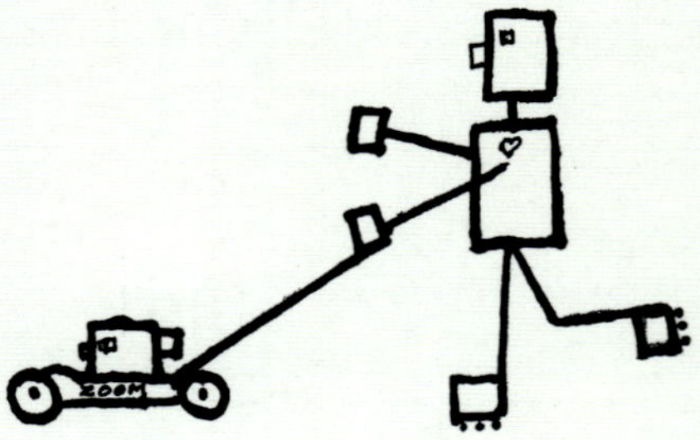

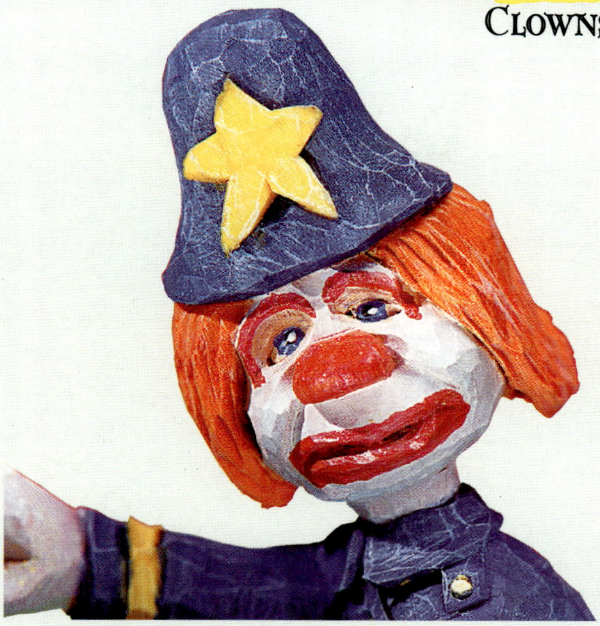

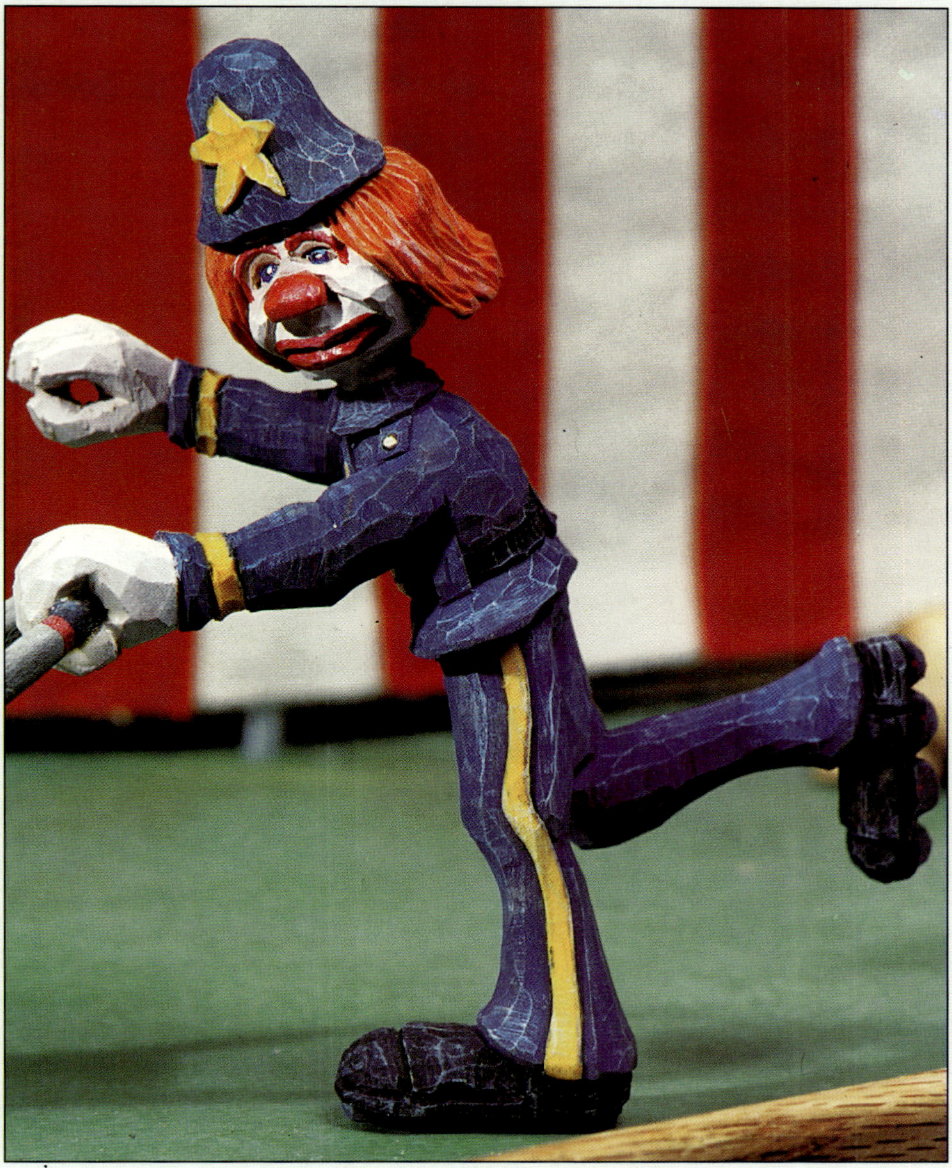

Tom Brown

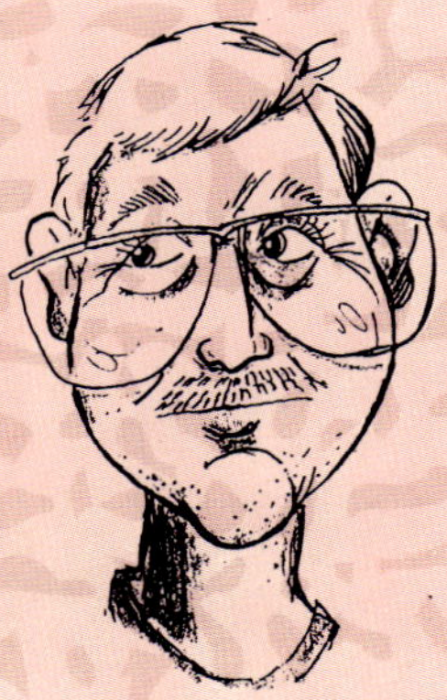

Tom, a resident of Converse, Indiana, began carving during his many years with the Boy Scout program, from Cub to Eagle to Scoutmaster. He rediscovered his love for caricature carving after retiring from Chrysler. Among his favorite subjects to carve are World War II pilots. Today, Tom is known for recognizing the humorous side of any situation, and his caricatures often reflect his unique view of life.

Tom's contributions to the CCA Circus appear on pages 14, 15, 48 and 49.

Tom is one of the founders and the president who started the Eastern Woodland Carving Club in 1988. He is also president of Affiliated Woodcarvers and International Woodcarvers Congress and a member of several other carving clubs.

Seminars, demonstrations, judging and promoting the art of woodcarving has kept Tom very busy these past few years. He is very proud to be one of the newest CCA members.

Cymbals the Clown by Will Hayden

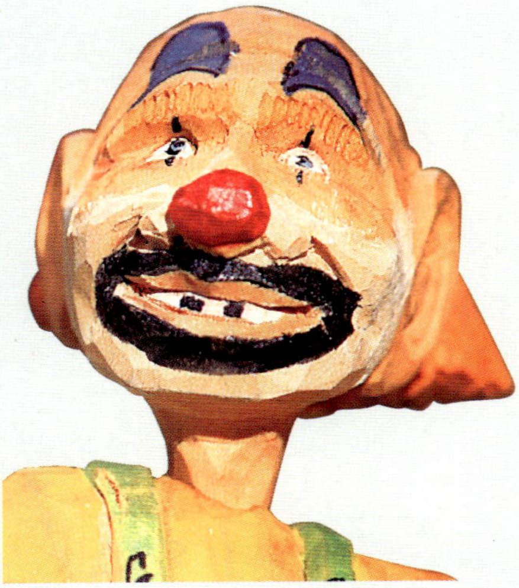

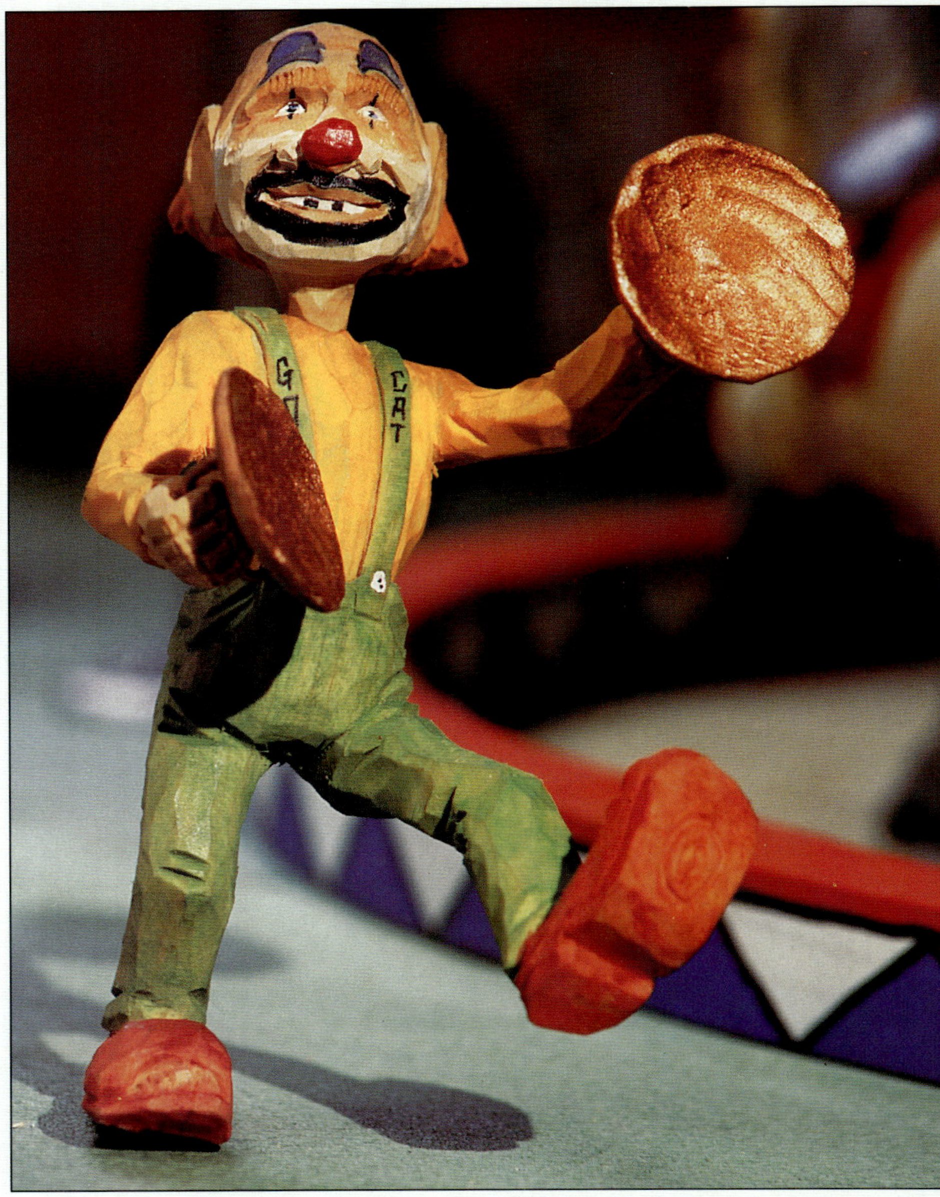

I was in Japan, 5,000 miles from my carving tools, when I received official notification that I was chosen as one of the new CCA members. So I decided to get a head start on the design of my piece and headed to the bookstore for a notebook and pencil. After a number of rough sketches, I settled on a band member with an instrument carved separately.

When I got home, I laid out my pattern on the block of wood. I always leave extra wood on my cutouts so that I have plenty of room to change it a little as I carve. For me, the pattern is like a road map... We can all get to the same destination, but by leaving the Interstate once in a while and taking the scenic route, you can make a simple carving into a real carving of your own.

I used a number of carving knives, three different sizes of v-tools, a fine-tipped flexible knife for the eyes and a couple of gouges. Total carving time was about three hours. I did the head separately because I had not seen the circus layout and had no idea as to the location of my piece or direction of movement. I used a $1^1/2$" by $1^1/2$" stick of wood for the head so I would have something to hold on to as I carved the face.

The hardest part of this carving was the raised foot due to the direction of the wood grain. The answer to any problem in carving is a very sharp tool, and more so when you must cut across grain or on very soft wood. Hard wood helps hone the blade and soft wood speeds up the rounding of the blade. So when carving softer wood, it is necessary to strop more often. The key for a nice, clean cut is a sharp knife.

To paint this piece, I used thinned-down acrylic paints. Extra coats were added to the folds and creases and on the lines in the face using the dry brush method. I used full colors for the eyes and buttons.

I antiqued my piece with a mixture of boiled linseed oil, turpenoid and burnt umber oil paint. I then sealed the carving with a spray matte finish. An extra coat of gloss varnish brightened up the red on the nose.

Up, Up and Away by Randy Landen

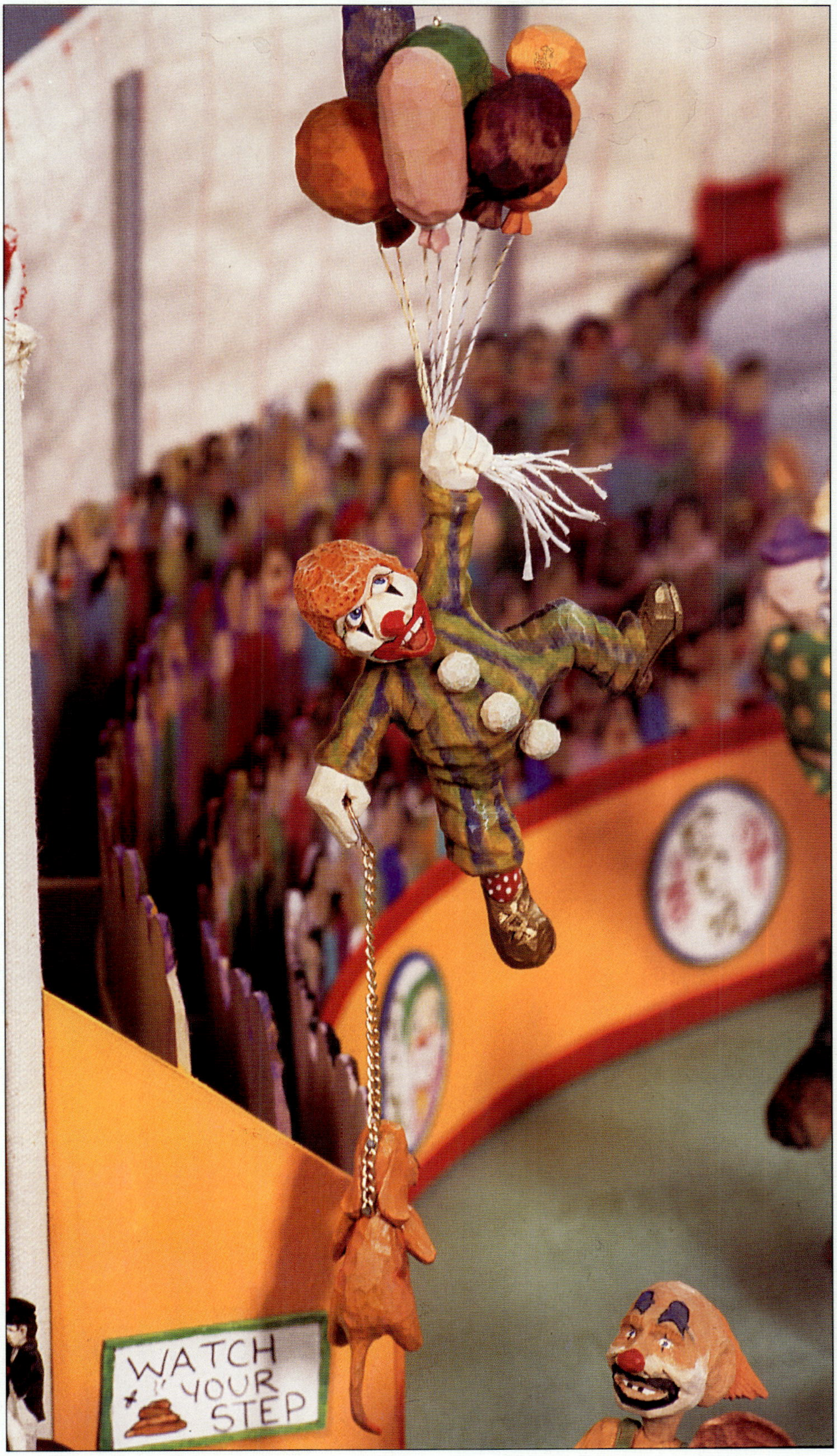

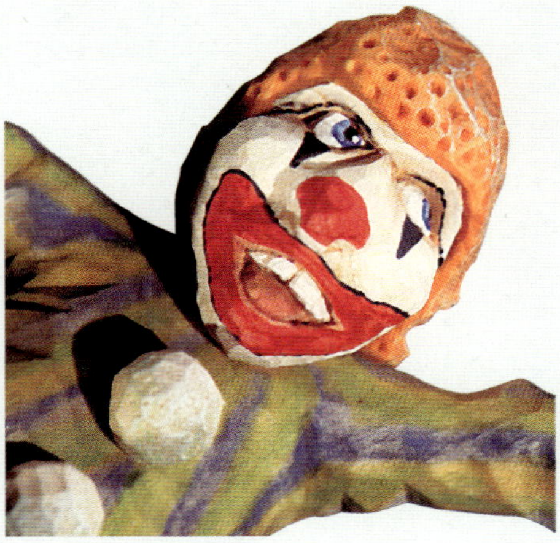

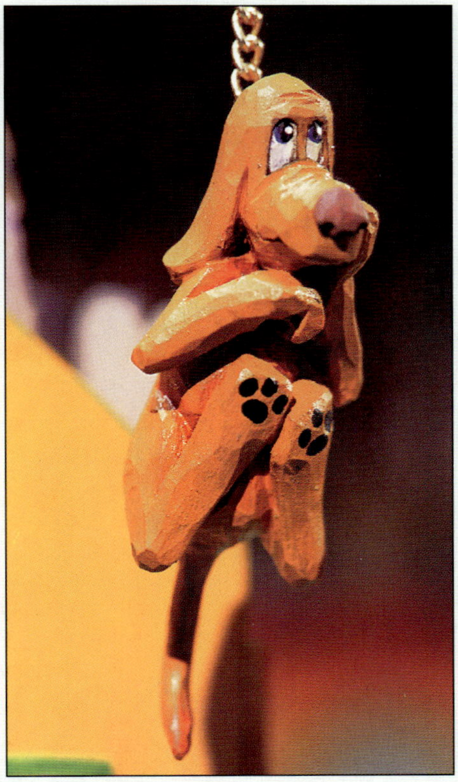

Too many "helium-filled" balloons have made this clown and his dog airborne. Clear fishing line attached to the top of the tent holds the pair in mid-aid. Artist Randy Landen used actual string for the balloons and a real chain for the dog's leash.

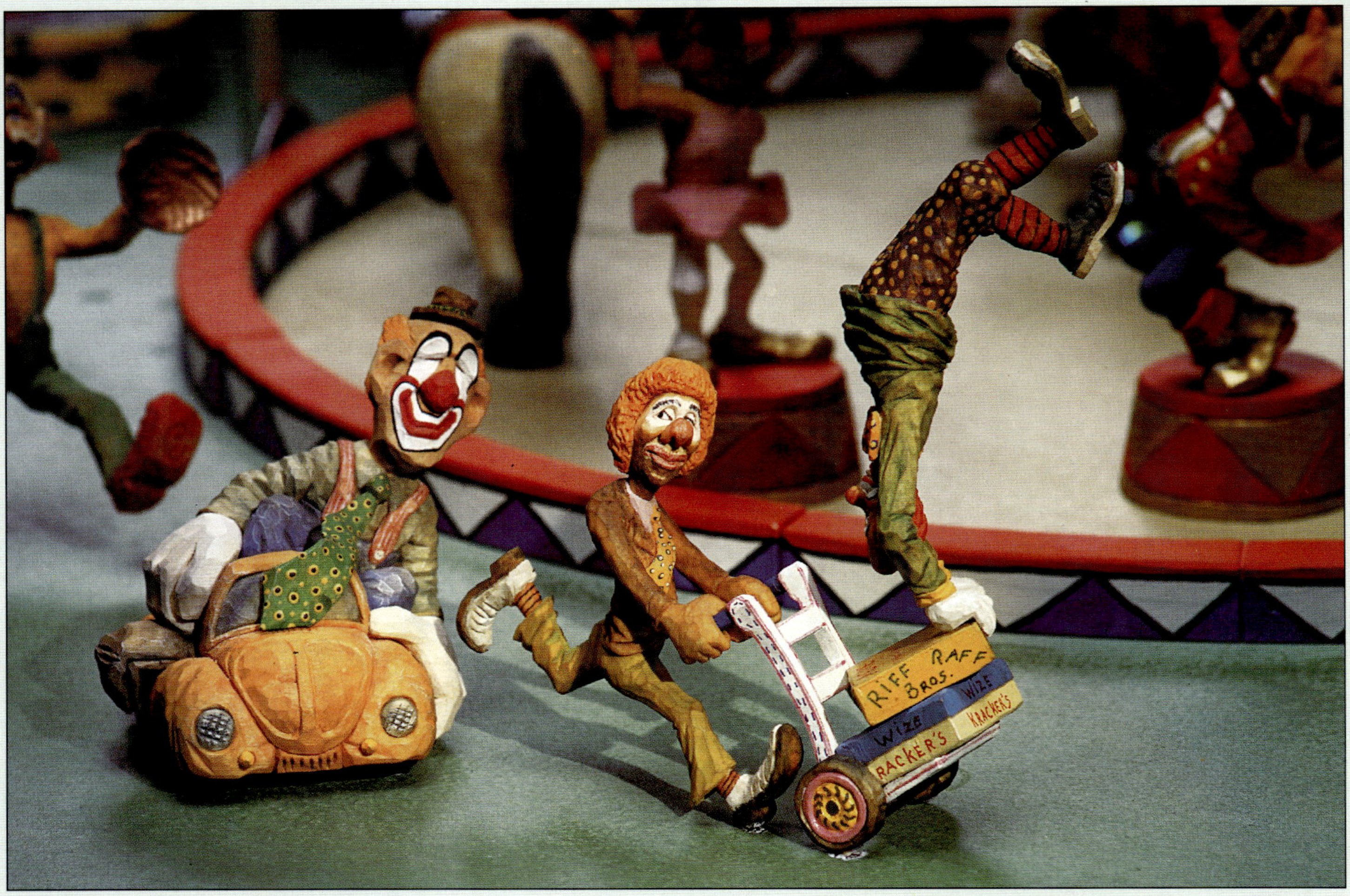

Buggin' Out by Randy Landen

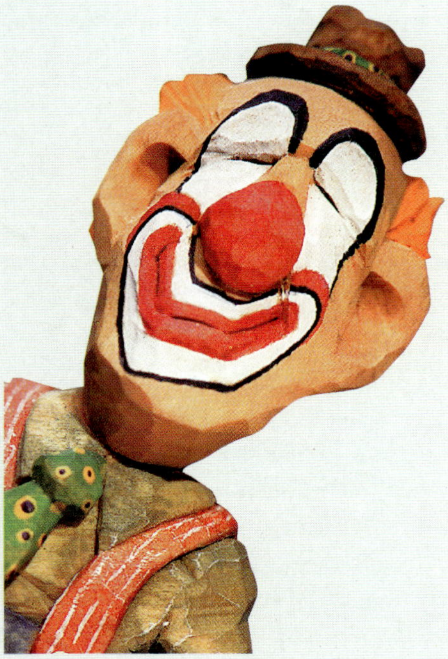

In the course of making the preliminary cut-outs for the CCA *Circus*, I began to develop the idea for a clown coming out of a Volkswagen. Since I worked for several years as a VW mechanic before joining the Police Department, I was intimately familiar with the shape of a VW Bug. This idea provided me with a project that would be more difficult than the piece I'd done for the *Full Moon Saloon*, yet still be fun to do.

Using my original drawing as a guide, I sketched the front view, minus the head, on a square block of basswood. The mental picture I have of a piece often changes as the actual shape changes during the roughing-out process. Sometimes the best ideas become apparent as you rough the carving out.

When roughing out the general shape of the piece, I used a 5/8 #9 gouge and a large v-tool. These tools allow for changes in the general shape of the carving without leaving deep cut marks. The remainder of

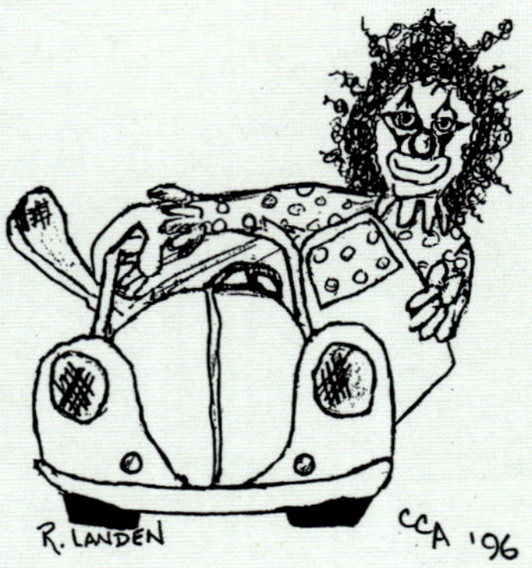

The Riff and Raff Brothers by W. "Pete" LeClair

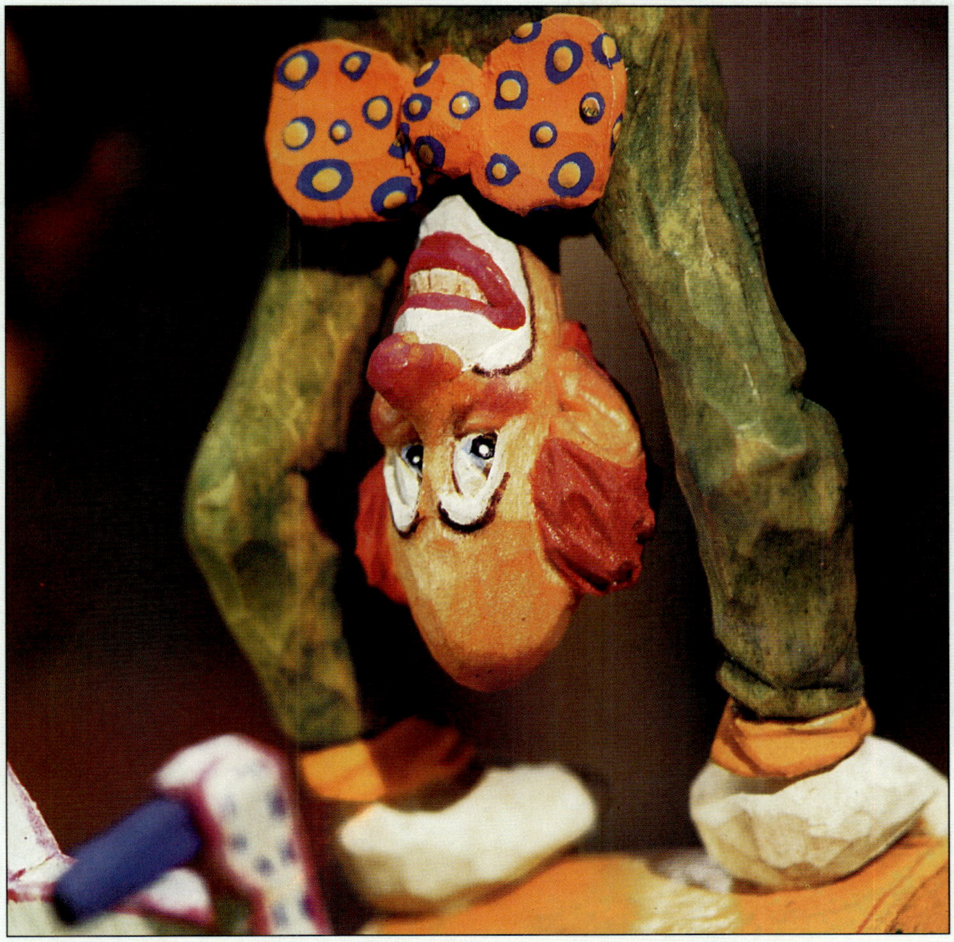

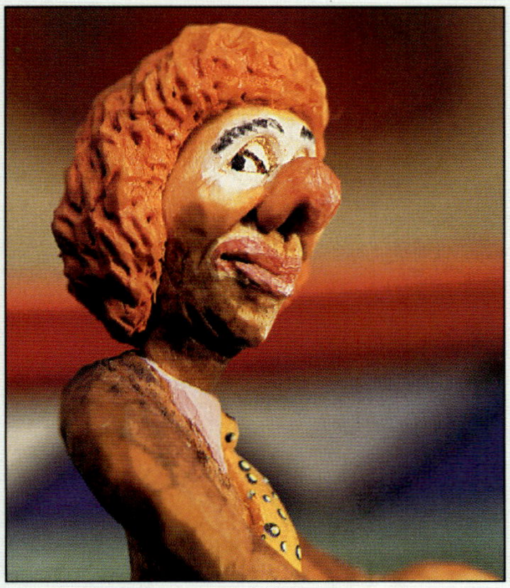

Intent on making the crowd laugh, Pete LeClair's pair of clowns joins fellow CCA member Randy Landen's clown on page 18 in a tour around the circus tent. To add the illusion of motion, Pete LeClair stretched the running clown's legs far apart and put just the toes of one foot and the heel of the other on the ground. The arch in the other clown's back and his tilted feet add even more motion.

the carving was done with a knife and various palm tools.

The small features of the piece can give it a great deal of character, so it's important not to rush in the final carving stages. Take time to put in fingernails, clothing seams and buttons. The last step is to add the wrinkles using a knife and several sizes of gouges.

On this particular piece, I chose to carve the head separately. This gave me the ability to carve faces until I got the one that captured my images of a clown. I carved about five heads before landing on my personal favorite.

As I've mentioned, the detail in a carving is essential to the character of the piece. Toward the end of the carving process, I realized the piece lacked that humorous appearance I was after, so I carved in suspenders and added on a wild necktie. These additions enhanced the detail of the piece and gave it the extra character I felt had been missing.

Unfortunately, I ended up having to carve another head for this clown because the original one seemed too large—even for a caricature. The completed piece took about 35 hours of carving time, provided you don't count all the time spent carving the extra heads.

Painting the piece took another 5-6 hours. I paint using water-based acrylics, watered down to a wash, then detail with heavier colors, and finally drybrush with white. On the circus project, I tried to use the brighter colors associated with clowns. For a sealer/antiquer, I used a mixture of boiled linseed oil and a small amount of oil-based brown paint. I painted the mixture on the carving, let it set for 10 minutes and wiped the residue off. The oil stain softens the acrylics and allows the wood to show through.

Toots by W. "Pete" LeClair

Pete LeClair

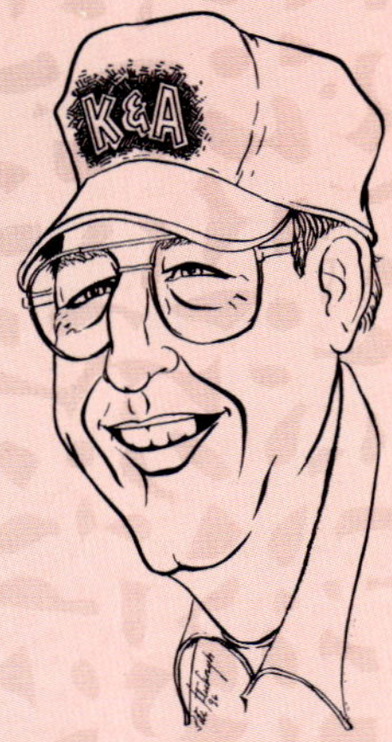

Pete, a resident of Gardner, Massachusetts, has been carving since 1979. After tiring of doing ships in a bottle, he decided to try his hand at carving caricatures. He tracked down a couple of basic books on caricature carving, then after several years of self study, he took a seminar with fellow CCA member Harold Enlow. Over the years he has developed his own unique carving style.

Pete's contributions to the CCA Circus appear on pages 18, 19, 20 and 33.

Pete began showing his work in 1990. In 1994 Pete claimed Best of Show for his caricatures at the Susquehanna Decoy and Woodcarving Show in Pennsylvania, and then won the Texas Carving Guild's Grand Champion Whittling Contest open division, the first non-Texan to win the award. Pete was inducted into CCA in September 1994.

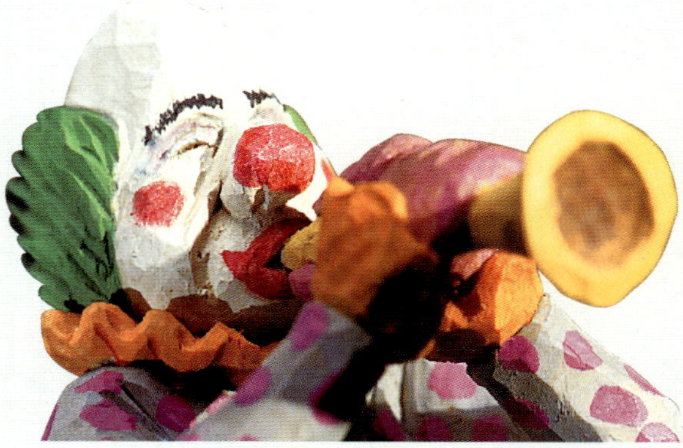

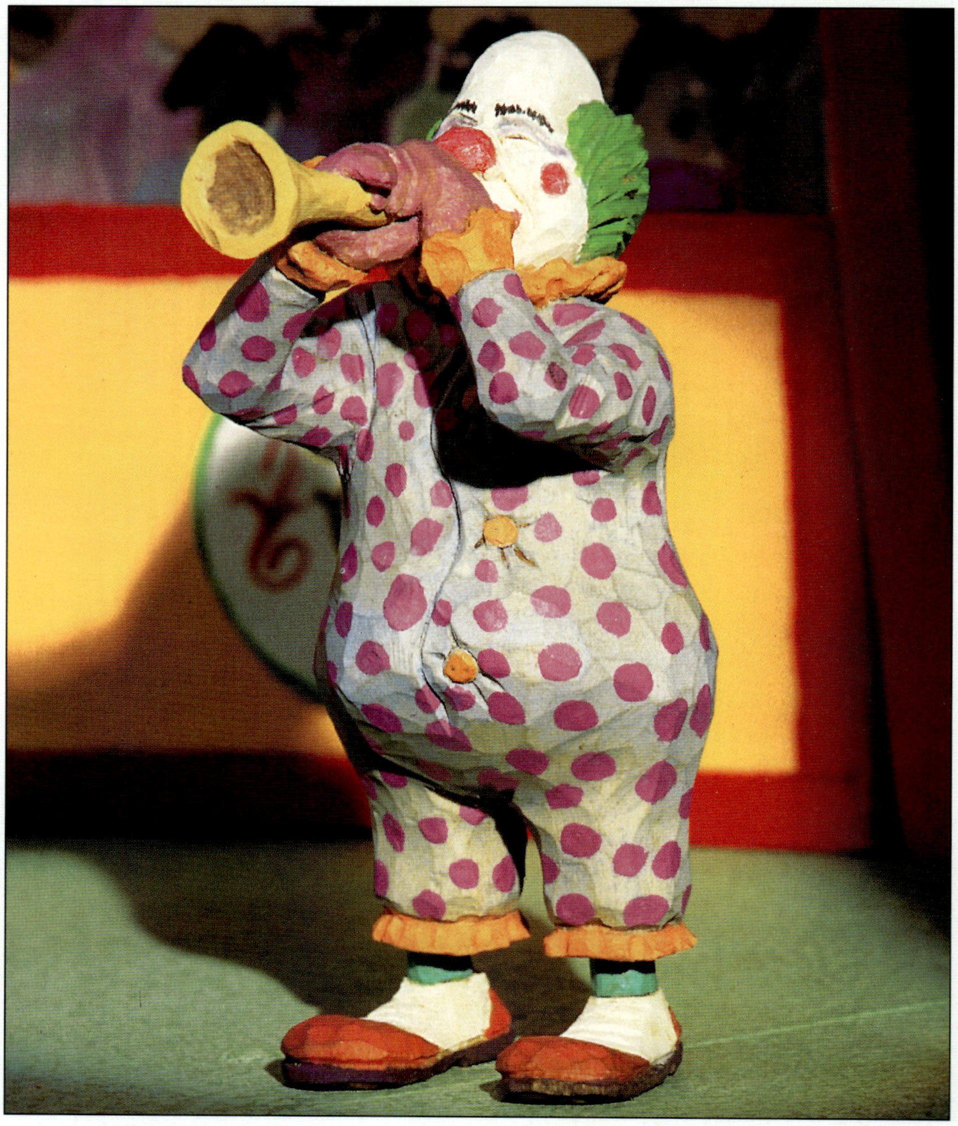

Pete LeClair's trumpet-playing clown helps keep the crowd entertained as he roams the tent making his own kind of music. Both the trumpet and the clown are carved from one piece of wood. Extra care had to be taken while carving the trumpet in crossgrain.

The Human Cannonball by Keith Morrill

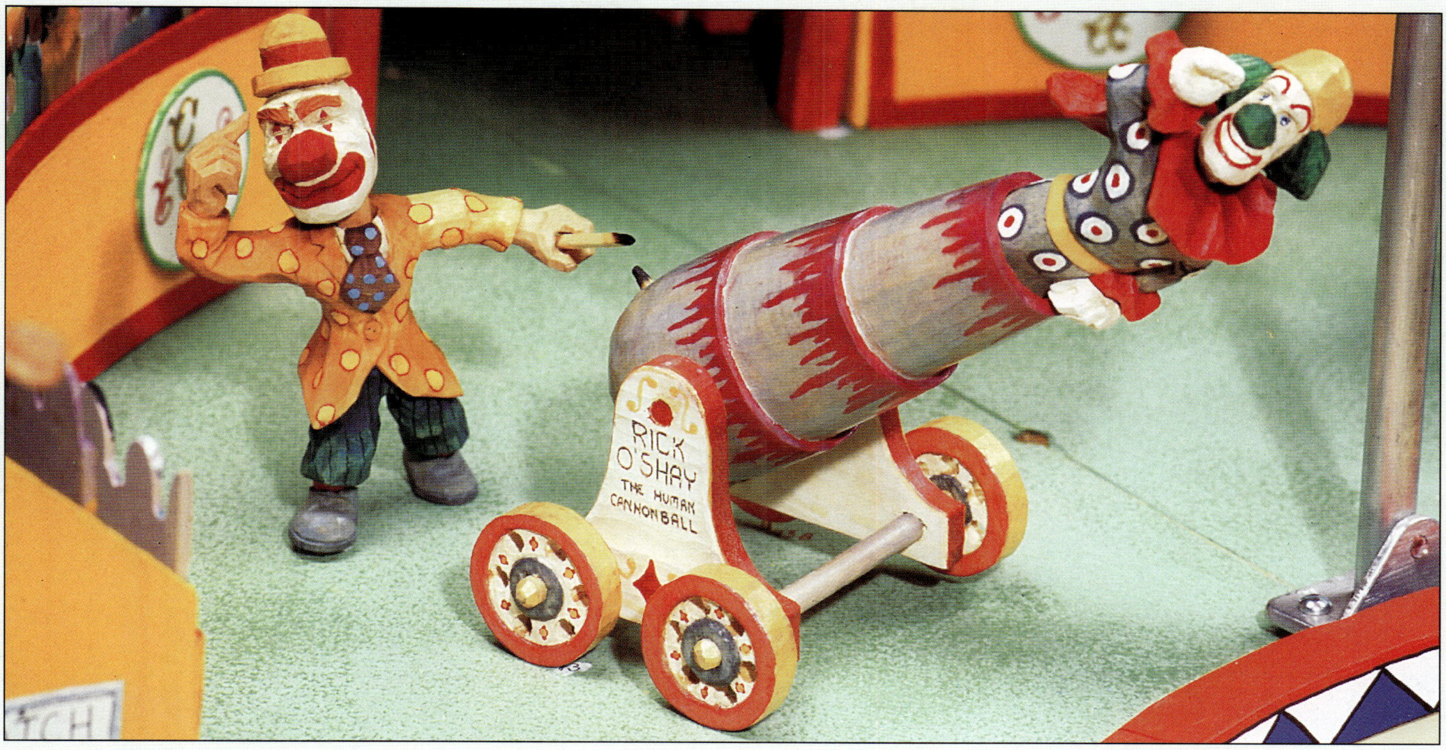

Who can forget the human cannonball? I recall a brightly costumed figure walking up the long, tilted barrel of a cannon, climbing into the muzzle of the cannon and waving to the crowd before disappearing from sight. The crowd collectively held its breath for a few seconds. Then everyone thrilled to the roar of the cannon, the flash of light and the large puff of smoke, followed by a live figure flying through the air and landing unhurt in a net at the other end of the tent.

I wasn't too sure how to accomplish a figure that would realistically appear to be flying, so I chose the easy way out and carved "Rick O'Shay" poised in the mouth of the cannon prior to sendoff. This was a relatively easy piece to carve. Because he's partially in the cannon, I only had to carve half a body. One arm is reaching forward, waving, while the other is grasping the mouth of the cannon. With this pose, the direction of the wood grain is not a big problem. The only place where I had to take particular care was on the curved bottom edge of his cape.

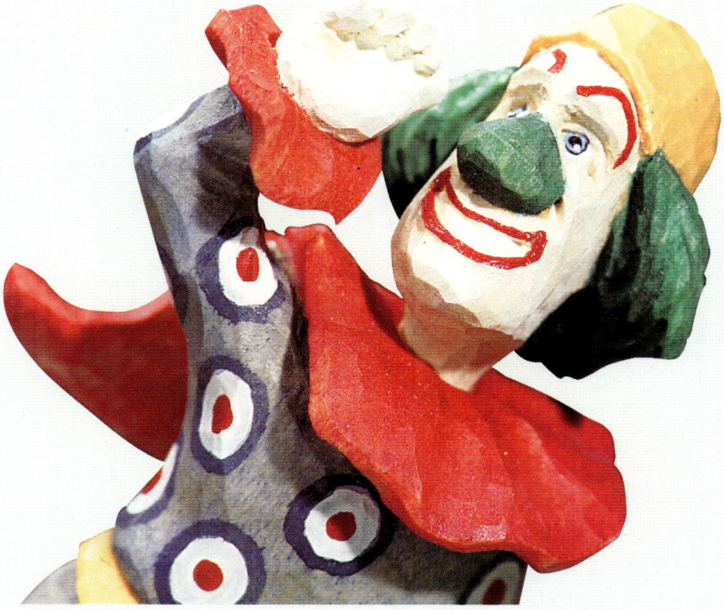

I chose to dress Rick as a clown because the choices of a brightly colored costume are endless. I painted this piece with thin acrylic washes and antiqued it with a mixture of boiled linseed oil mixed with a small amount of oil-based raw umber color.

Twinkle Toes by Keith Morrill

Keith Morrill

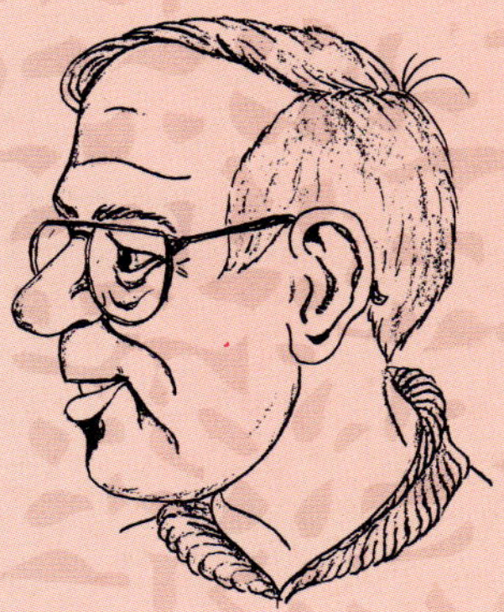

Keith, a resident of Albuquerque, New Mexico, and a retired teacher from the Biology/Microbiology Department at South Dakota State University, has had a life-long interest in carving wood. Only after attending a variety of classes and workshops did carving become a "serious endeavor." While he has enjoyed carving a wide range of subjects in a variety of styles, caricature carving is Keith's first love.

Keith's contributions to the CCA Circus appear on pages 21, 22, 69, 70 and 71.

Keith has taught carving classes in Brookings on a regular basis and has been invited to teach other seminars throughout the Midwest. Since 1986, he has been the summer carver-in-residence at the National Museum of Woodcarving in Custer, South Dakota. He was elected to membership in CCA in 1993.

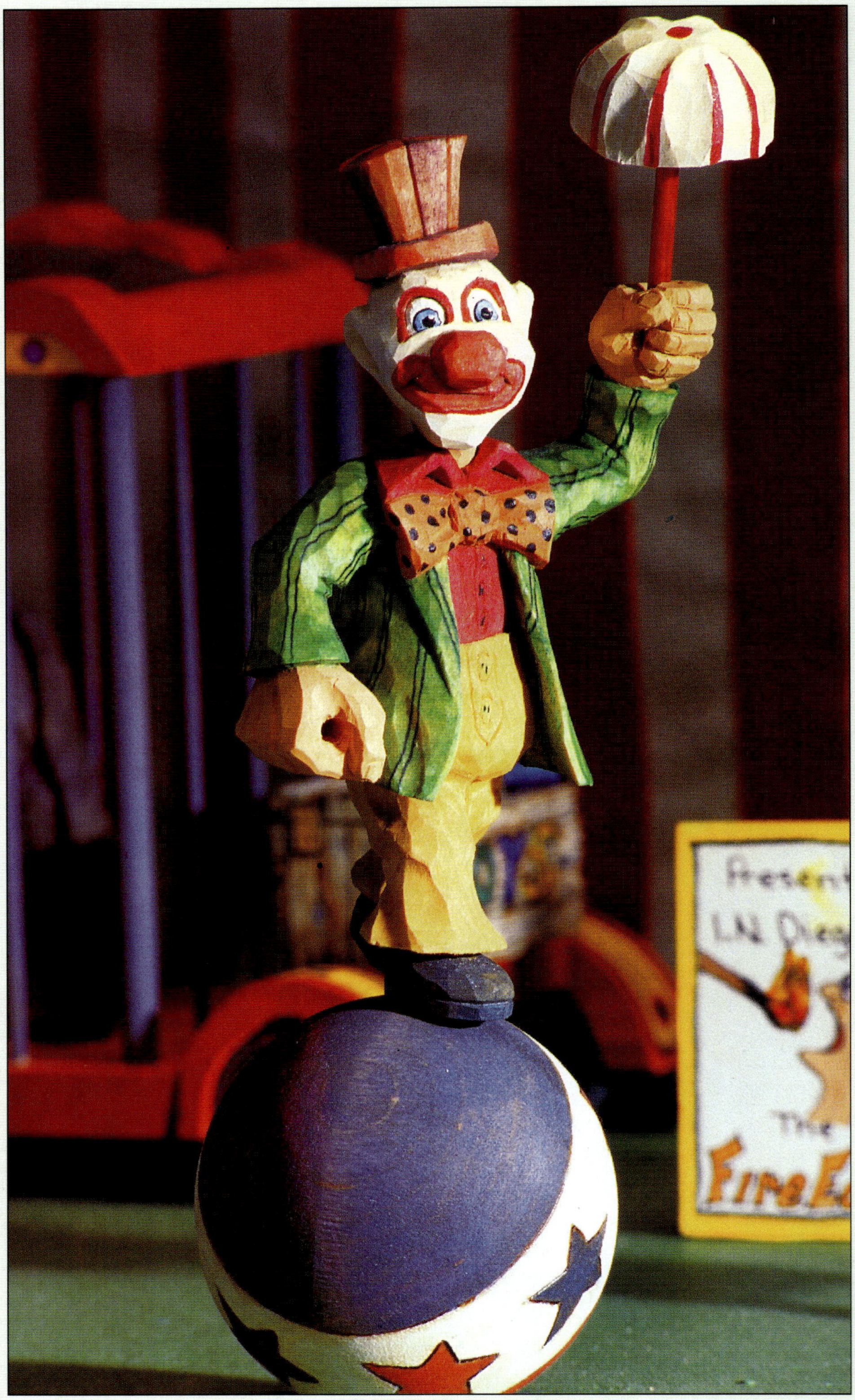

Balancing on a ball, or perhaps not balancing on a ball, will get this clown by Keith Morrill big laughs. The clown and the umbrella were carved separately. The ball upon which the clown balances was actually bought at a craft store.

Clown on a Unicycle by Dave Rasmussen

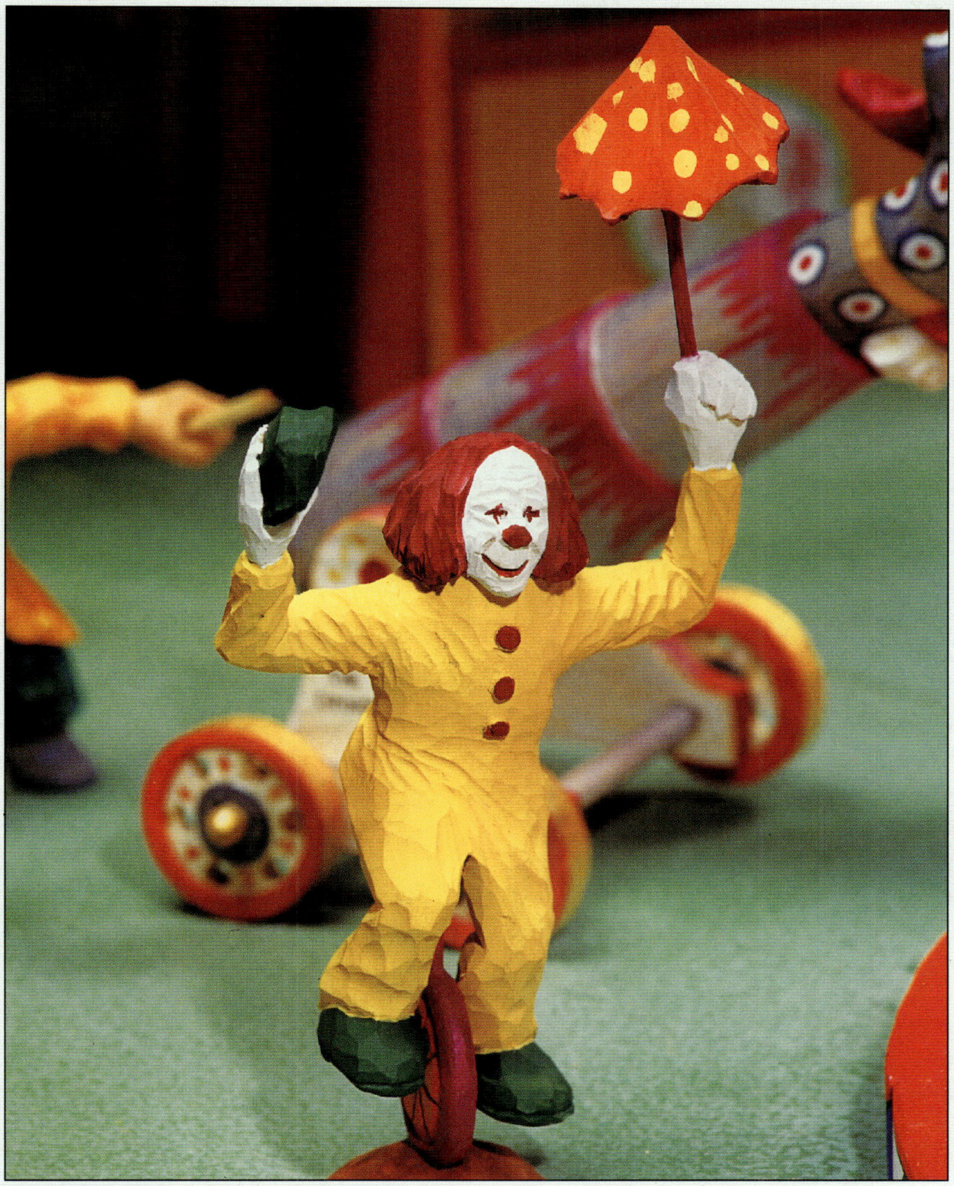

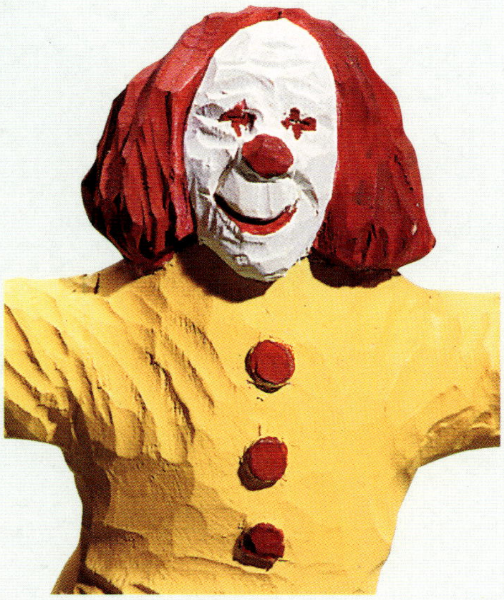

When considering what characters to carve for the circus project, I wanted one that was somewhat difficult. I chose a clown on a unicycle that could be made as difficult as I wanted and two simple figures, a boy with an ice cream cone and a Frankenstein-like spectator, that were much easier.

I made a clay model for the clown. By using the clay model as a guide, I could take measurements as needed while I was carving. I also used the model as a pattern to transfer the outside dimensions of the design, showing both front and side views, to a block.

I then bandsawed the block. Carving smaller figures goes quick, until the detailing. I always carve all over the piece until it looks in balance. Then I concentrate on one area, like the face, and carve it until it is about finished. I use a magnifying glass to correct any flaws before I continue on.

I carved the seat of the unicycle in place. The wheel was carved separately. To connect the two, I inserted a dowel into both pieces. The wheel could have had spokes, but I wanted to keep it simple. I carved the hat and the umbrella separately and placed them in the hands.

The clown took about two weeks to complete. I work on a carving for a while then work on another one. After a while the defects become apparent and I pick away on it in small time segments until I finally have a finished carving that I can then paint.

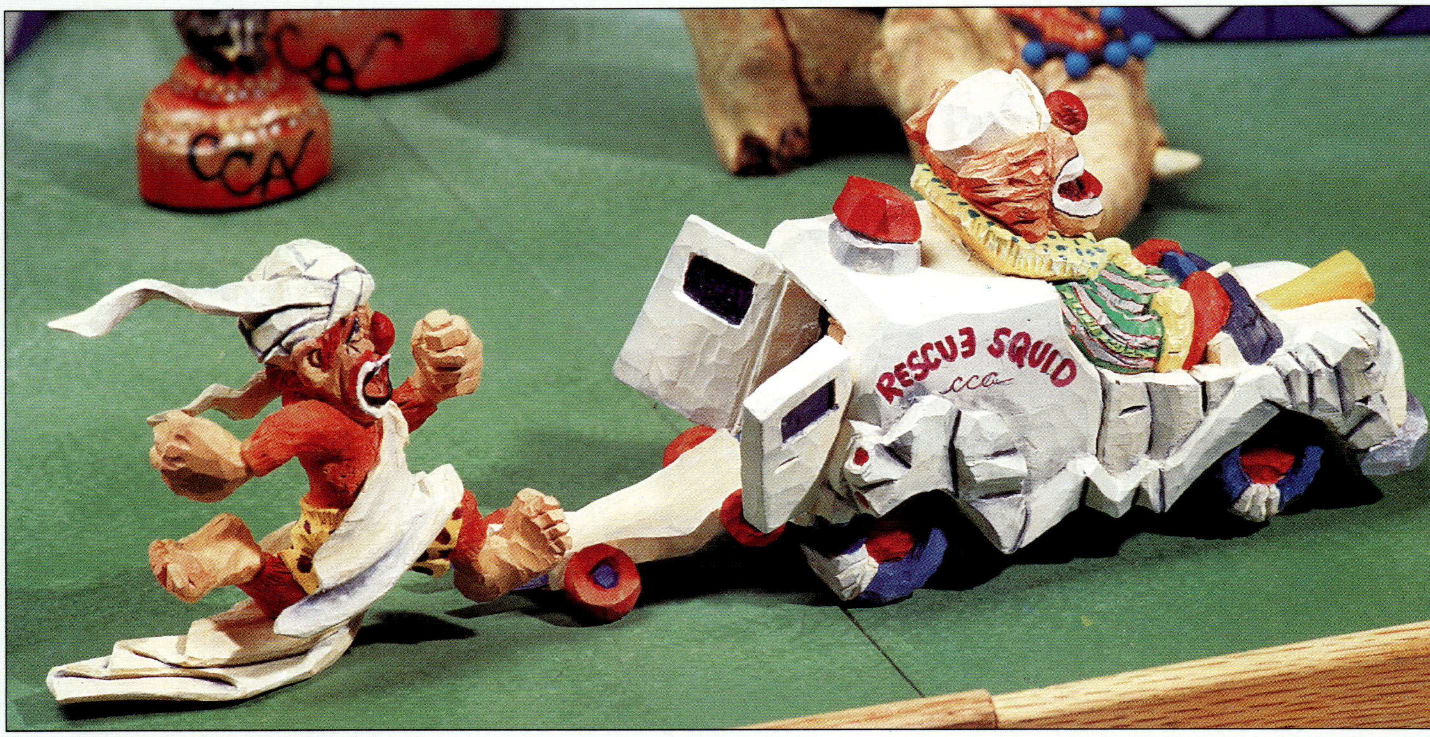

The Circus Ambulance by Pete Ortel

The CCA *Circus* was a great project to be involved with, but what does a guy from the Bronx in New York City know about circuses? I've spent a career with the cops, fire fighting, rescue calls... *Hey there's an idea!* (Yep. I talk to myself... Often too!) *How about a fire chief with a …? Oh, somebody's doing it. What about an elephant squirting water…? Somebody's doing that, too? I've got it! An ambulance!!*

Now I've got a subject. It's pretty serious stuff for a caricature circus, but that's what's exciting about carving caricatures. There are so many wonderful and exciting things going on around us all the time that are humorous or can be changed slightly to become truly funny. *So now I've got this ambulance. The driver is a clown. He's hysterical, laughing because he just crashed his ambulance, the back doors flew open, and the patient in the back… well he's no longer in the back. He fell out and he's running after the ambulance trying to get back in.* Now you see how an idea develops into a scenario. One thought gives birth to another thought. It's the first one that's sometimes a little hard to find.

Now I need to start carving. I wanted you to hear the hysterical laughter of the driver, but also to see the little guy running. The big laugh was my first step, then the damage to the vehicle was designed and carved. The back doors had to look like they were damaged and flew open, and the stretcher dragging behind had to tell you that someone was on it only moments ago.

Then it became more challenging. Making a figure run can be done many ways. *Spread his legs, both feet on the ground. Shift his legs, forward foot on the ground, second leg trailing, or put his forward foot and leg in the air and his second leg on the ground.* For this piece I decided to defy all the rules and pull both feet off the ground.

After much experimenting, I figured out a way to make my idea work. I placed a blanket around the patient's body and made it look like he was running out of it. I used a small dowel, placed into the bottom and extending into the ground, for mounting. By turning the wood so the grain ran horizontally, I was able to get the maximum strength out of the piece allowing me to extend the head bandage, for effect, as if it was trailing in the air due to the speed at which the figure is running.

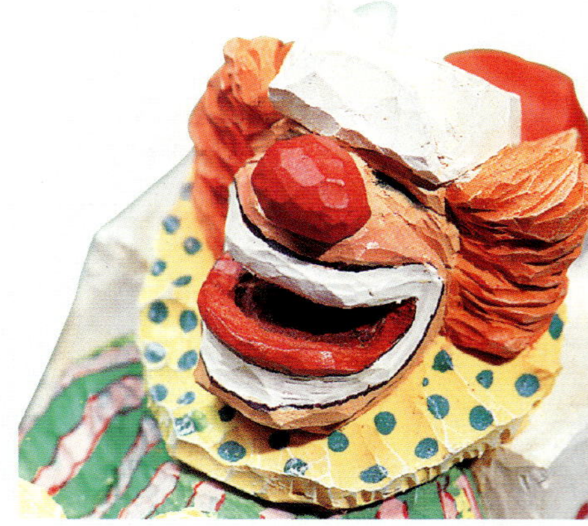

Pete Ortel

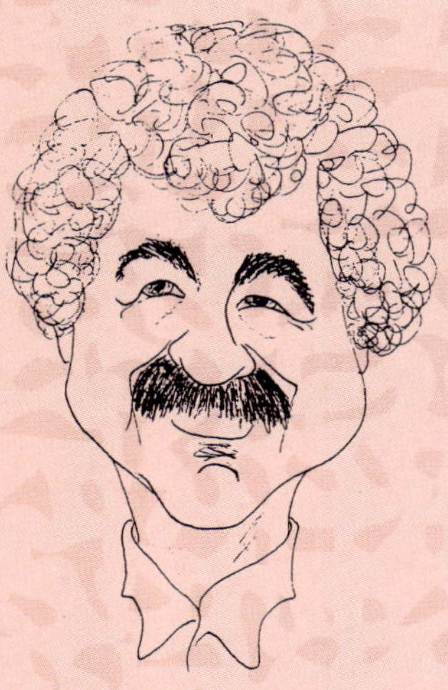

Pete, a retired New York City firefighter living in Monroe, New York, has always had an appreciation for all art forms, but holds a special affection for cartooning and woodcarving. Working in New York City, Pete could always find humor on the streets and in the firehouse and, when not fighting fires, he could be found sketching cartoons of the various situations he saw. His imagination and humor are reflected in the scenarios he creates.

Pete's contributions to the CCA Circus appear on pages 24 and 25.

Through reading books on caricature carving, Pete soon learned he could combine his fondness for cartooning with his love for wood. He took his first formal lesson in 1989 and was completely hooked. He's been carving ever since.

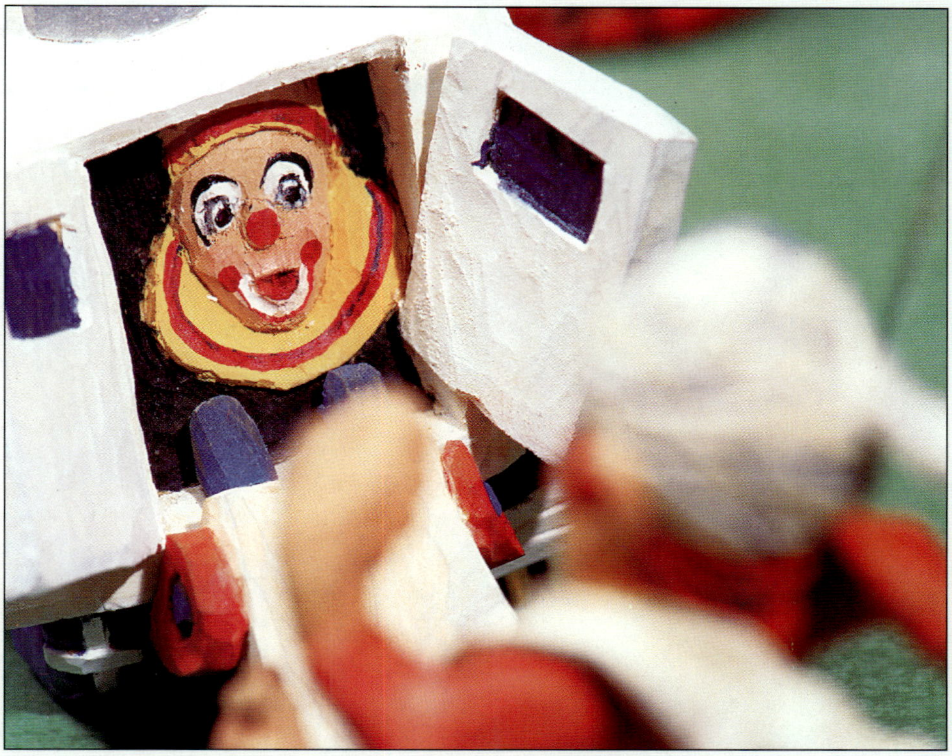

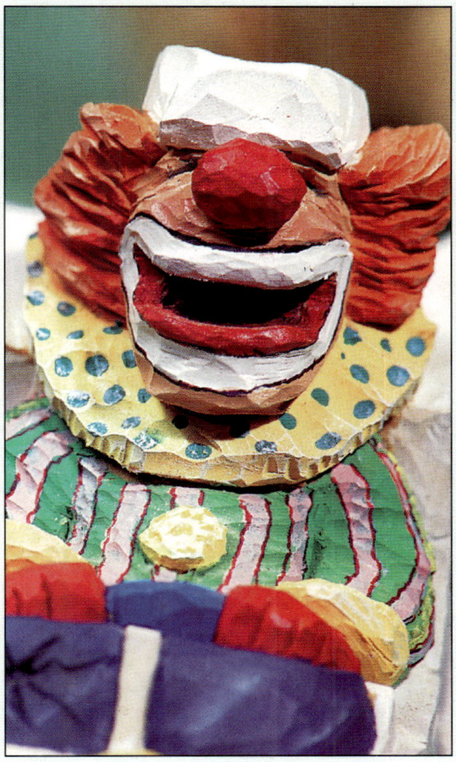

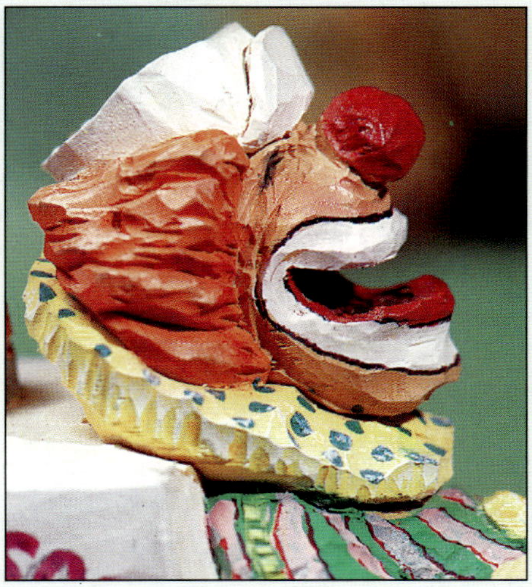

Clownin' Around by Doug Raine

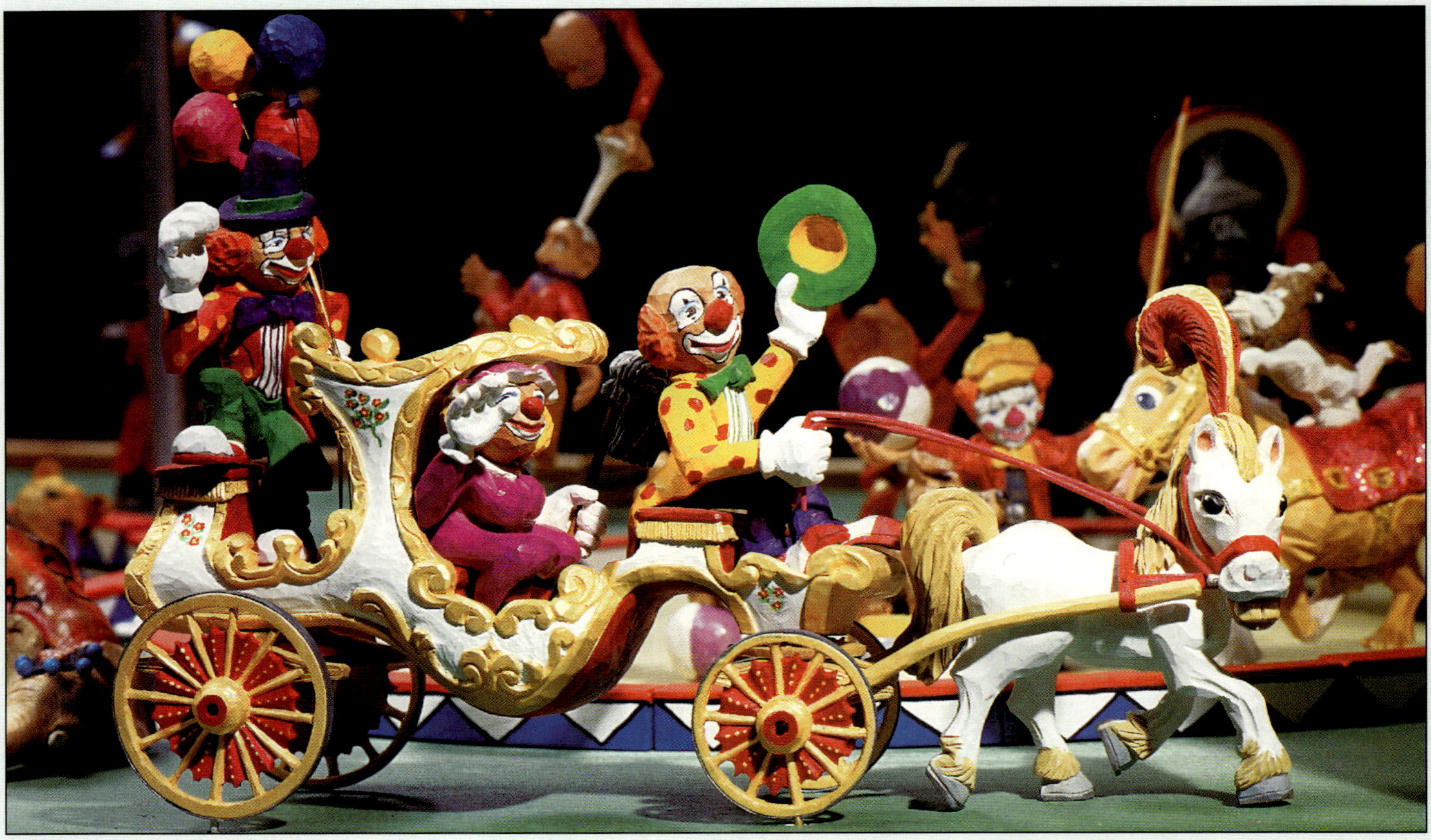

When I decided to carve a carriage with three clowns and a pony, I knew I did not want static figures. I carved the footman standing with one foot in the well and the other on the seat cushion. One hand is waving, the other clasps a string of balloons. The driver is clutching his hat in one hand; the other is holding the reins. The right shoulder down and the left leg and foot extended add a bit of action to the scene.

In clown fashion, Cinderella is a buxom maiden with a dirty old mop hanging off the side of the carriage. So far, all this nonsense was a lot of fun to think up, but oh, the carving!

A pony needed to be carved to haul this whole outfit. I turned the pony's head to the right, so he would be looking at the crowd along with the clowns. An ostrich plume gives the pony a touch of elegance.

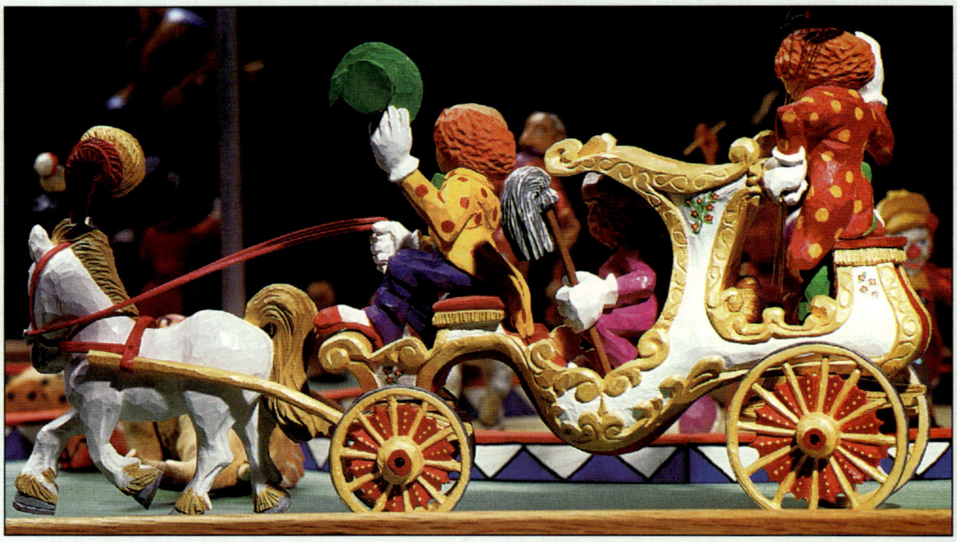

I had a lot of fun carving the hands. They are oversized and wearing white gloves. In carving the hands you have to consider the varying curvature of the back of the hand and the various planes formed by the position of the fingers and thumb. The best and closest model is your own hand.

I finished with Watco Satin Wax Natural. I like the satin sheen this gives my carving, and I find a piece coated with this is easier to dust and maintain.

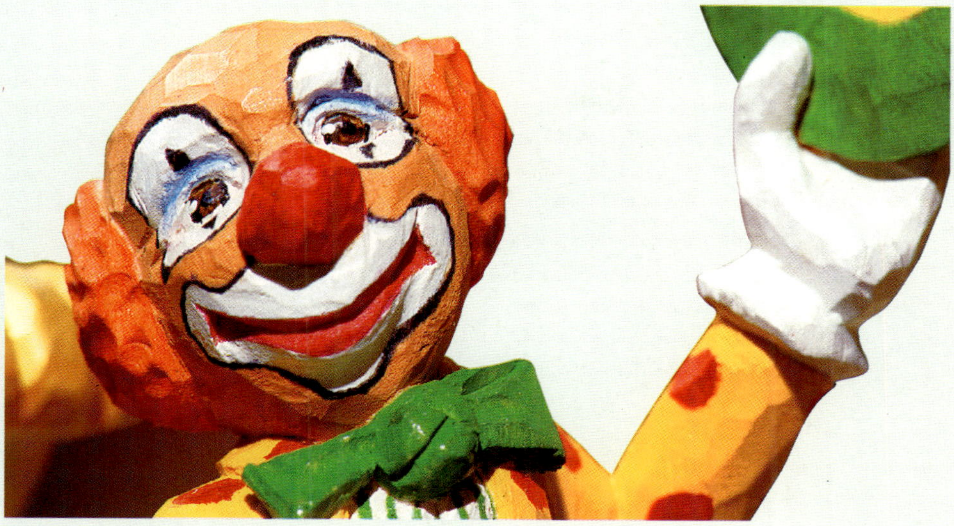

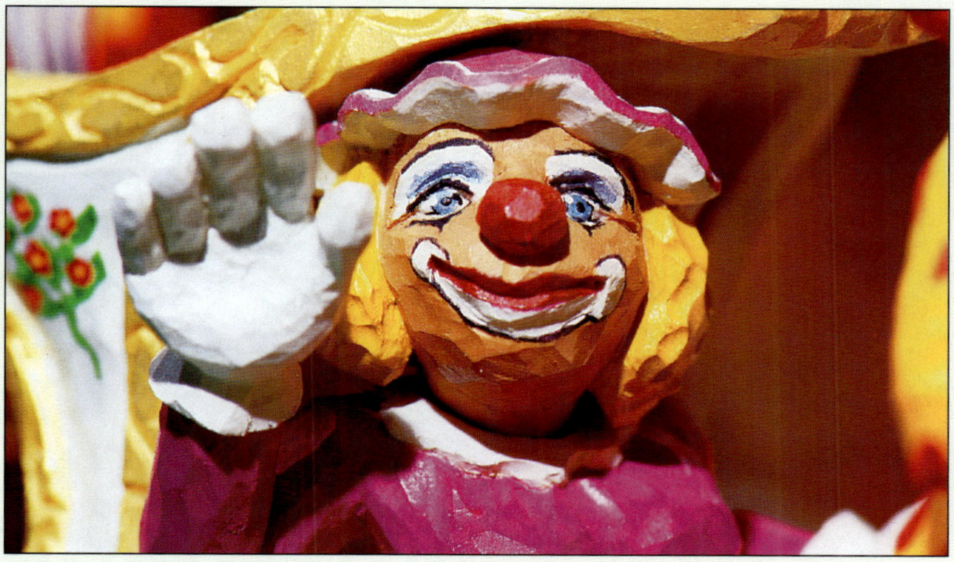

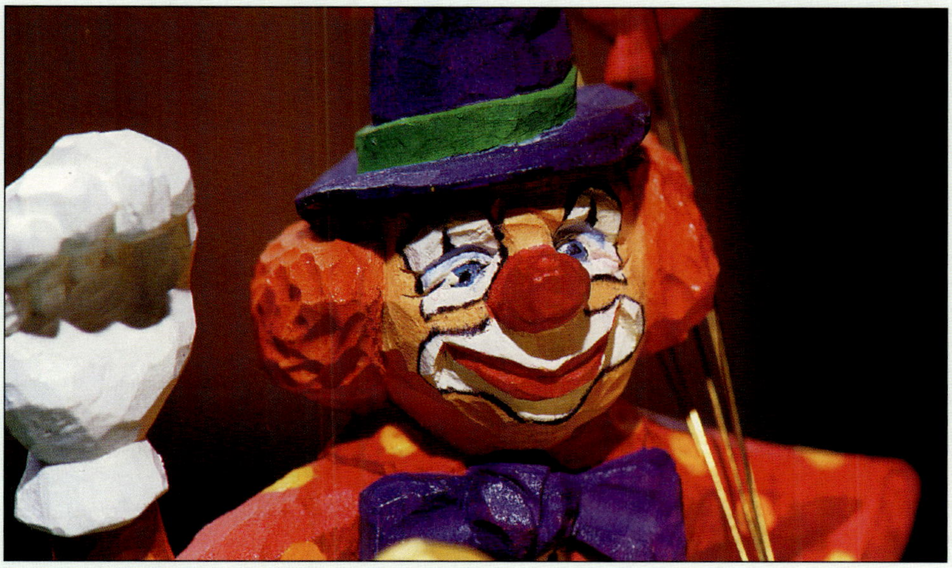

Doug Raine

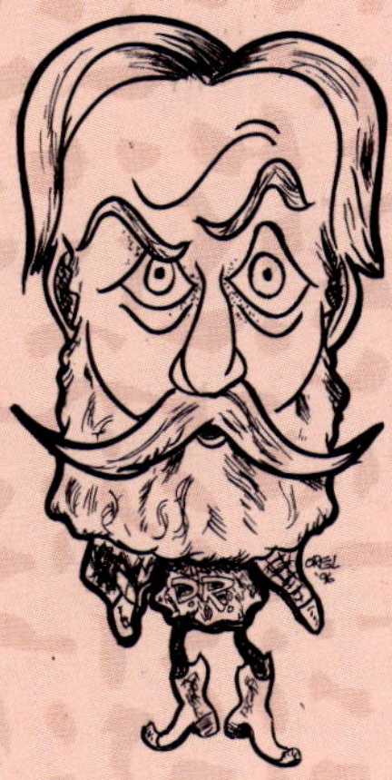

Doug began carving when not tending to chores on the family farm. At 16 he shipped out on a Great Lakes freighter and passed the time during off-duty hours carving small figures. After college graduation, he joined the U.S. Air Force and became a jet fighter pilot. He earned two combat decorations in Korea and again found himself passing time woodcarving. Doug later worked as an elementary and junior high school principal. He was active in Boy Scouting with his son, and campouts found him carving a caged ball and chain for the fascinated Scouts.

Doug's contributions to the CCA Circus appear on pages 26, 27 and 46.

Doug served as president of the Southwest Woodcarvers and is a member of the Arizona Woodcarvers, the National Woodcarvers Association, and the Affiliated Woodcarvers, Ltd.

Free Ride by Cleve Taylor

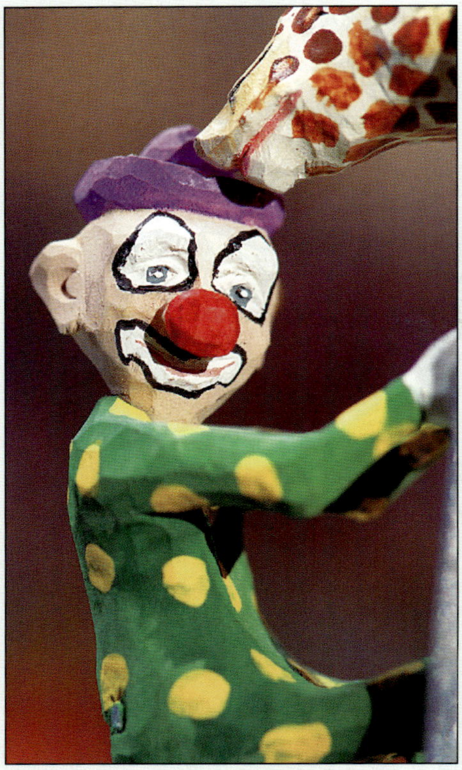

This very patient (and well-trained) giraffe becomes a make-shift sliding board for these two clowns. The ladder supporting the clown is resting between the giraffe's horns and his ears. The top rung of the ladder was inserted into the clown's hands.

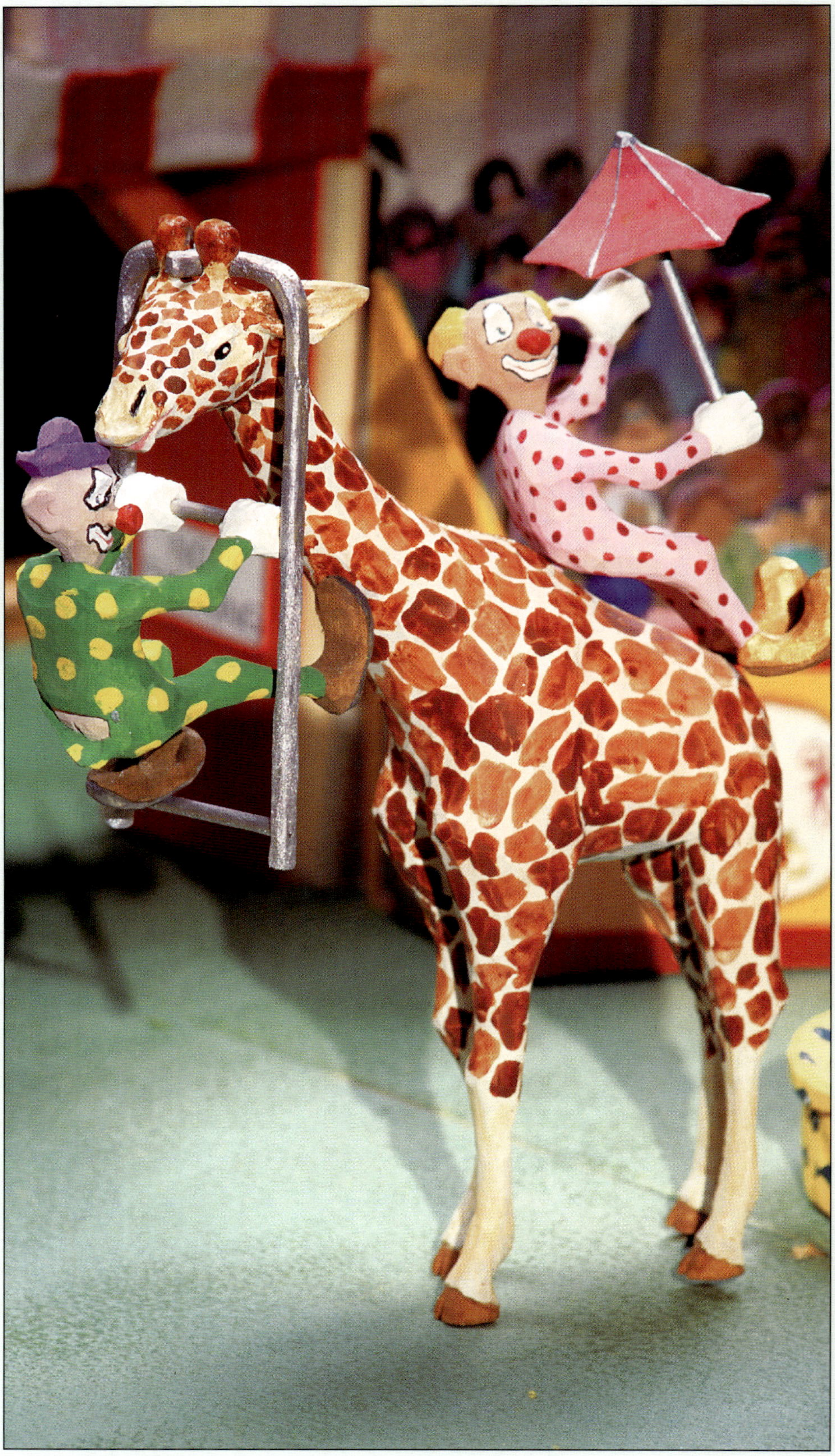

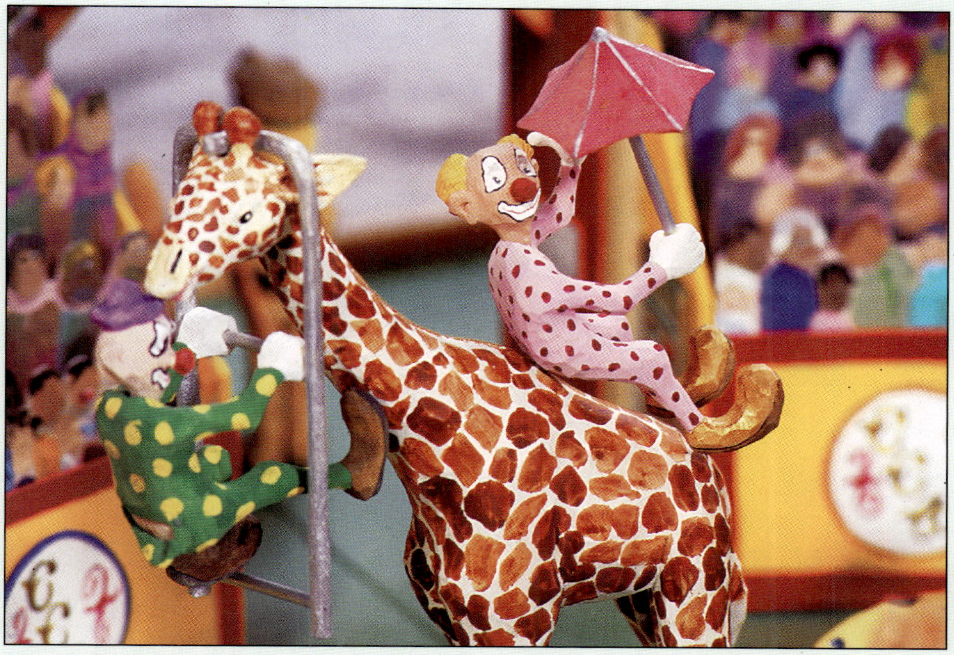

An umbrella helps Cleve Taylor's second clown keep his balance as he slides down the giraffe's back. The umbrella was carved separately and inserted into the clown's hand.

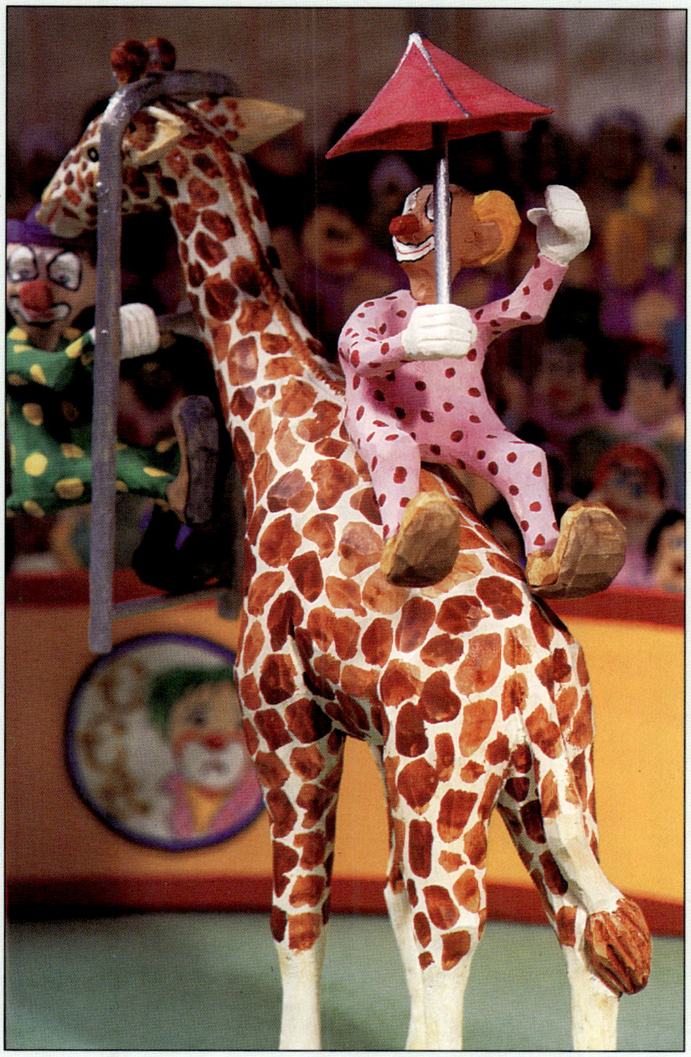

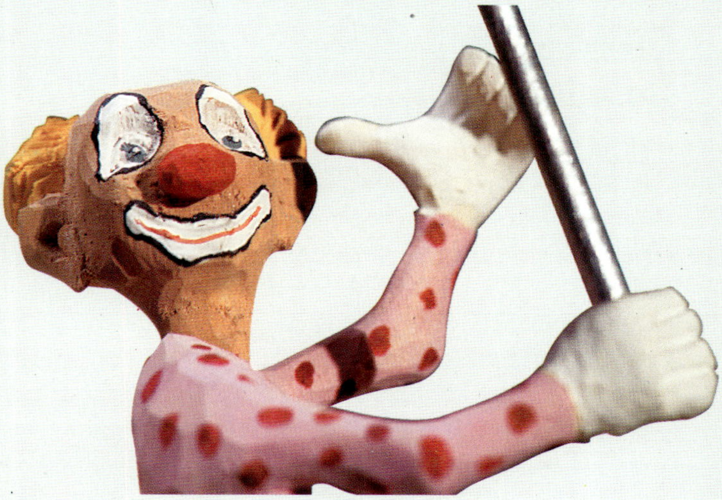

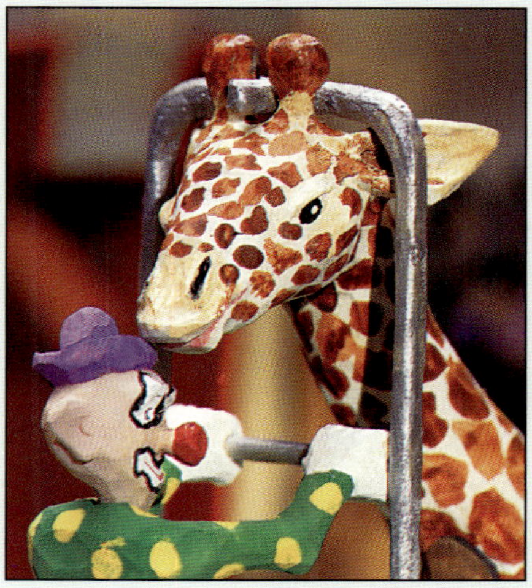

CIRCUS PEOPLE

The Brothers Gnomeaux by Marv Kaisersatt

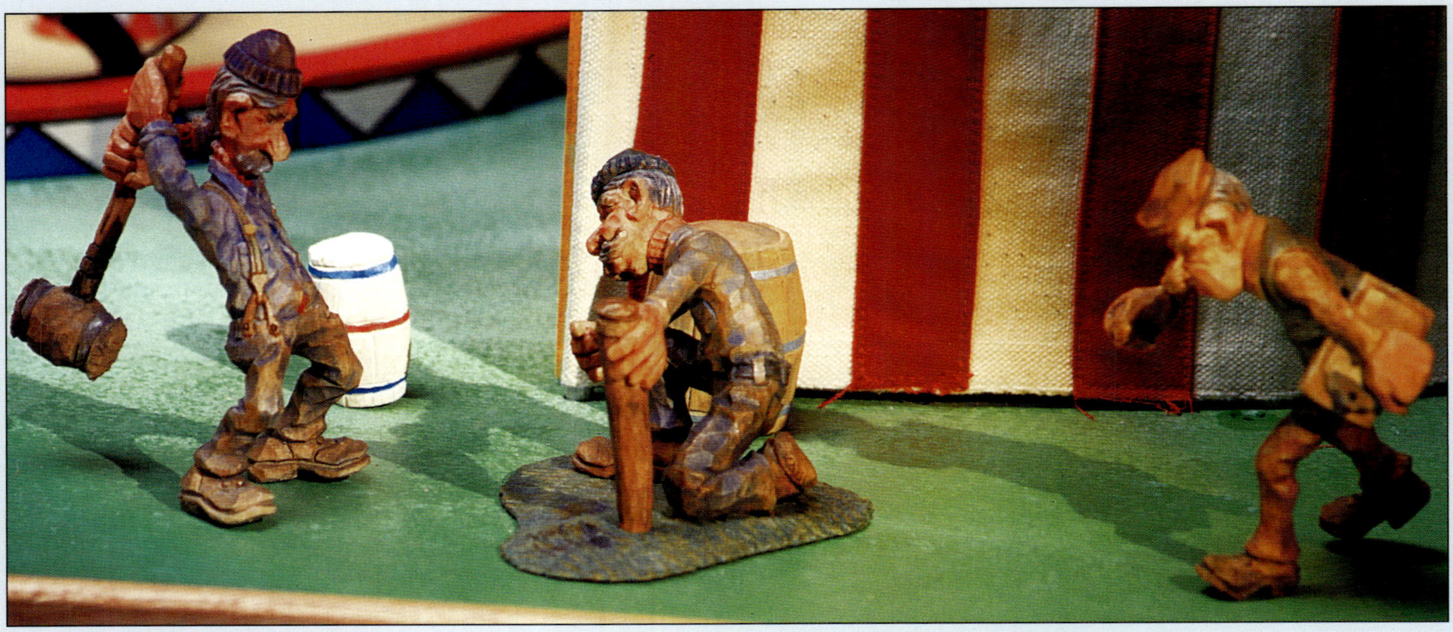

The Big Top is up, the show is moving along, and a workman is driving a stake outside the entrance! The incongruity of this situation didn't occur to me when I selected the sledge-wielding roustabouts as my contribution to the CCA *Circus*. I was on the verge of scrapping this character, however, my enthusiasm returned after exploring ideas involving crews of workers.

Translating my ideas of the three workers into three-dimensional models was my next step. For this, preliminary sketches were done with 10" flexible mannequins. My set of mannequins are assembled from pipe-cleaner-type wire, plastic tubes (ball point pen barrels) and scraps of wood, plus magnets for the bottoms of the feet. Setting up a mannequin of this type is quick and changes are easy. These sketches made from the model are used to make figures in clay. The clay models are then set aside, studied and revised as necessary.

Once the final poses are established in clay, I start thinking about details and clarifying them. Out comes the box of magazine clippings, photos and catalogs, or for those more organized, go to the appropriately labeled file folder and find the information exactly where you put it. Either way, pile or file, researching details is time well spent. The more you know about a subject, the more comfortable you'll be while carving. Carving will be more enjoyable, and the results will be closer to your expectations. Know how to cut and where to cut.

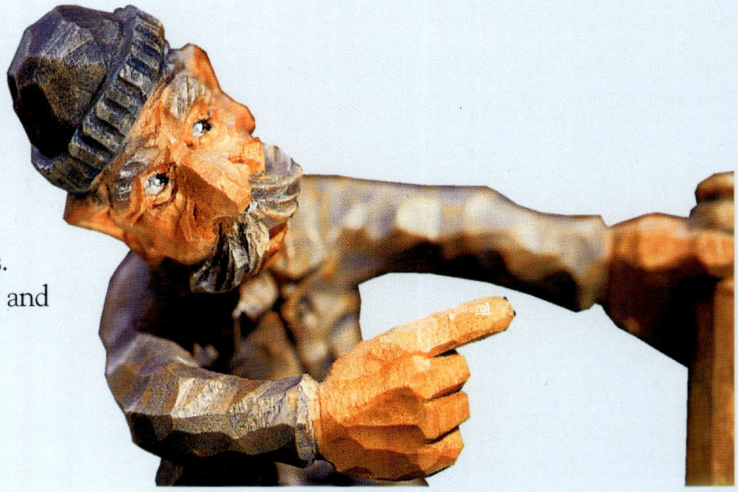

My carvings are sealed with tinted lacquer and stained with oil paint. The colors are blended into the wood and any excess stain is wiped off. A final matte finish is applied by spraying. Generally, I use a "carved finish," referred to by some as no finish or unfinished!

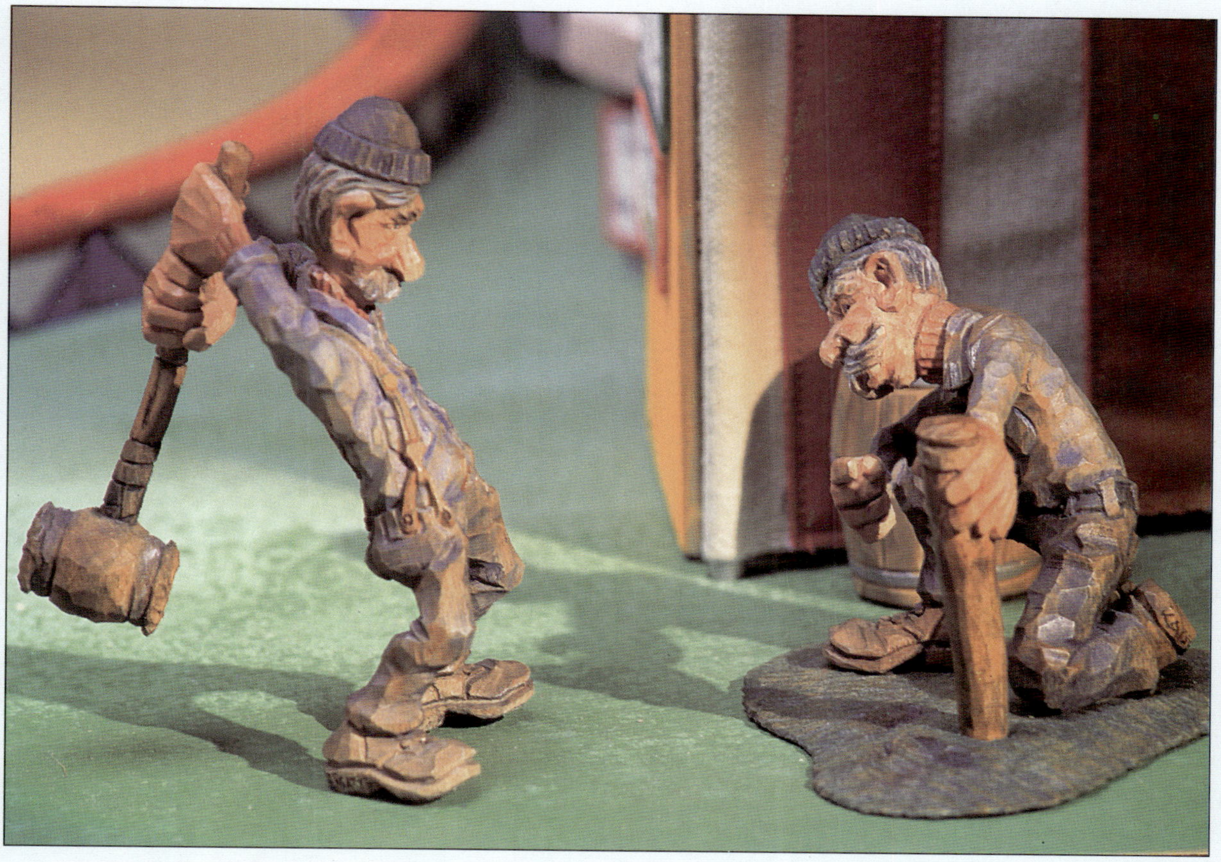

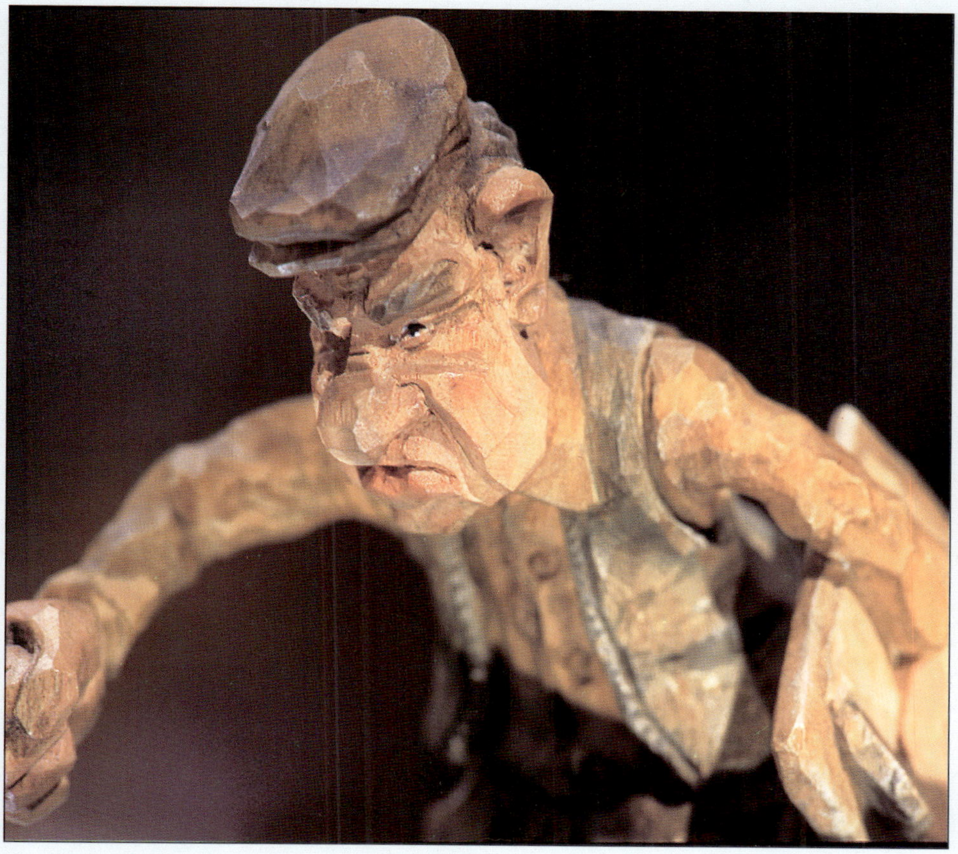

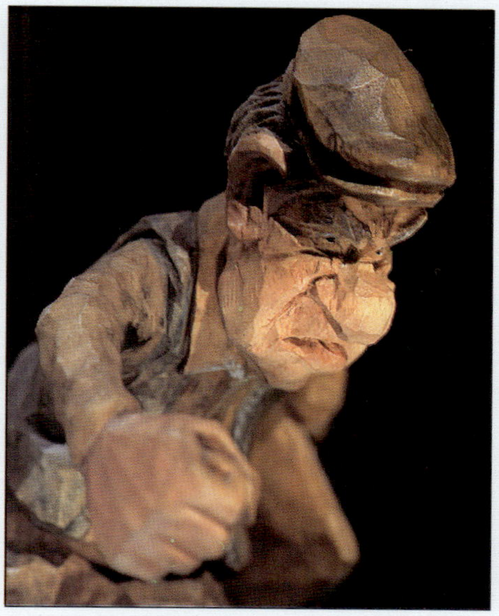

Carved from one piece of wood, Marv Kaisersatt's carving of the man holding the stake had to be reinforced to prevent breakage. A base and a metal pin, which runs through the base into the stake were added to make the left arm more stable.

Marv Kaisersatt

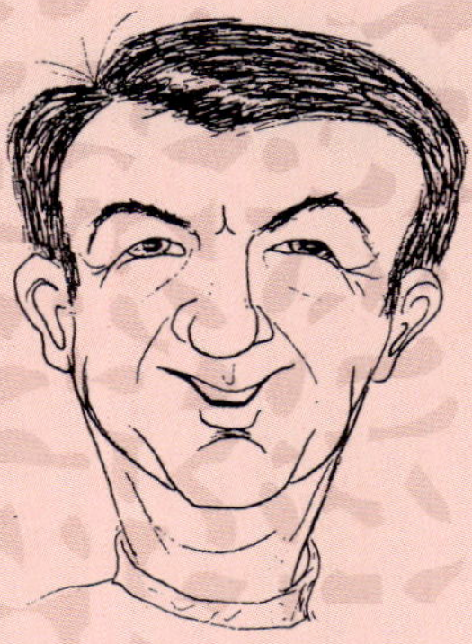

Marv, a Faribault, Minnesota, resident, is a retired junior high mathematics teacher and has been carving since 1976. Marv's caricature speciality is unpainted figures carved from a single chunk of wood. His figures depict "ordinary folks doing ordinary things in exaggerated ways."

Marv's contributions to the CCA Circus appear on pages 30, 31, 32, 44 and 45.

Marv is a founding member of CCA. He teaches several week-long seminars each year in Faribault. His awards are many and include honors from the International Woodcarvers Congress; the Upper Midwest Woodcarvers Expo in Blue Earth, Minnesota; and the Nordic Fest Woodcarving Exhibition in Decorah, Iowa.

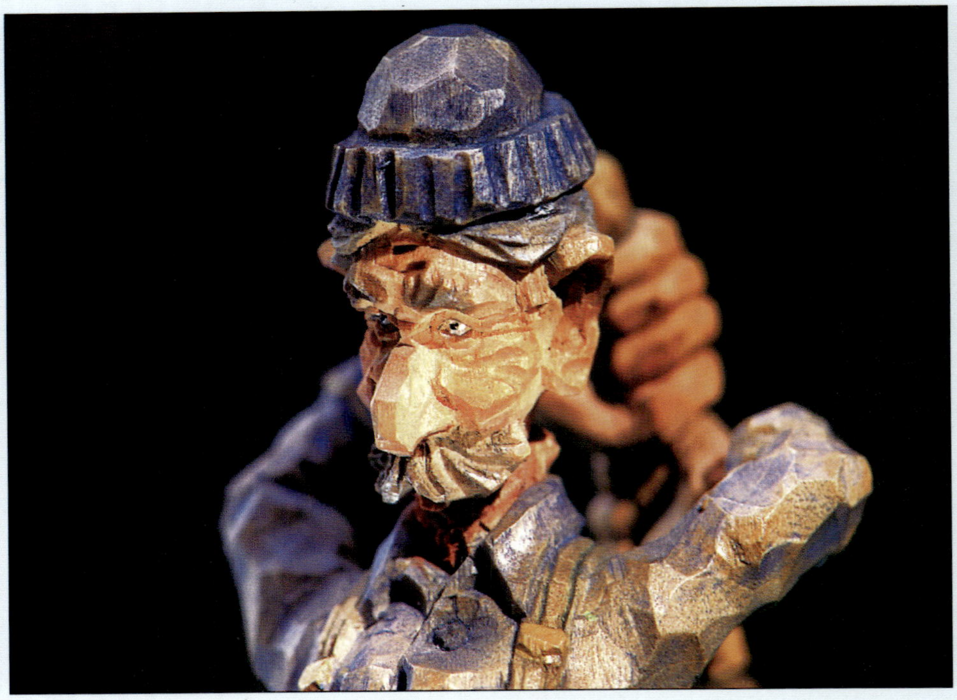

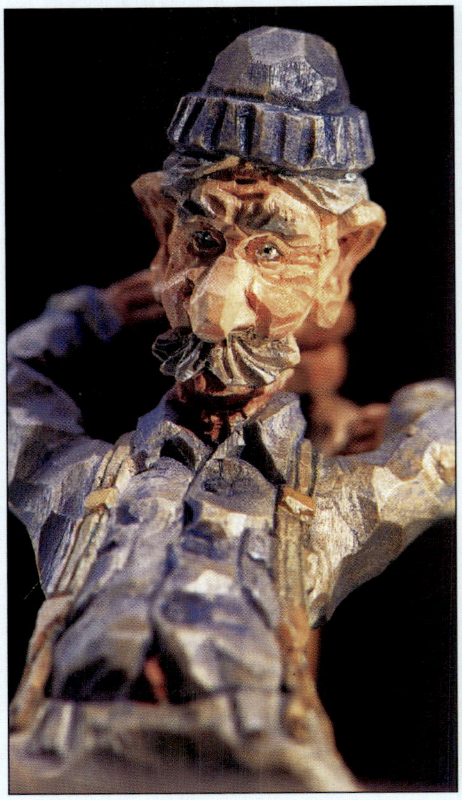

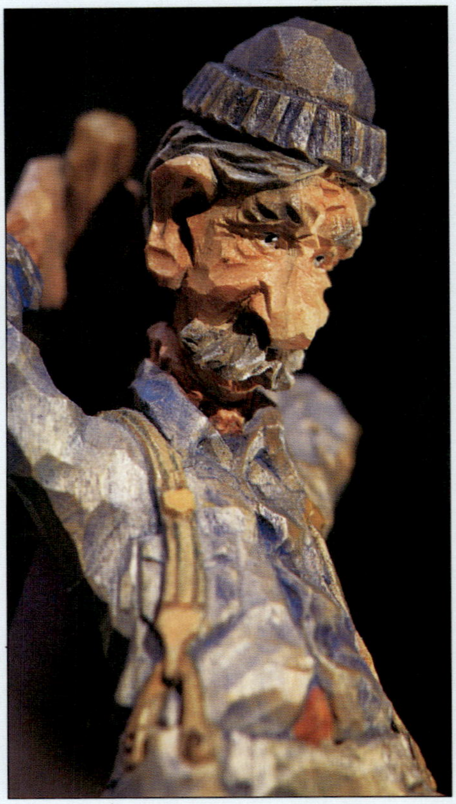

Keeping the hammer in this guy's hands took a little extra planning on artist Marv Kaisersatt's part. A metal pin connects the hammer to the hands to give the piece some added strength.

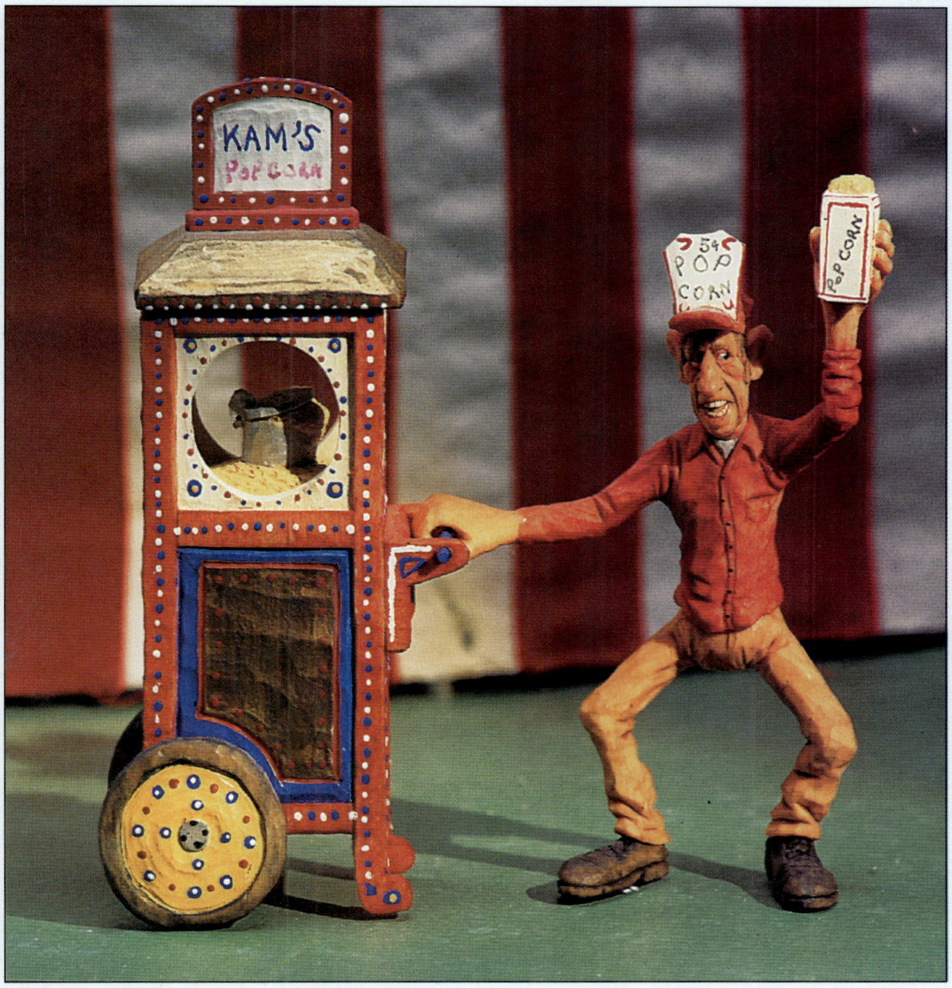

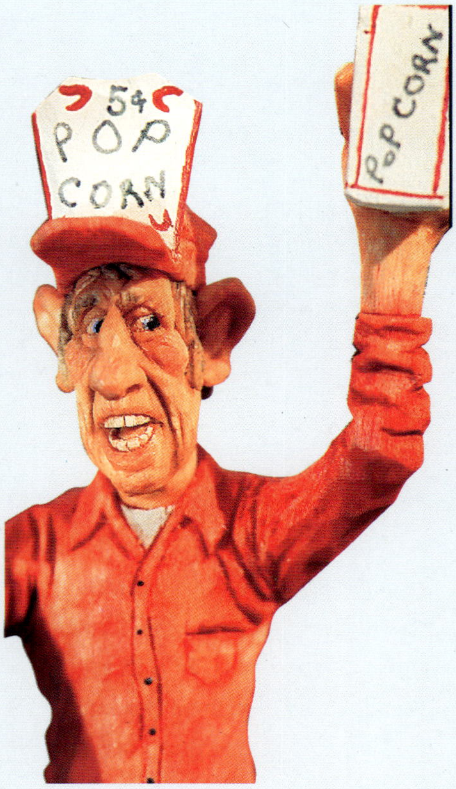

Kernel P. Cobb by W. "Pete" LeClair

When my Granddaddy was young, he operated a popcorn concession stand. Without hesitation, my first carving for the CCA *Circus* had to be a popcorn man with a push cart as a tribute to my Granddaddy. Once I knew what I was going to carve, I wanted to give my character a name. After much deliberation with friends, I settled on Kernel P. Cobb.

After my decision was made on what type of carving I would do, my first step was to draw the pattern. Drawing has always been a difficult task for me. I begin by drawing stick figures in the appropriate positions, then it usually takes several tedious hours to draw and refine the stick figures for my pattern. I then trace the pattern on a block of basswood and cut out on the bandsaw.

The tools I used for this project were a good knife and a 5mm #9, a 3mm #11 and a 4mm #12 Swiss gouge.

I begin carving the cut-outs by rough carving each into three-dimensional figures, always starting at the top and working my way down making as many as 8 or 9 passes before the figure is completed. At this point I put the carvings aside for a few days. This allows me to observe them from different angles and make minor adjustments, if needed, before they are painted.

I choose oil paints for my carvings. First, I apply a base coat to the entire carving. Once the base coat is dry, I begin painting the face. The eyes and teeth, as well as other small details are painted with fast-drying acrylics. The rest of the carving is painted with linseed oil washes, much the same way acrylic washes are applied.

Crowd Control by Randy Landen

Randy Landen

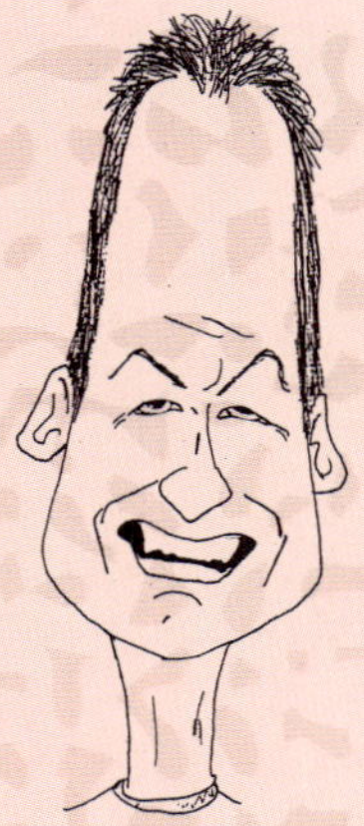

Randy, a Derby, Kansas, resident, is a Captain on the Wichita Police Department, in charge of the Special Operations Bureau. His interest in caricature carving began during a trip to Silver Dollar City in 1977. After collecting carvings for several years, Randy began carving in 1990. He typically uses a harder grade of basswood for his pieces. He finds the harder, yellowish-white basswood a little harder to carve, but feels the wood's ability to hold finer detail is well worth the trade-off.

Randy's contributions to the CCA Circus appear on pages 17, 18 and 34.

Randy has taught carving and painting classes at the Woodcarving Rendezvous and The International Woodcarvers Congress. He is a member of the National Wood Carvers Association and the Great Plains Wood Carvers. He currently serves on the Board of Directors for the Affiliated Woodcarvers, Ltd. and the International Wood Carvers Congress.

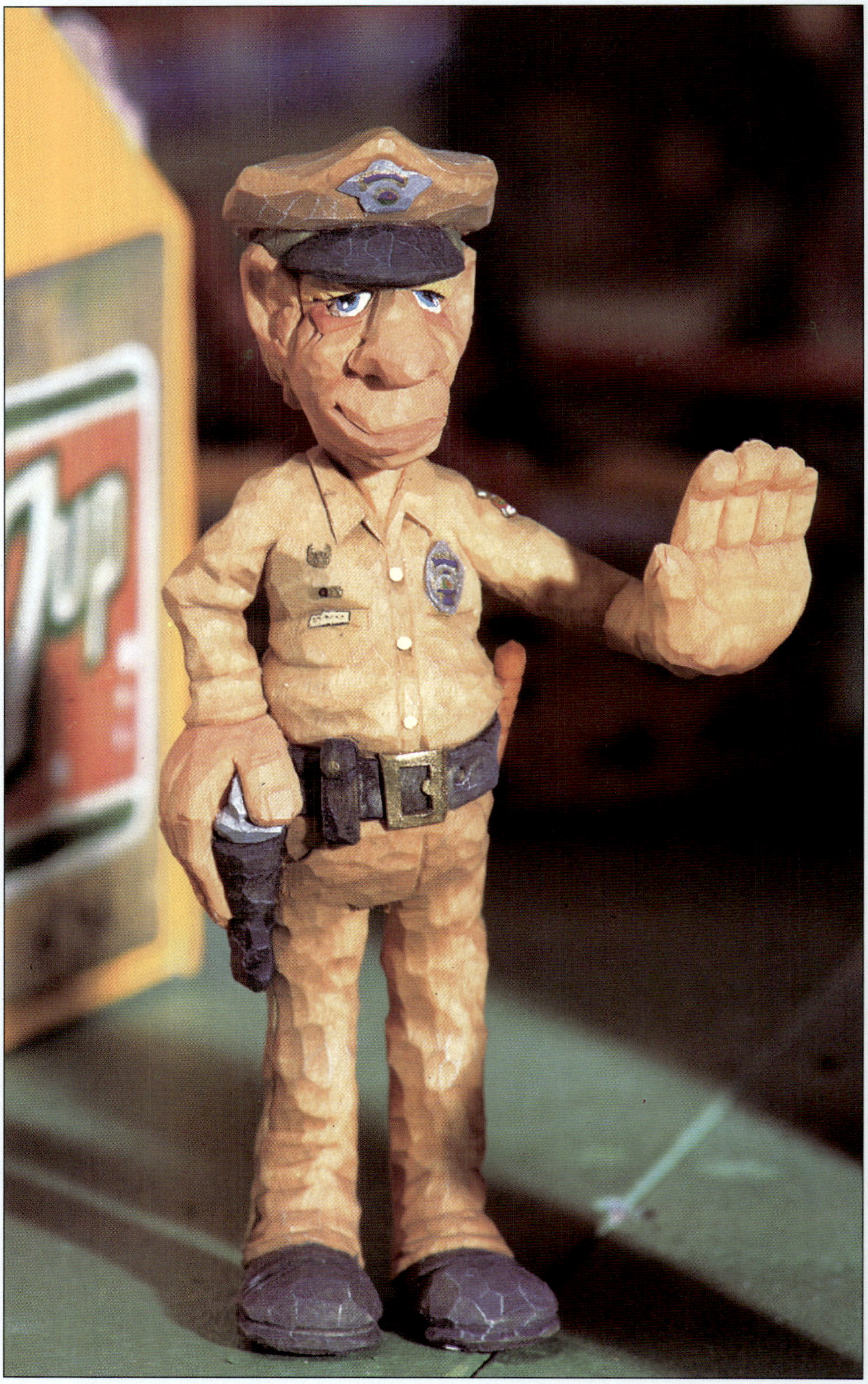

This policeman, dressed in the uniform of a Wichita, Kansas, policeman, was carved from one piece of wood, except for the raised left hand and the nightstick. The hand was carved separately, fitted into the sleeve and glued in place.

Dan by Harley Refsal

Harley Refsal

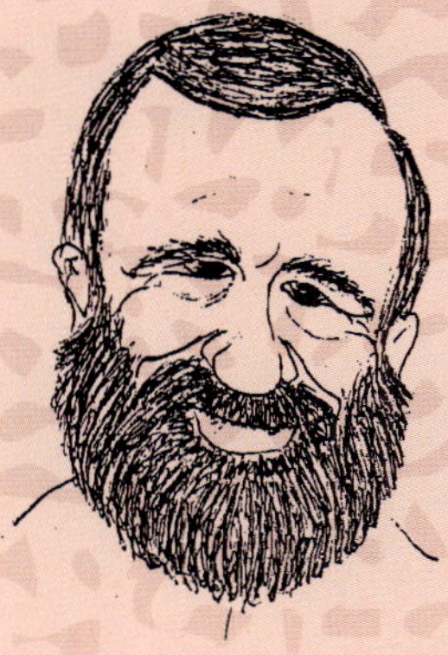

Harley was born and raised on a farm near Hoffman, Minnesota, homesteaded by his Norwegian-immigrant grandparents. He began working in wood as a young boy. His father, a carpenter and farmer, and a woodworker uncle who lived nearby kept him well supplied with wood, tools and encouragement. Today, Harley is an internationally recognized figure carver, specializing in Scandinavian-style flat-plane carving.

Harley's contribution to the CCA Circus *appears on page 35.*

Primarily self-taught, Harley began winning awards in regional and national carving exhibitions by the late 1970s. He teaches Scandinavian Studies at Luther College in Decorah, Iowa, where he also holds the title Resident Fellow in Scandinavian Folk Art.

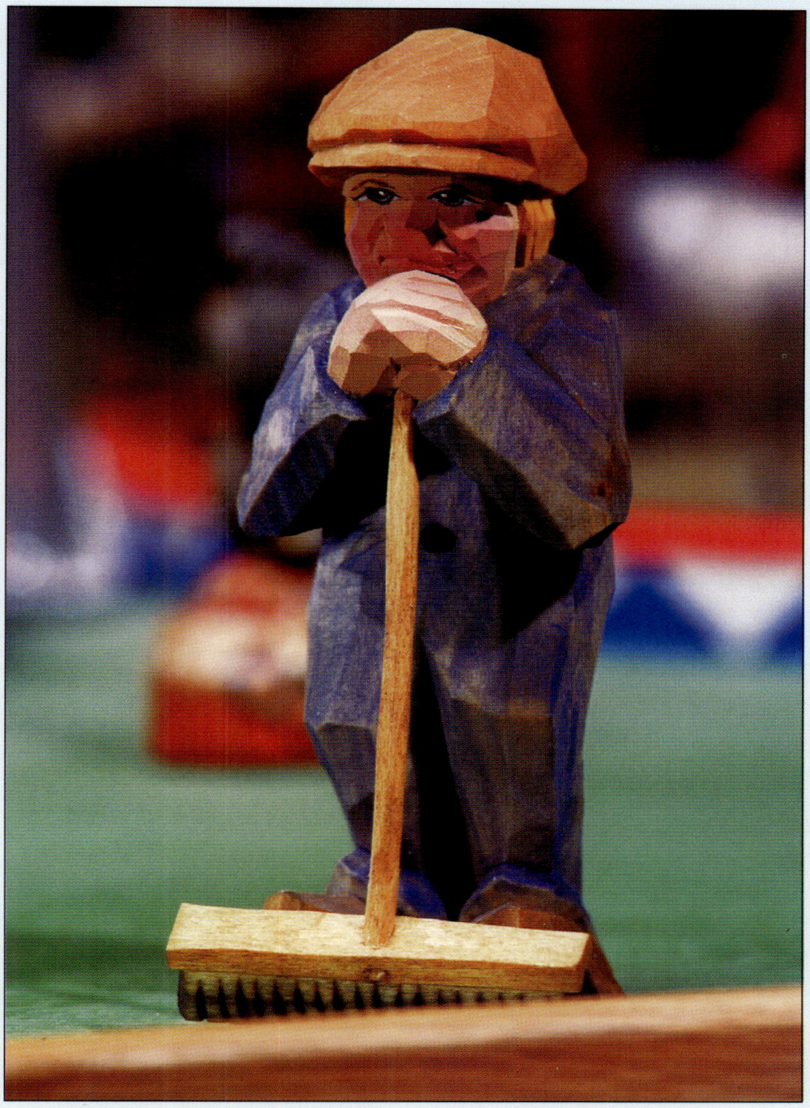

Someone always gets the job of cleaning up. And that someone is an especially vital person when the setting is a circus complete with live animals. For this character, I chose a stance that depicted him watching the show. He's relaxed, yet ready, leaning on a broom.

After bandsawing a rough shape, I began the actual carving. I typically use only a straight-blade bench knife, rather than a wider array of carving tools. The resulting figure has a minimalist or flat-plane look which I prefer, and the carving process affords the technical challenge of trying to say as much as possible with as few tools as possible.

In caricature, it is important to exaggerate physical features. I make the hands, feet and head larger than usual.

After finishing, I carved the two pieces of the broom, then glued the broom into place.

I painted this figure with acrylic paints. The final oil finish, applied after the paint was thoroughly dry, consisted of boiled linseed oil tinted with a bit of walnut-toned oil stain.

The Oompa Band by Dave Stetson and Harley Schmitgen

Dave Stetson

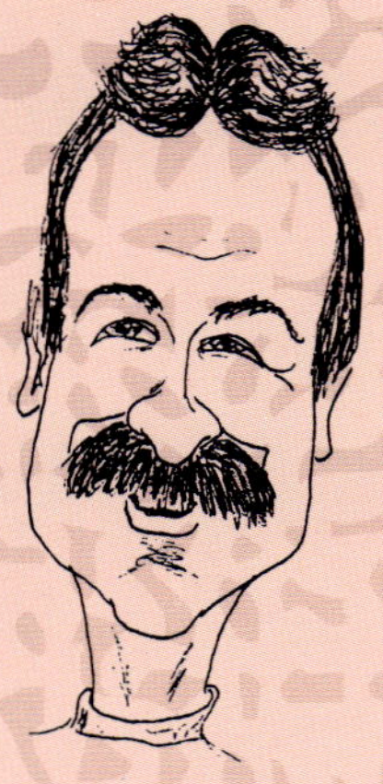

Dave is a bookbinder living with his family in Phoenix, Arizona. He has a flair for capturing humorous situations with figures in realistic poses. The western influence in his creations is derived from an admiration for the endangered species known as the "American Cowboy."

Dave's contributions to the CCA Circus appear on pages 36, 56, 57, 58 and 59.

Dave has studied with other wood carvers, but is essentially self-taught. He now teaches his carving style to others in his Phoenix studio. He has won many accolades for his caricatures including two best of show awards.

Dave is a founding member of CCA and the organization's second president. He is also active in several woodcarving organizations throughout the southwest.

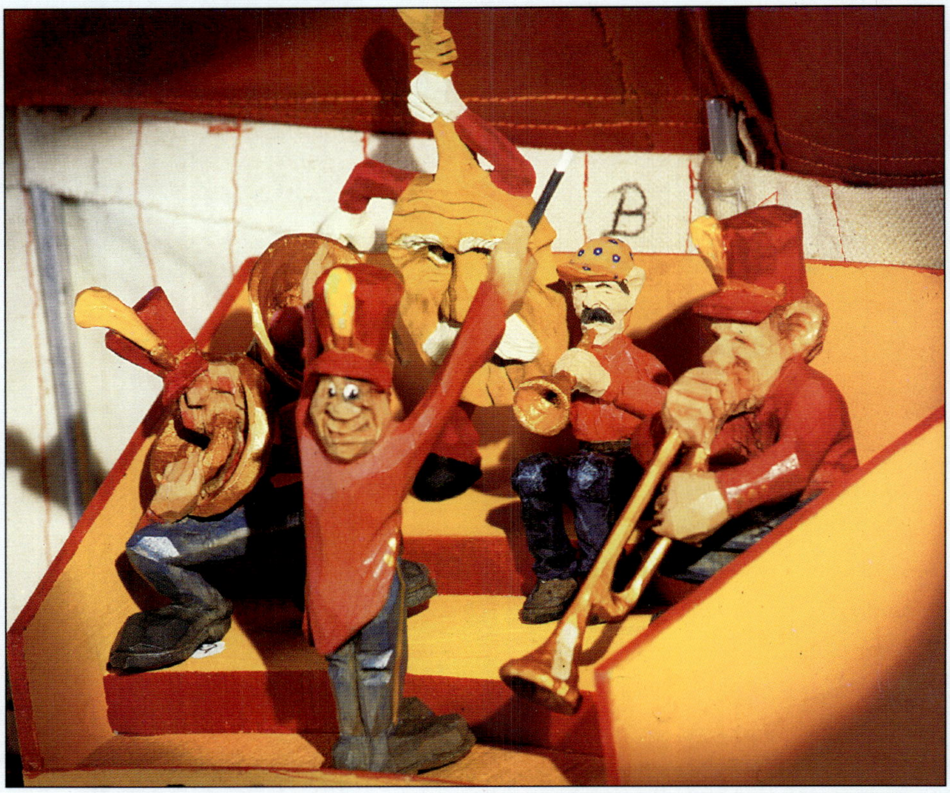

The tuba player, the trombone player and the band leader in the above photo were carved by Dave Stetson. The bass player and the trumpet player were carved by Harley Schmitgen.

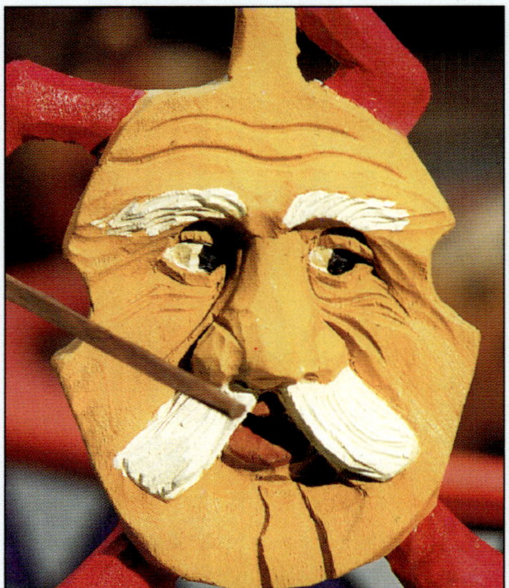

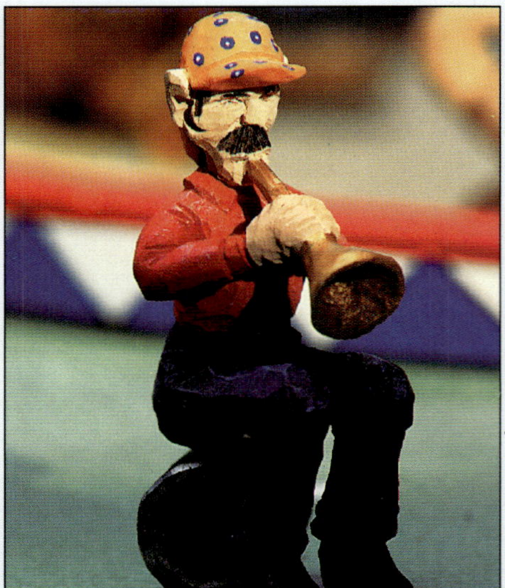

The band is an important part of the circus, heightening tension during death-defying acts and providing comical music for the many clown acts. The two musicians above and their instruments were carved by Harley Schmitgen from one piece of wood.

Circus Ringmaster by Gary Batte

Carving the circus ringmaster was appealing to me because of the importance of this circus character. The ringmaster helps to make the circus exciting by telling the audience about the history of an act and pointing out the things that make it especially dangerous or thrilling.

The most challenging aspect of this carving was positioning the arms and hands with the right arm and hand extended and holding a pointer and the left hand and arm slightly extended and holding a microphone.

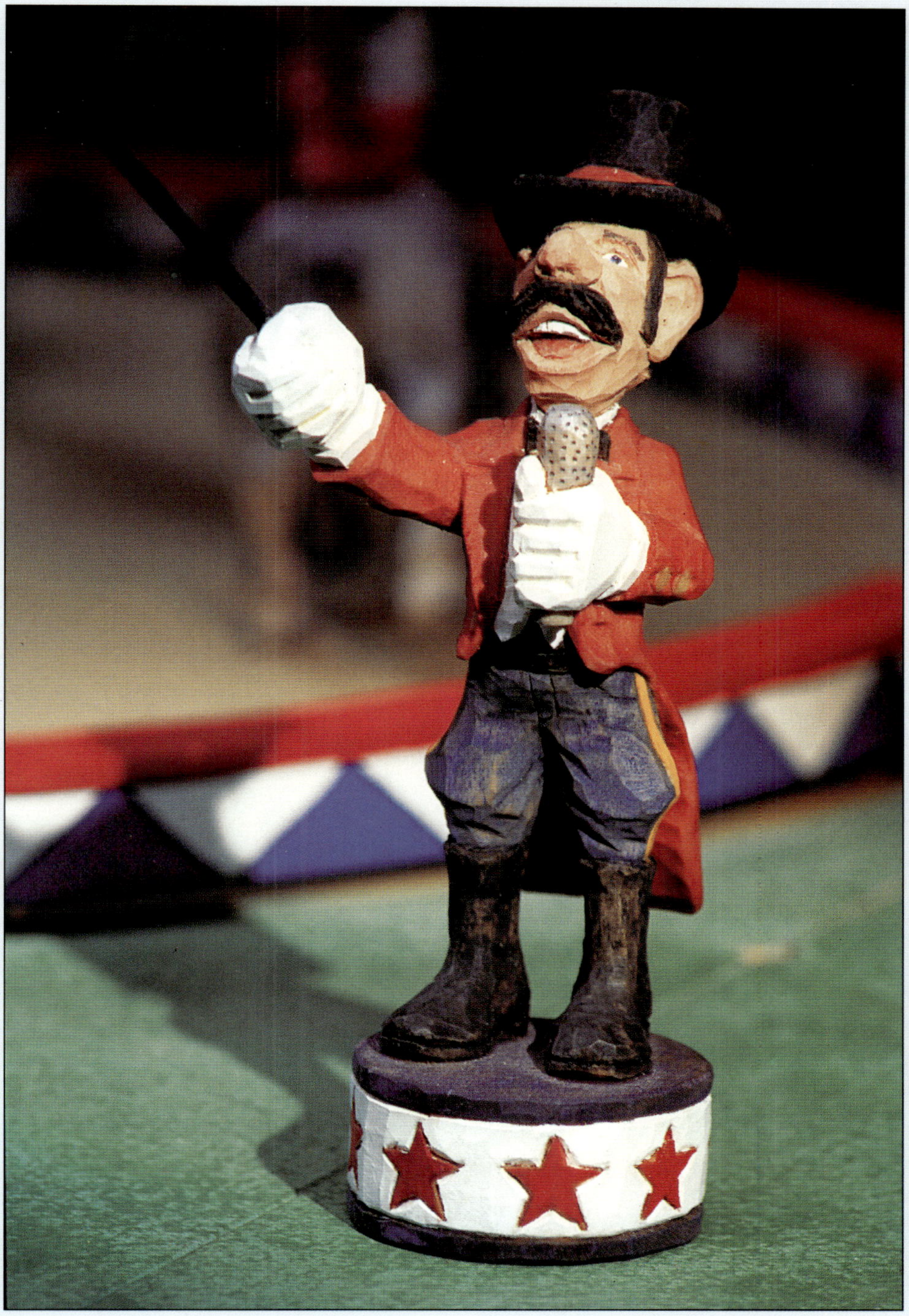

I used a wooden flexible model to help me determine the positions of arms, then transferred the ideas to paper. I left extra wood on the arms and hands when I bandsawed the blank.

Before beginning on the hands and arms, it was first necessary to carve excess wood from the sides of the head and to carve the ears in order to provide more working room.

I marked the top of the microphone and the outside edge of the right shoulder. Then I carved excess wood from above the microphone to the right shoulder line. After marking the left arm, I removed wood from behind and underneath the arm.

Next, I removed wood from all sides of the right arm. The arm is slightly bent and extended, and the hand is positioned so that it can hold the pointer. I carved the hand using my own hand as a model. A 1/16" hole was drilled to accommodate the pointer.

I then located the center of the microphone and marked the top and bottom view of the lower part, which is below the left hand. Leaving enough wood for the hand and fingers, I first carved wood away from the microphone, then shaped the hand holding it.

To carve the ringmaster I used a carving knife, 1/8 v-tool, 1/8 and 3/16 no. 9 sweep straight gouges, and a 5/16 no. 5 straight gouge. A 1/16 straight gouge came in handy for carving the eyes and several other areas.

The carving was painted with water-thinned acrylics. I sealed the circus ringmaster with a mixture of boiled linseed oil and umber antiquing.

Tickets Here! by Will Hayden

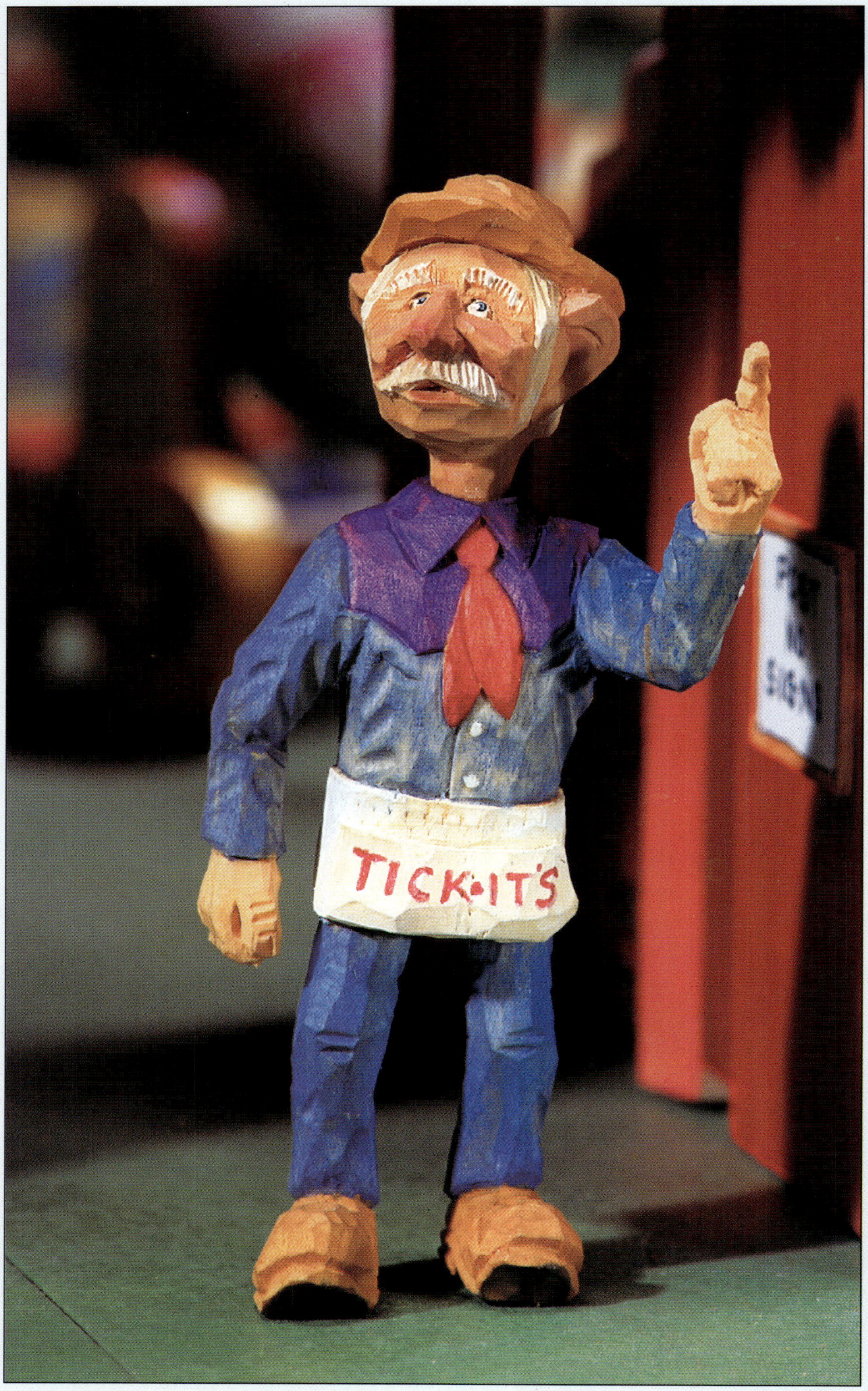

Arm upraised and finger outstretched, this ticket seller by Will Hayden is hoping to outsell all the other ticket sellers at the circus. The head was carved separately and inserted into the body.

Will Hayden

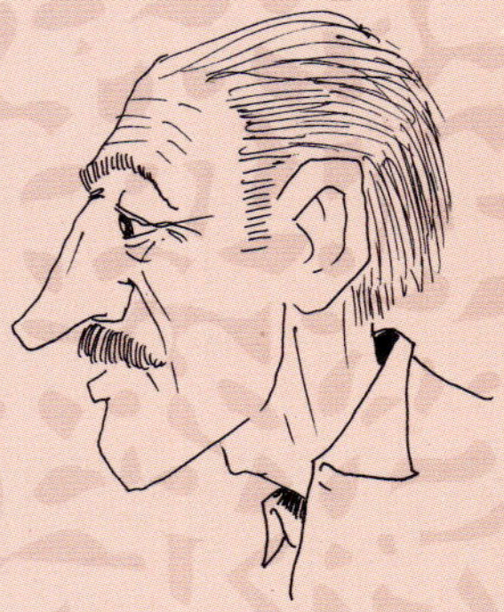

Will currently lives in Vancouver. He has been carving and whittling for the past 25 years, having started with a Boy Scout knife and "beaver wood" picked up along the banks of the Columbia River. Having tried all types of carving, Will always finds himself back with a caricature carving in his hands. Now retired from the U.S. Army, Will has plenty of time to carve. His philosophy on life is that one should give back twice as much as he has received. Through woodcarving, Will finds he can easily share his whimsical outlook on life with others.

Will's contributions to the CCA Circus appear on pages 16 and 38.

Will has taught all aspects of woodcarving at a local community college for 14 years and has judged and attended shows across the Northwest with his bird-carving wife, Kay. He is a member of the National Woodcarvers Association, the AWC, and the Midwest Carvers Museum.

Reggie Ringlet by Eldon Humphreys

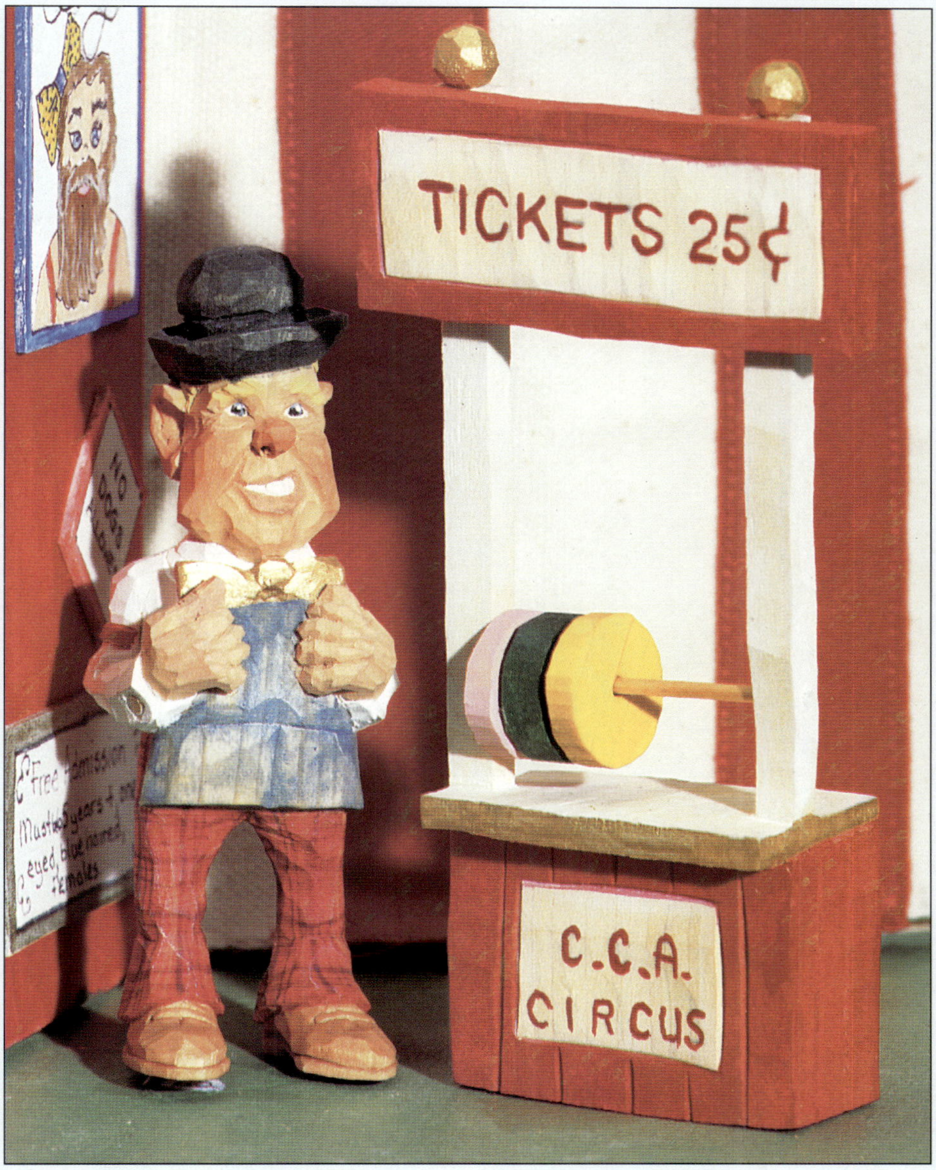

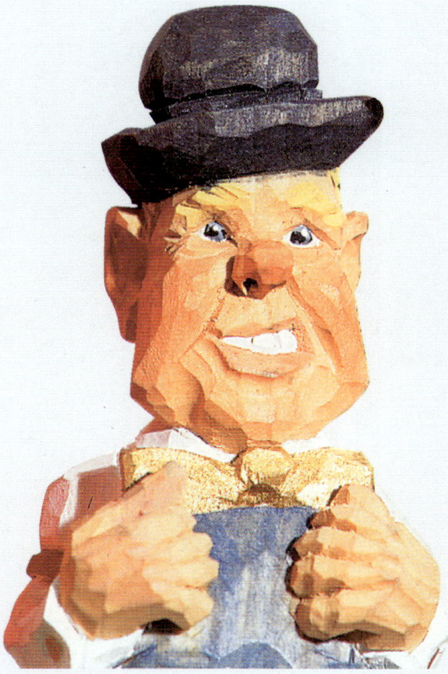

Reggie, but for an 'ing' instead of an 'et' might have been famous.

I find drawing my initial ideas and patterns the hardest part of carving. I don't draw especially well, therefore I need help in creating my patterns. Even though I am carving caricatures, they should be based on realism, having some of the proportions of human form. To ensure that I get the right dimensions, I use two cardboard templates designed and given to me by fellow CCA member Marv Kaisersatt. These templates, one for the front view and the other for a side profile of the human form, are hinged at the main joints. I can move the various body parts until I get the desired positions. Then I trace around the template onto the pattern paper. Once I get the basic body shape with the proper proportions, I can then exaggerate various characteristics, add clothing and make other changes.

After tracing on the front profile, but before tracing on the side profile, I first draw the lines on both the front and side of the blank. Now when I lay the side profile on I can align these points, thereby ensuring that I have matched the two profiles appropriately.

I'm sure all of us have experienced the desire to rush to see what the completed carving will look like. I'm also sure we have all cut corners or hurried our carving along to get it finished in order to see the completed project or meet a deadline. By doing so, we have probably not rounded off enough, got to detailing too soon, or left saw marks on. I find I have to stop every once in a while and remind myself that it's the act of carving I enjoy the most and to take that little extra time to make this carving the best one yet. The finished project will come along soon enough. Enjoy the process and you will probably have a better carving for it in the end.

Best Price by Bob Travis

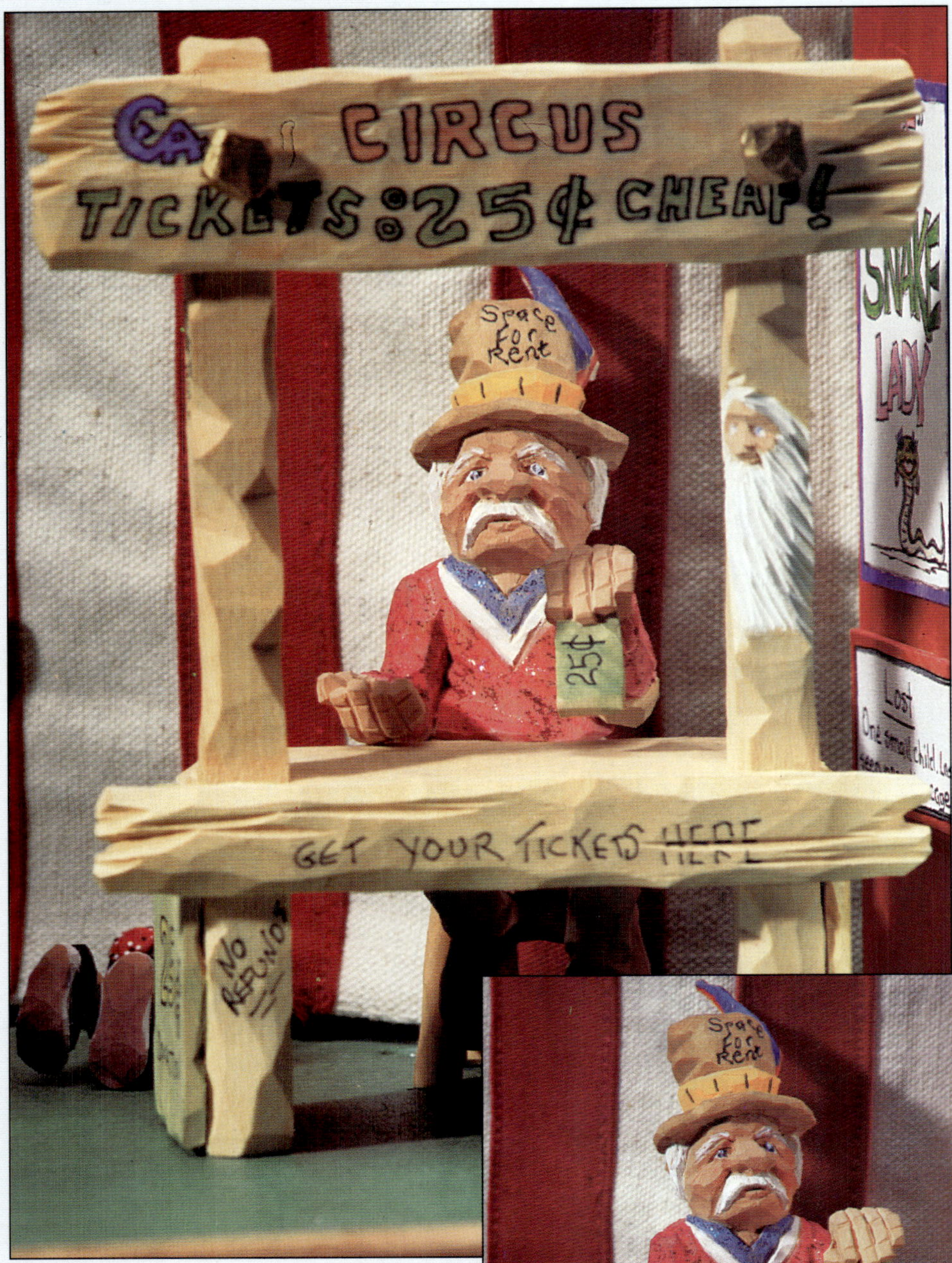

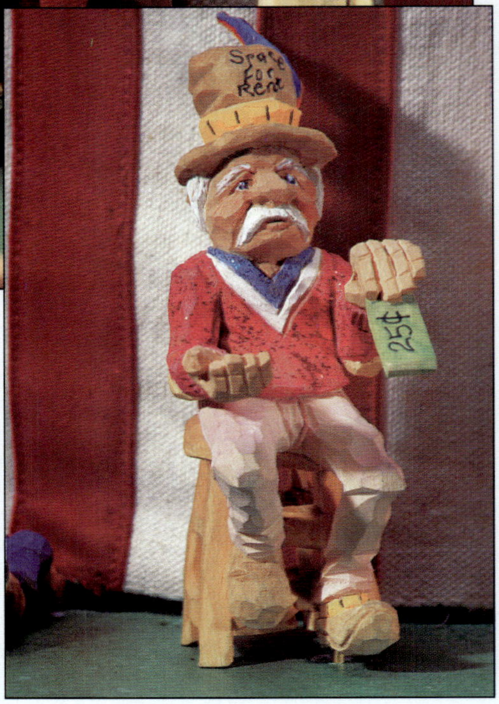

Palm out, this ticket seller by Bob Travis is just waiting for the quarter that will buy any spectator a ticket—cheap. The stand was constructed from several pieces of wood, but the ticket seller, his ticket and his stool were all carved from one piece of basswood.

Bob Travis

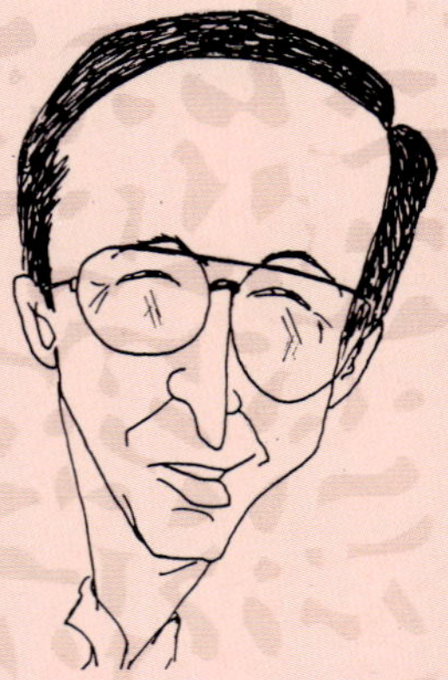

Bob, a resident of Davis, California, strives to capture in wood the type of humor that many of the modern western cartoonists express on paper. A professor of agronomy at the University of California, Davis campus, he fills the vast majority of his leisure time with carving and carving-related activities.

Bob's contributions to the CCA Circus appear on pages 10, 40 and 50.

Bob is a founding member of CCA and served as its exhibit chairman for 1992–94 and president for 1995–96. He is Chief of Education for the California Carvers Guild and writes a monthly column, "Talking Things Over," for the CCG publication, The Log. He has taught at the Doane Workshop in Crete, Nebraska, the Western and Wildlife Art Workshop, also in Crete, and the Missoula Carving Workshop in Montana.

Cotton Candy by Cleve Taylor

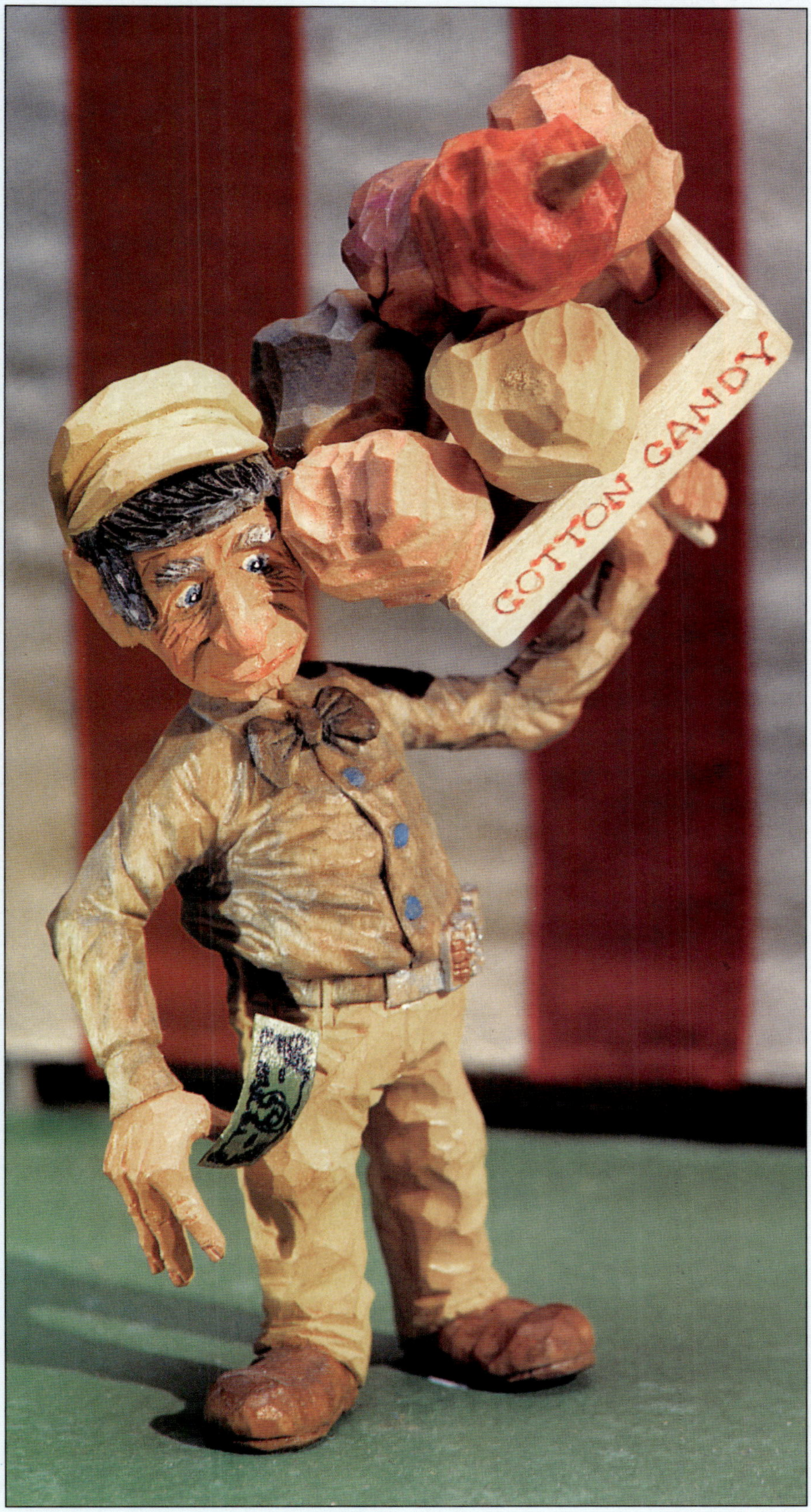

Cleve "Papa" Taylor

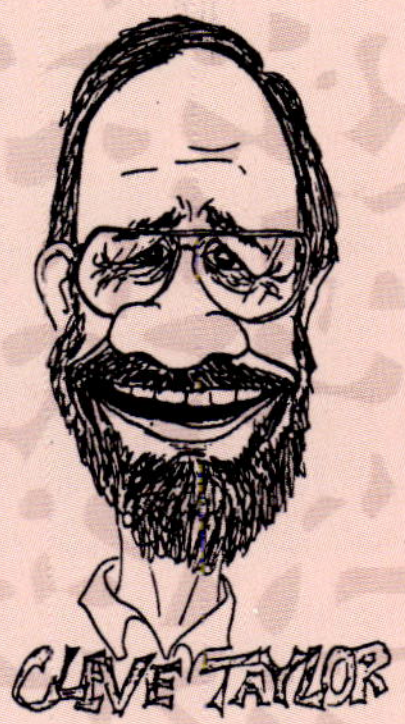

Cleve, a professor of adult education at the University of Idaho, started carving in 1986 after receiving a knife and a few gouges as a Christmas present from his wife and son. He describes his carving style as "eclectic," and admits that he uses "whatever works for whichever piece I'm trying to complete." He carves animals, golfers, fish and mountain men, but caricature cowboys are his favorite.

Cleve's contributions to the CCA Circus *appear on pages* 11, 28, 29, 41 *and* 65.

He has authored three books on caricature carving: Cowboy Carving, Hanging in There *and* Carving Fishermen and the Tall Tale. *He teaches classes and seminars regularly and judges carving shows when time will permit.*

Cleve is a member of the Idaho Woodcarvers Guild, Northwest Caricature Carvers Society, National Woodcarvers Association and the Affiliated Woodcarvers Ltd. Cleve became a member of the Caricature Carvers of America in October.

Arena Sanitation Engineer by Claude Bolton

Of all the performers, both animal and human, the one at the circus who grabbed my attention was the individual whose responsibility it was to maintain the arena. Most circus animals are apparently not house broken. Elephants are especially untidy. In observing this individual maintaining the cleanliness of the arena, I could not help but remember the old expression "Its a dirty job but someone has to do it."

I began to solidify my ideas for a carving by using a mannequin that Marv Kaisersatt so kindly helped several of us construct at a recent CCA meeting. I chose several poses but finally decided on the one depicted here. I then photographed the mannequin from several different positions with color print film. I made the scene as contrasting as possible by using a black background with the white mannequin. I then used the negatives in my enlarger to project the image on plain white paper so that an outline could be traced for my bandsaw pattern. An alternative method I have used is to shoot black and white film and actually print the pictures to scale for a pattern. Accuracy is not as important for this type of pattern since you will probably do as I usually do and make several attempts to get the final results that you want.

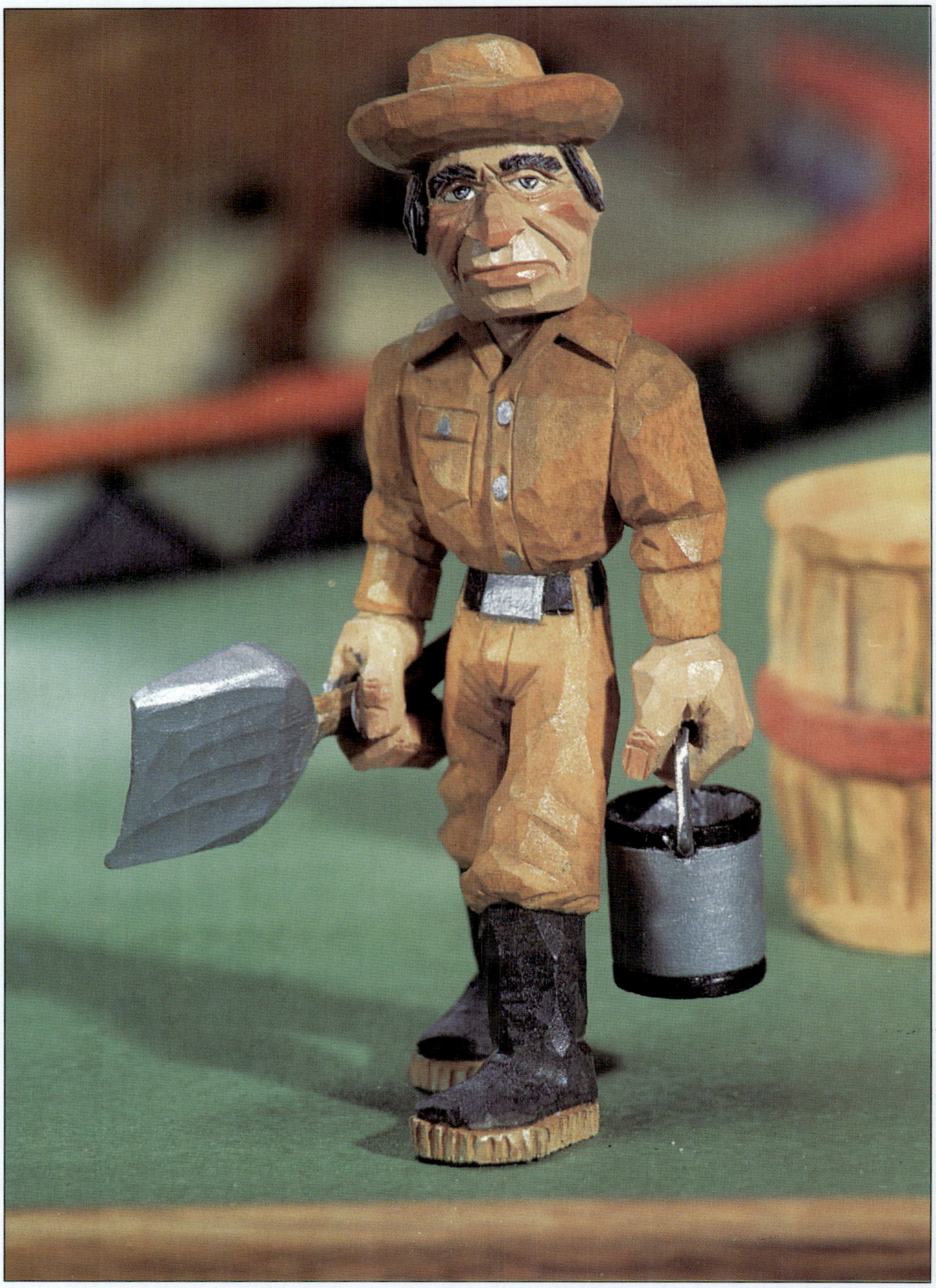

SPECTATORS

Cowboy by Dave Dunham

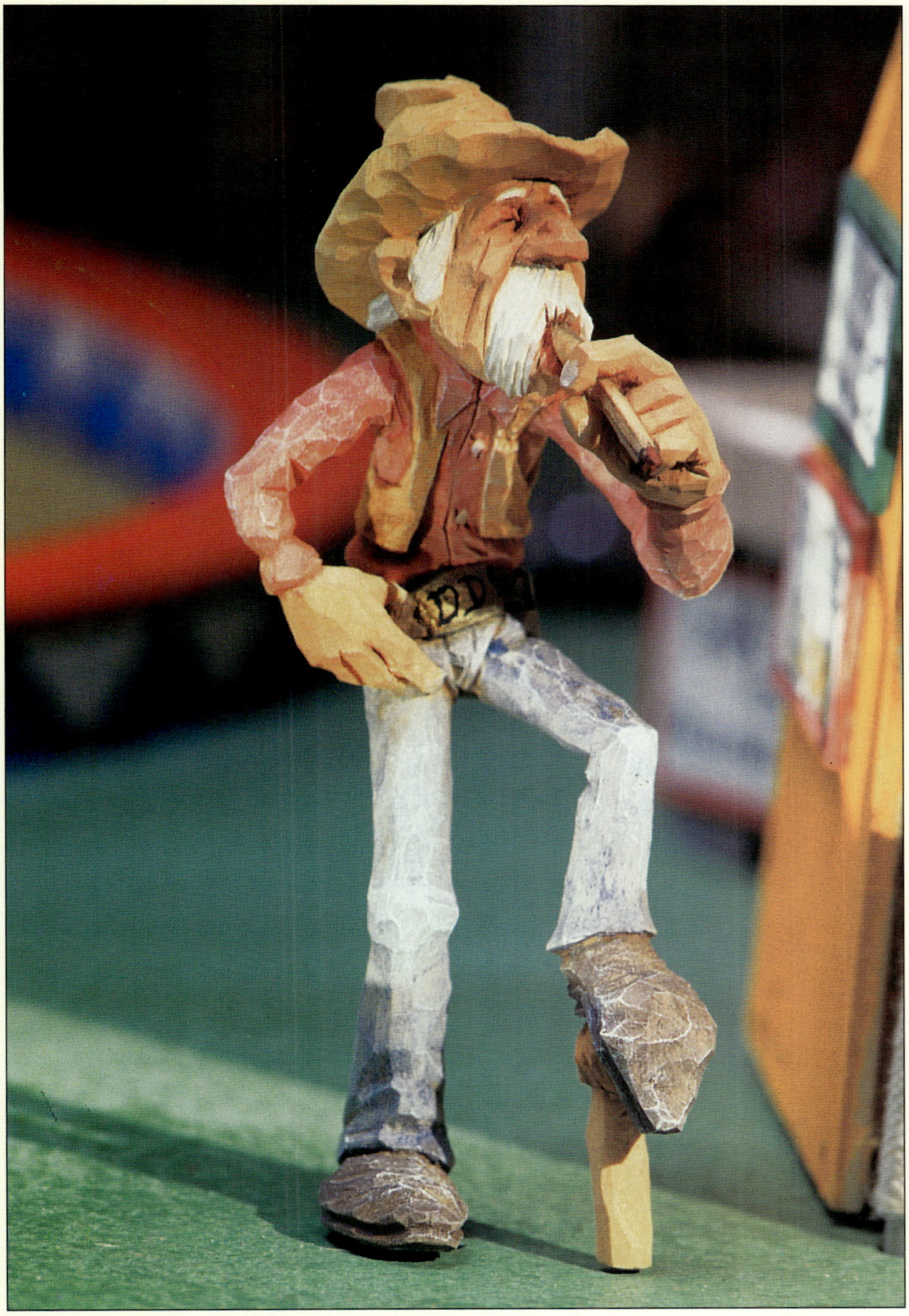

This old cowboy, carved by Dave Dunham, would rather be surveying the work it takes to raise the big top than see what's going on inside. The entire figure, including the cigar, was carved from one piece of basswood. Extra care had to be taken to carve the bent left leg so it wouldn't break as the piece neared completion.

Dave Dunham

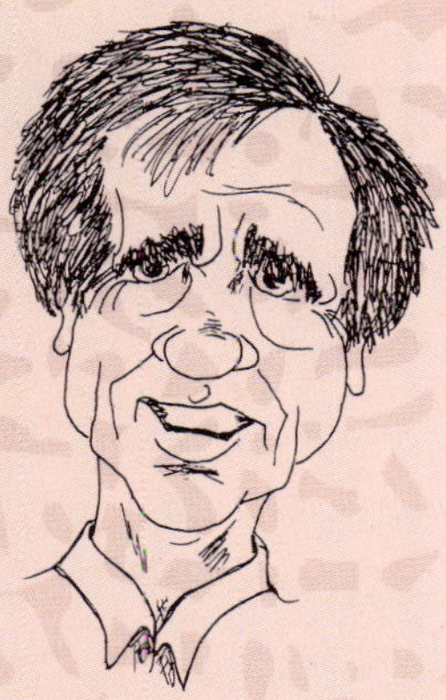

Dave, a resident of Cleburne, Texas, is a Diplomate of the American Board of Orthodontics and maintains an active practice in Cleburne. His extensive studies in human anatomy have stimulated his interest in carving facial features and expressions. His special interest is in caricaturization. Along with carving caricatures in wood, Dave also draws caricatures. Many of the caricature drawings of the CCA members, including Dave's own, were drawn by him.

Dave's contributions to the CCA Circus appear on pages 43 and 64.

Dave regularly conducts classes and seminars on caricature carving. Dave is a frequent blue-ribbon winner and has won several awards at the International Woodcarvers Congress over the past several years. He is a founding member and Corresponding Secretary of CCA. He also has held offices in the Affiliated Woodcarvers, Ltd. of Davenport, Iowa, and the Texas Woodcarvers Guild.

The Con Man by Marv Kaisersatt

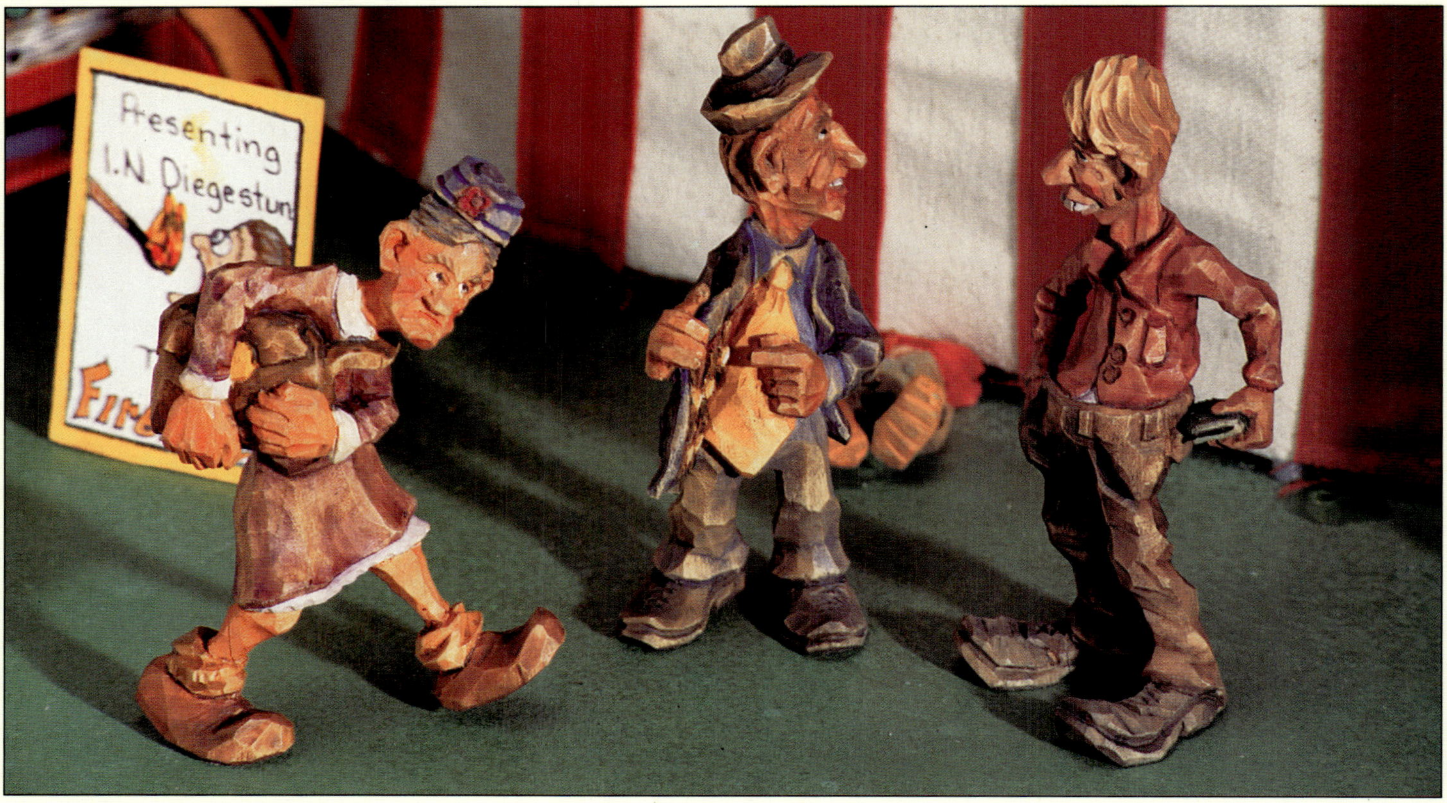

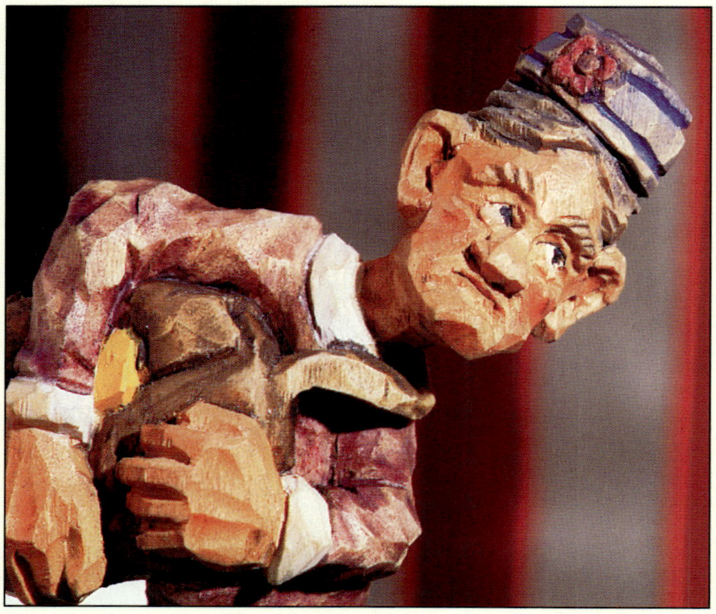

This woman knows a con man when she sees one, and she's not letting her purse out of her sight any where near this character. Because of her twisted position, Marv Kaisersatt made a clay model to help him visualize the piece before he began carving.

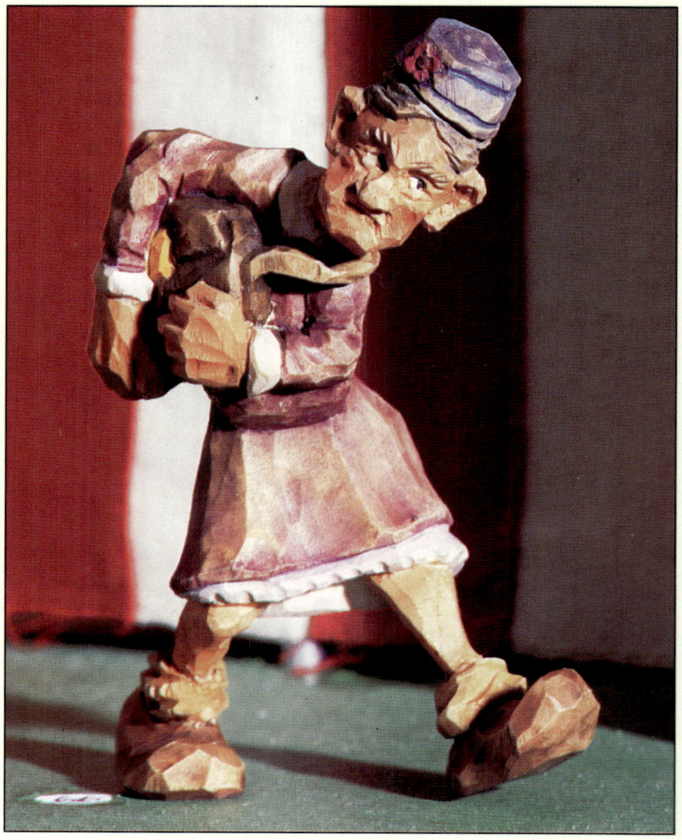

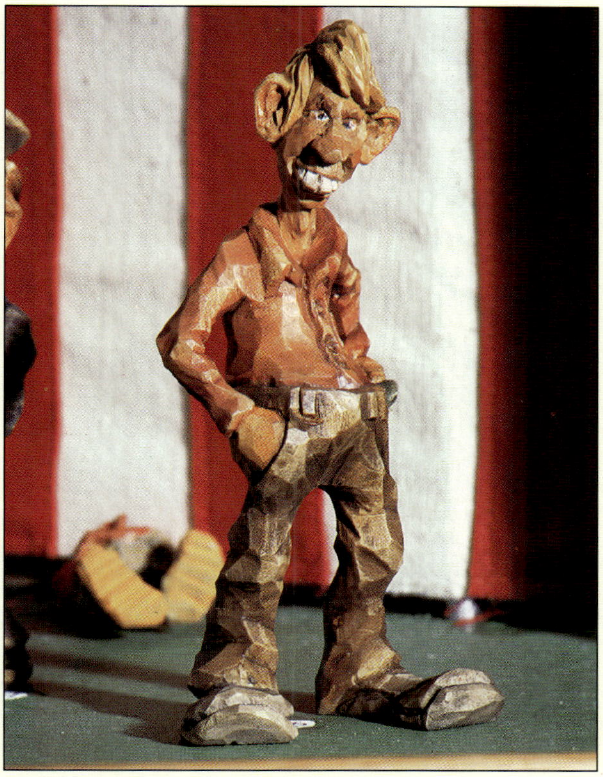

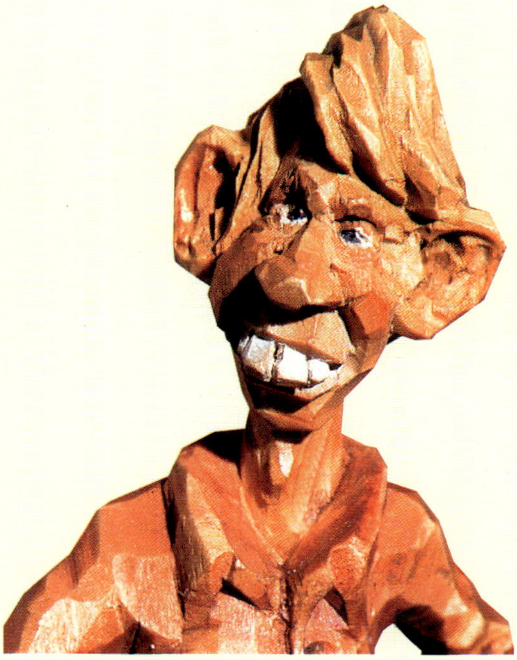

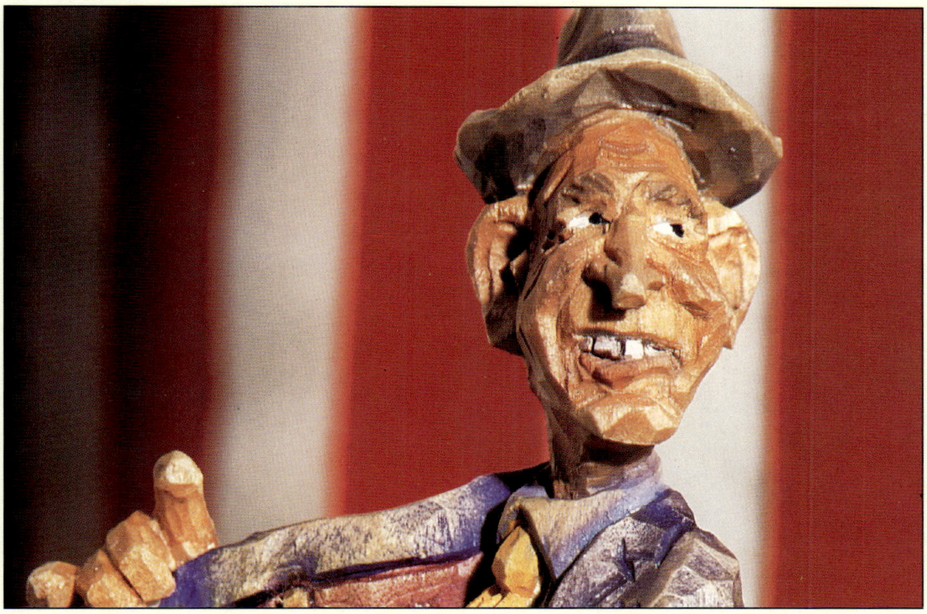

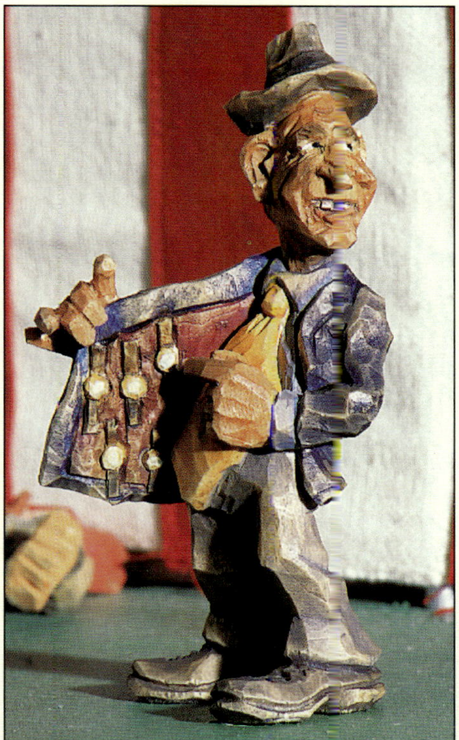

To make the watches under this con man's coat stand out, Marv Kaisersatt first outlined them with a v-tool and then relieved the wood around them.

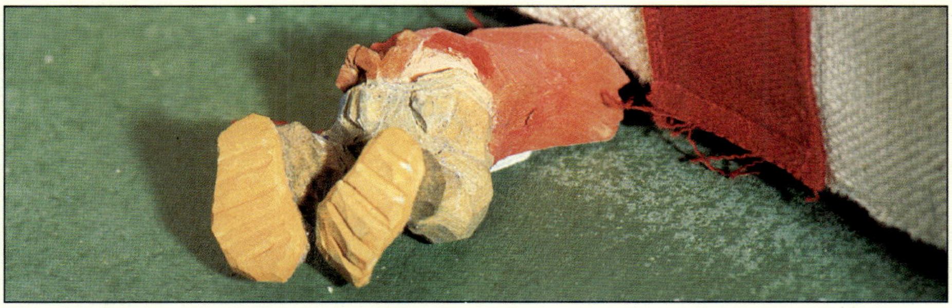

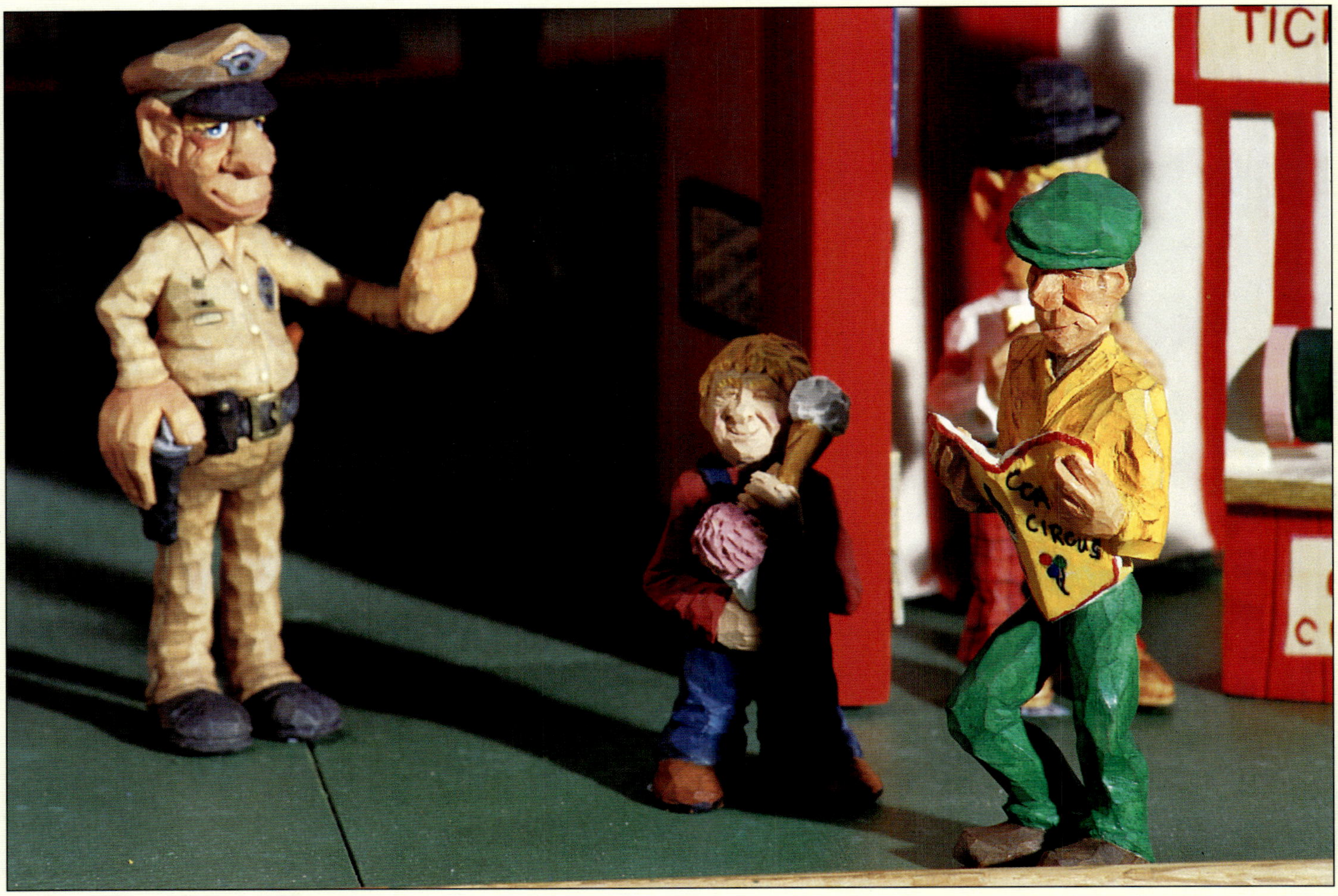

The Next Act by Doug Raine

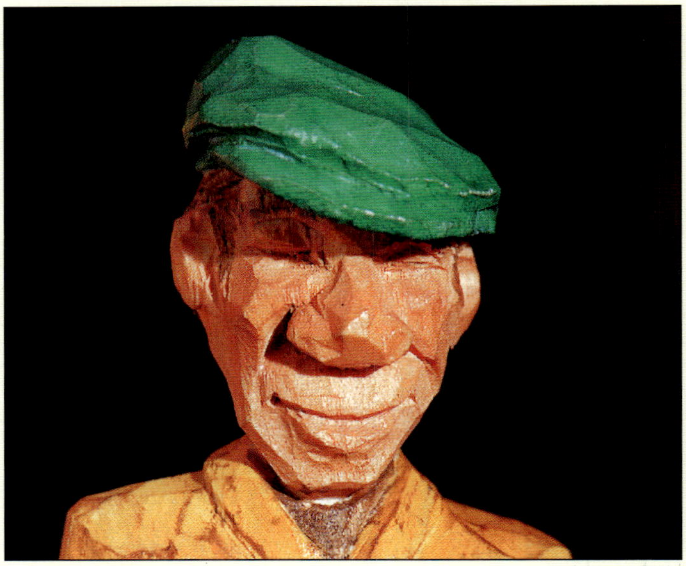

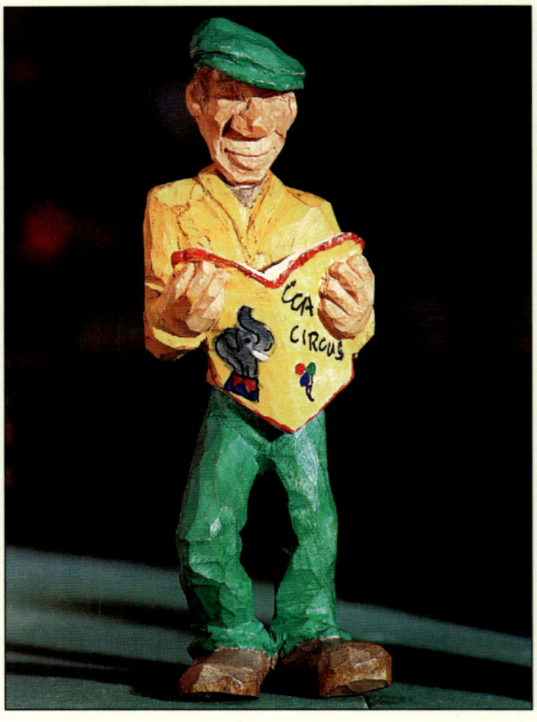

This gentleman, with his eyes downcast, is concentrating so hard on the circus program that he's missing all the action around him. The figure and the program were carved from one piece of wood.

I Scream by Dave Rasmussen

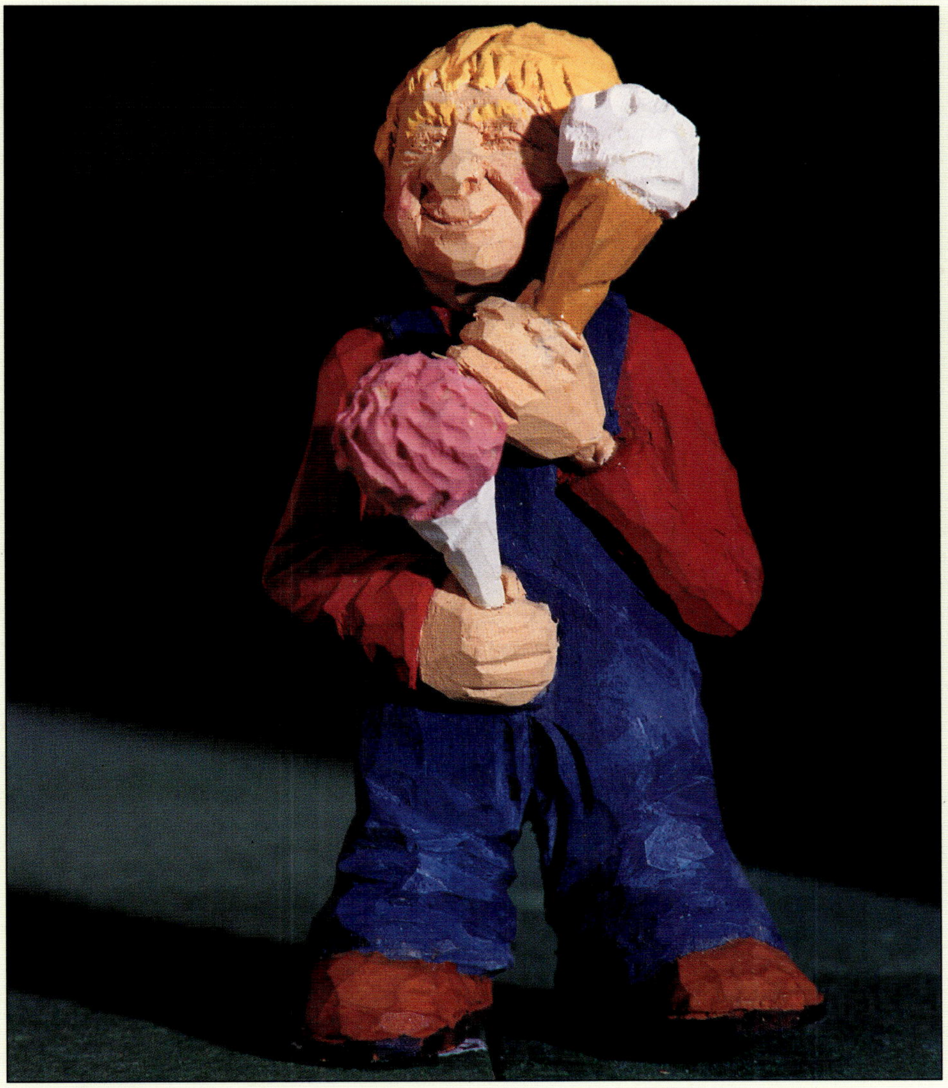

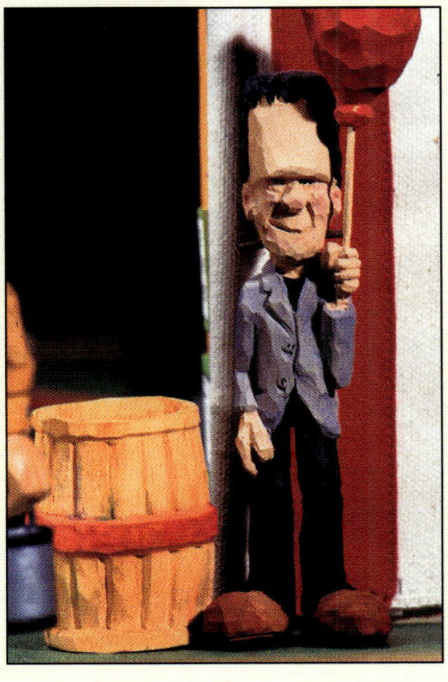

Dave Rasmussen's inspiration for this piece came from his childhood days when a kind gentleman at the local pool hall used to buy him ice cream cones. The two ice cream cones were carved separately and inserted into holes carved in the boy's hands.

Frankenstein by Dave Rasmussen

This circus is so good that even Frankenstein wants to attend. Dave Rasmussen carved the balloon separately and inserted it into the figure's left hand. Carving a caricature in pieces can lessen the degree of difficulty without compromising the complexity of the carving.

Dave Rasmussen

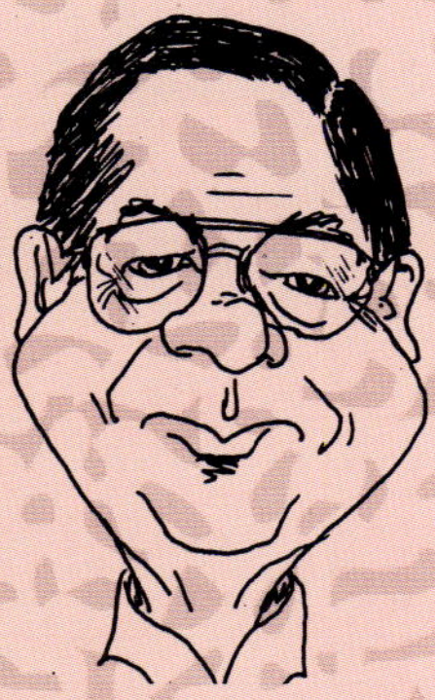

Dave, a resident of Cokato, Minnesota, began carving in 1978 and has since studied the classical Acanthus style with noted Norwegian carvers and Dovre graduates. Using mostly basswood or butternut, his carvings range from traditional Norwegian kubbestols, to reliefs and carousel horse restorations. In caricature carving he enjoys presenting "ordinary people in ordinary settings."

Dave's contributions to the CCA Circus appear on pages 23 and 47.

Dave received the 1990 Gold Medal for excellence in woodcarving awarded by the Norwegian-American Museum in Decorah, Iowa, as well as many first place awards in competitions throughout the nation. He is a founding member of CCA and a member of the National Wood Carvers Association, the California Carvers Guild, and the Allied Artists of America, and an associate member of the National Sculpture Society.

Mr. Tubs and the Little Boy by Tom Brown

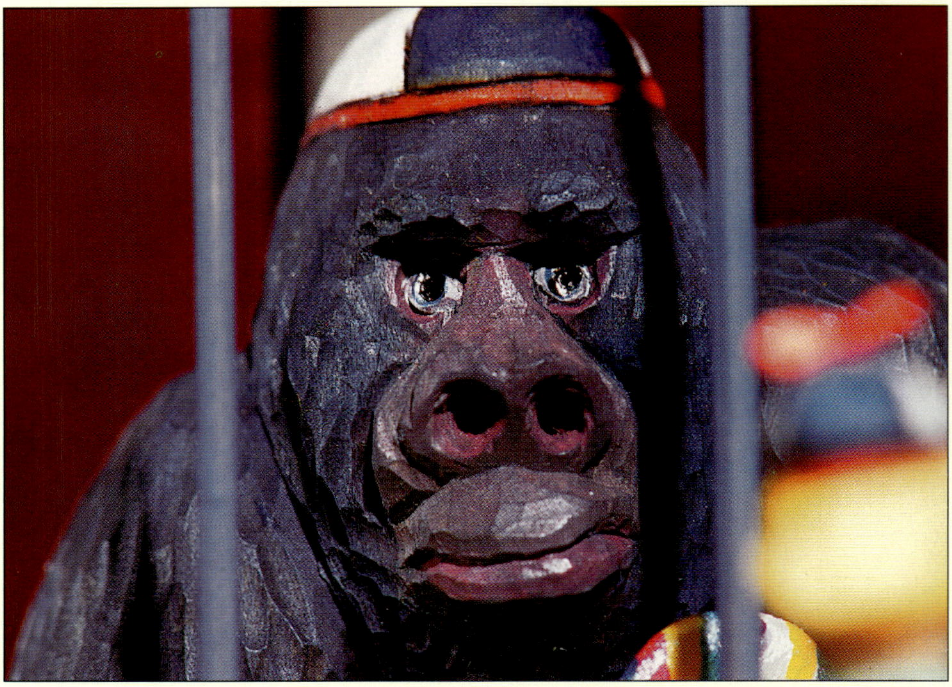

This gorilla and the little boy in front of him are so intrigued with each other, perhaps because each is noting more similarities between the species than just their tastes in lollipops and caps.

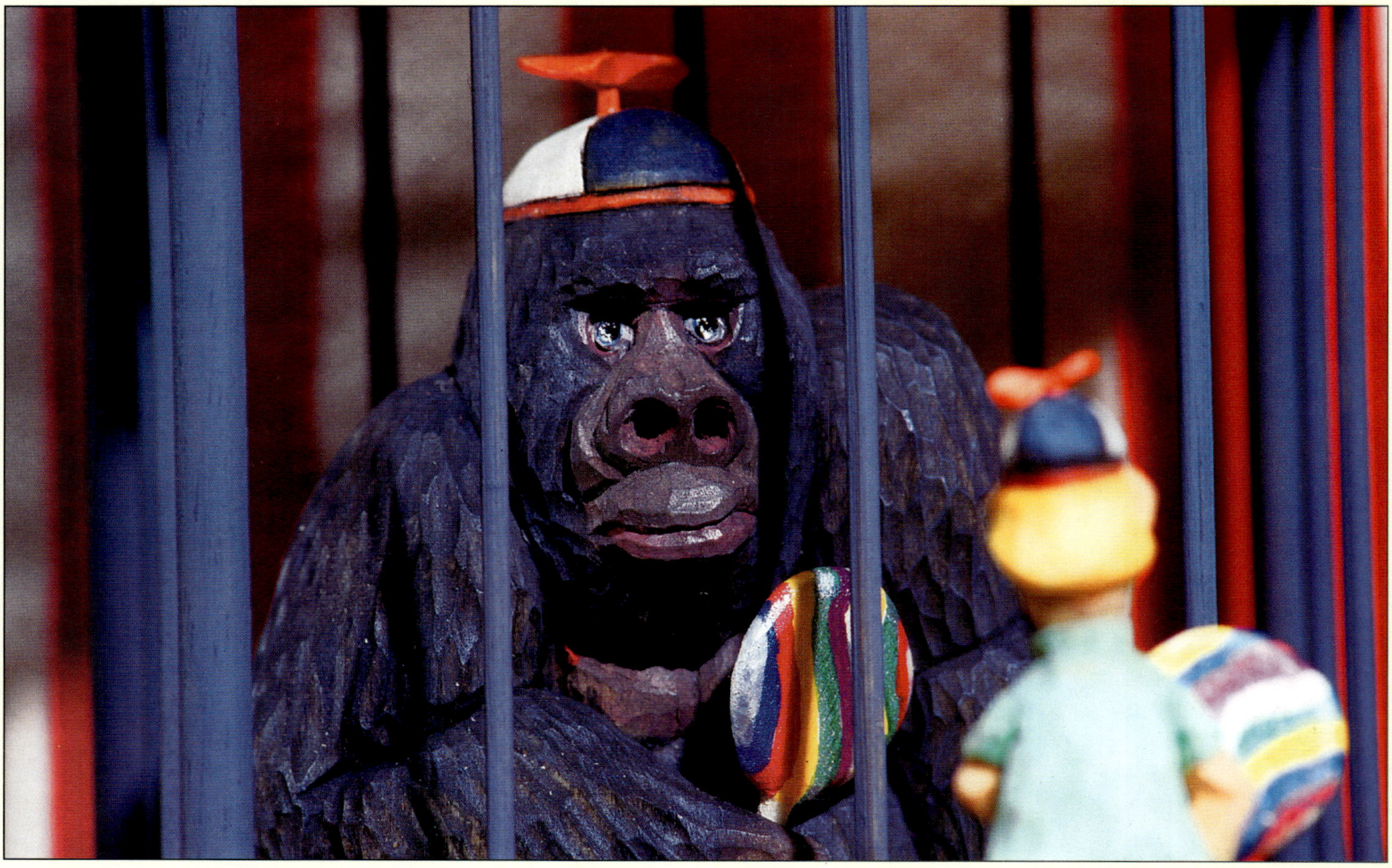

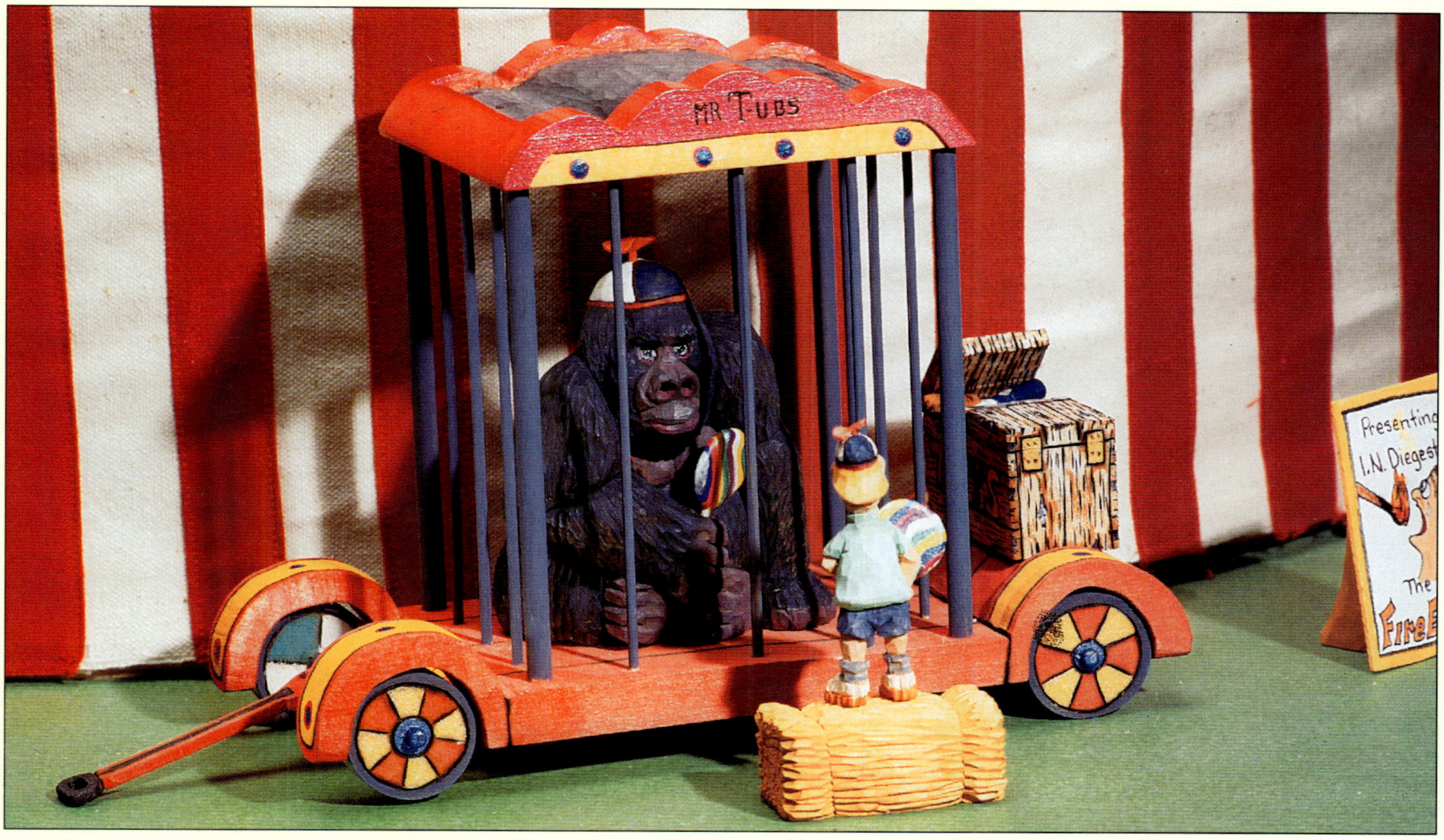
MR TUBS
Presenting
I.N. Diegest
The

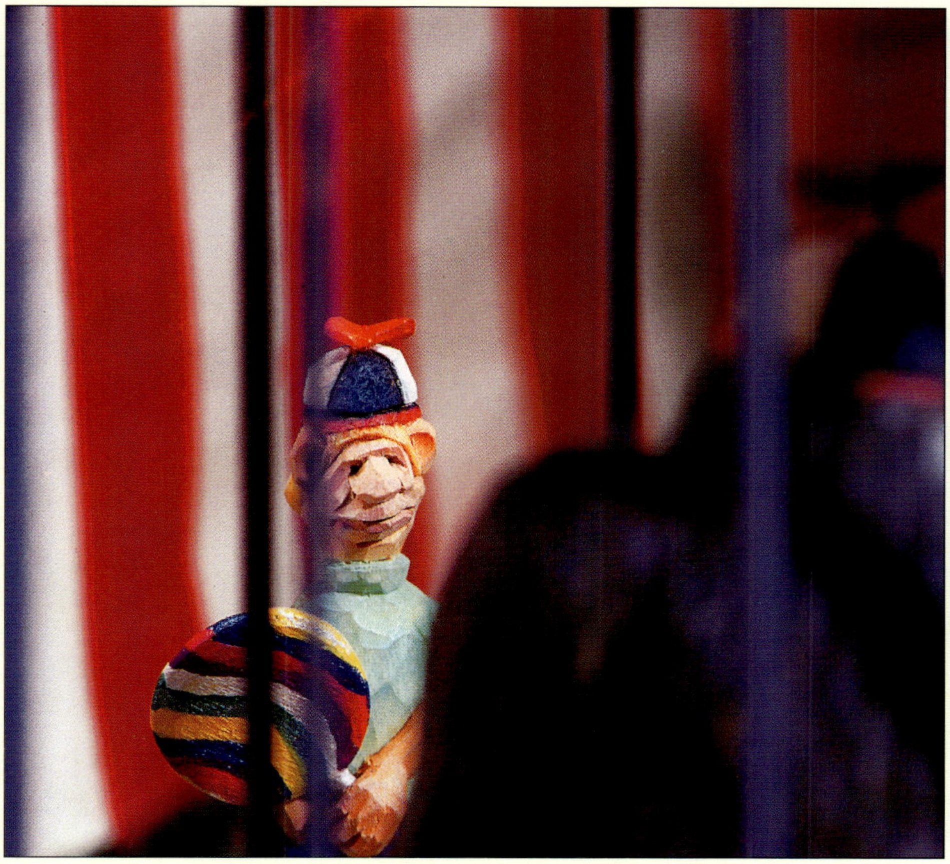

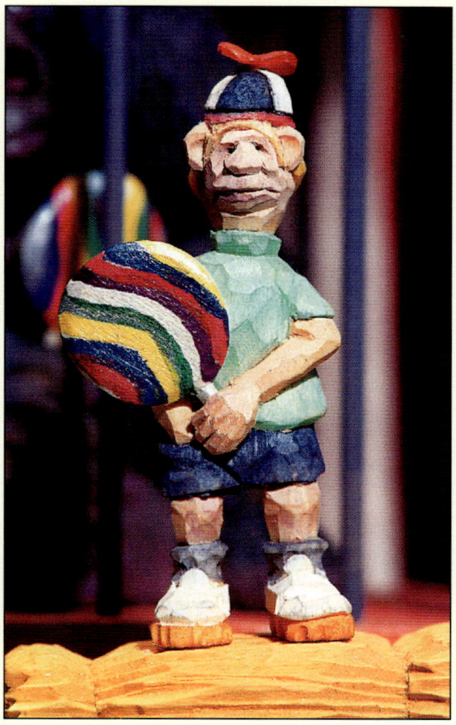

ANIMAL ACTS

Dog and Pony Show by Bob Travis

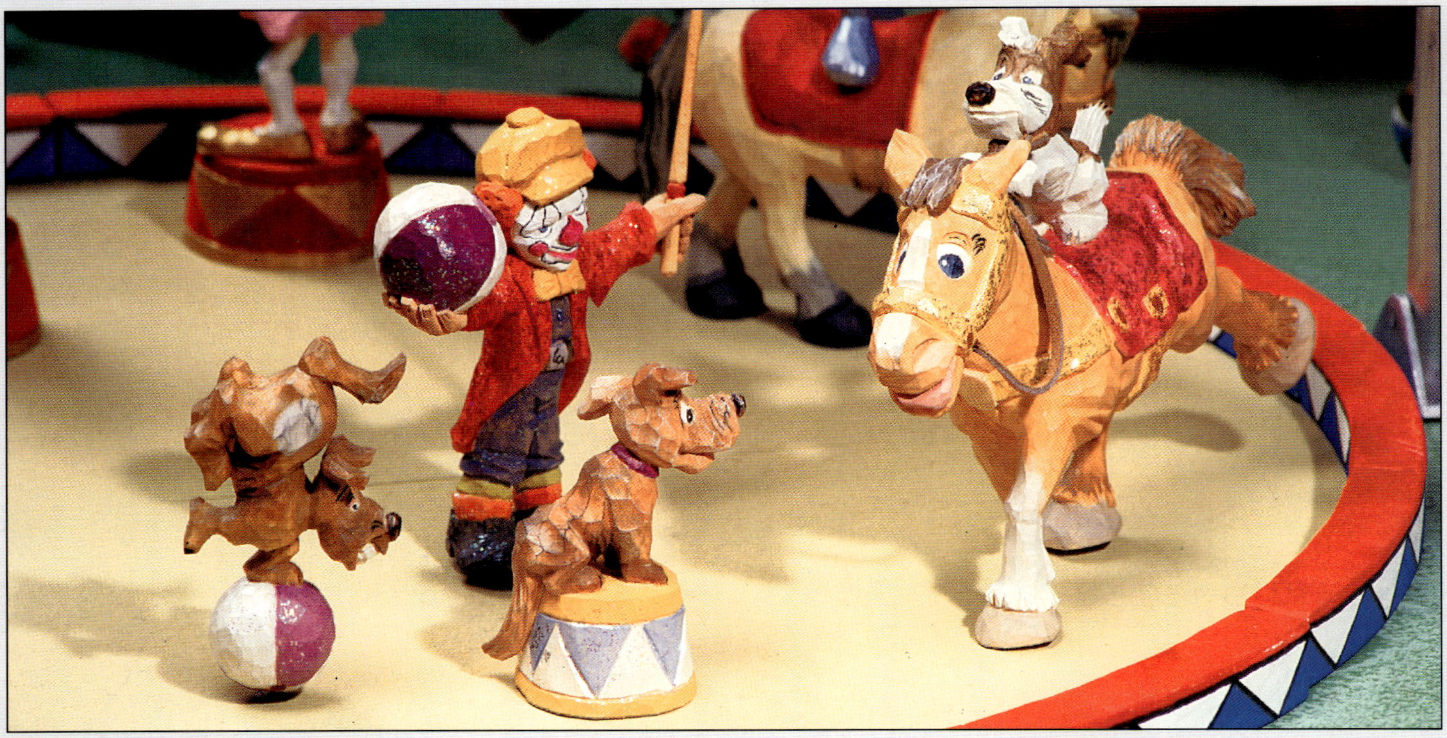

Determining the proper leg position of the pony as he trots around the ring was somewhat of a challenge. My first thought was that this would be easy, that was until I tried to sketch the pony. How are the legs positioned on a trotting pony? I made a trip to the club library to find out. Then I sketched the pony and added the dog sitting in the saddle. The carving is a single piece with the grain running in a vertical direction. Most of the major components are carved with the grain so breakage was not a problem. The dog's tail was the only area where the piece was delicate because of cross grain. To eliminate this problem, I blocked in the tail then drilled a 5/32" hole the length of the tail, and into the dog's body, then inserted an 1/8" dowel coated in carpenter's glue.

The dog balanced on one foot on the ball and the dog sitting on the stool are both one-piece carvings. Both are fairly simple. The grain direction for the first dog runs lengthwise through the balancing leg. The grain runs vertically for the second dog.

The grain direction for the clown is also vertical. While this makes most of the carving fairly easy to do, it does present a problem with the arms. Because they are extended out to the sides they are in cross grain and very delicate. To alleviate this problem the left arm was doweled from the knuckles into the shoulder before the final detail was carved. The right arm could have been strengthened in the same manner; however, in this case I used a different approach. The hand holding the ball was carved separately. An 1/8" dowel was then inserted through the arm, into the shoulder and into the wrist attached to the hand. If care is taken to carve the wrist so that it fits neatly into the sleeve, the finished carving will appear to be in one piece.

All the figures were painted with acrylics. I usually use very light washes of acrylic paints, but in this case, I wanted the circus figures to be brighter and didn't dilute the paint quite as much. The horse blanket, the dog's ball and stool, and the clowns clothes were coated with an acrylic glitter paint after the base color was applied. Glitter paints come in several colors but they really don't cover well without a base coat. The clown's coat, for example, was painted with naphthol crimson first followed by a coat of red glitter. I always finish off a western caricature with a coat of antiquing mix to dull the bright acrylic colors. However, in this case I omitted the antiquing as I wanted the colors to stay bright.

Dimbo the White Elephant by Desiree Hajny

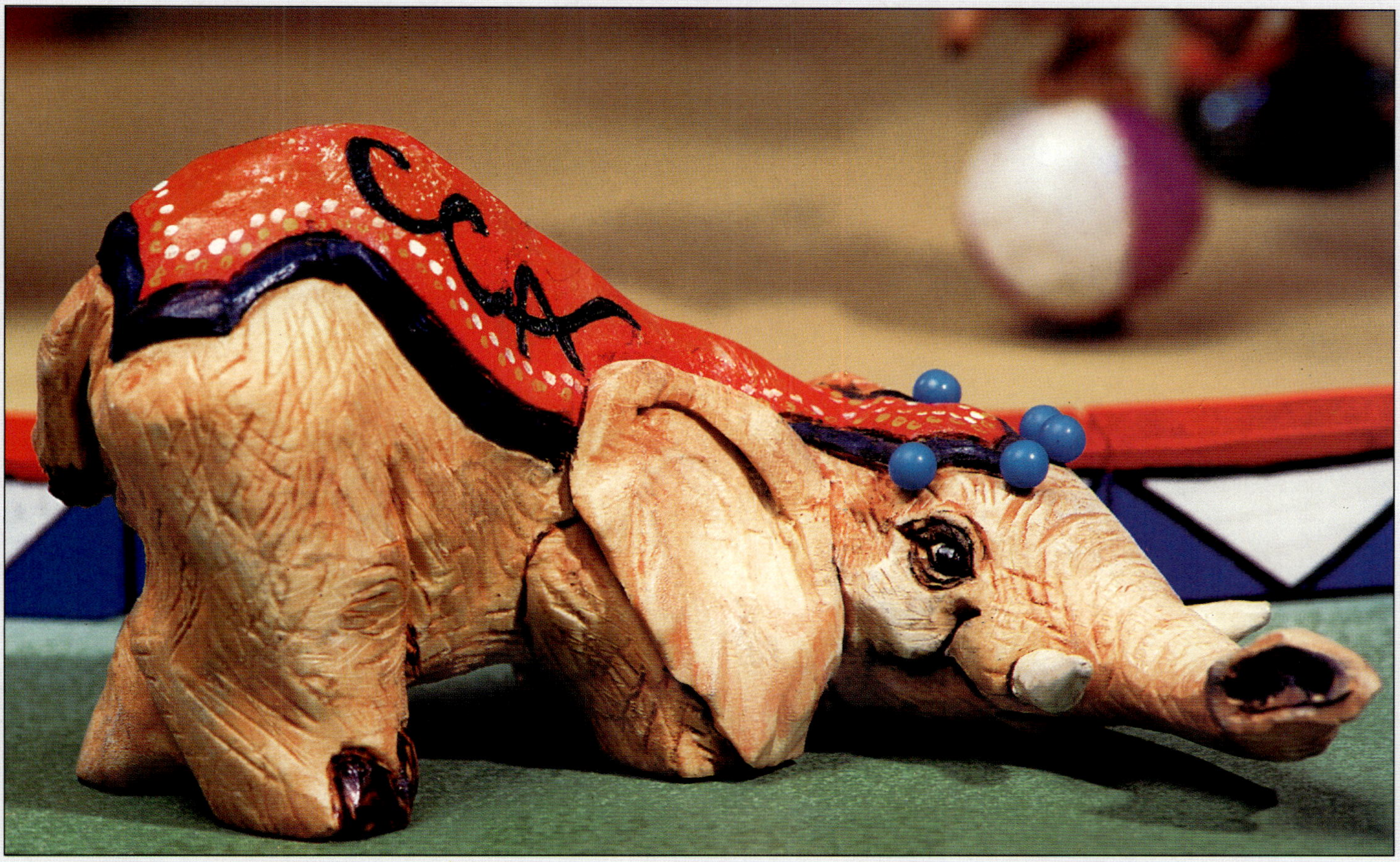

The study for this project was a lot of fun. In caricature, you'll find if you exaggerate the features that are special to that animal you'll be more successful in capturing its personality. Studying the animals will show you which features to focus on.

The wrinkles have a definite rhythm throughout an elephant, whether it be Indian or African. They're soft wrinkles, so using just a parting tool wasn't enough. After studying the direction of the wrinkles and marking them with a pencil, I cut into them with a parting tool. Next, I used a rotary bit over all the wrinkles. This softened all the harsh cuts left by the parting tool, leaving the result I wanted.

A wood burner came in handy for Dimbo's eyes and toe nails. I burnished both with high heat to get the effect I wanted.

The African elephant has one dome on the top of the head. The trunk is snakelike and offers many possibilities for redesign. It is used much like a hand with two finger-like parts at the tip of the trunk. The ears are like sticks with flags hanging from them. I worked in wrinkles and folds in the ears using a gouge or, if you prefer power carving, rotary balls.

The eye sockets are somewhat deep-set to protect the eyes from the sun. They also have very long eye lashes which offer even more possibilities. Both male and female Africa elephants have large tusks. The tusks grow on either side of the trunk and are like long cones in shape. The mouth is under the tusks and trunk.

The drapery and decorations sometimes can get quite ornate, but that's what makes a circus so fascinating. Remember that the covering lays over the animal and isn't skin tight, so you'll probably do some undercutting around the bottom of the blanket.

The baubles on the head piece can be carved, or push in some pins with fancy balls at the end. Hat pins would be too long, but with a little ingenuity they can be cut down and used.

For the sparkly blanket, I first painted on a base coat. Then I chose a lighter color and used a sponge to dab it on. This will give the illusion of sequins and sparkles. After it was dry, I painted in the lettering with a spotter brush.

The Three Leopardo Brothers by Harold Enlow

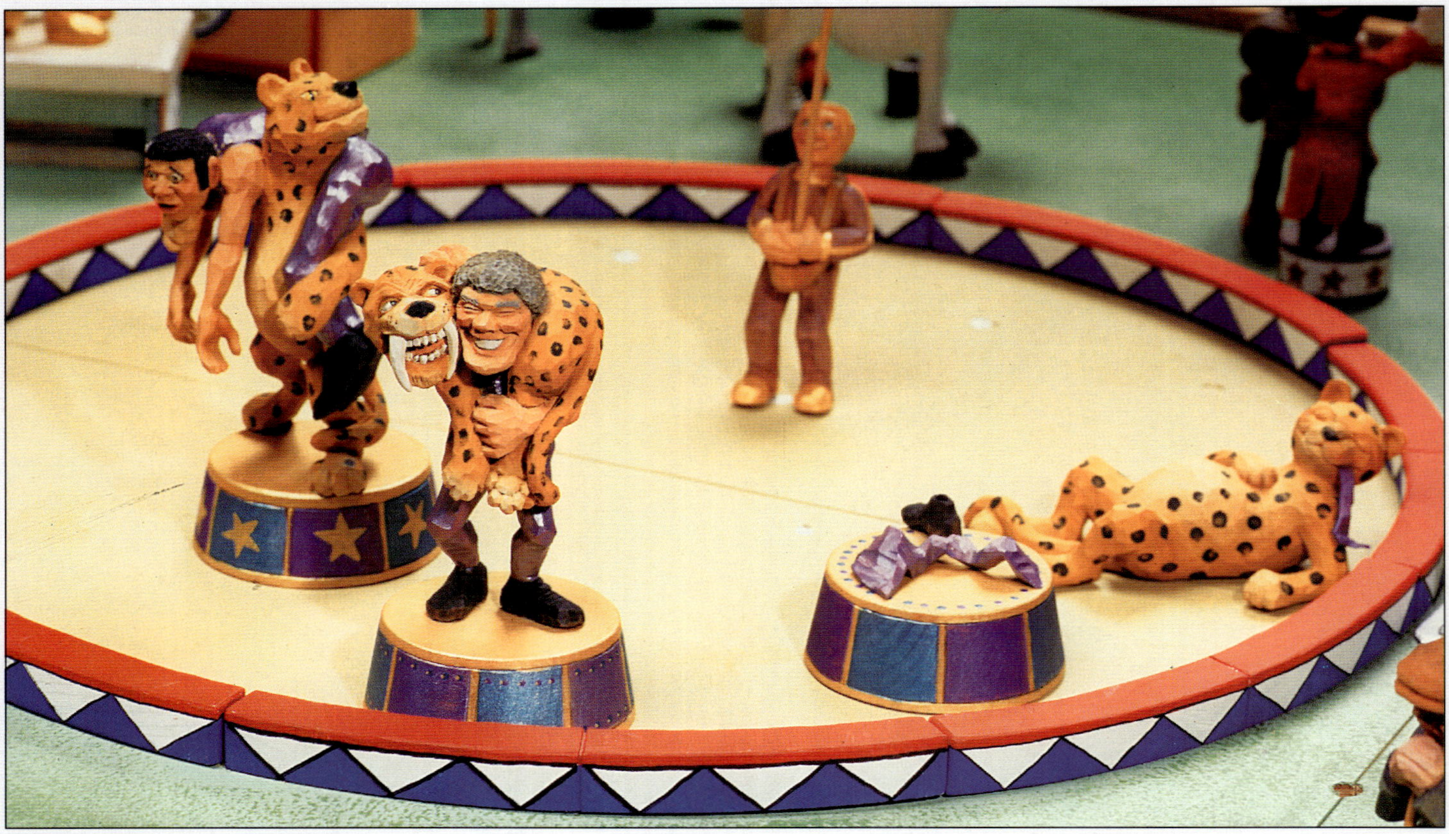

Doing my three carvings for the CCA *Circus* was probably the easiest project I've ever done as far as getting the ideas. Of course, I had a lot of help. I arrived home with a good idea of what I would do and talked to my wife, Elaine, about it. That was the end of my pondering. She took over and kept getting these ideas.

The first was a performer holding a leopard on his back. "Why don't we do a cat holding a man on his back to go with the first one?" she said. "Oh, then we could do a big cat lying on his back with a 'pooched' out belly like he's eaten the third fellow." (Good idea, I wouldn't have to carve the third brother.)

While doing the first carving of the man holding the cat, I added some sabre teeth. Recently I had seen a casting of a sabre-toothed cat skull. This was probably in the back of my mind and just popped out. There may never have been a sabre-toothed leopard, but if there had been we now know how he probably looked.

One of the things you may have noticed on all of these carvings is that they are all doing something other than standing with their hands in their pockets. This makes them a little more difficult. Another thing you may have noticed is that my animals look a little on the human side. But that is the beauty of caricature; I can carve them as I want.

All my carvings are done in basswood because it is my favorite wood. It takes any kind of finish well. In this case, I used acrylic paints. The pedestals are simple pieces, but they need to have enough room for the figures. A good way to cut the pedestals is to draw them on wood with a compass, tilt your bandsaw table slightly and saw them out. All you will have to do is clean off the saw marks and put the detail on with a v-tool. The detail could even be painted on.

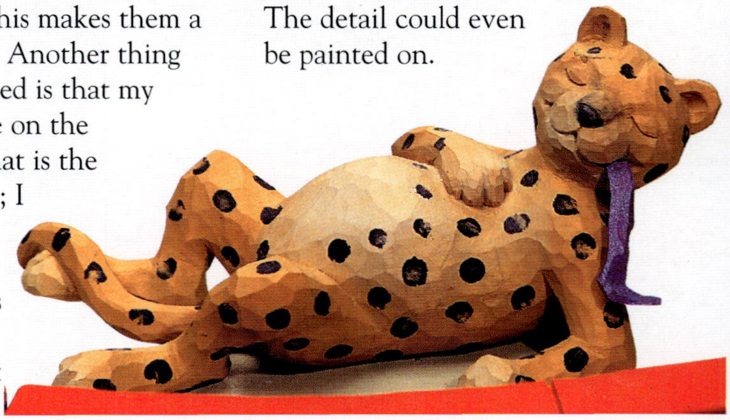

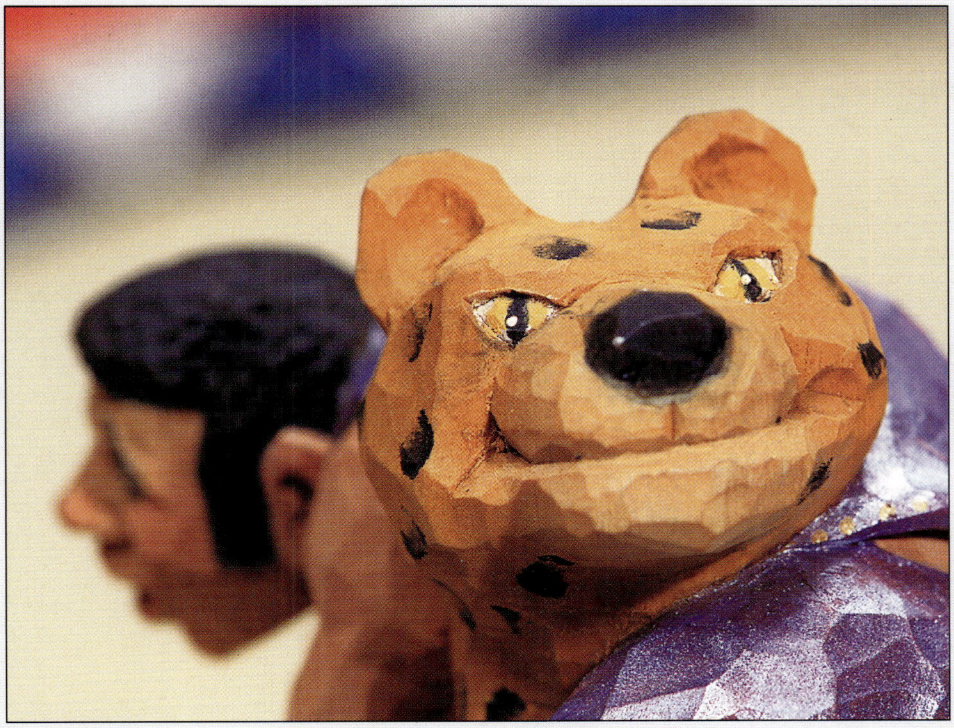

With such a smug look onn his face, Harold Enlow's leopard is quite proud of the role reversal he pulled on this unsuspecting Leopardo Brother. Harold carved this figure, and the other Leopardo Brothers and their cats, from basswood.

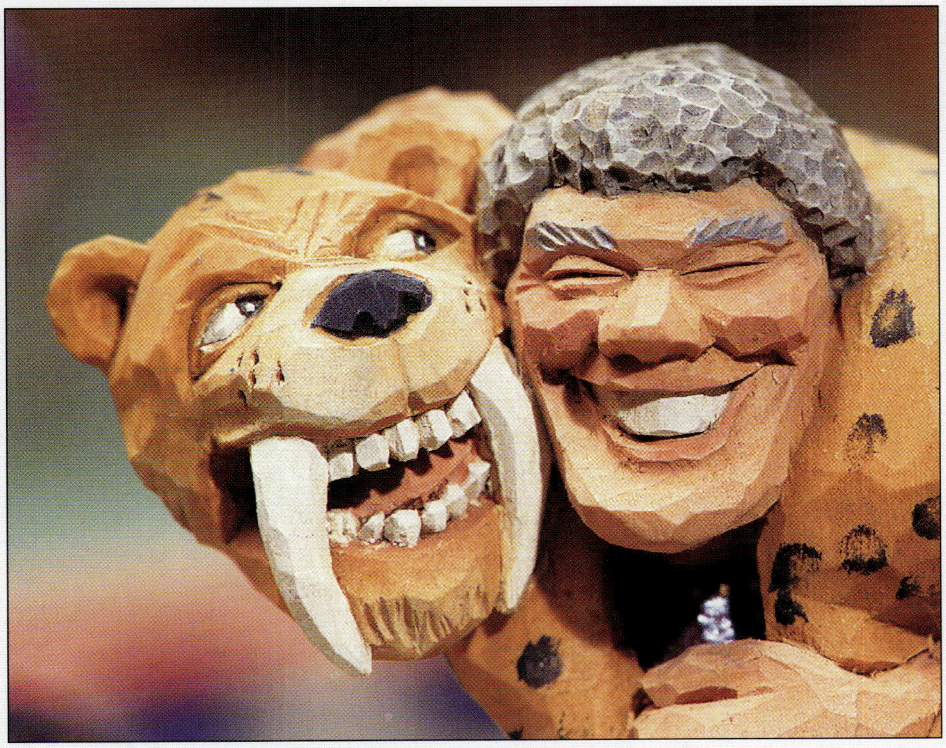

It's hard to tell just who has the bigger smile—the Leopardo Brother holding the leopard or the leopard. The artist has seen a casting of a sabre-toothed cat just before designing this piece and, even though leopards don't sport such incredible teeth, incorporated them into his design.

Harold Enlow

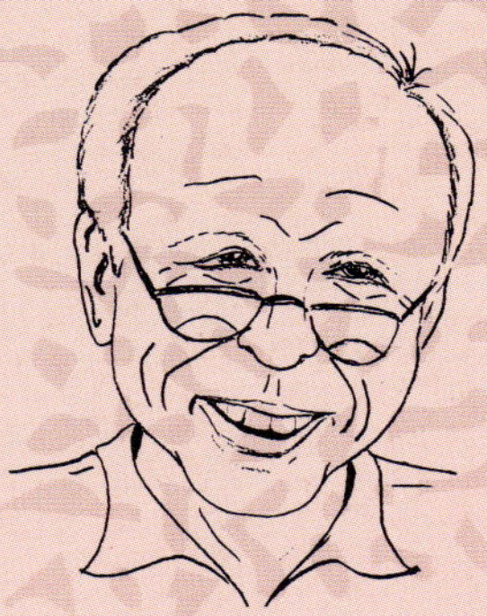

Harold, who now lives in Dogpatch, Arkansas, was born on Friday the 13th in the Ozark Mountains. Although he became interested in carving while quite young, he did not do any serious carving until he was stationed with the U.S. Army in Okinawa. Harold began carving professionally in the early 1960s. Humorous hill folks are among Harold's favorite subjects to carve.

Harold's contributions to the CCA Circus appear on pages 52 and 53.

Harold has written nine woodcarving books and teaches 30–35 woodcarving seminars each year. He is a founding member of CCA and a member of the National Wood Carver's Association, the Ozark Whittlers and Wood Carvers and several other carving groups around the country.

Bazel and Hazel Gazel by Eldon Humphreys

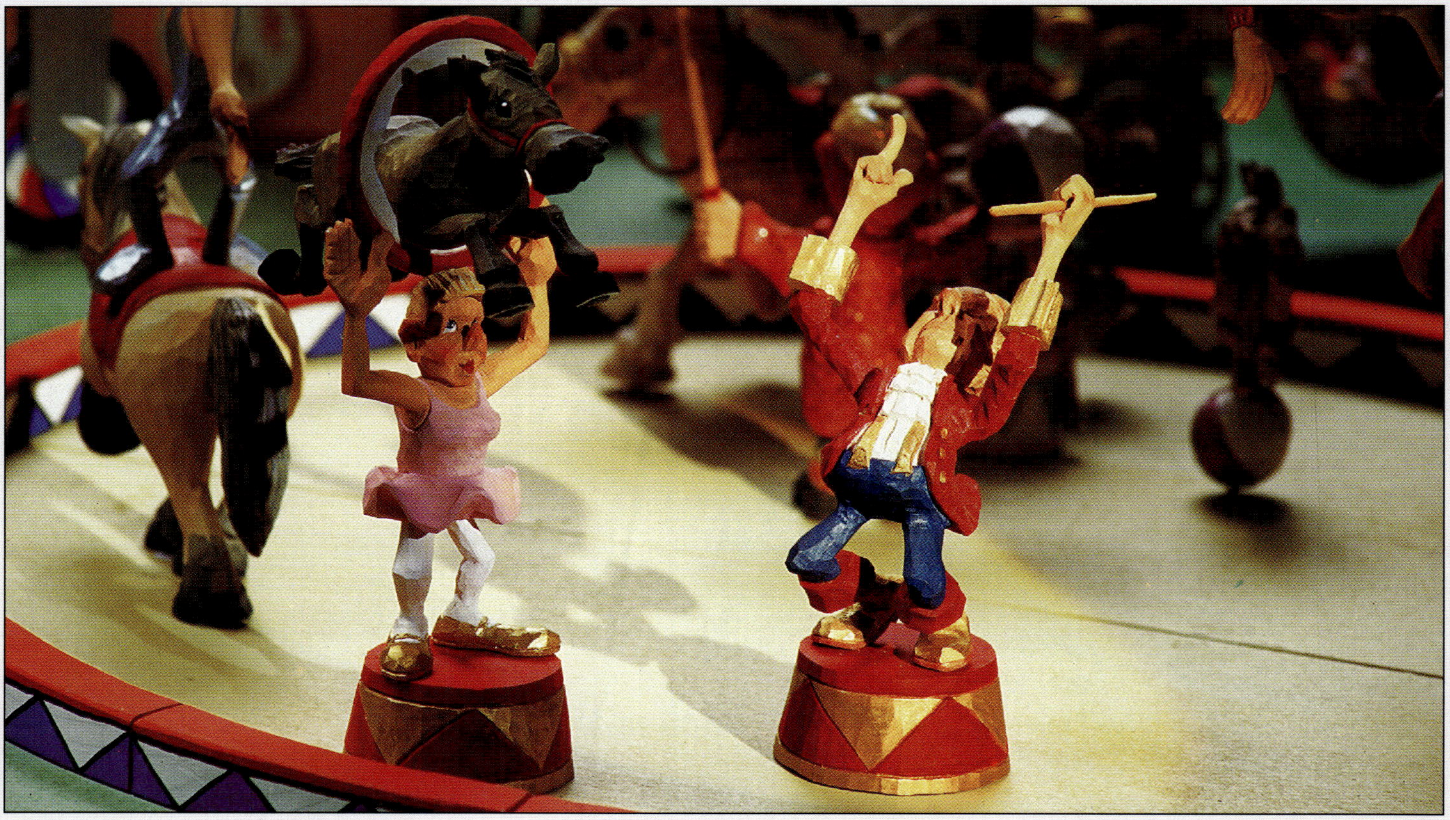

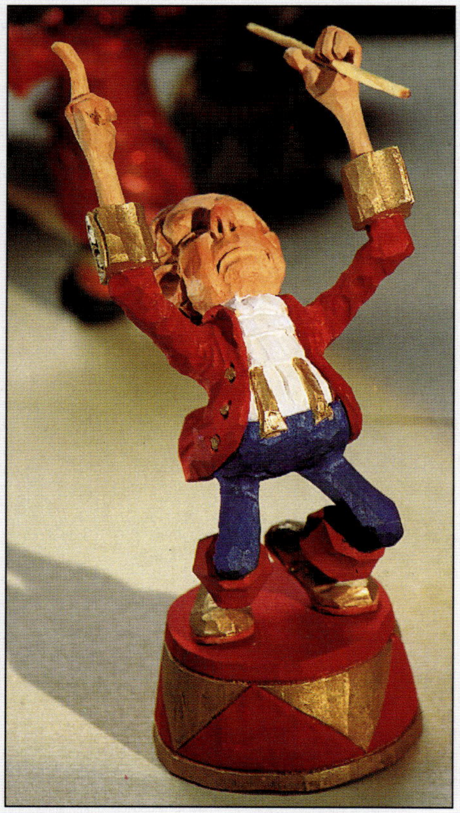

For my circus subject, I wanted to reflect the action and excitement of a multi-ring circus. An animal trainer and his partners would do that easily.

When transferring a complicated pattern, like the animal trainer, to a block of wood, it is important to use the comparative lines. In the case of the animal trainer, he is bent backwards and is standing on his toes, making it more difficult to align the patterns. If the side profile pattern is not lined up properly with the front profile, the blank will be difficult to carve. For instance, the arms, already fragile, could be cut too thin. One way to overcome this would be to only bandsaw the blank in one dimension. The other way is to use the comparative lines to align the two profiles.

The most difficult aspect of carving these three pieces was overcoming the problem of breaking off an arm or leg while carving some other part of the body. Because of the small size, the arms and legs were very fragile. Bandsawing was a challenge, too. I intentionally left extra wood around both the arms and legs on the two human pieces, and on the legs of the horse. I carved those parts last.

On the animal trainer, I carved the hands separately and pegged them in afterwards. This allowed me to ensure that the grain was running properly for maximum strength.

I used acrylic paints watered down to a wash. I finished the carving by dipping it into a container of boiled linseed oil, wiping off the excess with paper towels. Linseed oil removes the sheen and deepens the color.

Eldon Humphreys

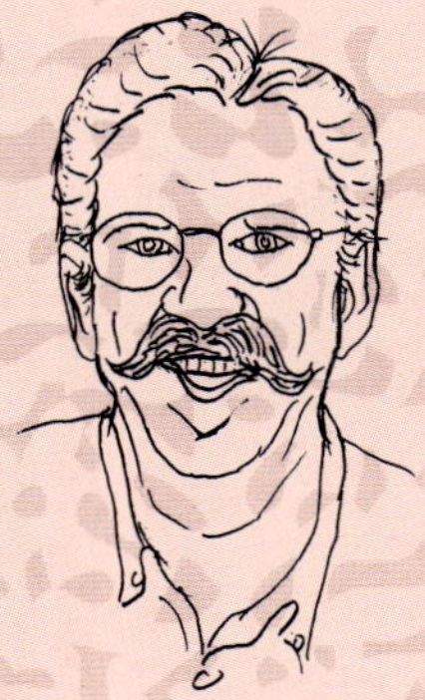

Eldon Humphreys, a resident of Kincardine, Ontario, is a retired Chief Superintendent of the Ontario Provincial Police. When he started carving in 1983, he soon found out that the art of caricature carving fit right in with his ability to see the humorous side of things. He used caricature to show the funny side of police-work—something he knew very well. He soon began carving a wide variety of subjects in this style and found caricature carving to be a wonderful new career.

Eldon's contributions to the CCA Circus appear on pages 39, 54 and 55.

Eldon is past-president of both the Mississauga and Lake Huron Wood Carvers and a former vice-president of the Ontario Wood Carvers. He is a member of the Affiliated Woodcarvers and the National Wood Carvers and was invited to become a member of the Caricature Carvers of America in 1996.

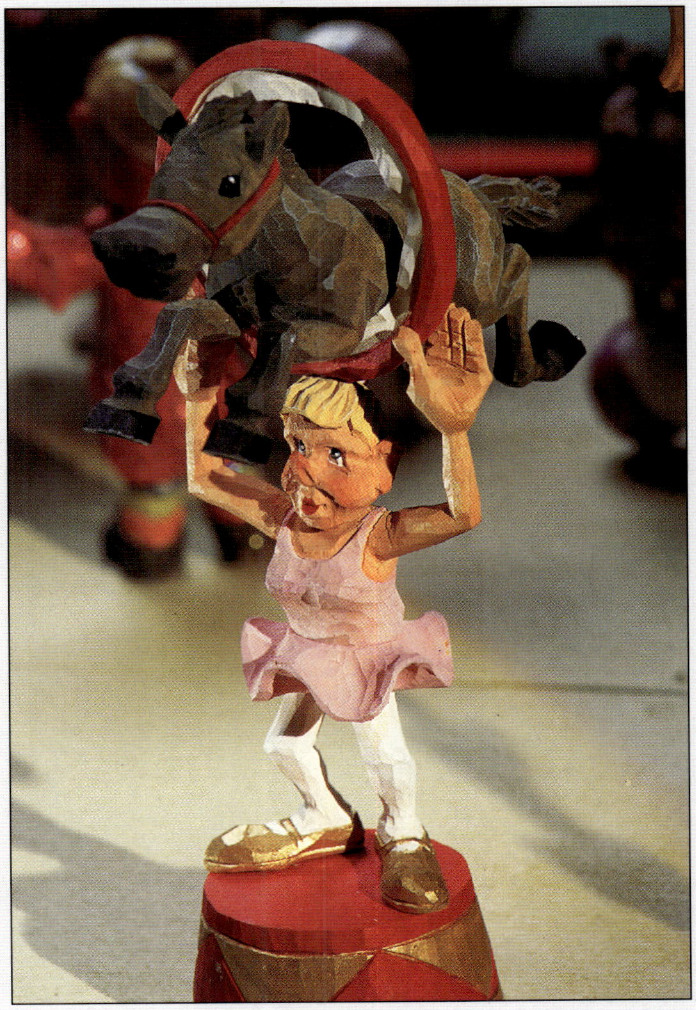

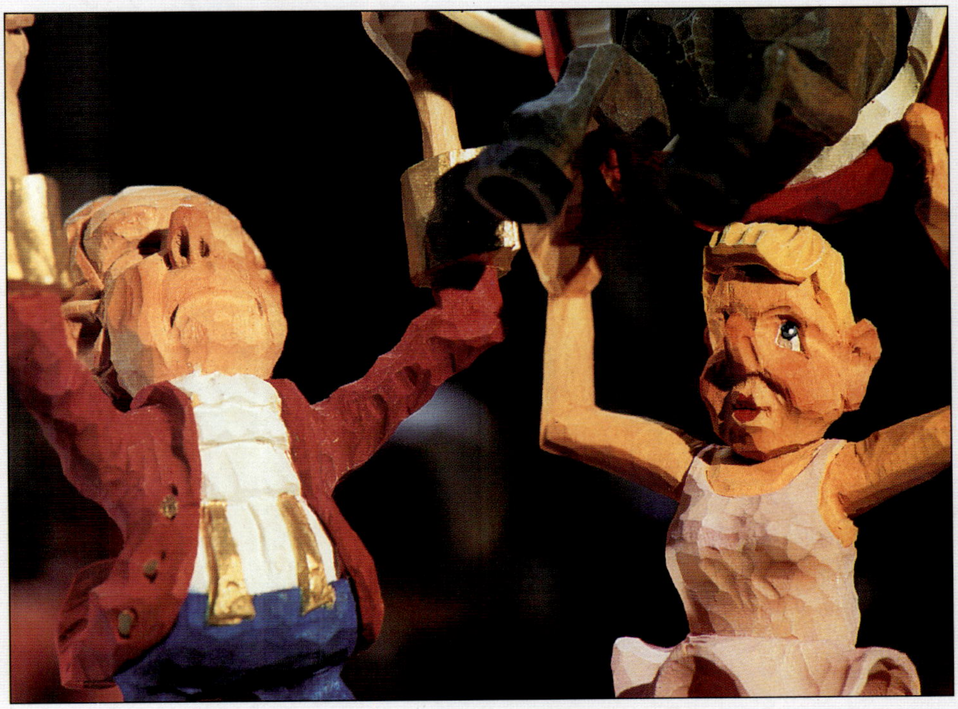

The Stetsonious Brothers by Dave Stetson

If it's unsafe to walk under a ladder; is it more dangerous to walk under an elephant that's under a ladder? Not if you're a member of the stupendous, fantabulous, ever exciting and devil may care (but never on Monday) Stetsonious Brothers.

The scene was not totally planned in the beginning. The original idea was to have three guys standing on each others shoulders and it seemed appropriate that the guy on top should be holding an umbrella to assist him with balance. The guy in the middle is more of an involved observer. And the guy on the bottom, well, he'd need big feet for stability.

The idea was first drawn out on paper and then drawn onto the block of wood. The idea of the elephant squirting water on the umbrella came to me as I was carving, and a flame on the umbrella seemed to be a logical thing for her to squirt at.

I had to do some research into what elephants really looked like, and picked one that's used to harvest banana wood (a great wood for prime caricature carving).

So then it just happened that the Stetsonious Brothers were looking for work when the CCA *Circus* came to town. They were hired as tent packers because of their unique ability to put ten pounds in five pound sacks. One day as the brothers were about to put the last panel of the Big Top into the last five pound sack, a fire broke out in the hay trailer. While everyone was frantically running around looking for something to smoother the fire, an enormous flood of water doused the flames. There stood Bimbo the elephant. The circus owner was so overwhelmed that he hired Bimbo as the manager of the Traveling Circus Fire Department (TCFD) - in fact, she was the entire department.

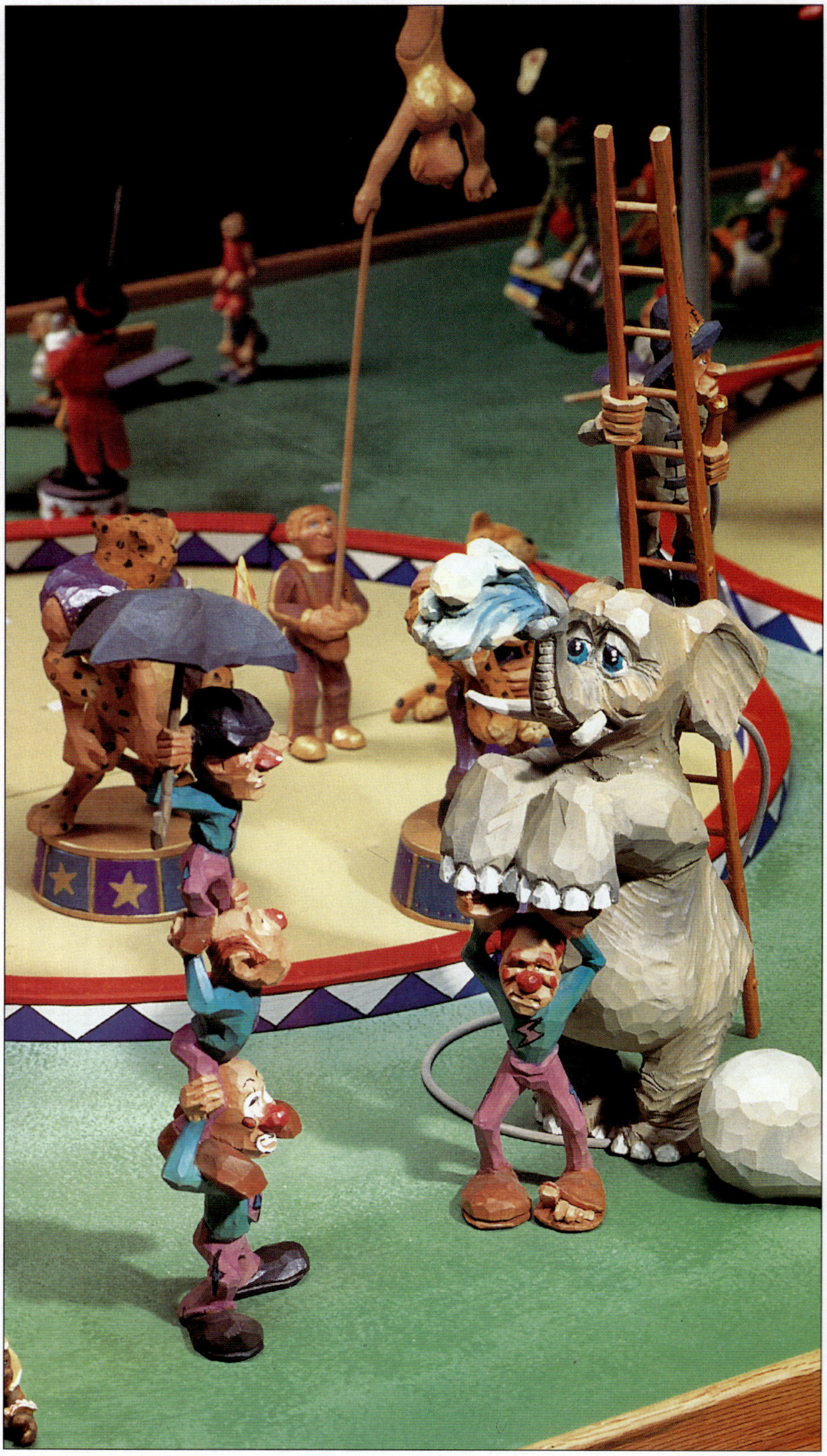

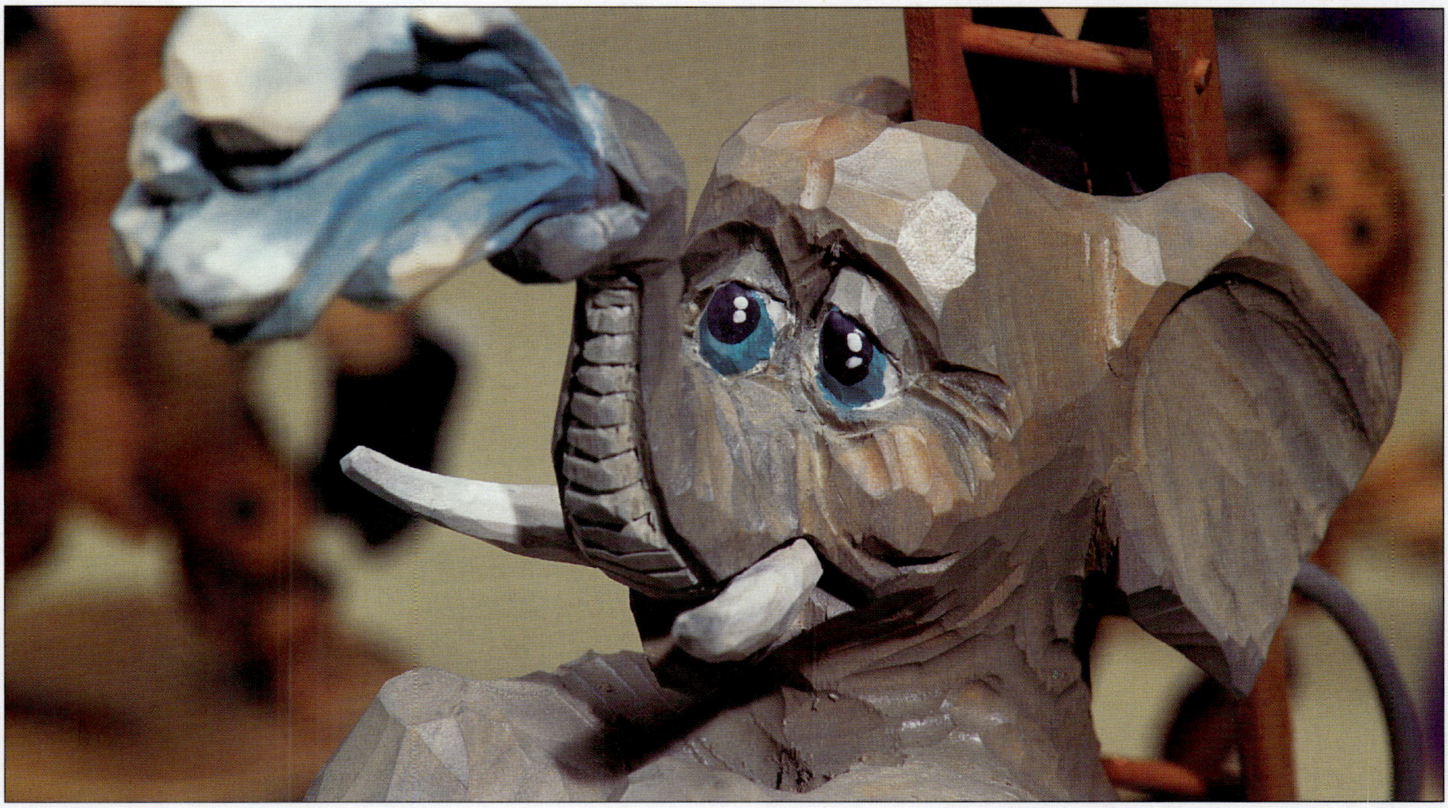

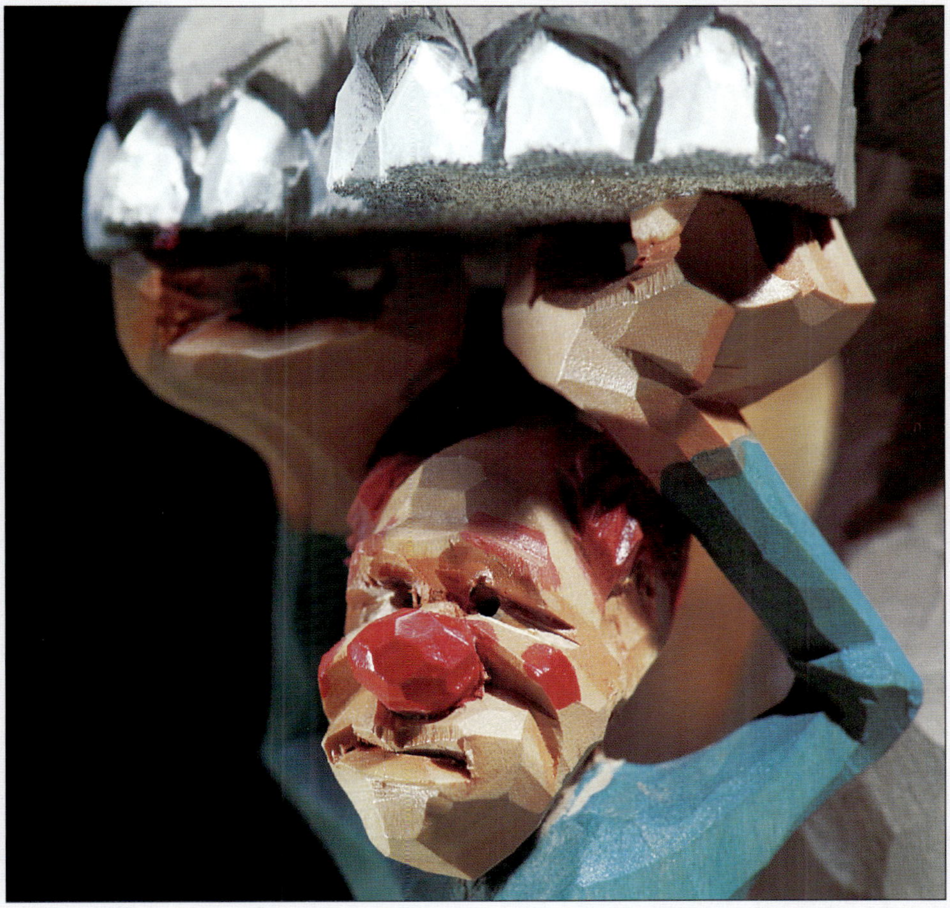

This unlucky guy isn't the only thing "underfoot." The elephant is also standing on the water hose, cutting off the supply of water to the dismay of the fireman on the ladder.

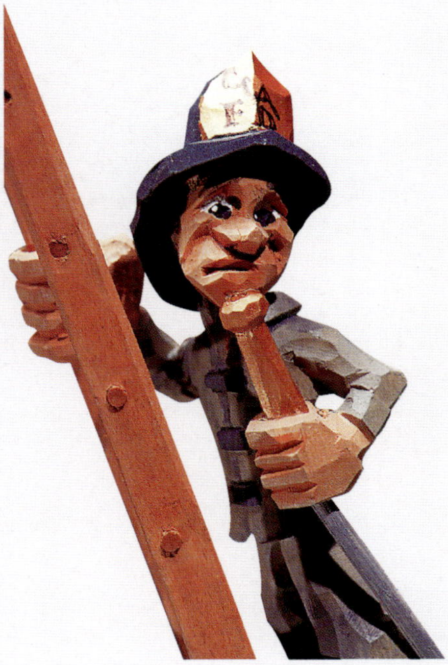

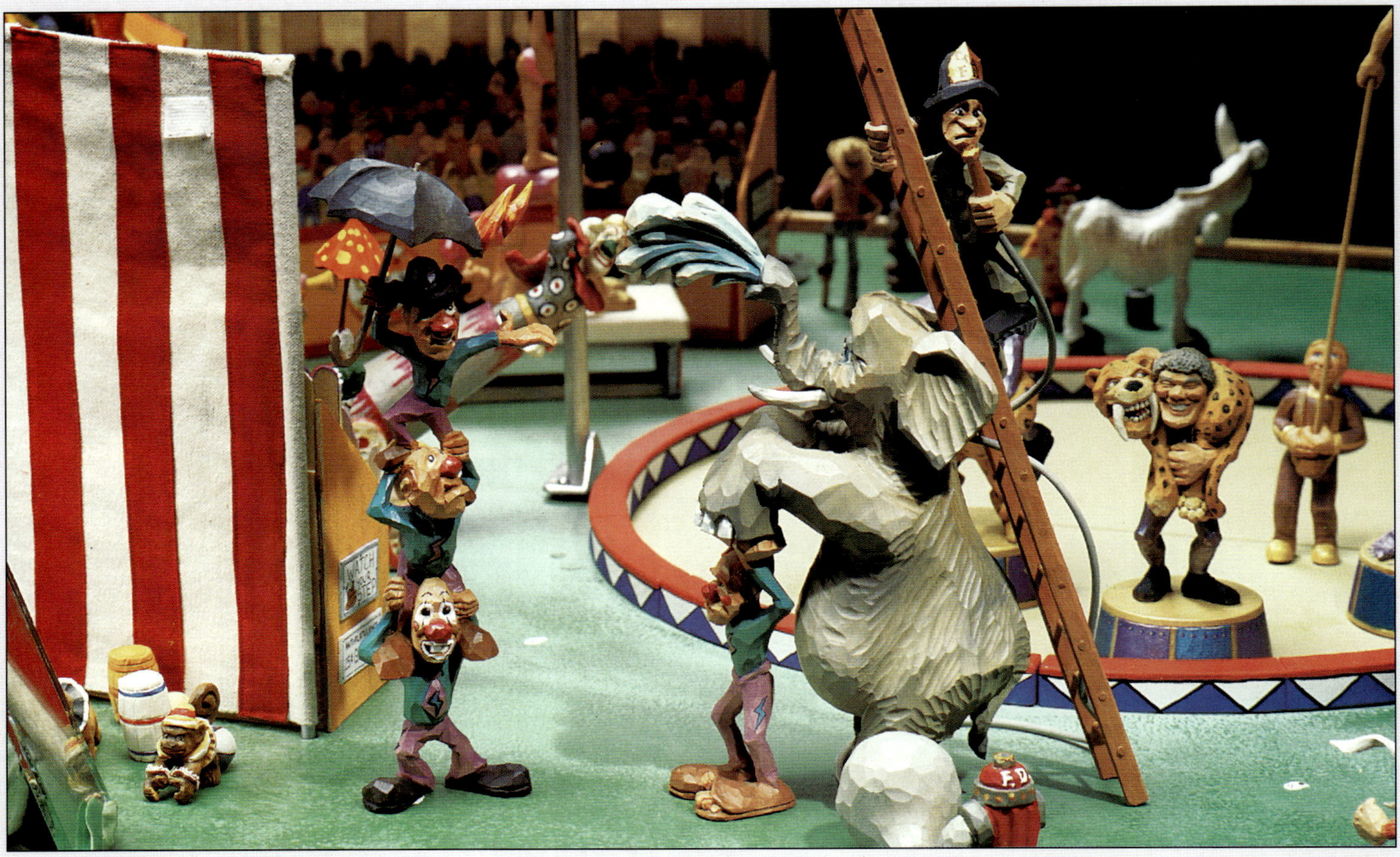

Dave Stetson wanted his carving of three men, one on top of the other, to be the tallest in the circus. He added the ladder and the fireman later as extra insurance, just in case someone else carved a giraffe or a figure on stilts.

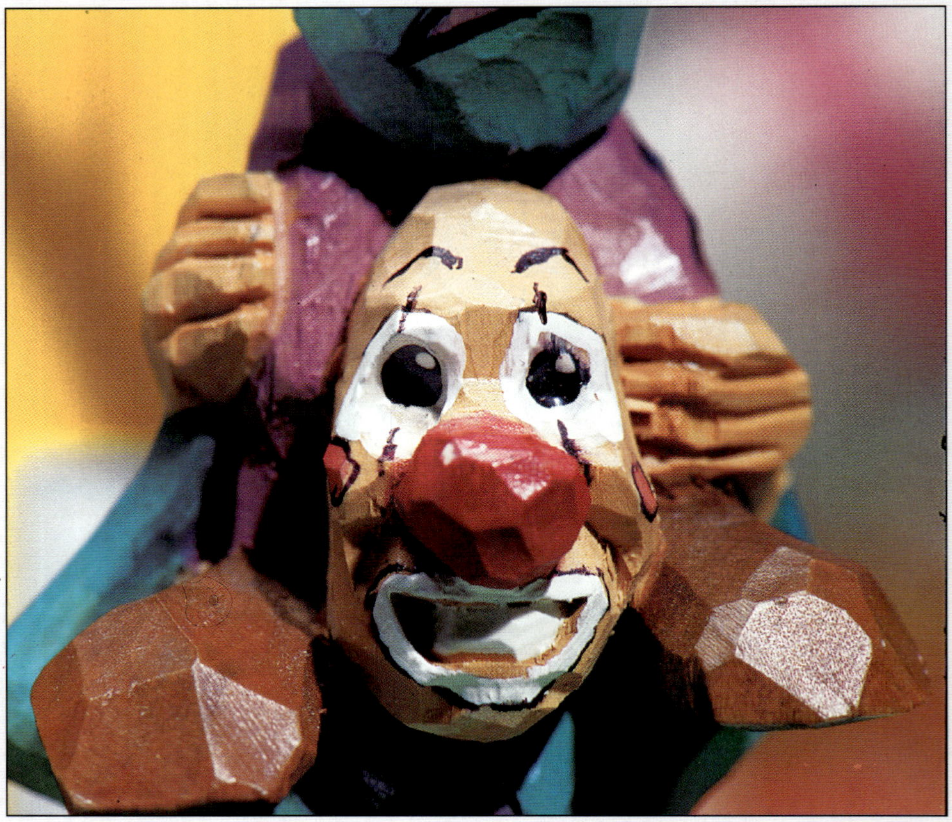

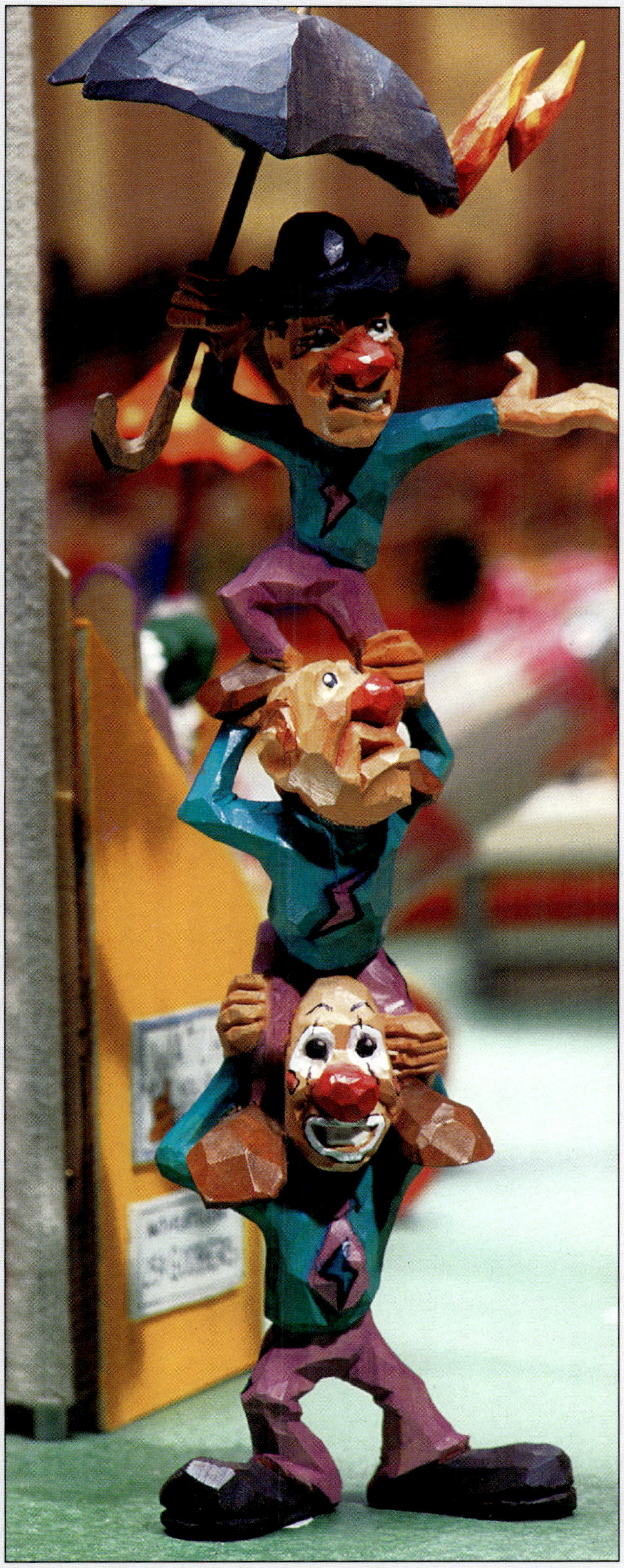

These three brothers are carrying an awful lot of weight on their shoulders. Dave Stetson carved the bottom brother with extra big feet to help him balance the weight of his other two brothers.

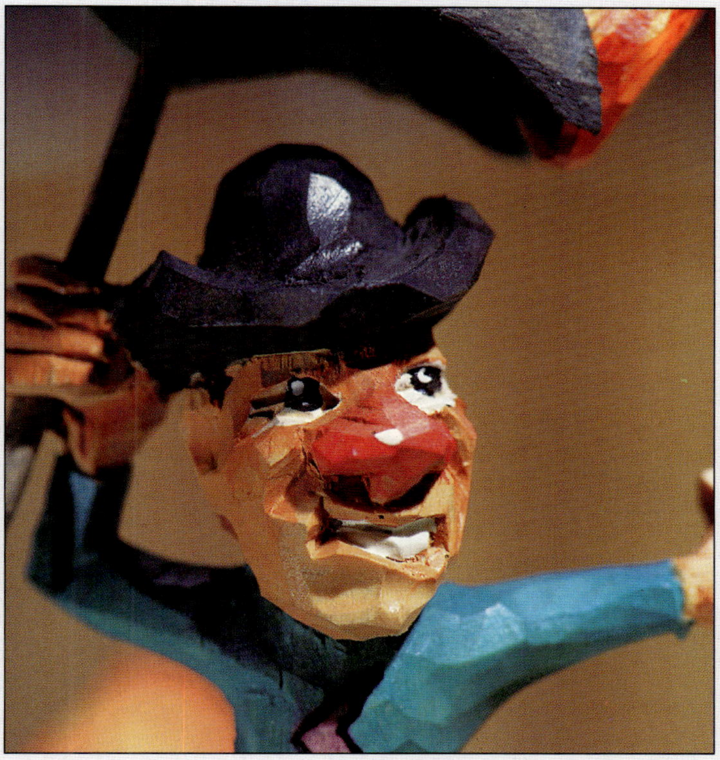

In another second, this poor fellow will be doused with water. The object of the fire-fighting elephant's water is the flame attached to this brother's umbrella.

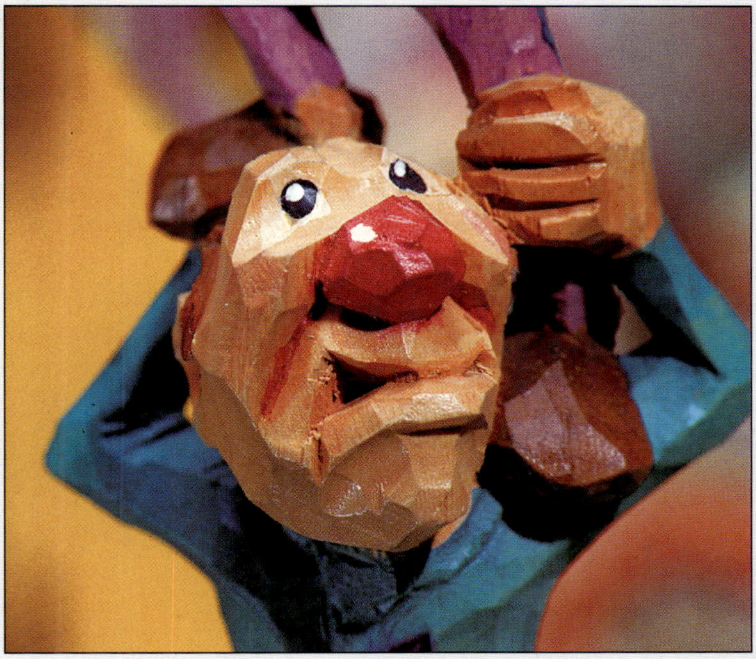

The middle brother is definitely caught in the middle of this situation. Dave carved the expression on this brother's face to portray his uncertainty of what will happen next. Perhaps the top brother will take a tumble before the water hits his umbrella?

Clive Batty by Tex Haase

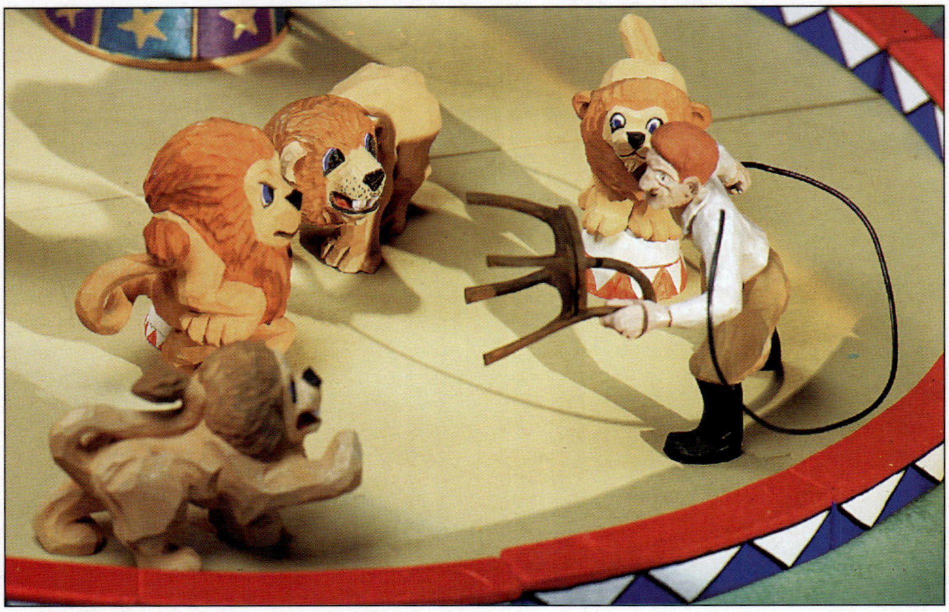

I went to my only circus when I was 10 years old. Our family went in and sat on the bleachers ready for the excitement to begin. When it finally began, there was a parade of clowns. Horses with pretty girls on top, dogs running and jumping and the band playing were all part of building suspense for the big acts to come. It was a splendor of color and dynamic motion.

As the show went on, everyone began to get hungry and thirsty, especially me. The circus was over four hours long, and all I could think about was my ever-growing thirst. Then the lion tamer came in. I don't recall who he was, but he was awesome. He was tall, splendidly dressed in a white costume with tall black boots, a wide black belt with a gun, a long, loud cracking whip and a strong left arm waving a chair in front of real lions. There must have been a dozen lions, all man-eaters, and he was in complete control. Instantly, he became this little boy's hero and a source of many a pleasurable daydream. This man was the inspiration for my part of the circus.

The carvings were fun and as we were all trying to meet a deadline, carving each correctly the first try was important. All went well with the cats. They were pretty straight forward because I wanted to keep them simple. The lion tamer was also to be simple. He is, only I missed his center of gravity and the chair in his left hand kept making him fall over. So, I needed to add a counter weight, something to change Clive's center of gravity.

Now most everyone knows from elementary physics, that the high wire walker carries a long heavy pole to lower his center of gravity, thus, making it easier to walk the tight rope, if this can be easier. So, I took a piece of black bell wire and made Clive's whip long enough for the counter weight I needed. Then I adjusted the curve behind Clive so he balanced while addressing his cats. There's nothing magical about the curve; I just adjusted the wire until the carving stood the way I wanted it to.

Tex Haase

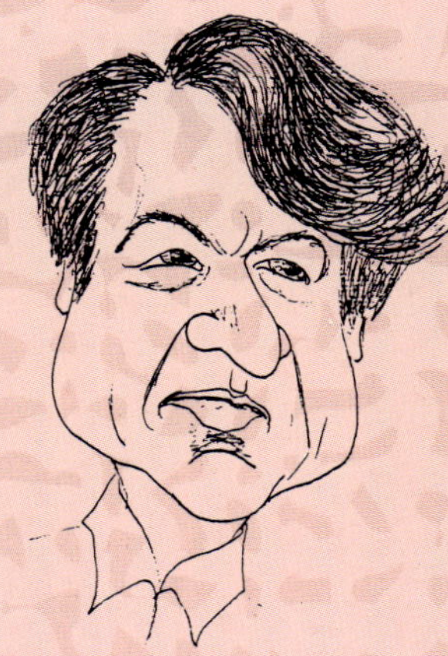

Tex, a resident of Tucumcari, New Mexico, started carving at the age of eight. After high school, three years in the U.S. Marines and a B.S. in mathematics, he began carving professionally. Tex expanded his knowledge with an M.A. in art in 1976. He has taught art and woodcarving at the vocational school, high school and college levels in Tucumcari since 1976. Tex teaches woodcarving seminars, judges carving shows, and is a frequent blue-ribbon and best-of-show winner throughout the Southwest.

Tex's contributions to the CCA Circus *appear on page 60.*

Tex is a founding member of the CCA and a member of the International Woodcarvers Congress and several other organizations.

Bear Acts by Gary Batte

Gary Batte

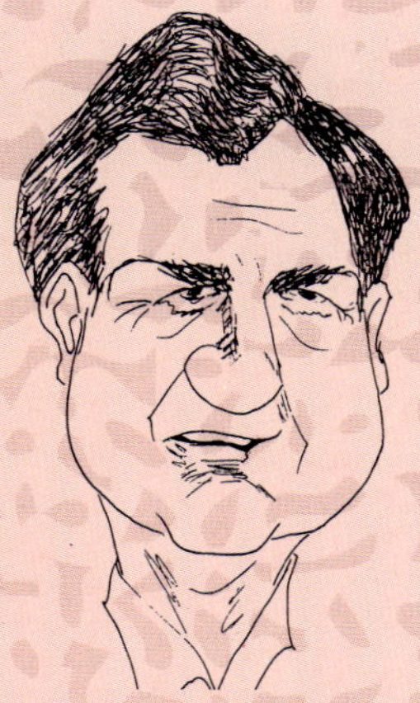

Gary, a resident of Stephenville, Texas, retired from USDA Natural Resources Conservation Service in 1994 and now spends much of his time on woodcarving-related activities. His caricatures are created from original designs and are noted for their humor and detail. They have been exhibited at a number of galleries, museums and universities. Gary has won numerous awards at major carving shows, and his carvings can be found in many private collections throughout the United States.

Gary's contributions to the CCA Circus appear on pages 9, 37 and 61.

Gary is a woodcarving instructor and has authored a book titled Carving Critters, Cowboys and Other Characters. *He is a founding member of the CCA, and is a member of the National Woodcarvers Association, the Affiliated Woodcarvers, Ltd. and the Texas Woodcarvers Guild.*

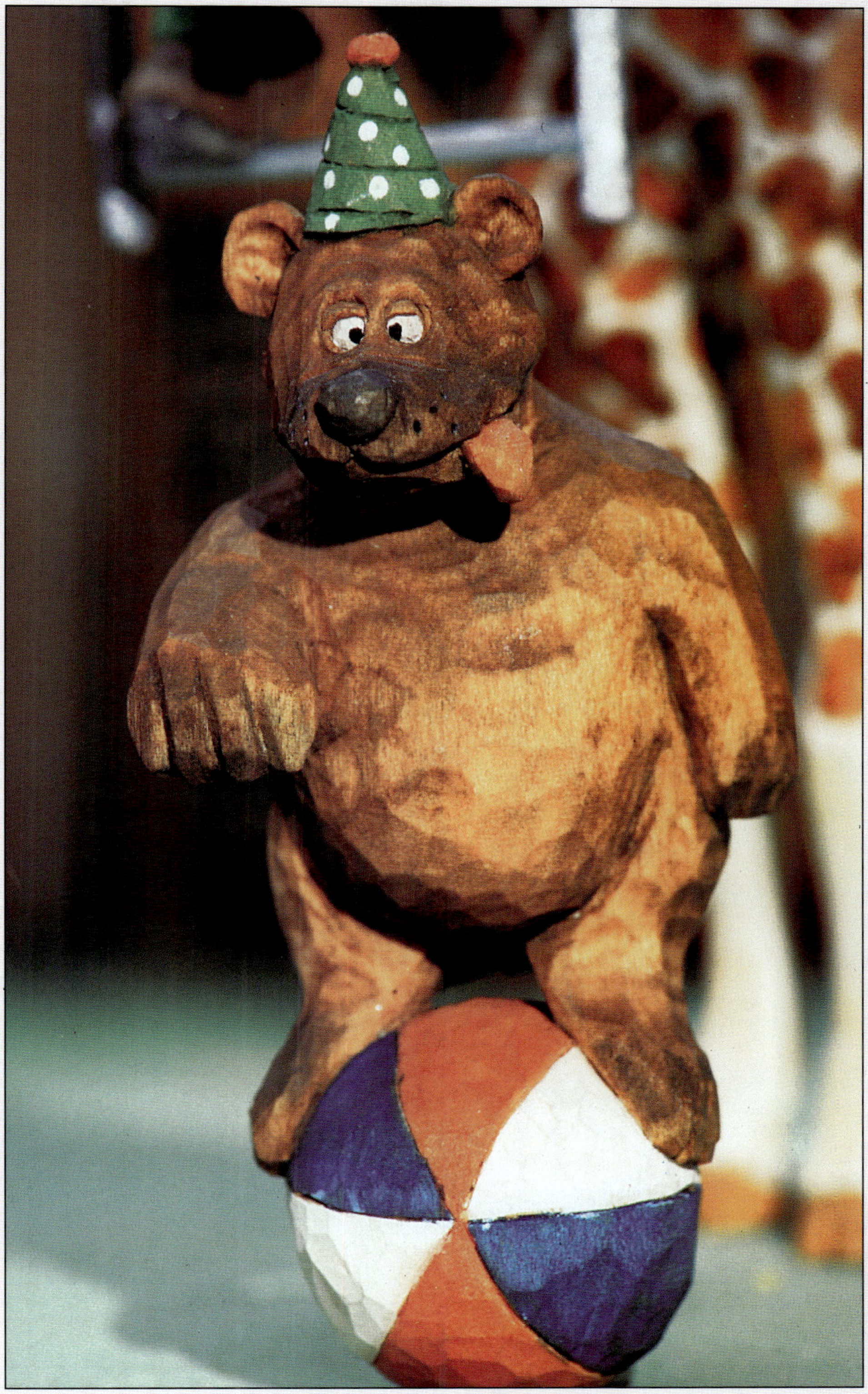

Balancing on a ball is a tough act for this bear, as evidenced by the look on his face. The bear and the ball were both carved from one piece of wood. Gary Batte carved the ball first to help him keep the rest of the carving in proportion.

Ronald by Desiree Hajny

Desiree Hajny

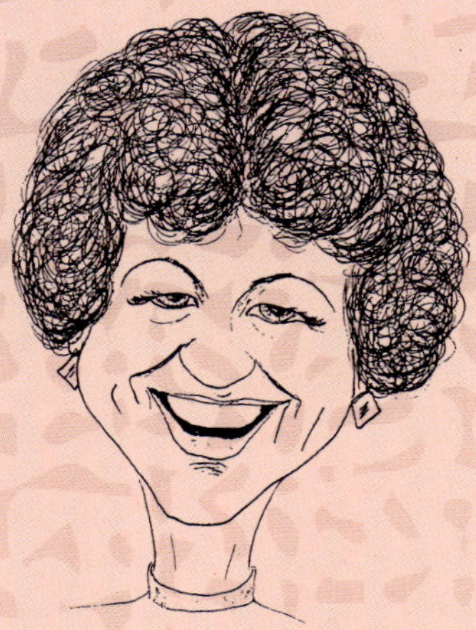

Desiree, a resident of Eckert, Colorado, is a wildlife artist, specializing in carving mammals in a realistic style. She finds the research involved in creating these pieces to be engaging and an important part of the carving process. Desiree also enjoys cartooning and frequently carves caricature animals. Her research for realistic mammals also helps her decide what features to exaggerate on a caricature animal.

Desiree's contributions to the CCA Circus *appear on pages 51 and 62.*

Desiree has written three books on carving realistic mammals and one book on carving caricature animals. She is the American representative in the new international woodcarving magazine published in England. She is also a founding member of CCA and is a member of several other organizations throughout the United States. She has exhibited nationally and internationally and has won over 70 first place awards, including 11 best of shows, since 1985.

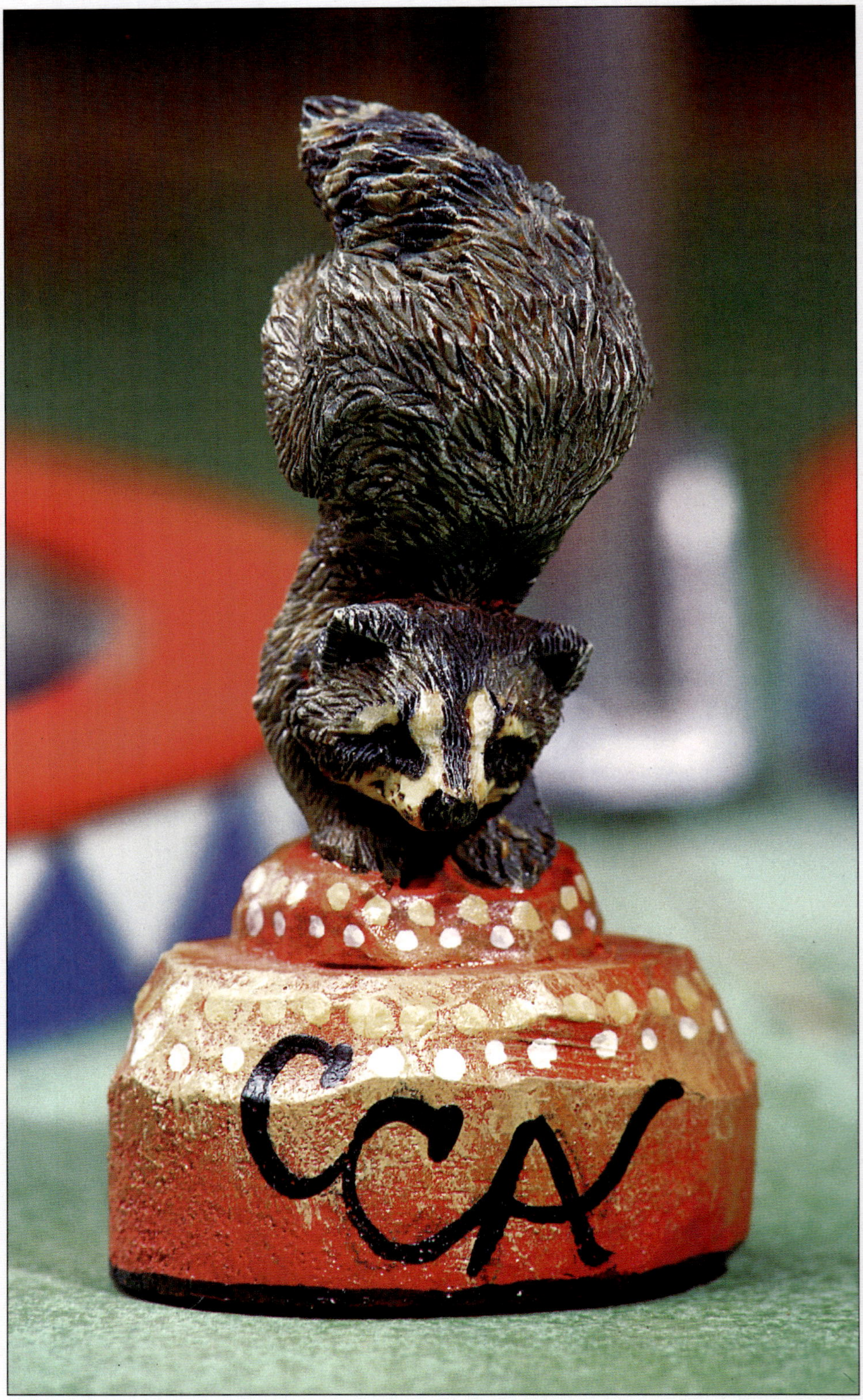

A "trained" raccoon by Desiree Hajny shows off for the audience at the CCA Circus. The fur was detailed with a v-tool and burning tool in a random pattern to make it appear as realistic as possible.

ACROBATS

Balancing Act by Steve Prescott

As I was researching my subject for the circus scene, I had the opportunity to take my daughters and a couple of neighborhood kids to the Shrine Circus. Ideas for potential carving projects were abundant, but the act that really impressed me was called "The Golden Aztecs." It consisted of two men and a woman acrobat completely covered in gold body paint. I don't know if acrobat is the correct description. They were more like amazing contortionists. Carving this act would be a real challenge!

My first attempts at a design involved the two males that form the base of the carving. The bigger, stronger man was always at the bottom of the pyramid, while the taller, more slender young man balanced on him. Several of the patterns I developed proved to be too fragile for this kind of traveling exhibit. (Always keep in mind how the carving will be displayed or handled when planning your design.) I compromised with a square base for strength and balance.

The third figure, the beautiful girl perched on top of the two men, should exhibit balance and grace even as a caricature. I just couldn't visualize in my mind a human being in such a distorted position until I saw a young cheerleader at my school perform this stunt. It's called a "scorpion." My first clay models kept falling over until I finally discovered that this figure is just a diamond on a stick. This figure is balanced on top of the two male figures, and the three figures together form a pleasing triangular form.

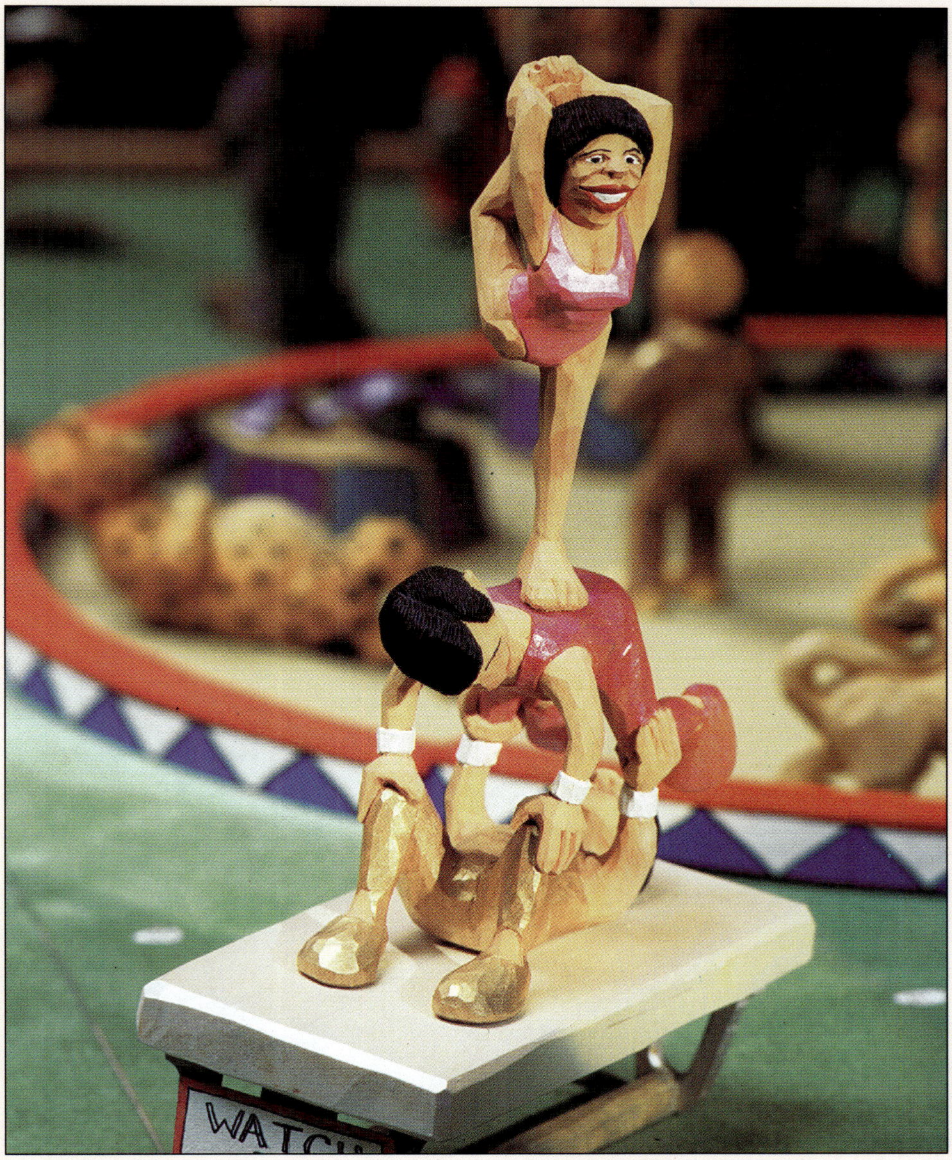

All three figures can be carved as one piece if you want that kind of challenge. I chose to carve it as two pieces, rationalizing the carving would be stronger for a traveling exhibit this way. The heads of the men were carved separately. The girl isn't hard to carve except that the bent leg and hip are in a weird position and the arms and shoulders almost appear to be dislocated. A little study of human muscle anatomy may be useful since the form-fitting costumes cannot hide the muscular shape of these figures.

I feel that circus figures need to have bright, almost outlandish colors. I decided to paint a little heavier than usual and used colors which have a metallic or pearlized sheen when dry. I painted each performer a different color. I did not antique these figures as I usually do since I did not want to dull the vivid colors.

Girl on the Flying Trapeze by Dave Dunham

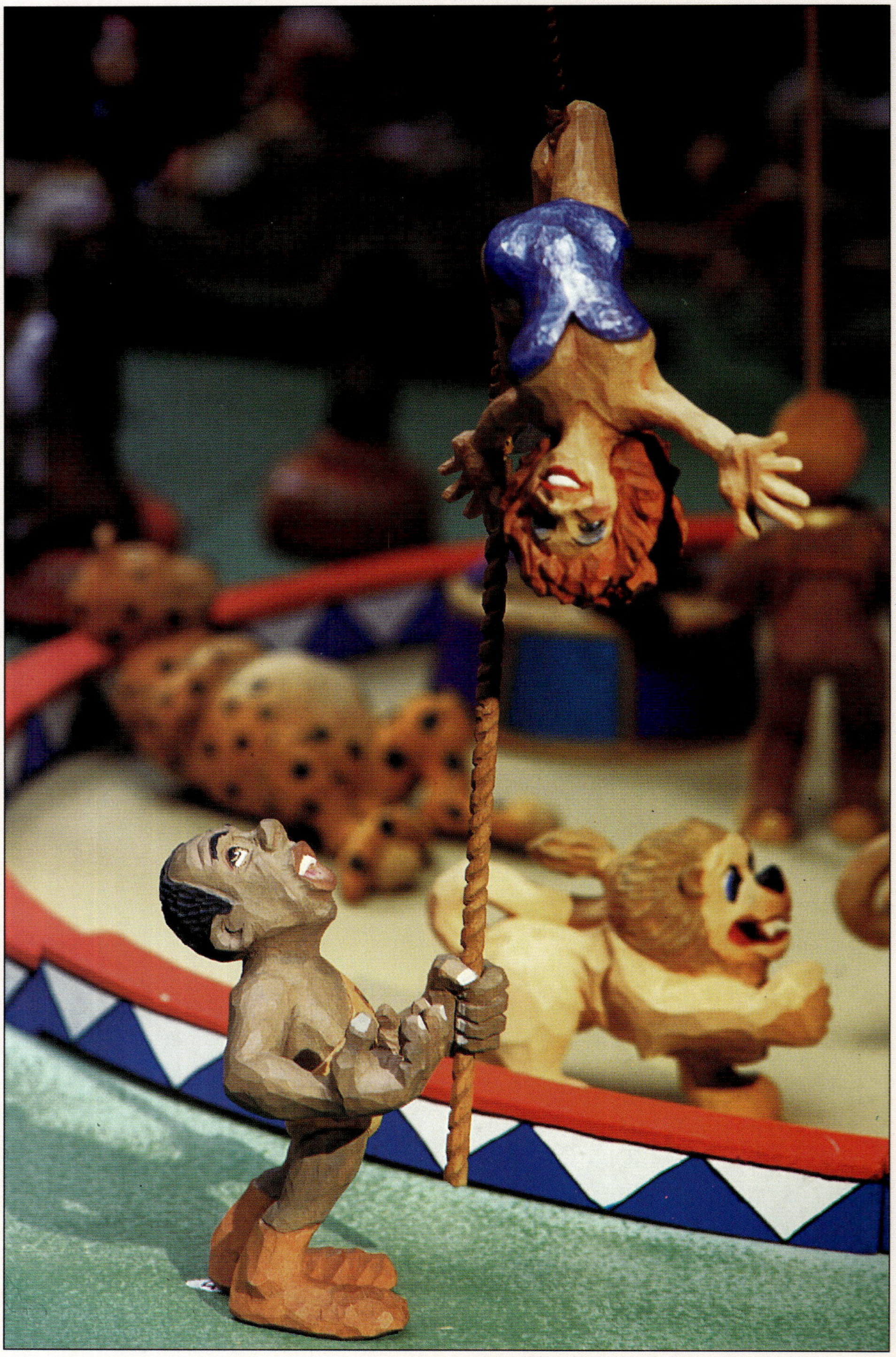

A trapeze aerialist hanging by the legs from a vertical rope and a strongman looked like a challenging project, especially with the girl's feet and legs intertwined with the rope, so I decided to carve it as my primary project.

I had a good mental image of this project, but due to the complexity, I also needed a visual, three-dimensional model from which to work. I made a model out of pipe cleaners and then made a detailed drawing of the figure, filling out the body contours and showing the facial expression that I wanted.

I also made a detailed drawing of the legs intertwined with the vertically suspended rope. I suspected, correctly, that this would be the most difficult part of the carving, and I would need a good visual reference to construct it properly.

Finally, I reduced the finished pattern drawing to scale, made the properly sized bandsaw pattern and cut the profile figure from basswood stock.

Much of this carving would be in direct cross-grain, which means easy breakage. The very thin arms extended to the sides would be especially vulnerable, so I drilled 1/8" dowel holes through the long axis of the arms, extending the holes into the shoulder and chest area. I then glued tight-fitting dowels into the holes to increase the strength of these appendages. The torso, also in direct cross grain, was thick enough to resist easy breakage so it was not reinforced.

I carved the hands last, after all of the other details were finished. I wanted the fingers separated, as they were going to be in cross grain. After carefully carving the fingers, I soaked the fingers, hands and arms in superglue. This substance penetrates the wood fibers and bonds them as it sets up, adding much greater strength to the entity and increasing resistance to breakage.

Unfortunately, superglue is difficult to paint using thin washes, so paint has to be applied in a thicker coat over these areas. However, with careful blending, the paint can cover nicely without appearing like porcelain.

On the Move by Cleve Taylor

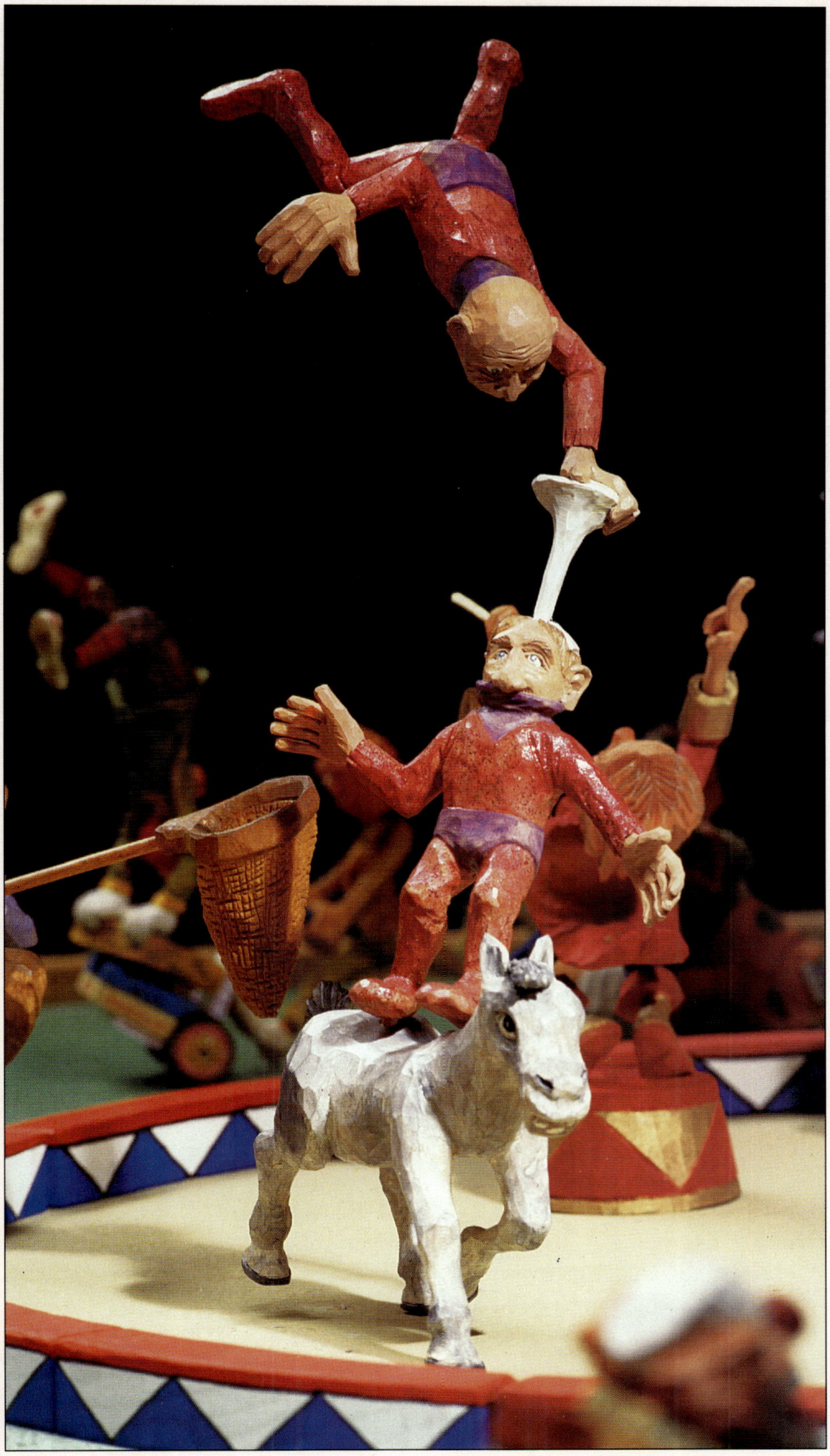

Freehand sketching without a model has always been a problem for me. Rather than working directly on this deficiency and learning to draw, I have compensated by developing mechanical devices.

The most helpful mechanical device I've come across so far is Melrose the Marvelous Maniken, a bendable, three-dimensional model. The lengths of the various body parts were approximated using the scale of 7/10 inch equals 1 foot, cut from a 1/4 inch diameter dowel and connected together with copper wire. I drilled a small hole in the appropriate location on each part, sanded the ends to allow for three-dimensional movement and epoxied copper wire into the holes. The advantage of Melrose over pipe cleaners is stability; and over clay is the speed in which a model can be constructed. Melrose is not an original idea, but with him I can make patterns without too much frustration.

All of the human subjects in my scenes were designed using Melrose. I attempted to lay out the figures for my bandsawed blanks to take advantage of the wood grain in the basswood for maximum strength. Weak limbs and joints were reinforced with 1/8 inch dowels.

I used acrylic paints on the finished unsealed wood carvings. Brightly colored washes were selected for the tights worn by the acrobats, and DecoArt Craft Twinkles (DCT 1-6) were used to add glitter to the base colors of the tights. After all the coloring was finished, I antiqued the carvings with a mixture of linseed oil and dark walnut stain. The final sealant was a thin wash of matte finish.

Princess Teena by Jack Price

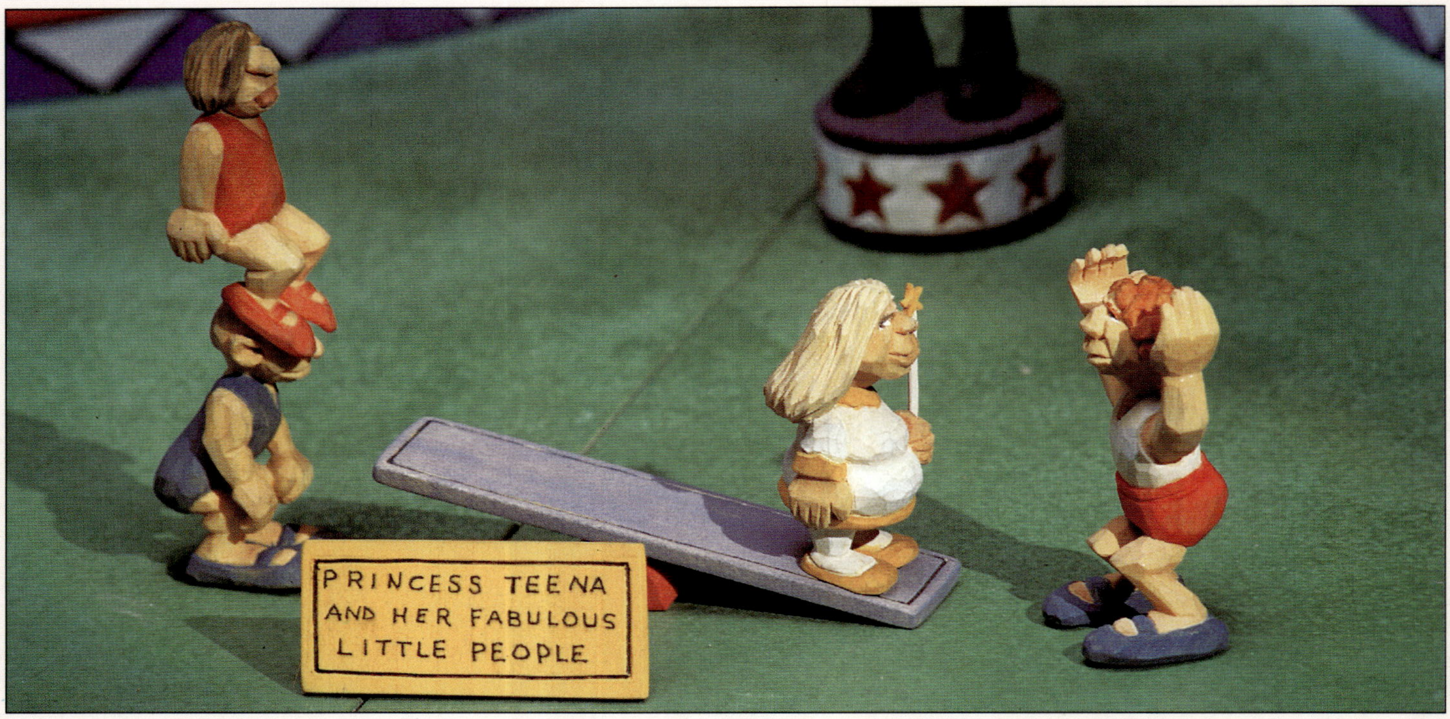

In my older years I have become a practicing ne'er-do-well who has developed procrastination into a fine art. Thus, the hardest part of any project for me is just getting started. You'll see from this essay that the majority of my work goes into deciding and planning.

How to portray my Little People was the first and hardest part of the creative process. Several ideas immediately came to mind and all of them looked good at first. After a bit of thought several ideas were discarded because they were either impractical, too complicated, too large for the space allowed, or beyond my level of carving ability.

Three ideas remained viable. I drew each of the ideas on paper using stick figures. Then, I studied each idea carefully. My wishy-washy mind favored first one idea then another. So I wrote a scenario for each idea in order to explain what the characters were doing. A lot of time was spent with each idea, adjusting and refining, playing with them, trying to make each better. I almost "whatifed" them to death. Finally, in total frustration, I decided to put the project aside for a while and let it gel.

For a few days, I carved figures that were not related to the ideas proposed for the circus project. This respite helped. When I examined the ideas this time, a clear favorite emerged almost immediately.

Princess Teena and her fabulous Little People are members of the clown troupe. As a unit they have developed several routines that are humorously done and highlight their athletic prowess. They appear in this skit to be an inept group of acrobats trying to do a routine that has little chance of succeeding.

Most of the onlookers are convinced that the act will be a disaster. Teena is so fat that when Rocky, the top guy, drops on the inclined board, the audience expects the board to break. Few believe that Teena will become airborne.

Rocky is another part of the problem. He can't even get in position to do his drop. Instead of being on Samson's shoulders, he is squatting on his head.

Curly, the catcher, is shown grimacing as though he expects to be crushed when Teena's bulk crashes down on him. What the audience doesn't know is that Teena, who is a superb athlete, is wearing a body suit to make her look obese. Rocky is only pretending to have difficulty climbing on Samson's shoulders, and Curly is a strong and experienced catcher. They will see Rocky drop on the seesaw. This action will propel Teena into the air where she will do a double flip with a half twist and land lightly on Curly's shoulders. The audience will, of course, be surprised and delighted.

Using stick figures as guides, I developed patterns and carved the figures from basswood. All four characters are painted with acrylics.

Jack Price

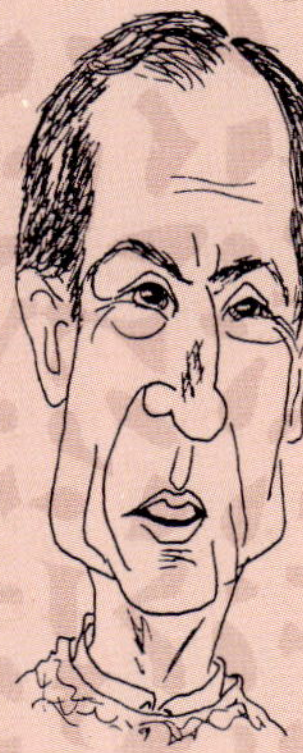

Jack, author of three carving books is a retired Texas public school administrator living in Cleburne, Texas, He began carving in 1975 and has specialized in compact figures since 1978. Jack definitely doesn't believe that "bigger is better" as most of his carvings are only 2–3 inches in height. As he travels to display his carving talents, Jack is more than willing to share his carving knowledge with others.

Jack's contributions to the CCA Circus appear on pages 66 and 67.

Jack is a founding member of CCA. He also belongs to several woodcarving groups and is past-president of the Texas Woodcarvers Guild.

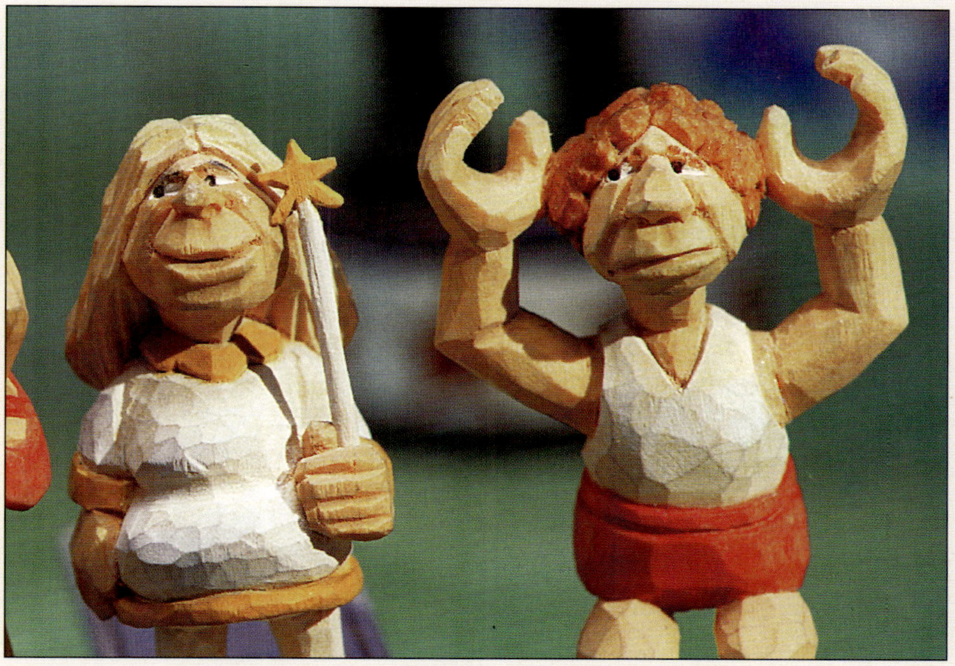

Seeming quite ungraceful, Princess Teena may just need that magic wand in her hand to complete this trick. Unbeknownst to the audience, the princess is actually quite slim. Jack Price carved her wearing a body suit to make her look ungainly.

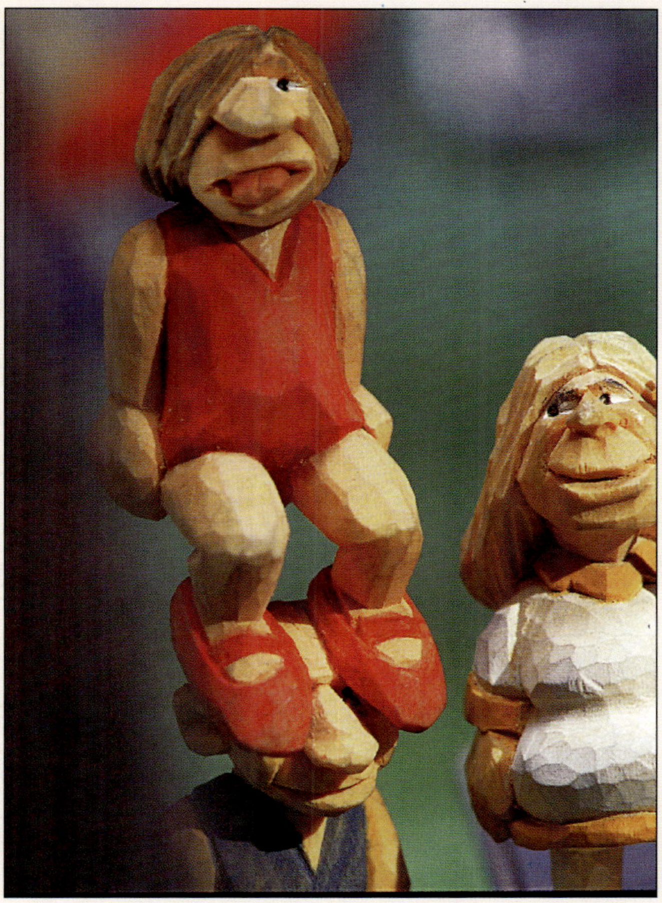

Furthering the impression of an inept group of acrobats, Rocky appears to be having trouble getting into position on Sampson's shoulders for the jump to the board. The two figures were carved from one piece of basswood.

Look Ma by Steve Prescott

Steve Prescott

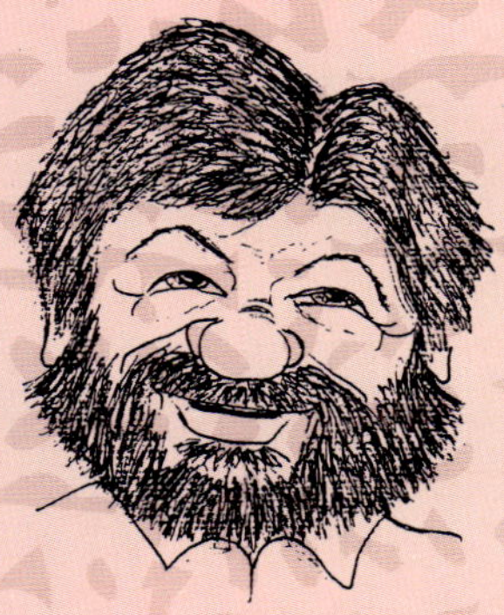

Steve, a resident of Fort Worth, Texas, is a junior high life science teacher with over 20 years of experience as a professional educator. He began carving in 1982 when his doctor advised him "to find something to do with your hands other than feeding yourself." Steve is now recognized as an outstanding carver of western humor. His caricatures typically feature oversized heads and exaggerated hands.

Steve's contributions to the CCA Circus appear on pages 63 and 68.

Steve began teaching carving in 1987. He has won numerous awards in carving competitions, the most notable being the Texas Whittling Championship in 1990 and 1993, and has written two books, Cowtown Carving *and* Carving Blockheads. *Steve is a founding member of the CCA and served as its first president. He also serves as Regional Advisor for the Texas Woodcarvers Guild.*

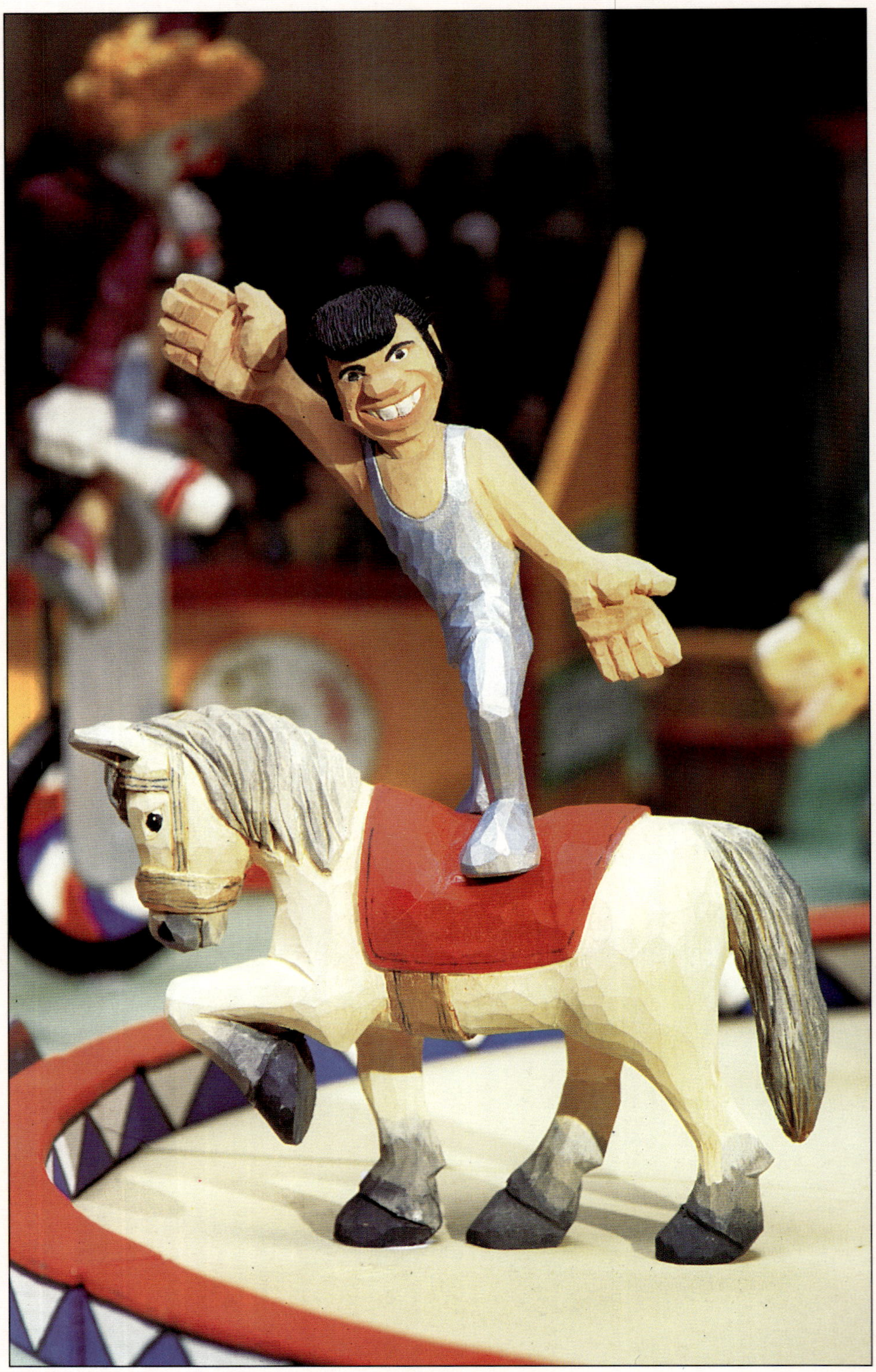

For this acrobat, carved by Steve Prescott, balancing on the back of a horse is no small feat. Notice the large hands on this figure. Heads on caricatures are typically larger in proportion when compared to the body. Hands are carved in proportions to match the head.

Going, Going... by Keith Morrill

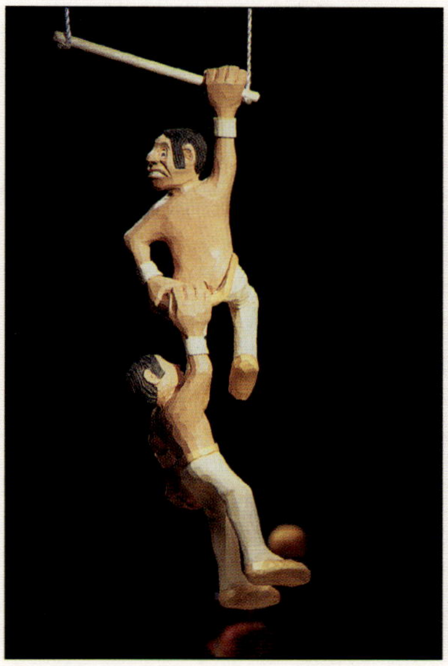

...Gone by Harley Schmitgen

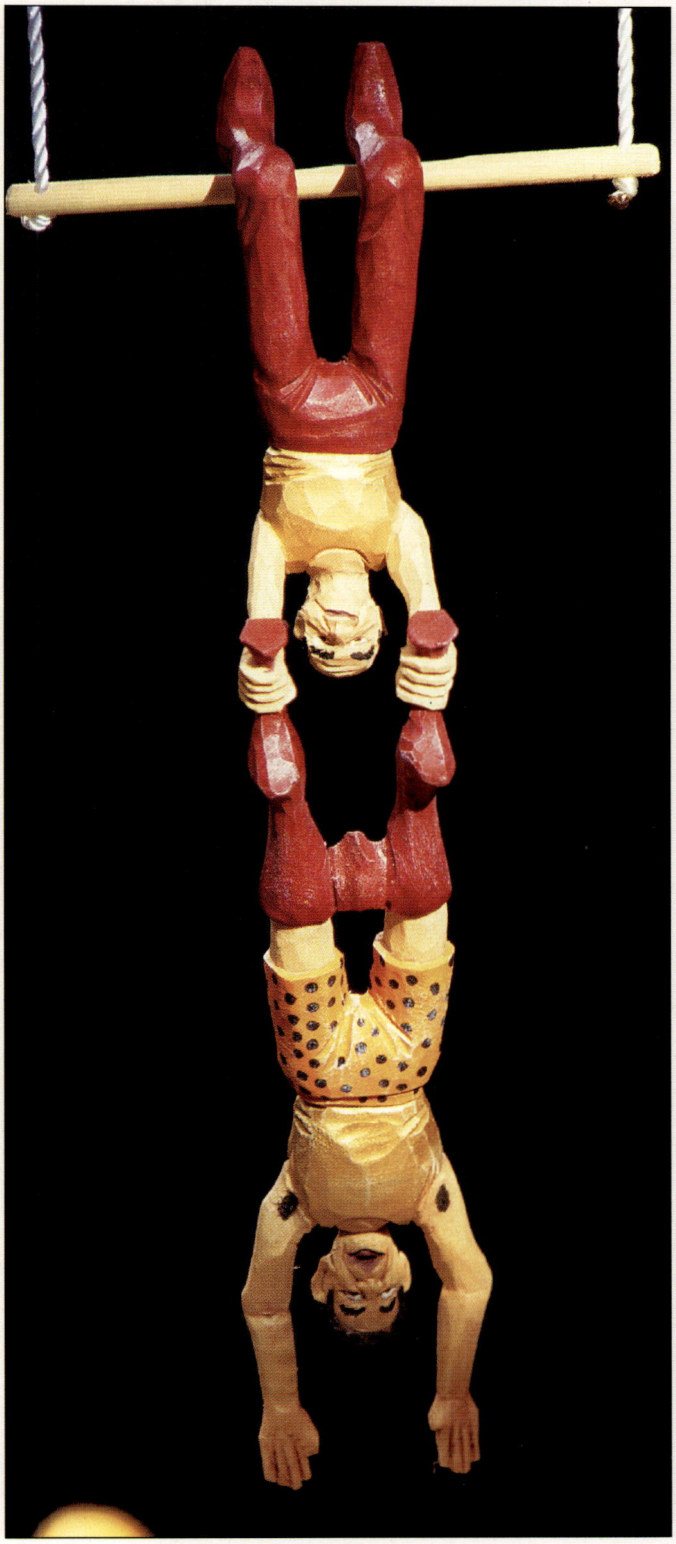

Upside Down by Keith Morrill

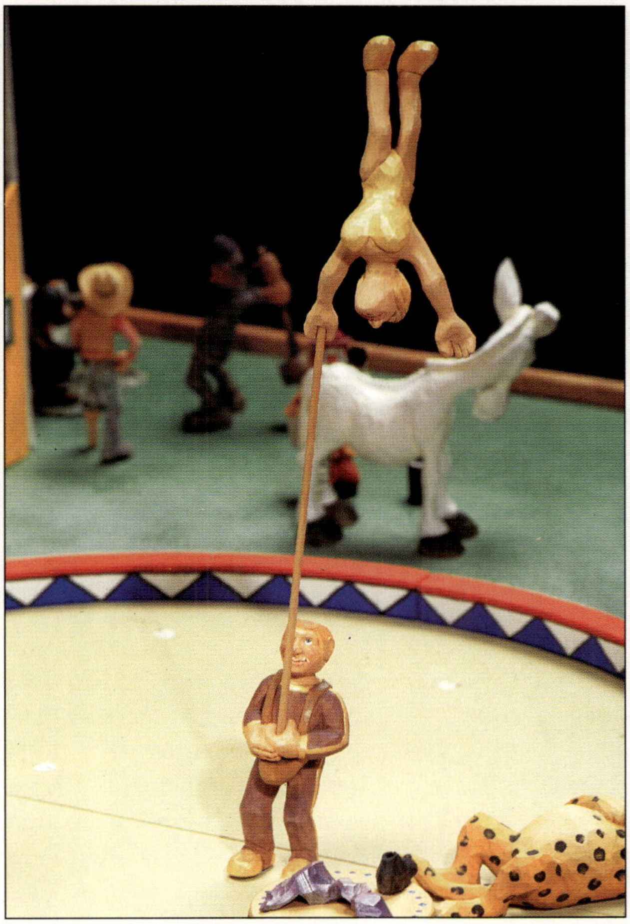

SHOW STOPPERS

The Knife Thrower by Keith Morrill

Although it has been many, many years since I have seen a circus, I can remember one act distinctly: the knife thrower and the human cannonball. I can still see in my mind a woman strapped to a large turning wheel with arms and legs extended while her partner threw knife after knife, outlining her body, barely missing her with each terrifying throw. I saw this type of knife-throwing act several times and recall one of the throwers doing it blind-folded! It was this image that inspired one of my carvings for the CCA *Circus*.

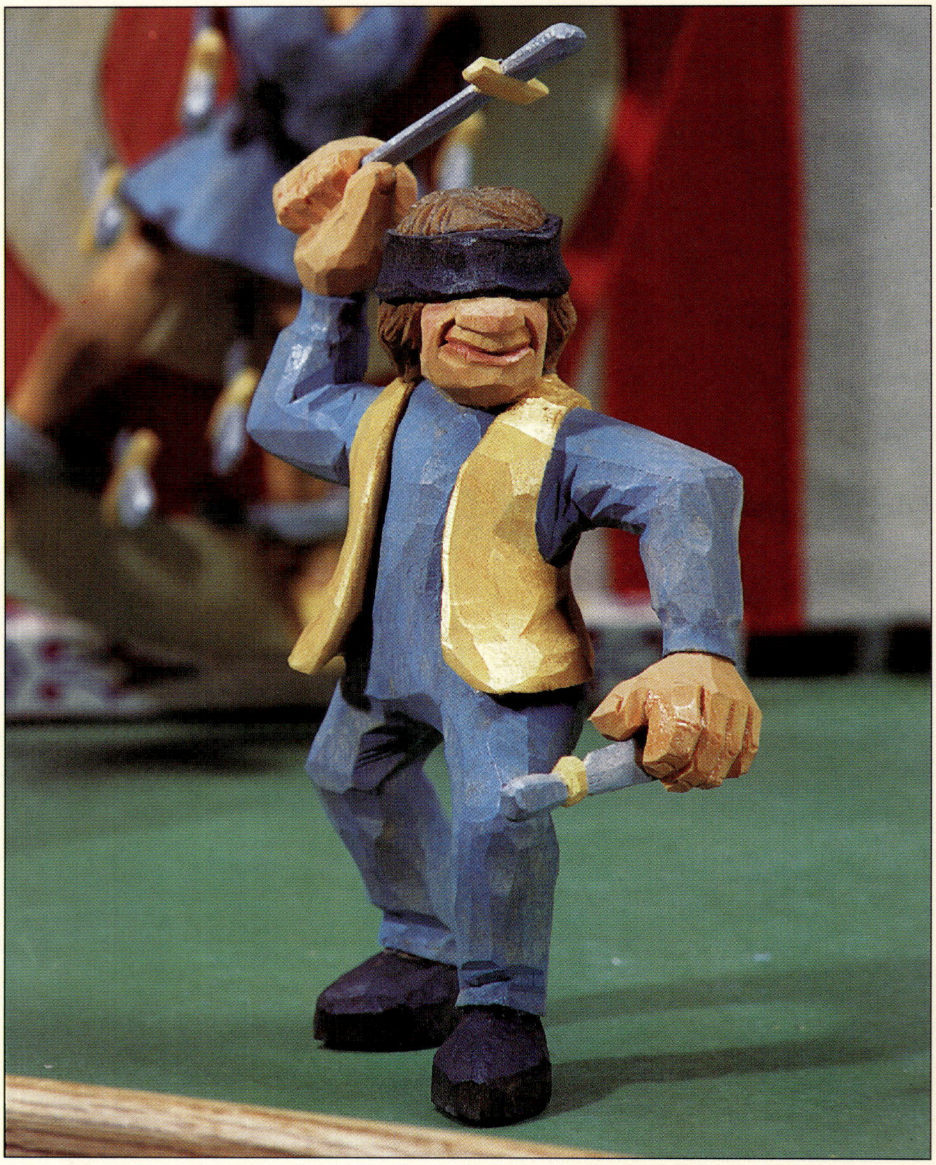

I used a plastic action figure, such as those sold in toy stores to design my circus carvings. These figures are very helpful as models because many of them are jointed and can be twisted, turned and positioned to suit your needs. Luckily, the action figure I chose was almost the exact sized specified for the circus.

Converting the model to a drawing began by placing the figure on a piece of paper and tracing around it. I usually draw front and side views then transfer the drawings to a suitably sized piece of wood. I then bandsawed the front and side views.

Carving the knife-thrower and lady required extra care because their arms and legs extend from their bodies at various angles and are not straight with the wood grain. This can cause problems during carving as the limbs can break if too much pressure is applied in the wrong direction. I sometimes reinforce extended arms or legs by drilling and doweling the protruding appendage. On these carvings, however, I went ahead and carved without doweling, concentrating a little harder than usual and carefully holding the piece.

Most of these carvings were done with a detail knife and a 3 or 4 mm v-tool and u-gouge. I do not sand my carvings, preferring to leave the tool marks. I paint my carvings with thin acrylic washes (approximately 10 parts water to 1 part paint). I then antique them using boiled linseed oil to which a small amount of oil-based raw umber was added.

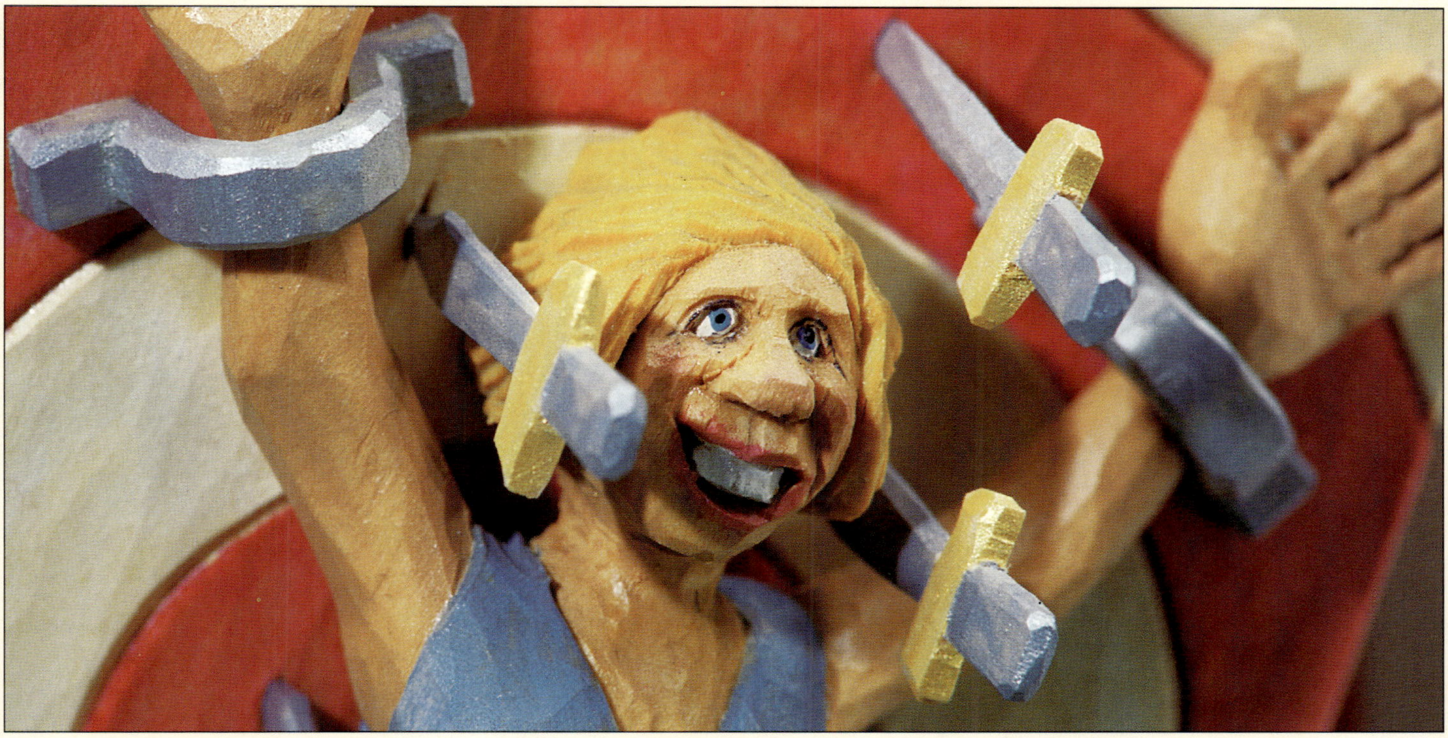

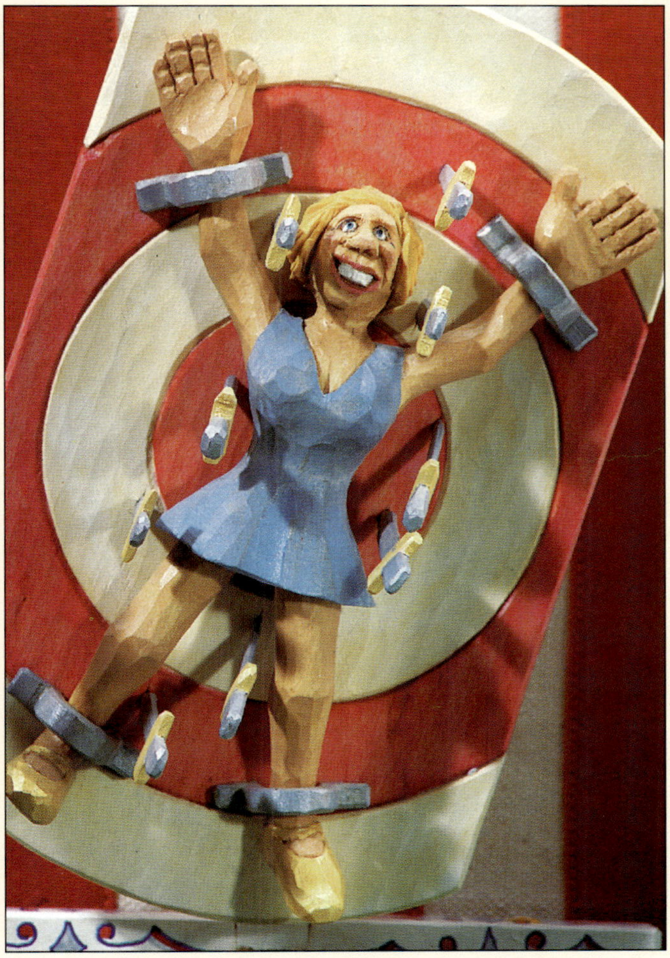

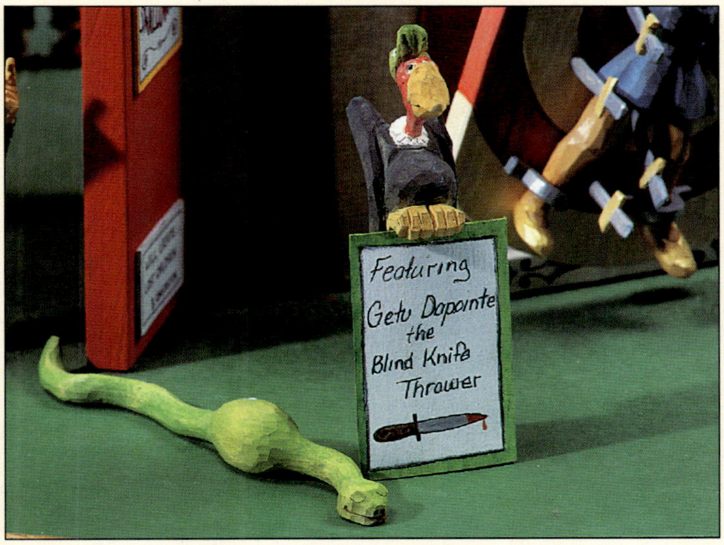

The buzzard sitting atop the sign for the knife thrower's act is patiently awaiting... for something other than supper, we hope. It was carved by Gary Batte for inclusion in this scene.

The Tallest Man at the Circus by Harley Schmitgen

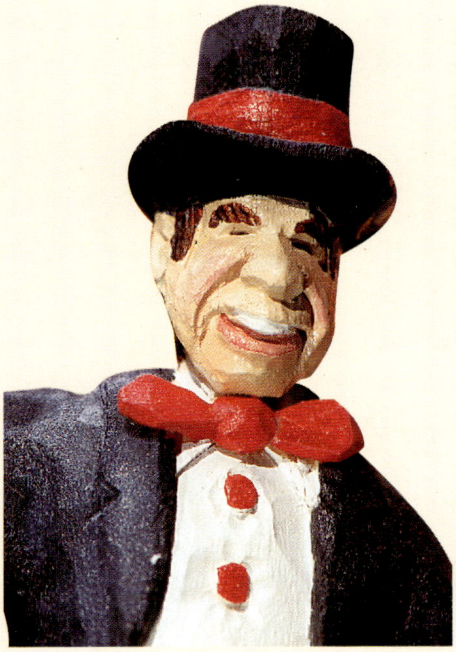

Everyone knows that stilts give the tallest man at the circus his added height, but how do you make that obvious in a caricature carving? Harley Schmitgen decided to use dowels between the pants and the feet. Making the pants a little short allowed the dowel to show, giving the appearance of stilts.

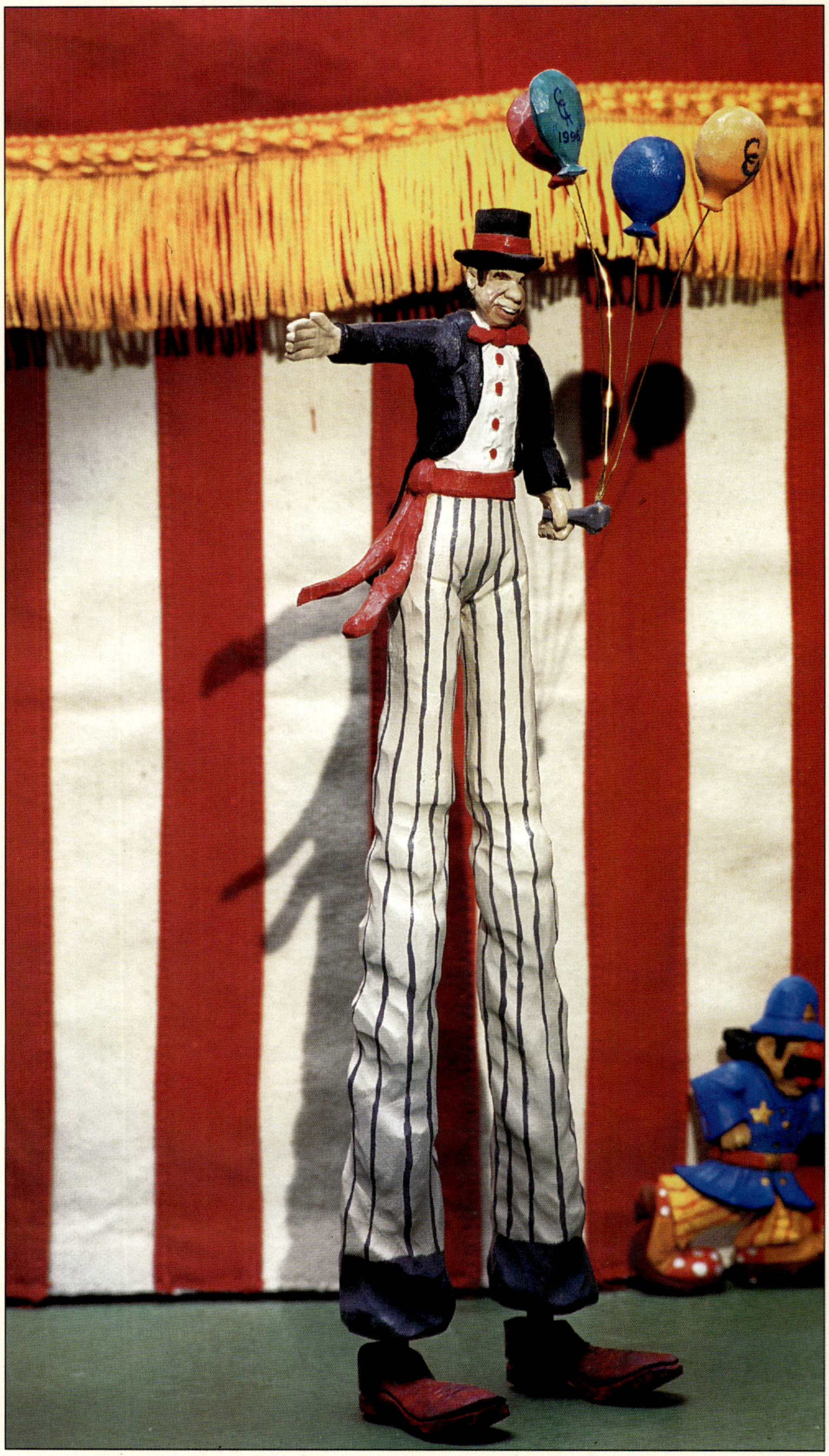

World's Smallest Man by Harley Schmitgen

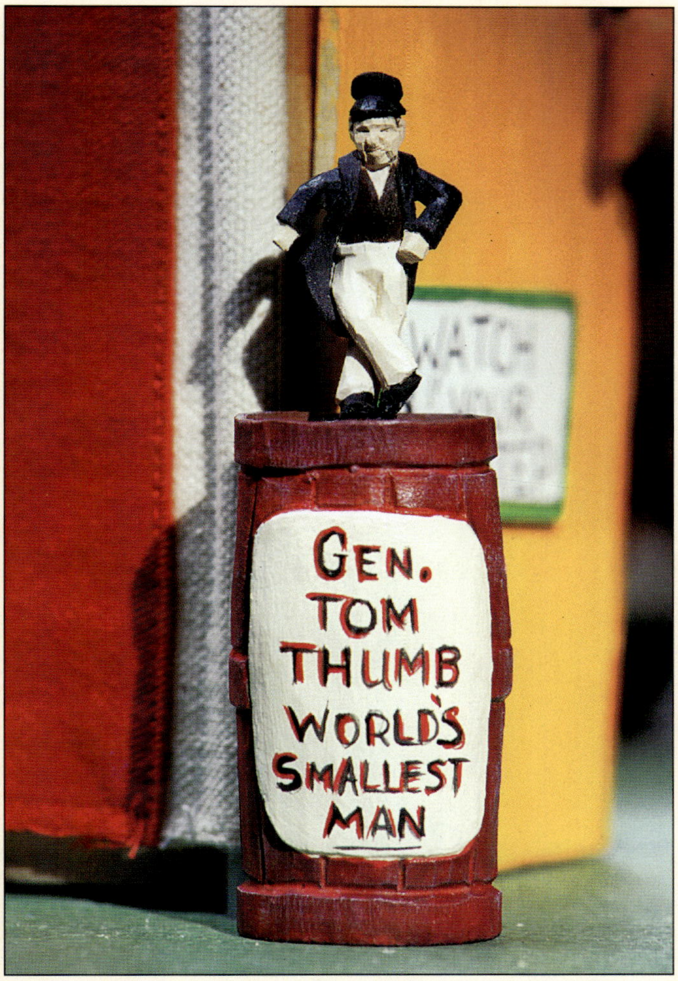

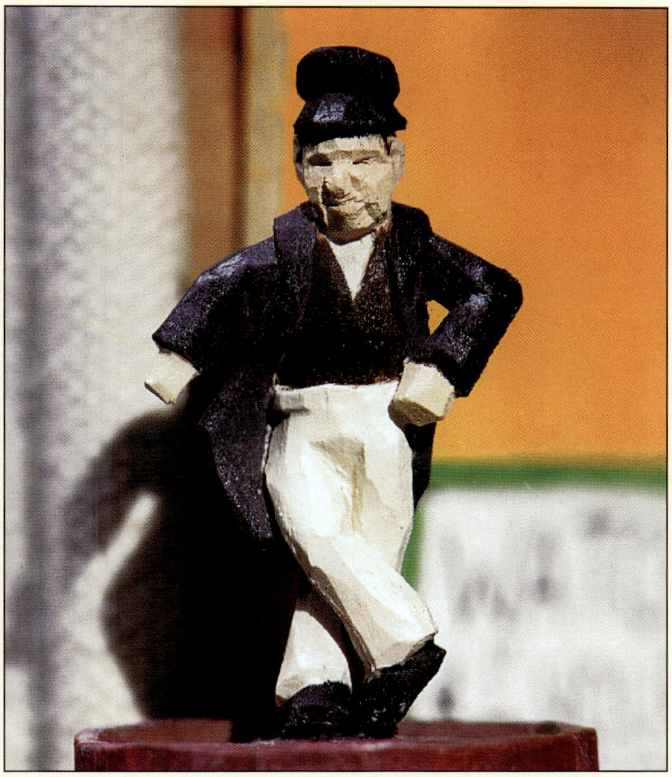

The smallest man in the CCA Circus *stands only about* $1^1/_2$*" small. For Harley Schmitgen, putting a face on General Tom Thumb was the biggest challenge of this carving. He used a special pair of glasses to magnify the face and add detail.*

My idea for the man on stilts came from an ad I saw in a tennis magazine that was advertising tennis shoes. I also got ideas from researching the life of P. T. Barnum and from various circus books and magazines. I put all the ideas on paper, making simple sketches until I had one I liked. I had to make sure that the scale model was in the correct proportion to fit in with the other carvings in the circus.

I did not do any clay sculpting for this carving. When I visualize a carving in my mind, I immediately sketch it onto the basswood and begin to carve. I have no special tools that I use for this. I make sure my tools are sharp and use mid-size gouges, knives and v-tools. I block out the entire carving, doing no detail until I have it in proportion. Then I begin putting in the details. I leave the face and hands until the very end.

For this carving, I had to do some extra planning in order to make the character appear to be walking on stilts. I decided to use a dowel between his pants and feet to give the illusion of the stilts. I also decided to add something to one of his hands so that he would look "busy." I carved four balloons and attached them to wires to make them appear as if they were circus balloons.

I painted this carving in the same manner as I have all my other carvings. I "wash" the entire carving with burnt sienna mixed with water. I use approximately $^1/_4$ teaspoons of acrylic paint with 1 cup of water. I test this mixture on scrap wood to make sure it gives the color I'm looking for. It's important to let the paint dry completely because it always dries lighter than it first appears.

For the rest of the carving, I used the acrylic paints right from the tube so that the colors would be vivid and resemble the bright colors that circus performers always wear.

Uncle Sam by Harley Schmitgen

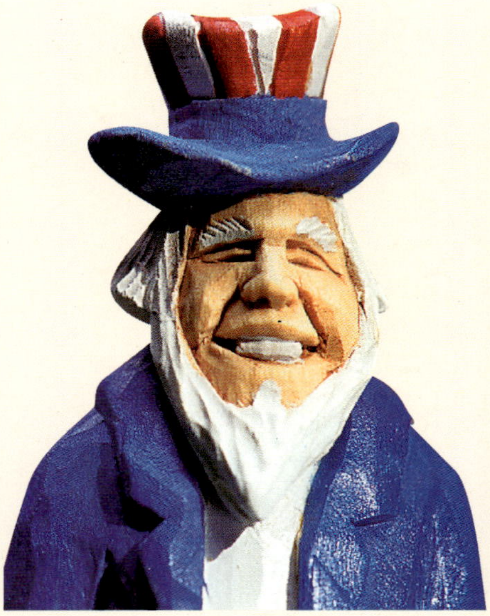

Every circus needs an Uncle Sam, says Harley Schmitgen. The Uncle Sam at the CCA Circus was carved from one piece of wood and painted with acrylics. Getting the proportions correct on this extra tall figure was a challenge for the artist.

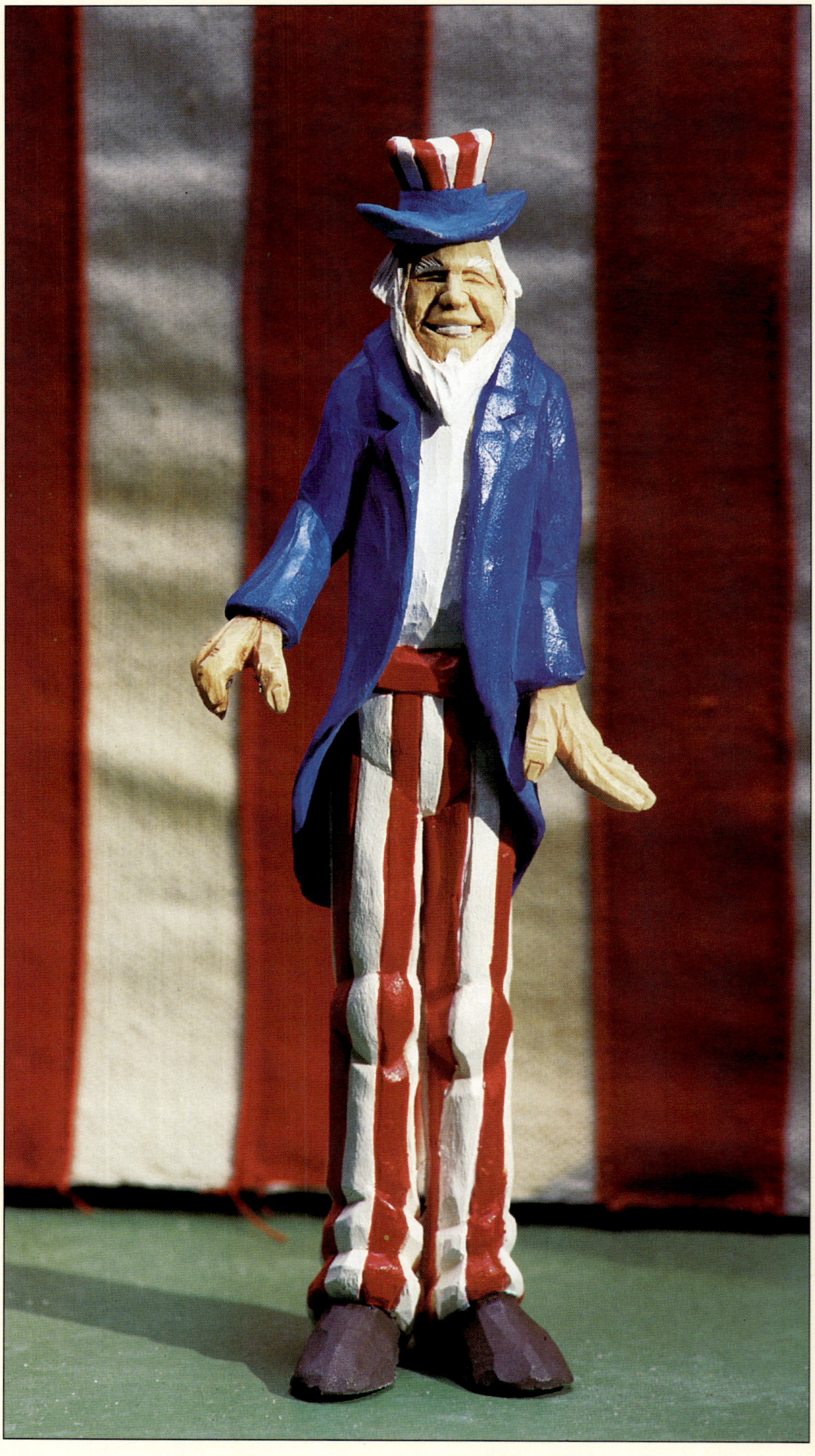

Arena Sanitation Engineer
by Claude Bolton

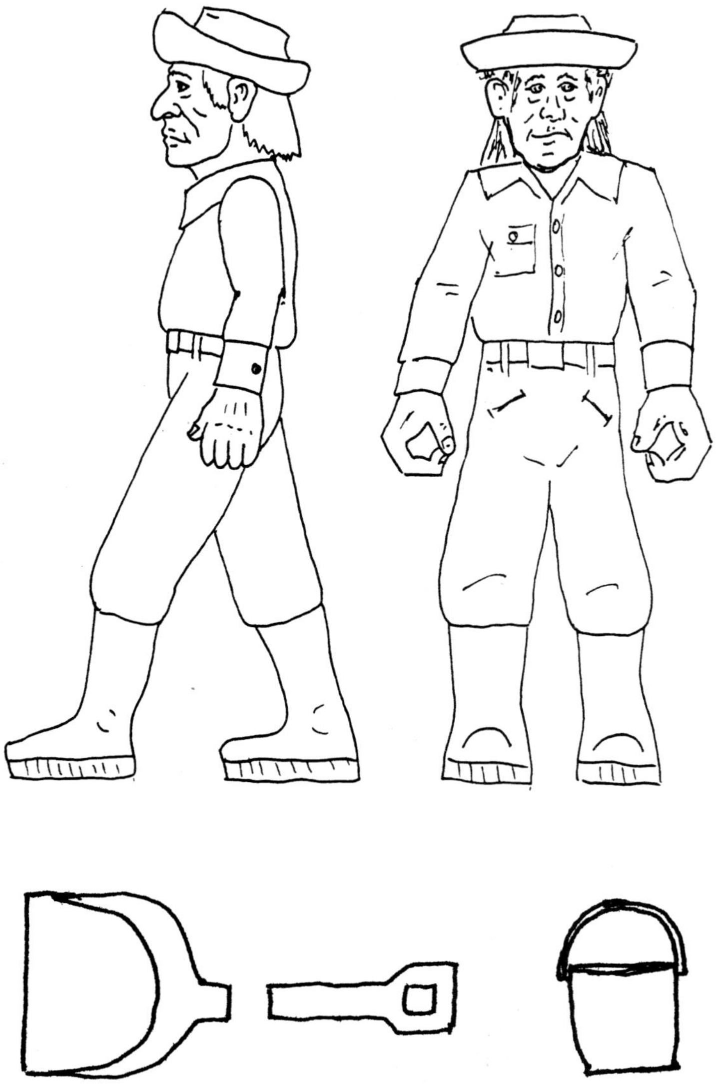

Best Price
by Bob Travis

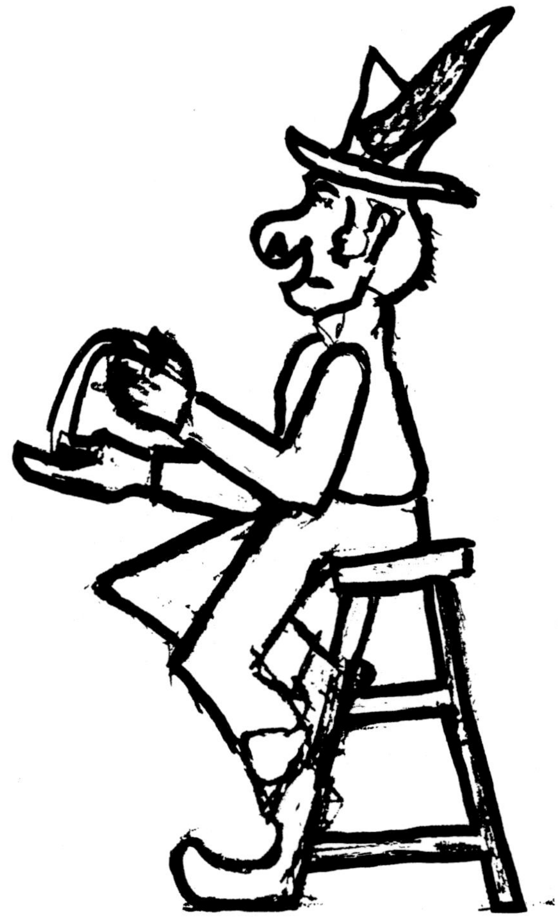

Balancing Act
by Steve Prescott

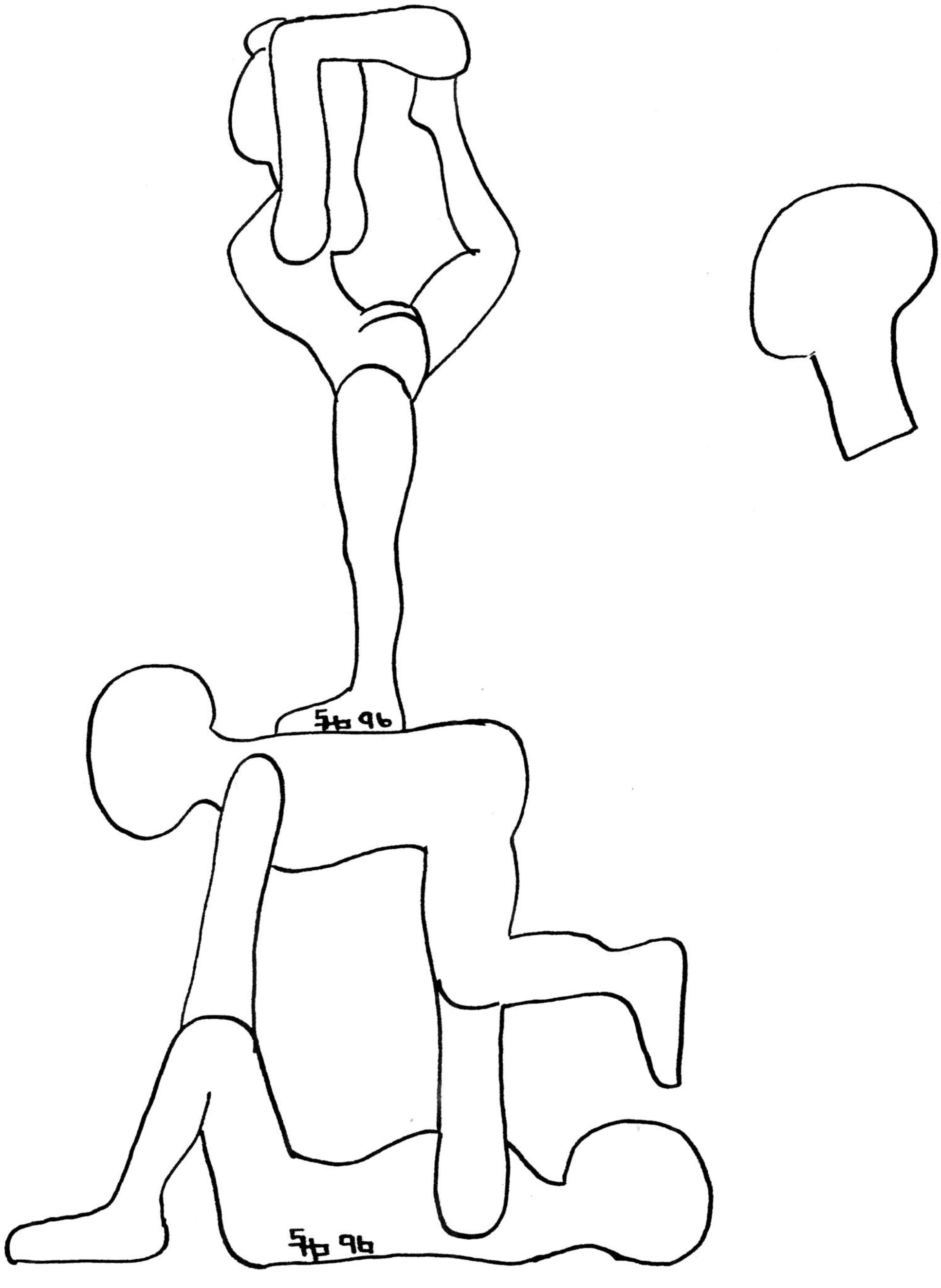

Balloons
by Claude Bolton

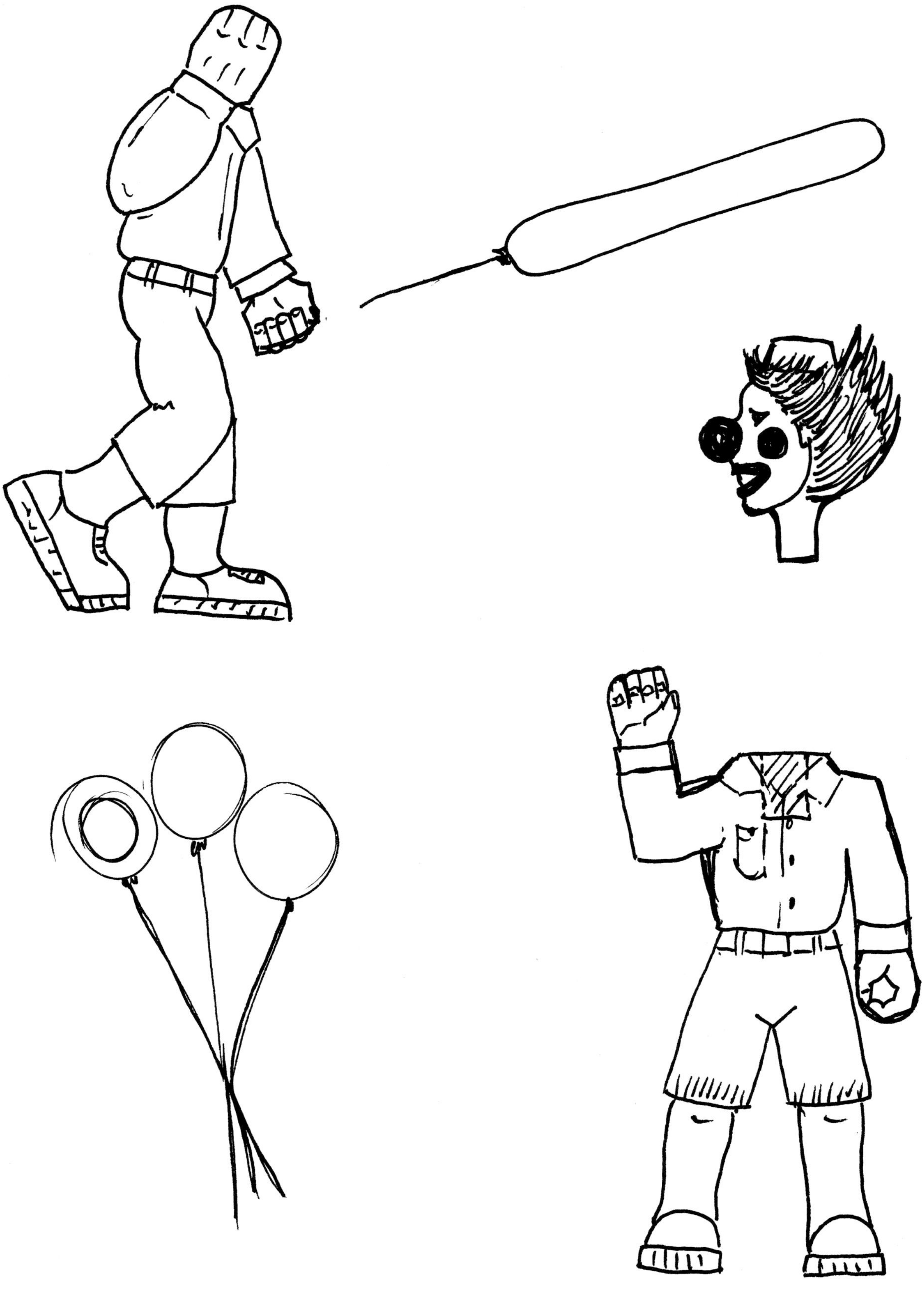

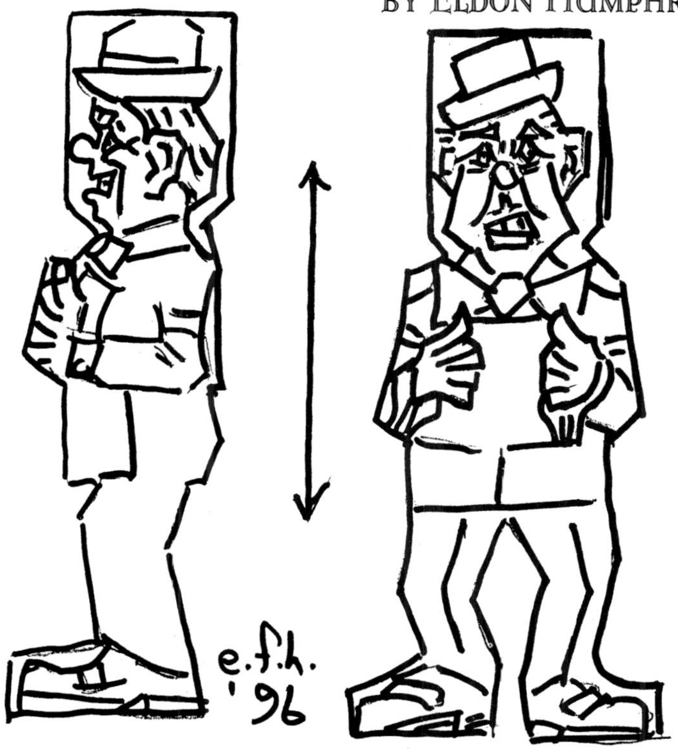
e.f.h.
'96

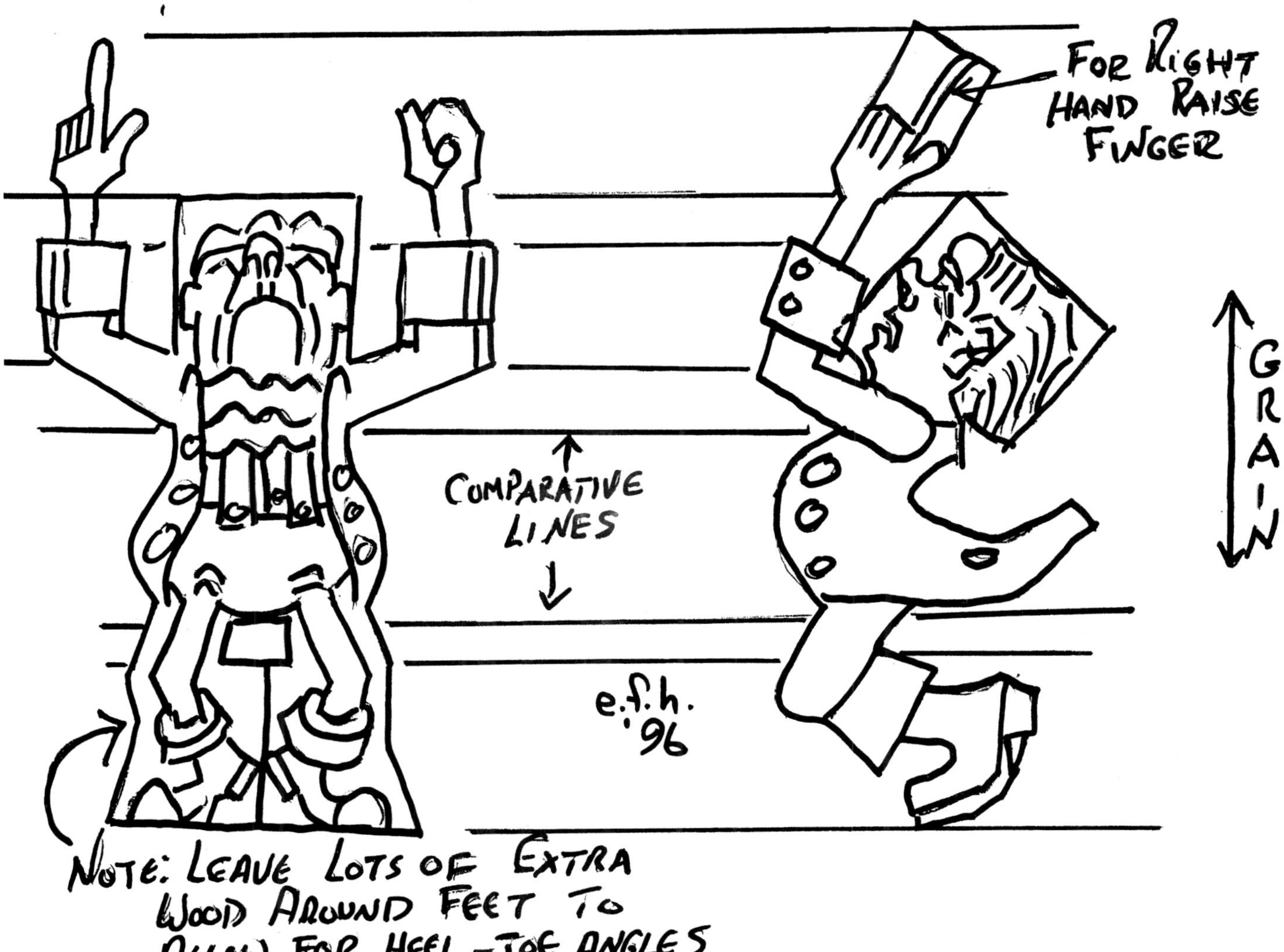
FOR RIGHT HAND RAISE FINGER
GRAIN
COMPARATIVE LINES
e.f.h.
'96
NOTE: LEAVE LOTS OF EXTRA WOOD AROUND FEET TO ALLOW FOR HEEL-TOE ANGLES

Bazel and Hazel
by Eldon Humphreys

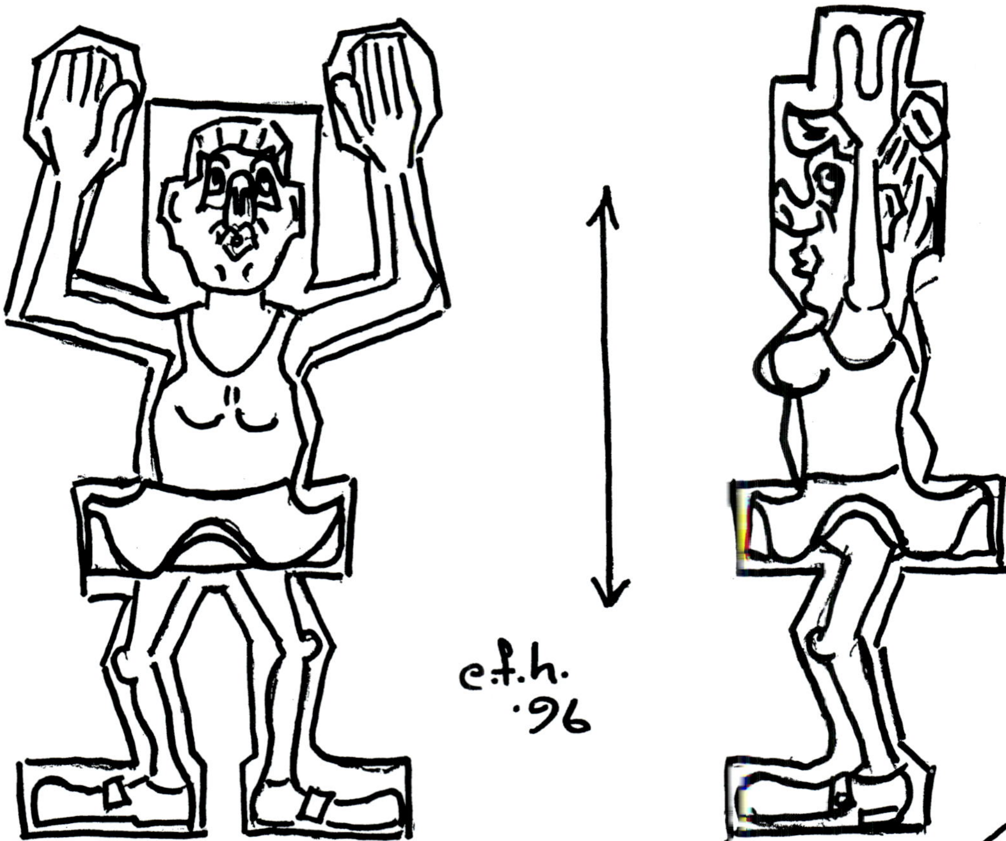

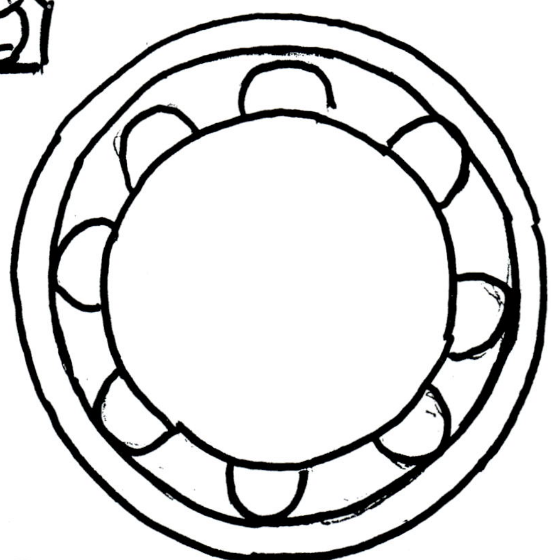

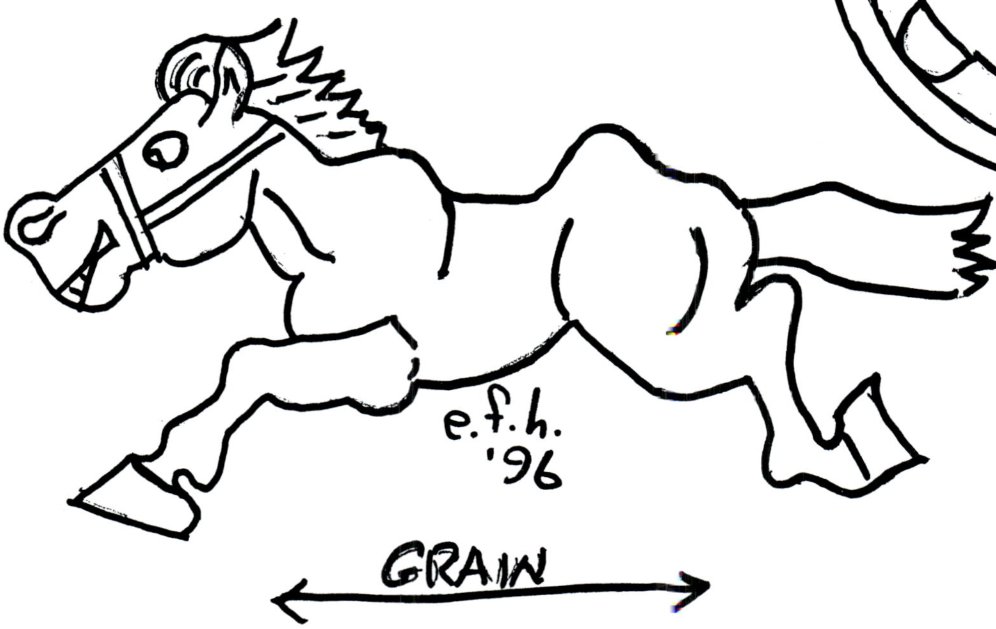

Bear Acts

by Gary Batte

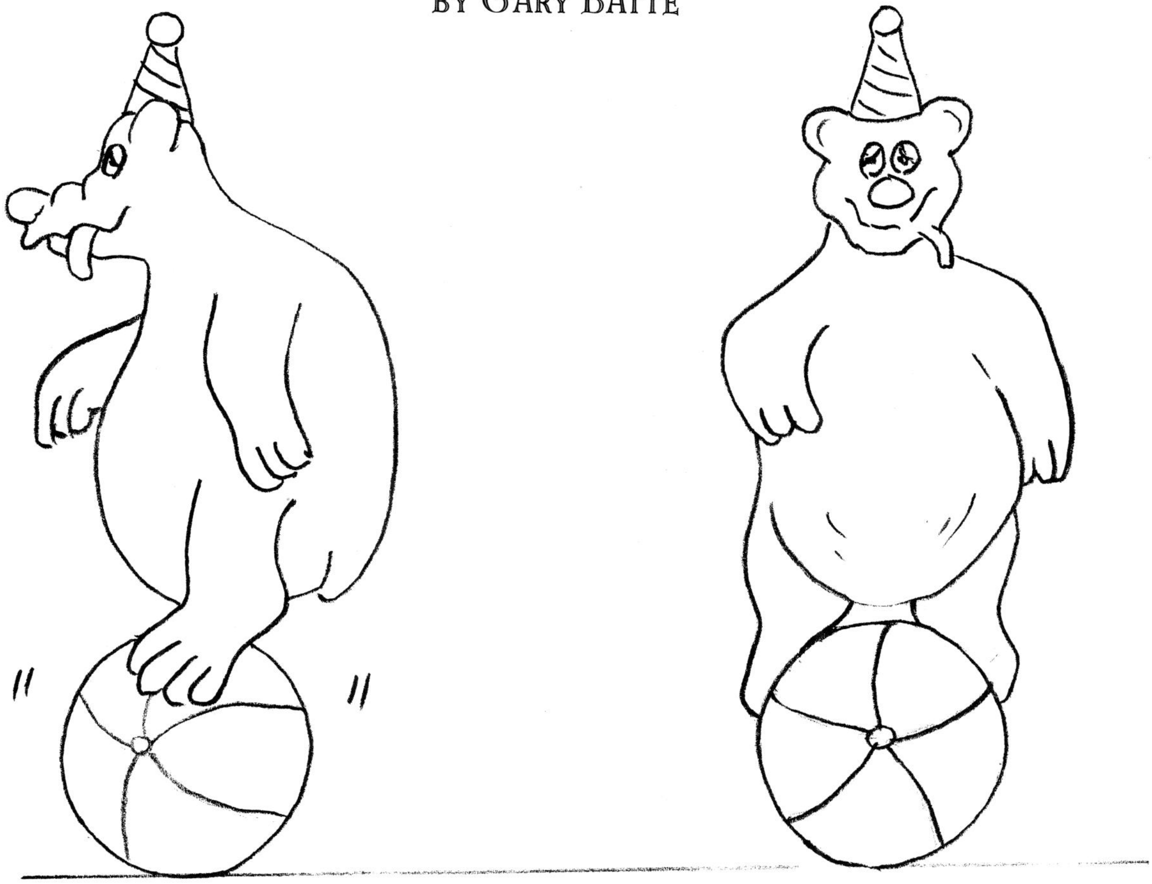

Buggin' Out

by Randy Landen

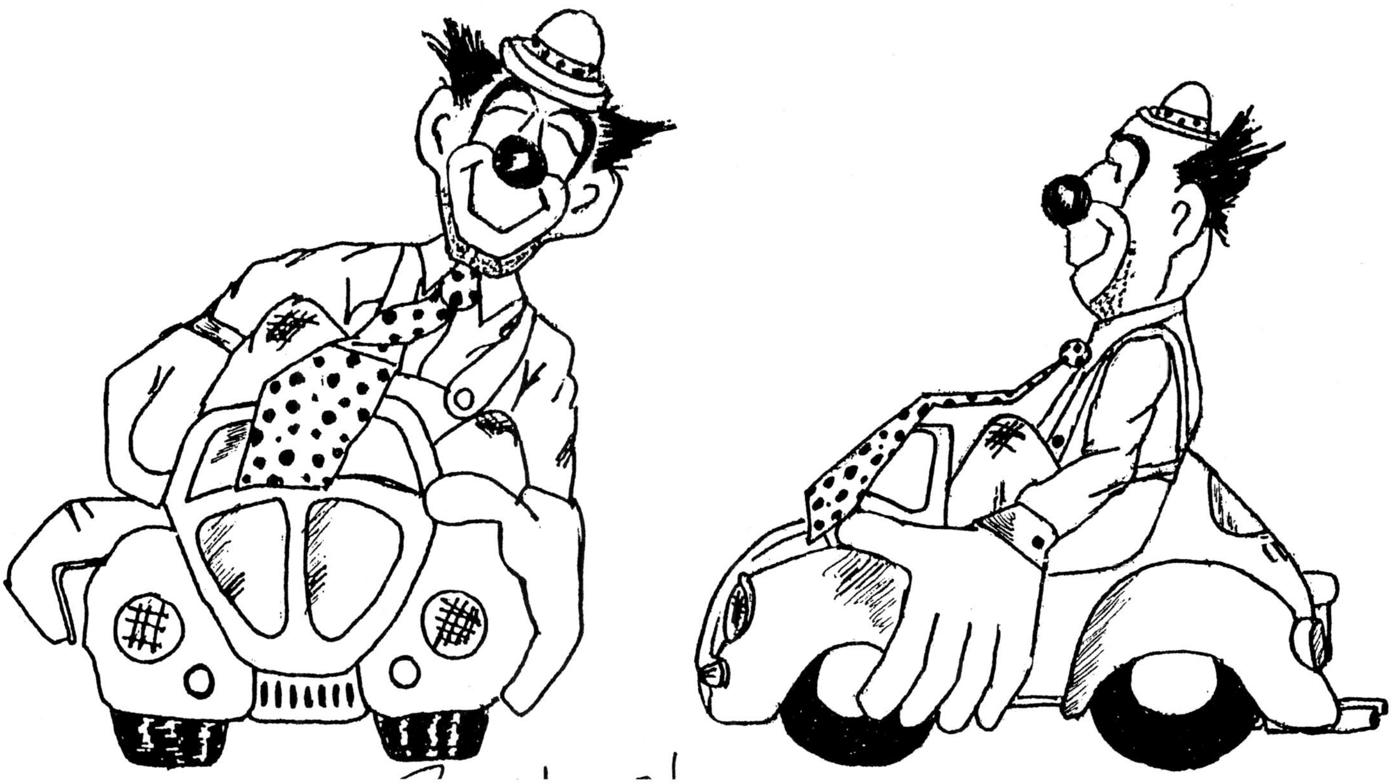

Clive Batty
by Tex Haase

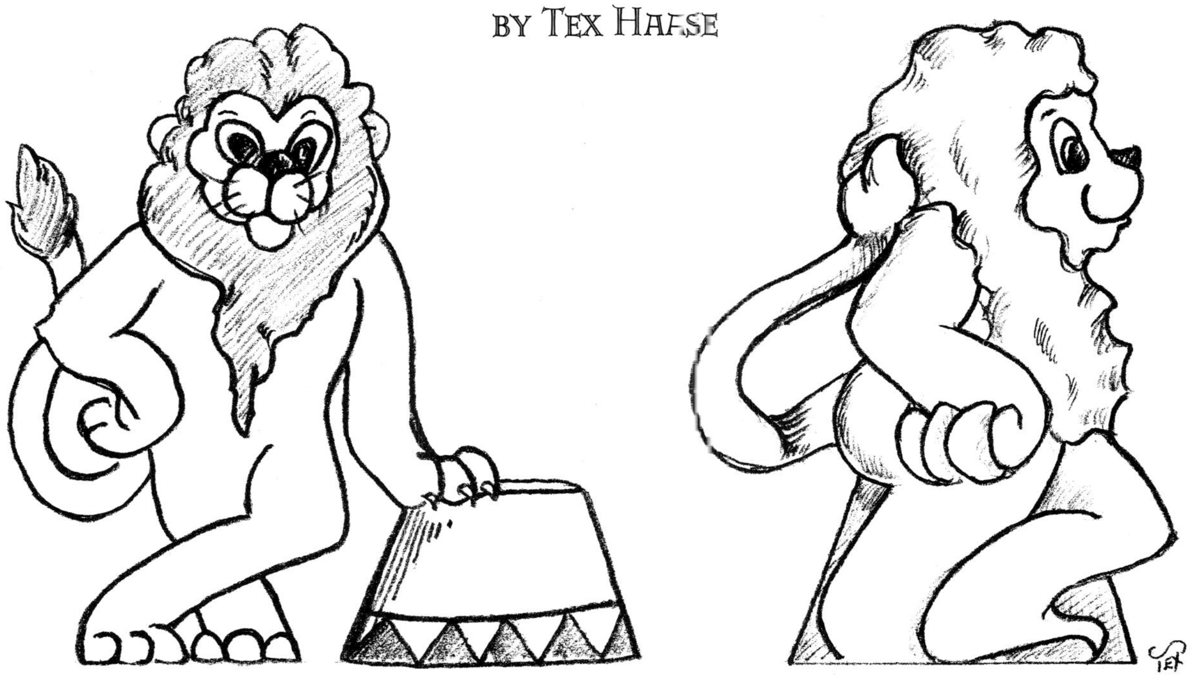

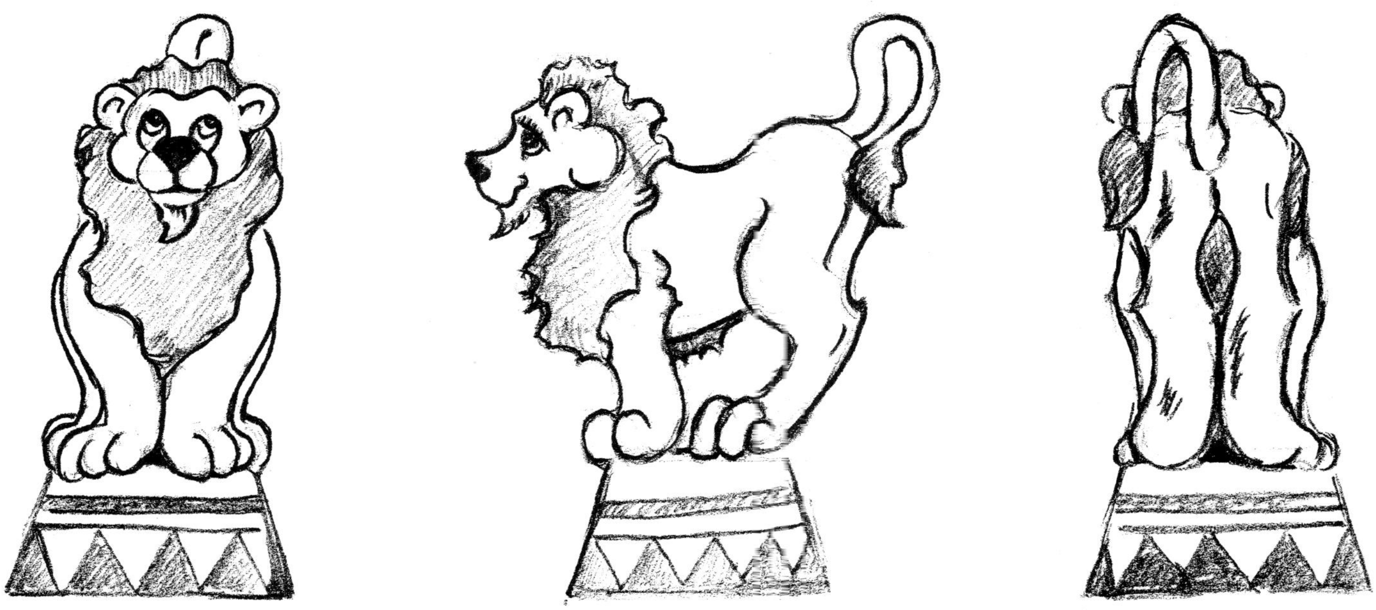

Clive Batty
by Tex Haase

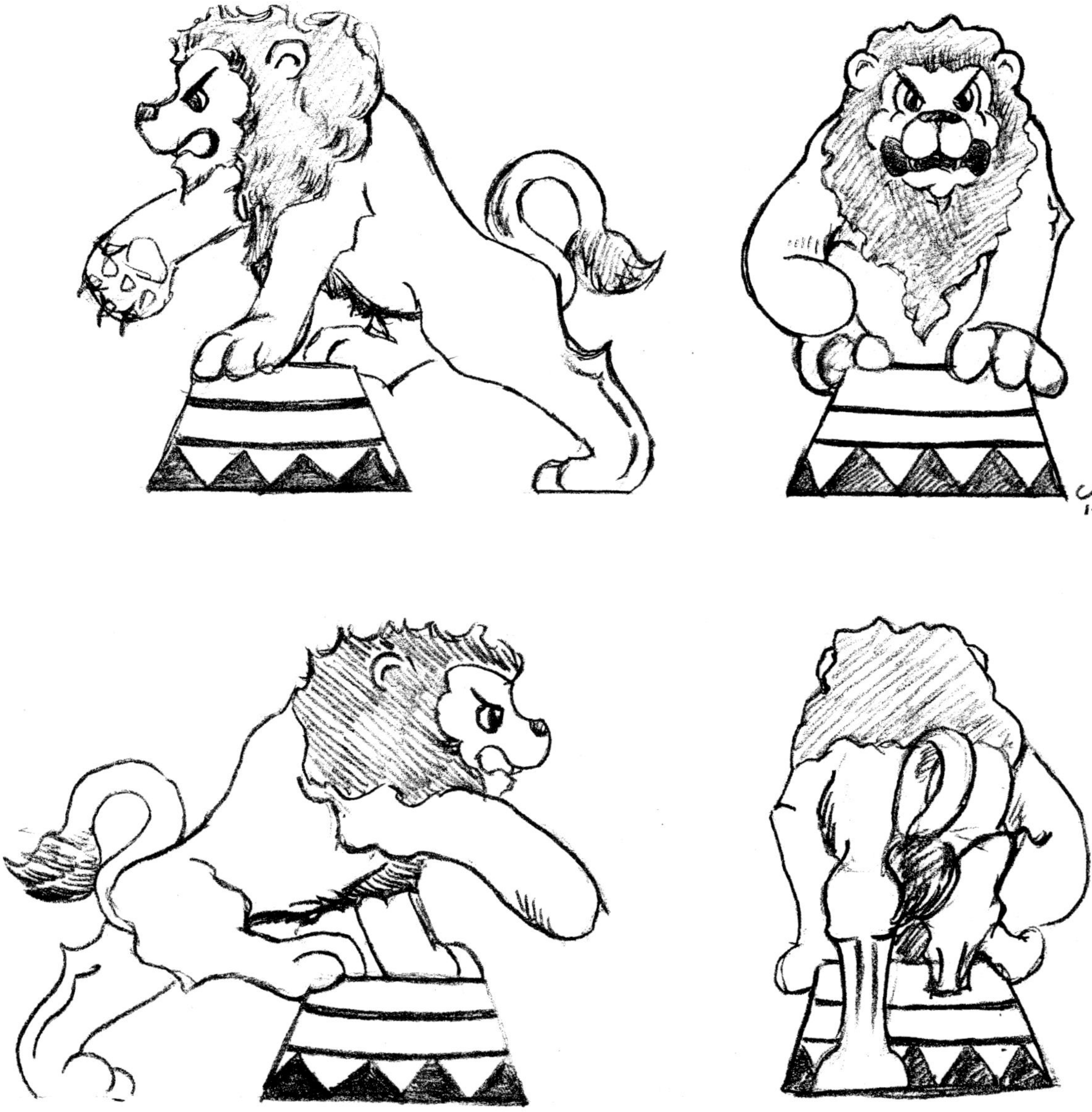

Clive Batty
by Tex Haase

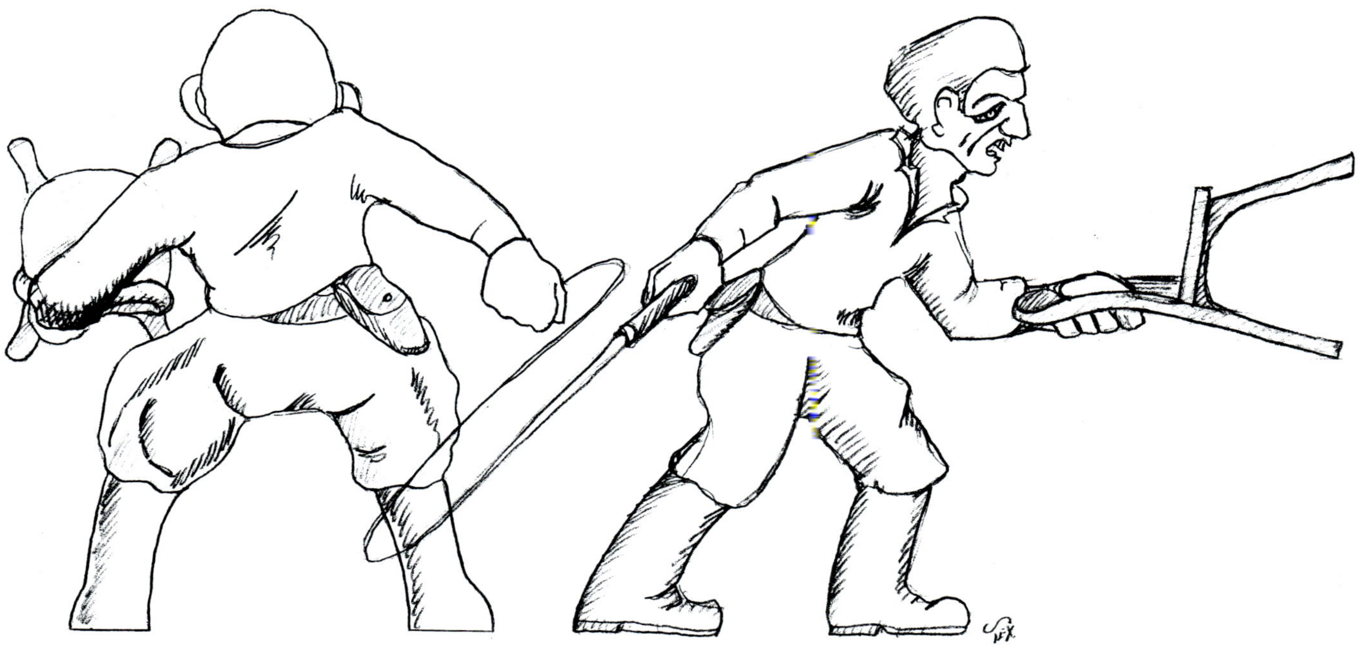

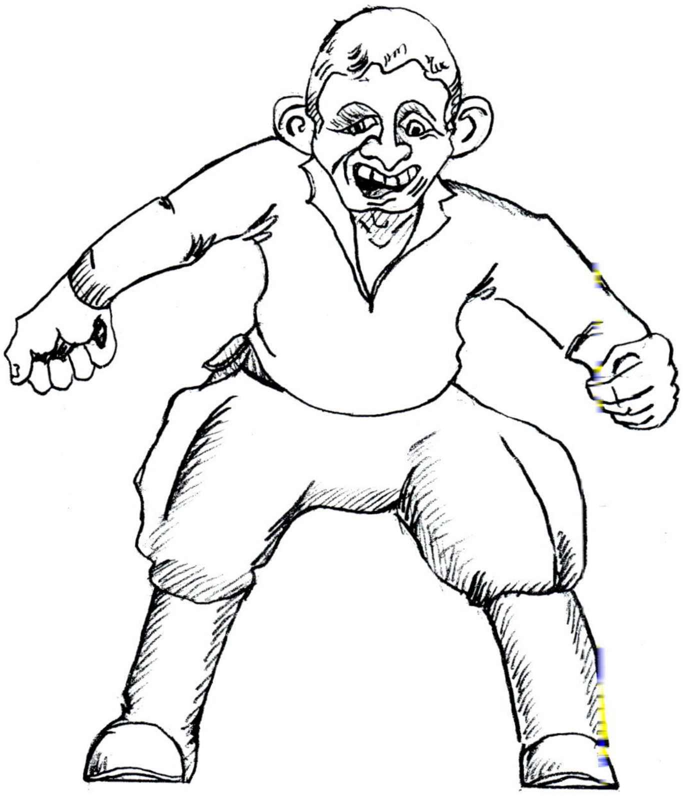

Clown on a Unicycle
by Dave Rasmussen

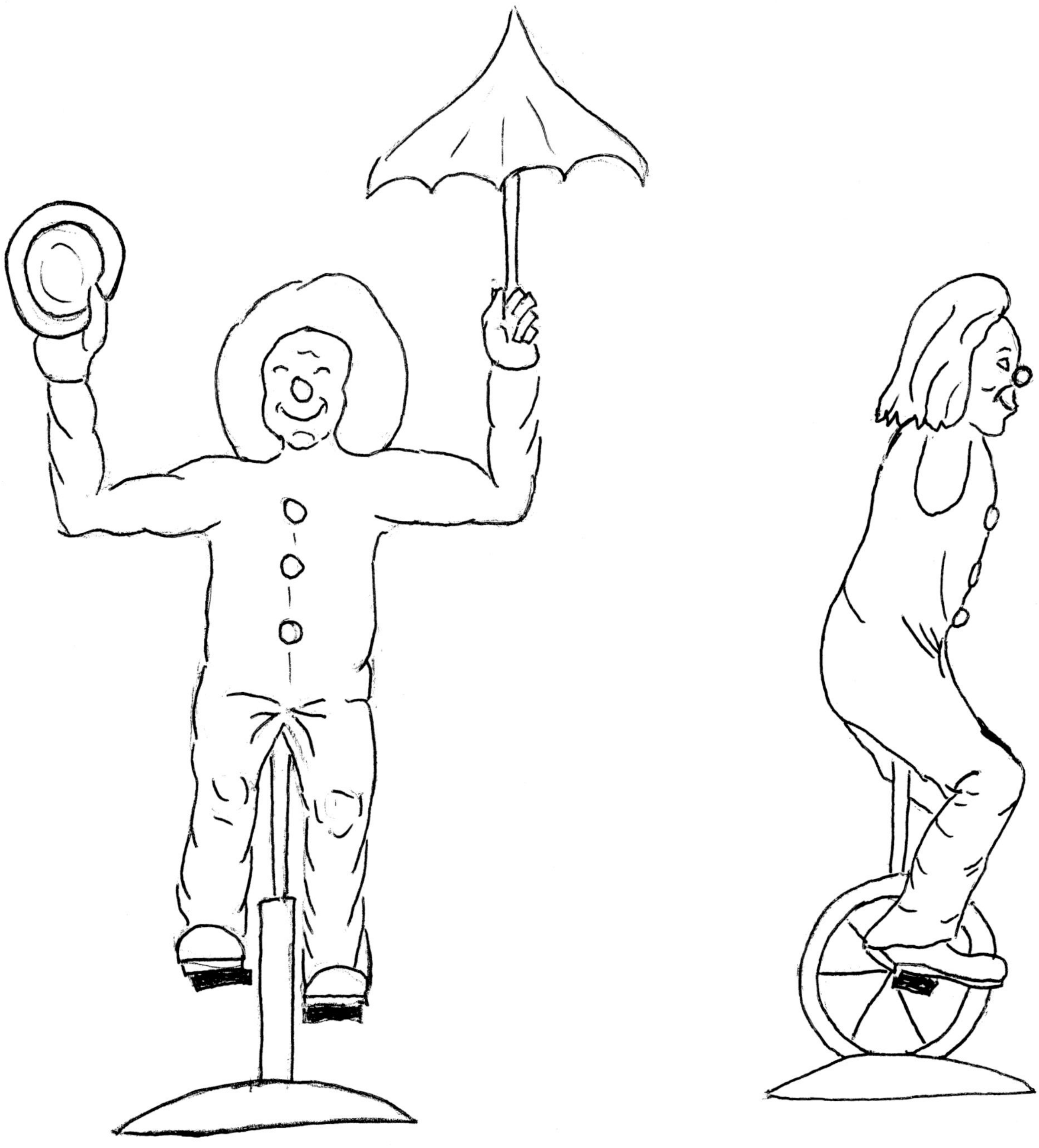

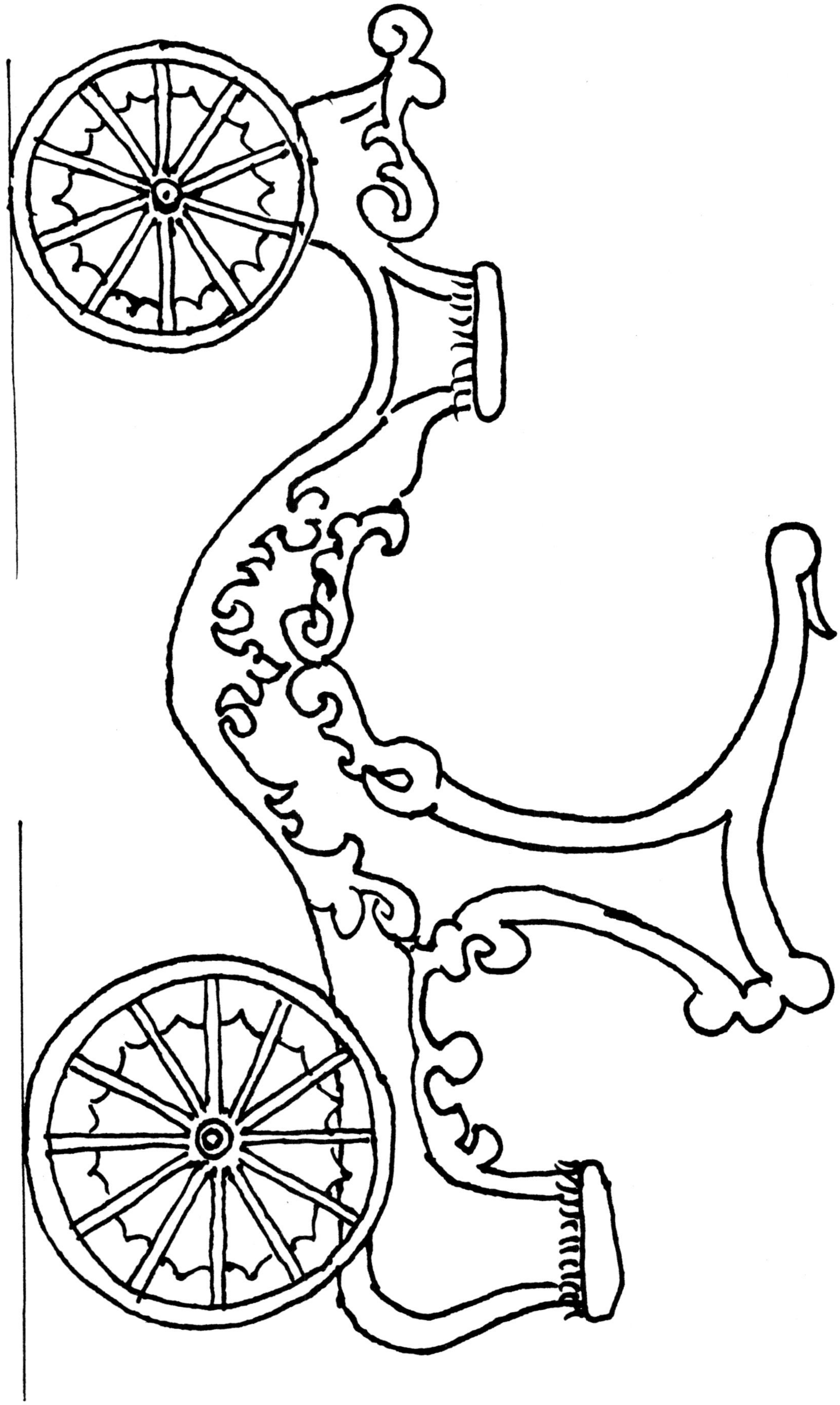

FRONT VIEW

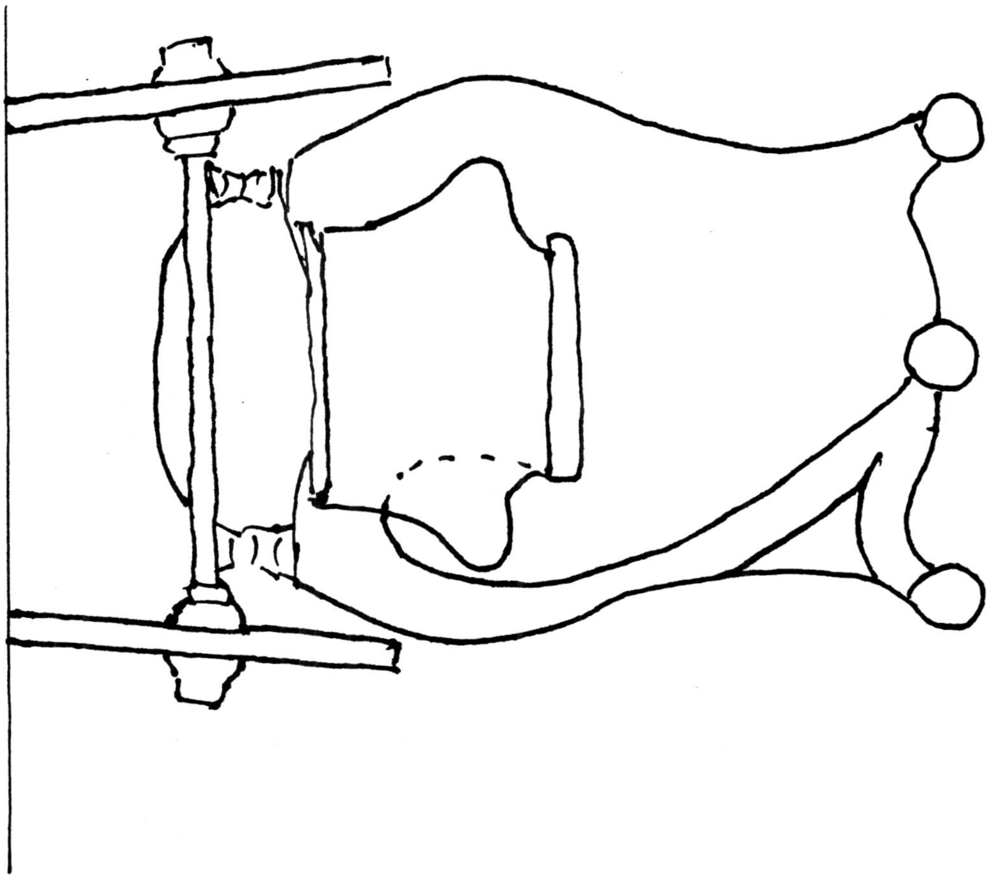

REAR VIEW

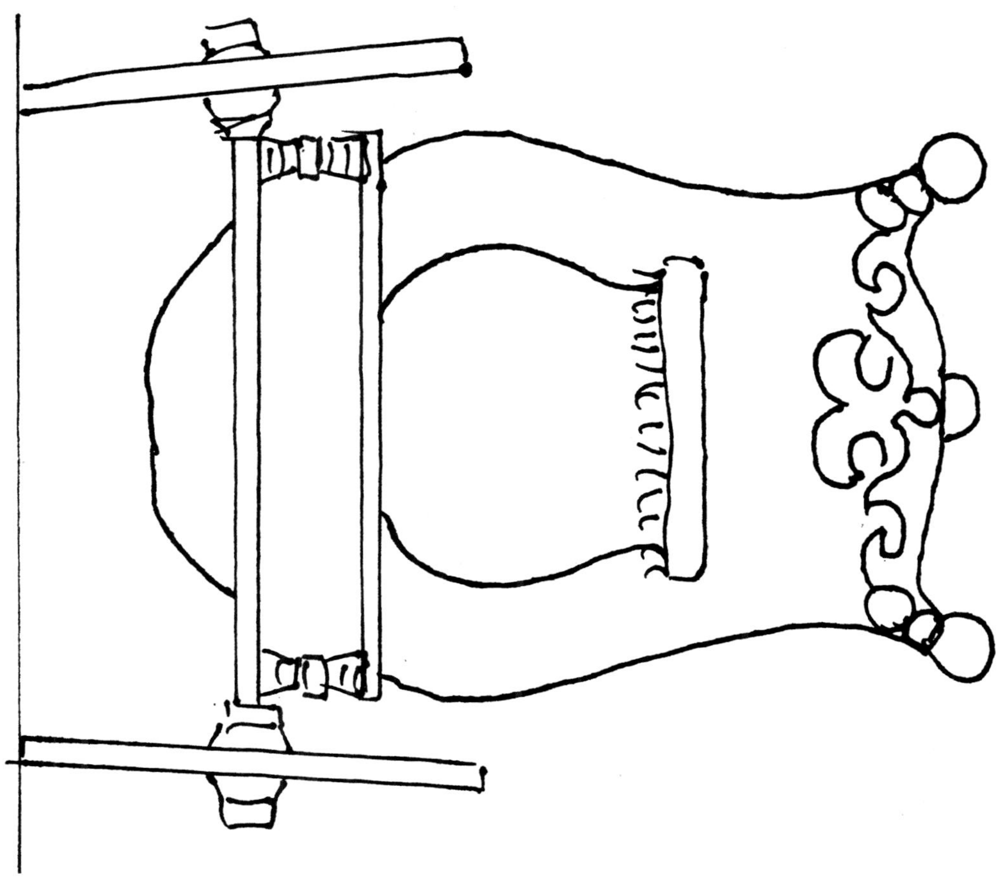

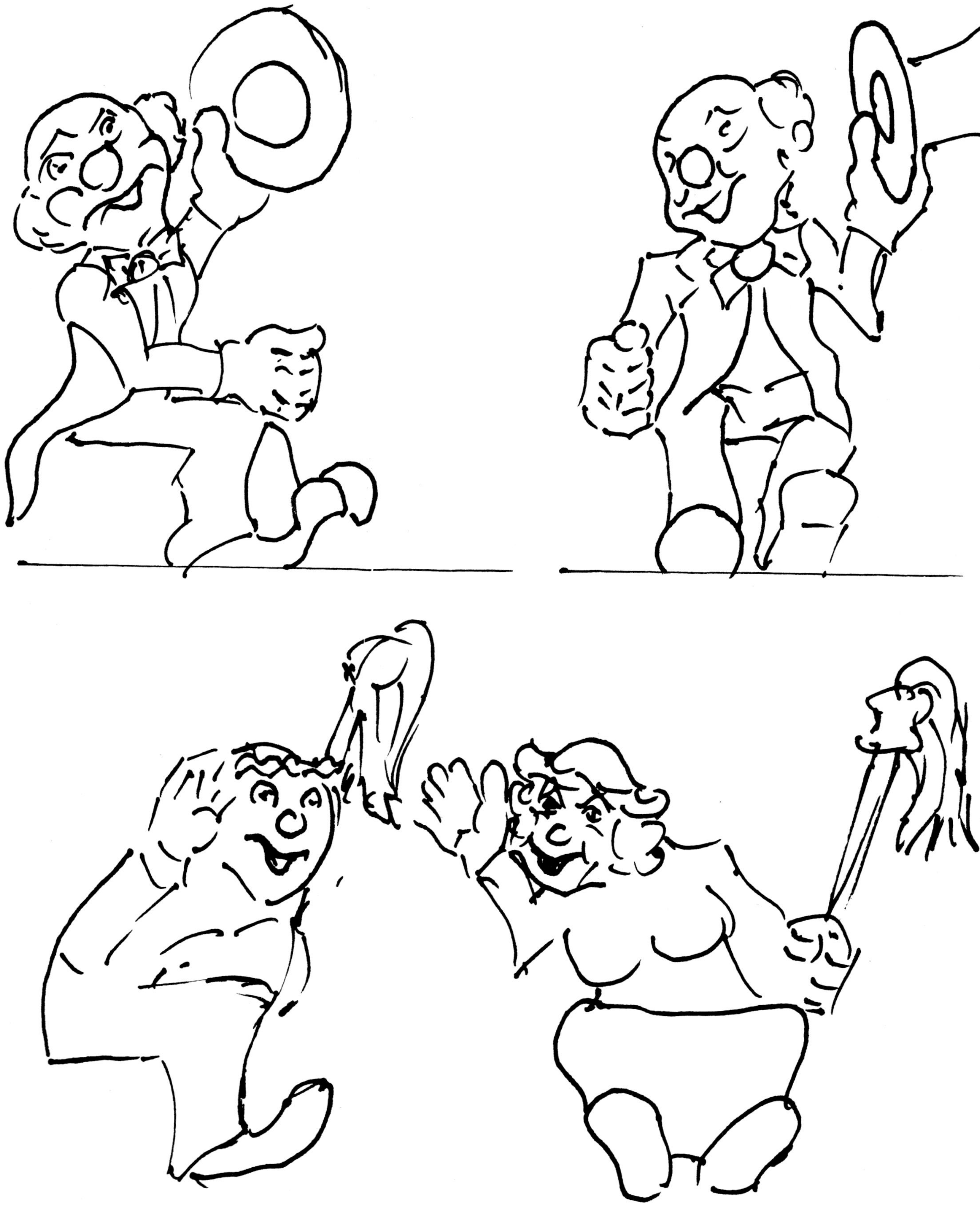

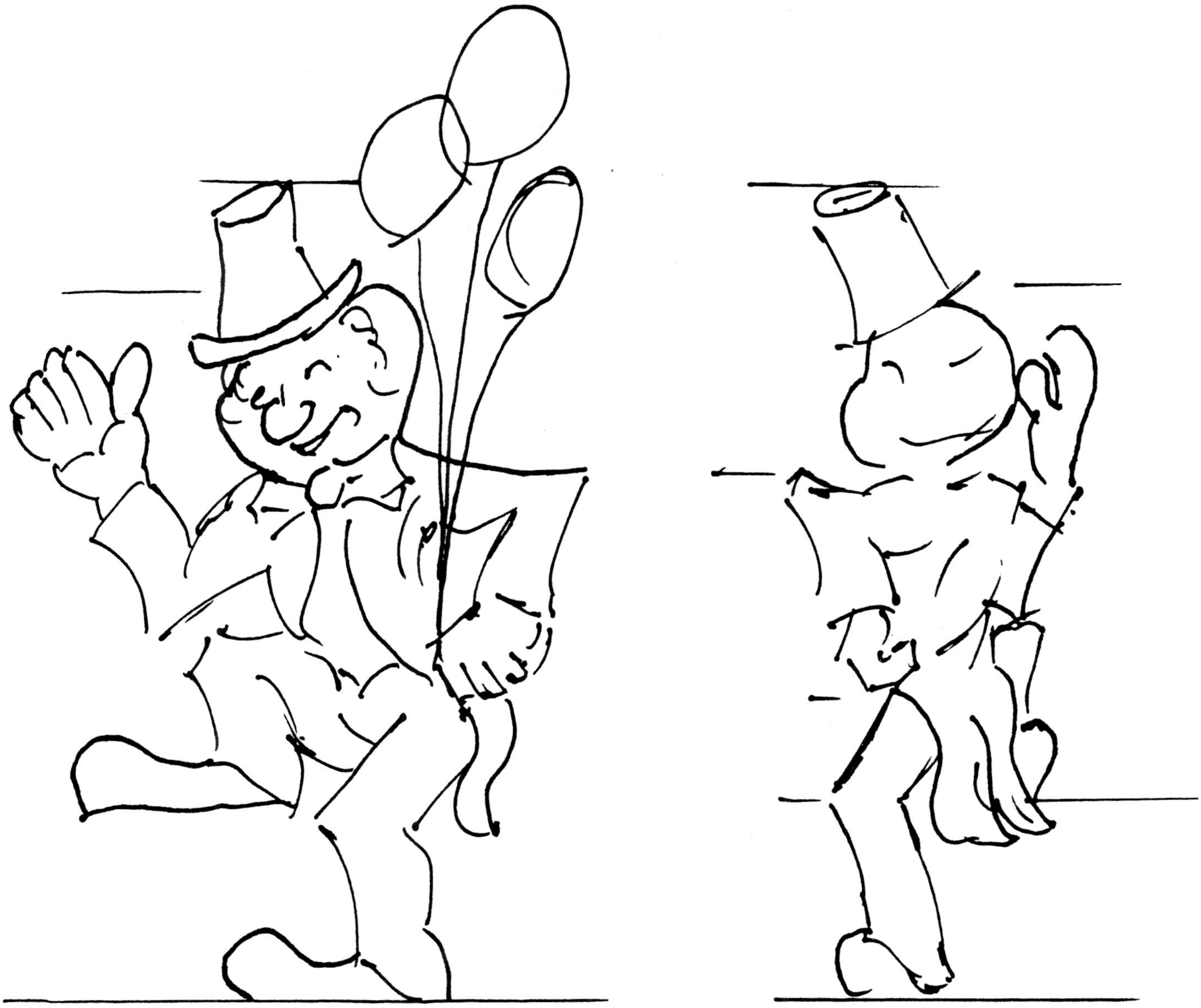

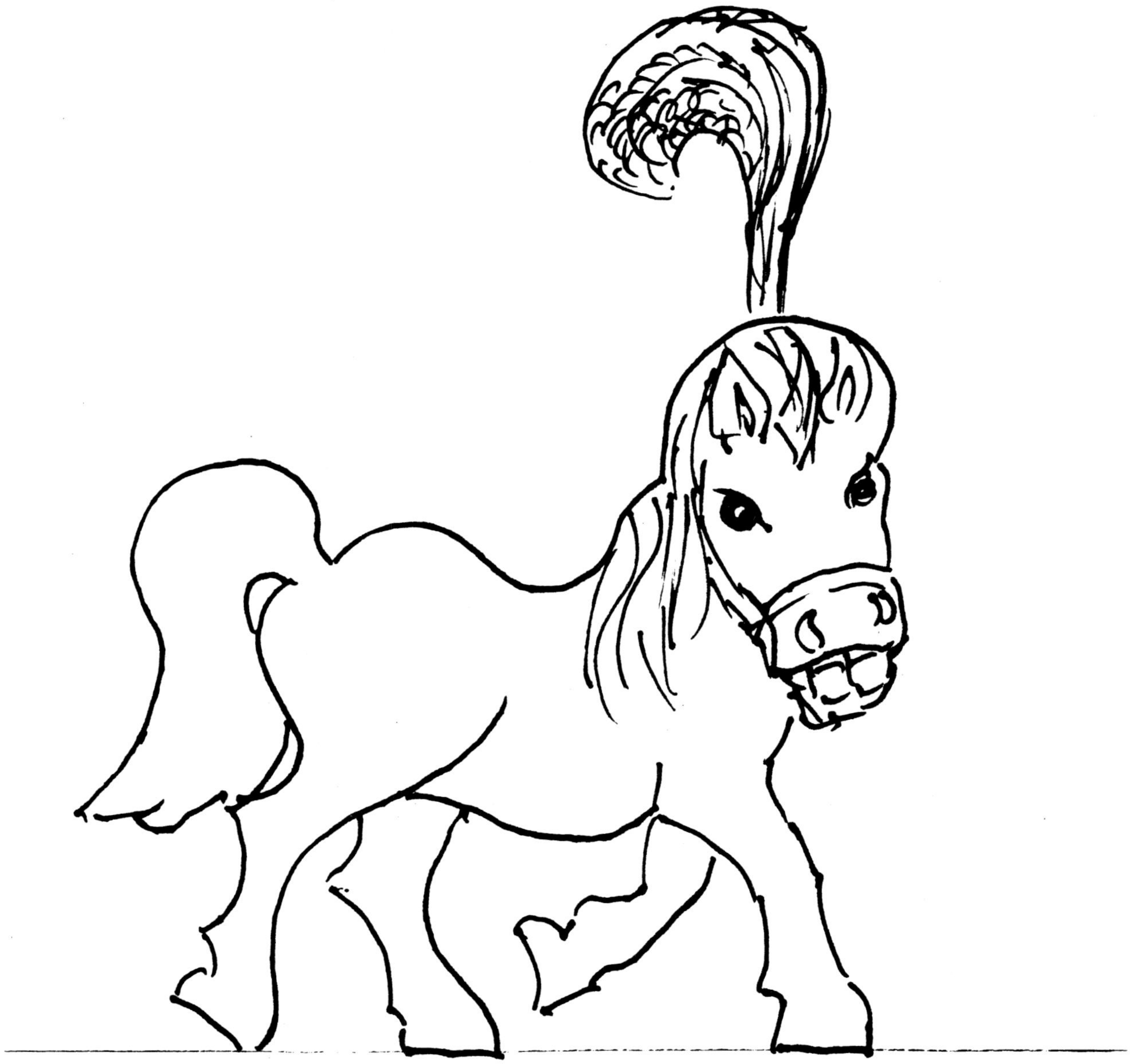

Crowd Control
by Randy Landen

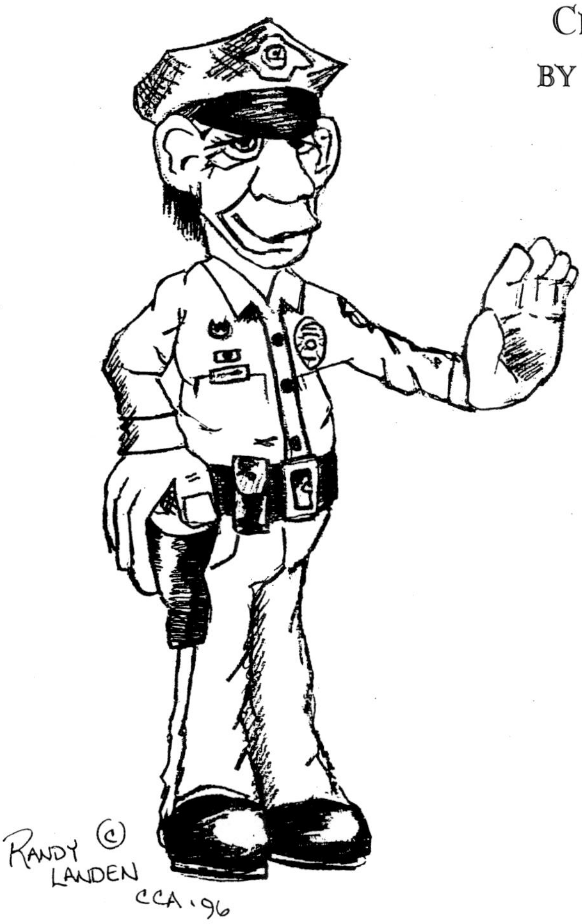

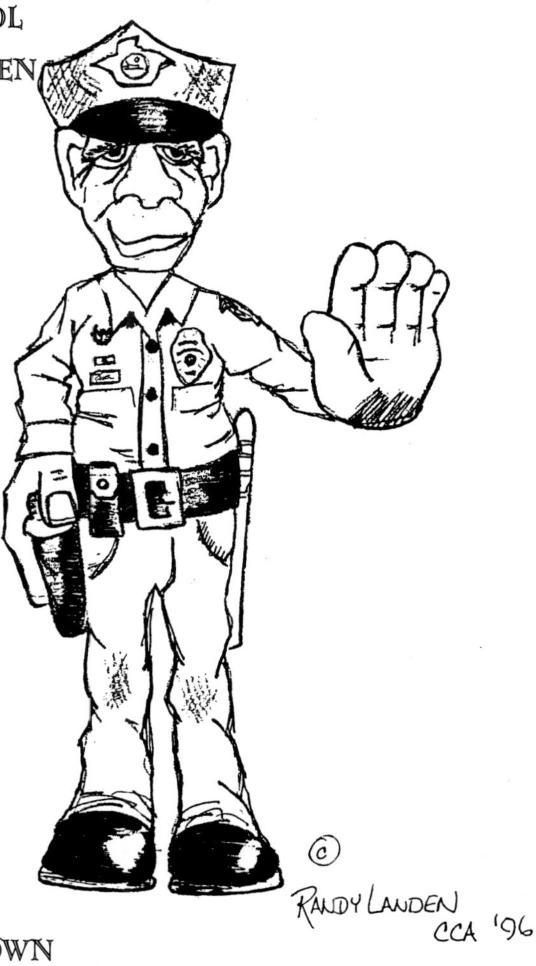

Cymbals the Clown
by Will Hayden

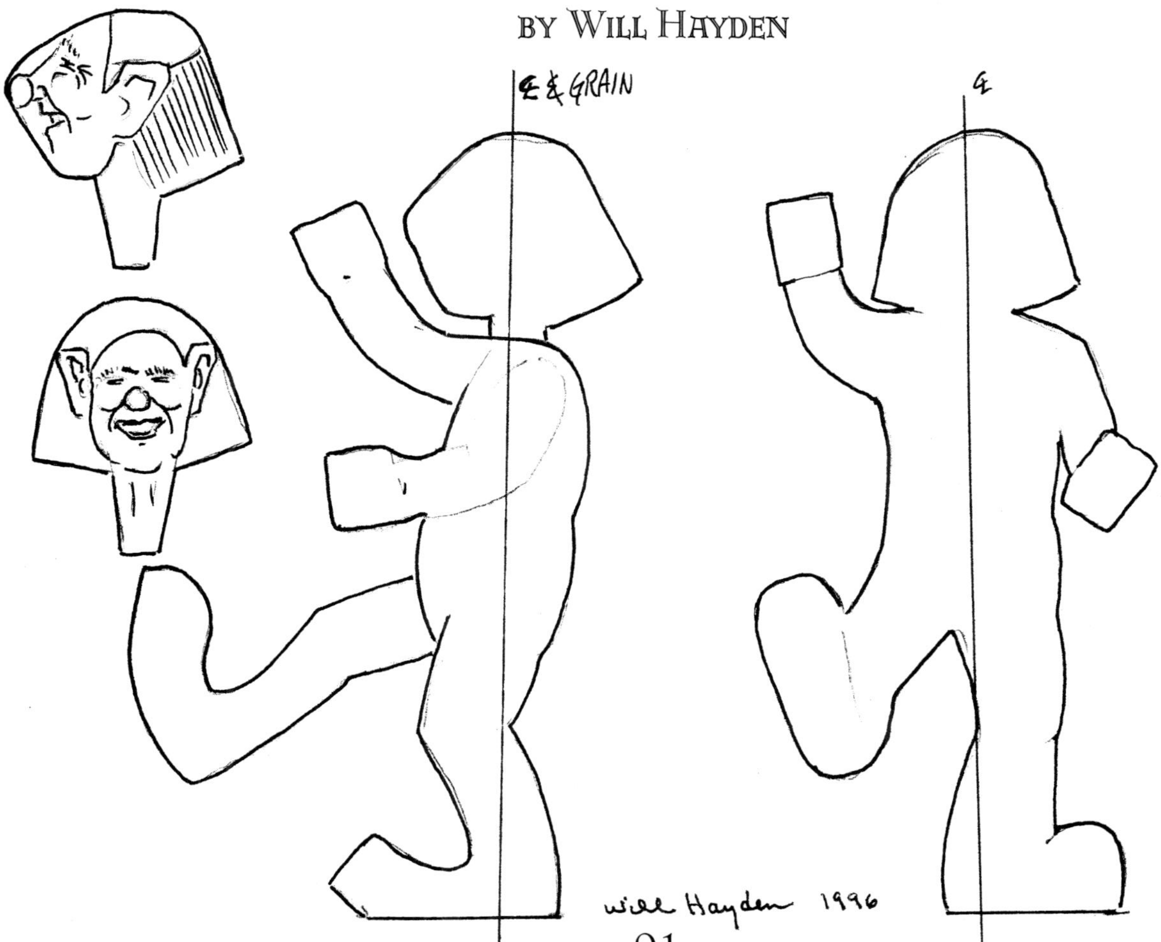

Dan
by Harley Refsal

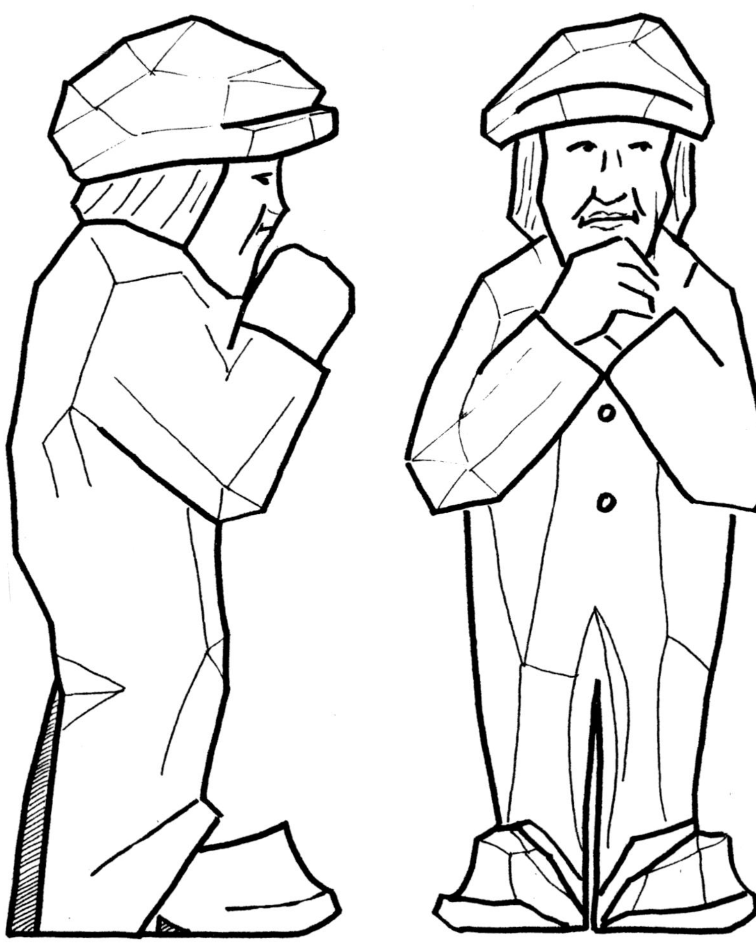

Dimbo the White Elephant
by Desiree Hajny

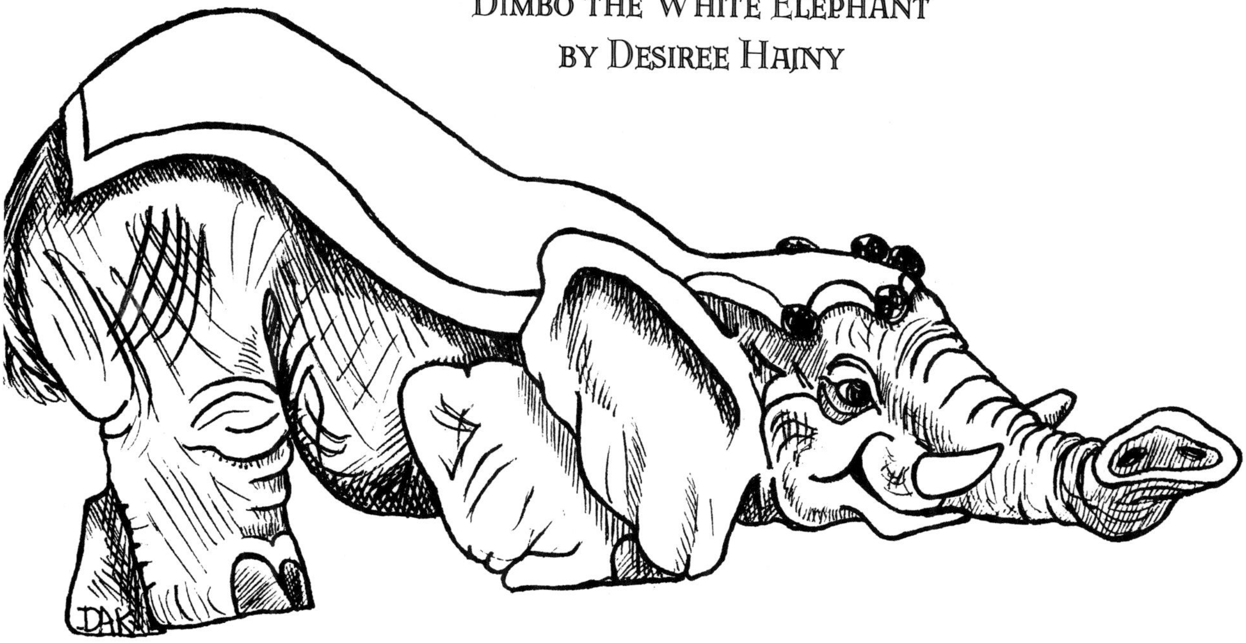

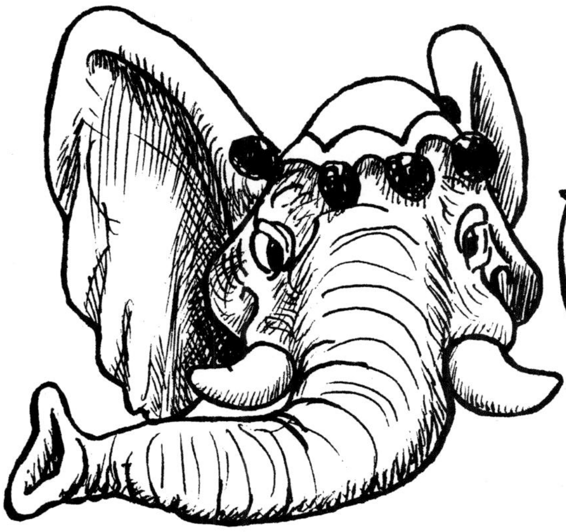

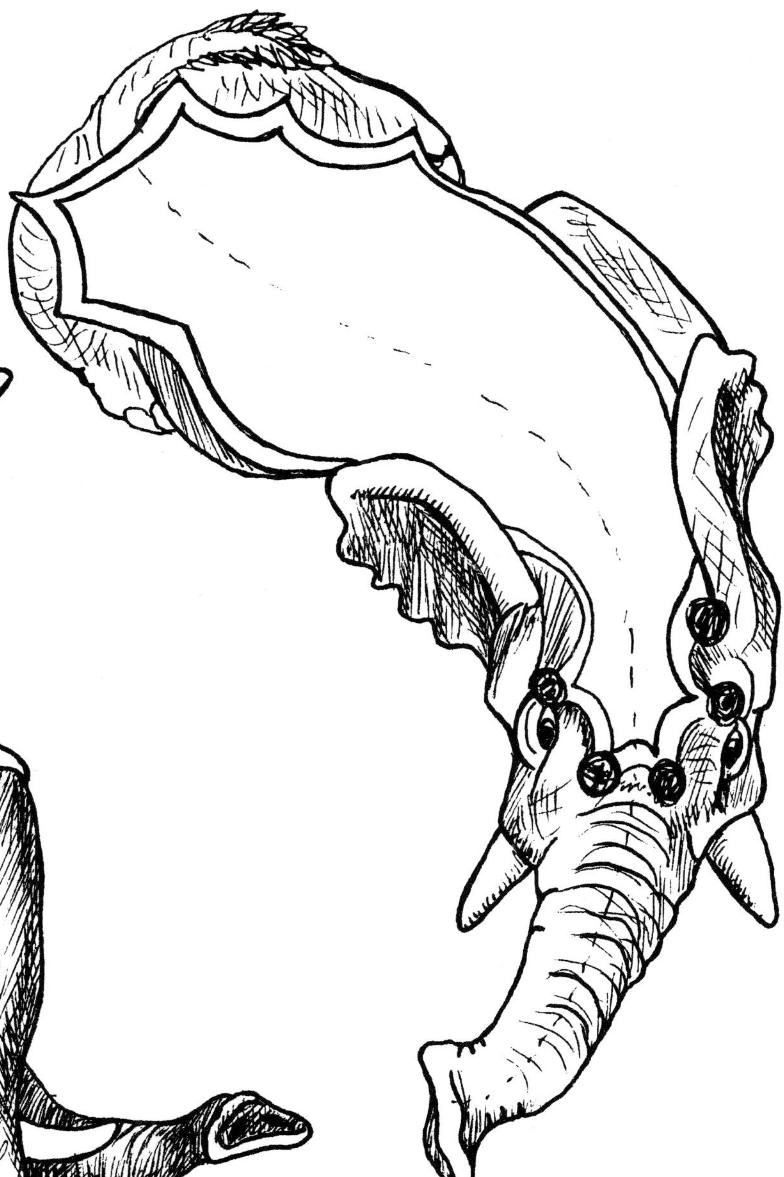

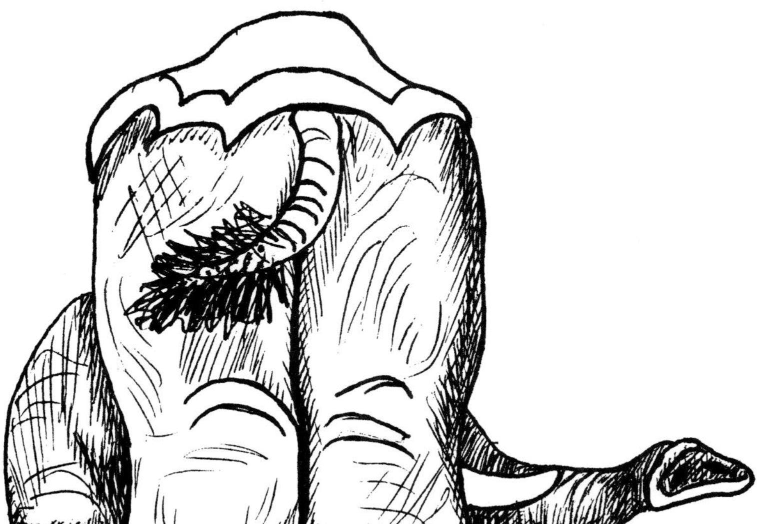

Dog and Pony Show
by Bob Travis

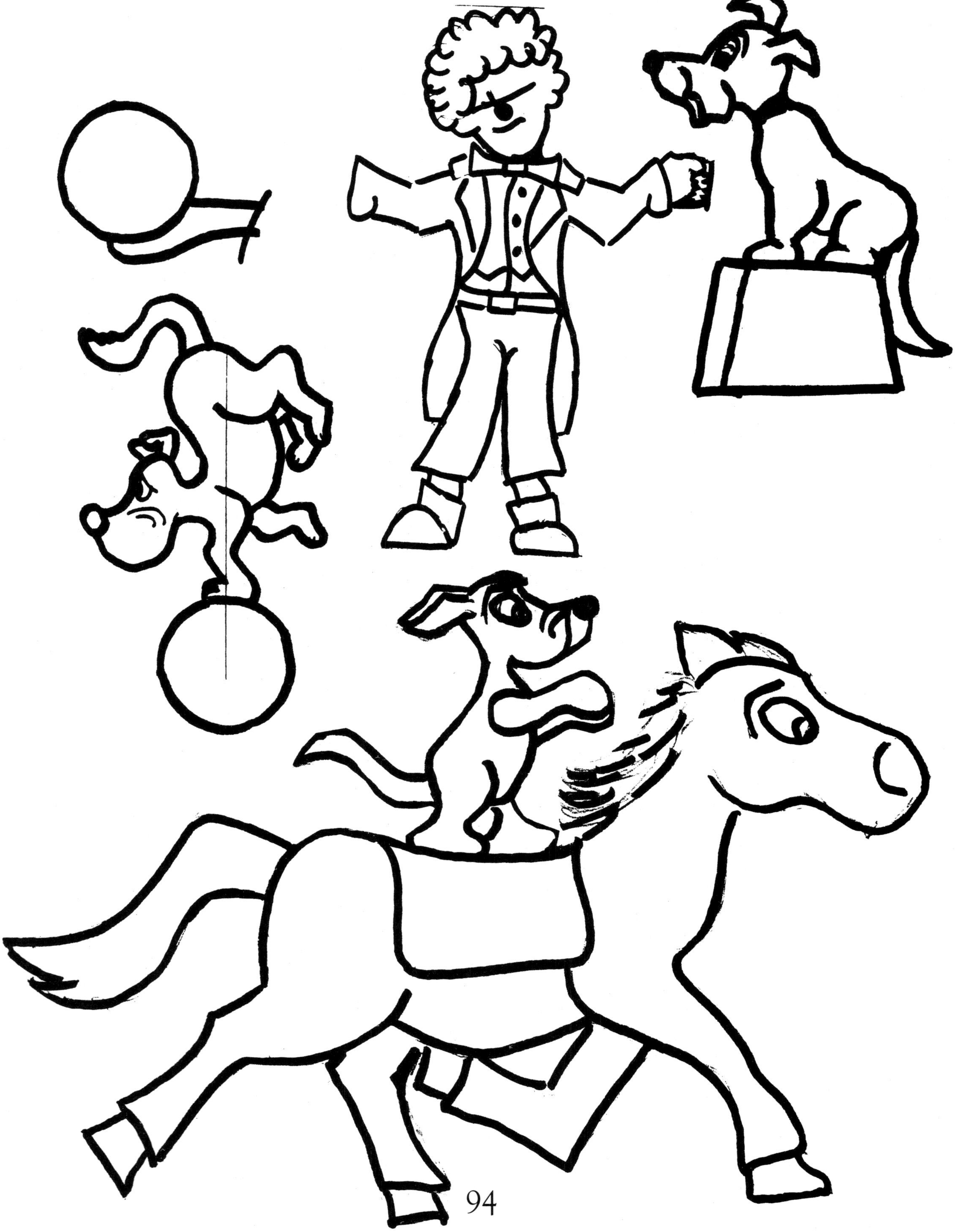

Frankenstein
by Dave Rasmussen

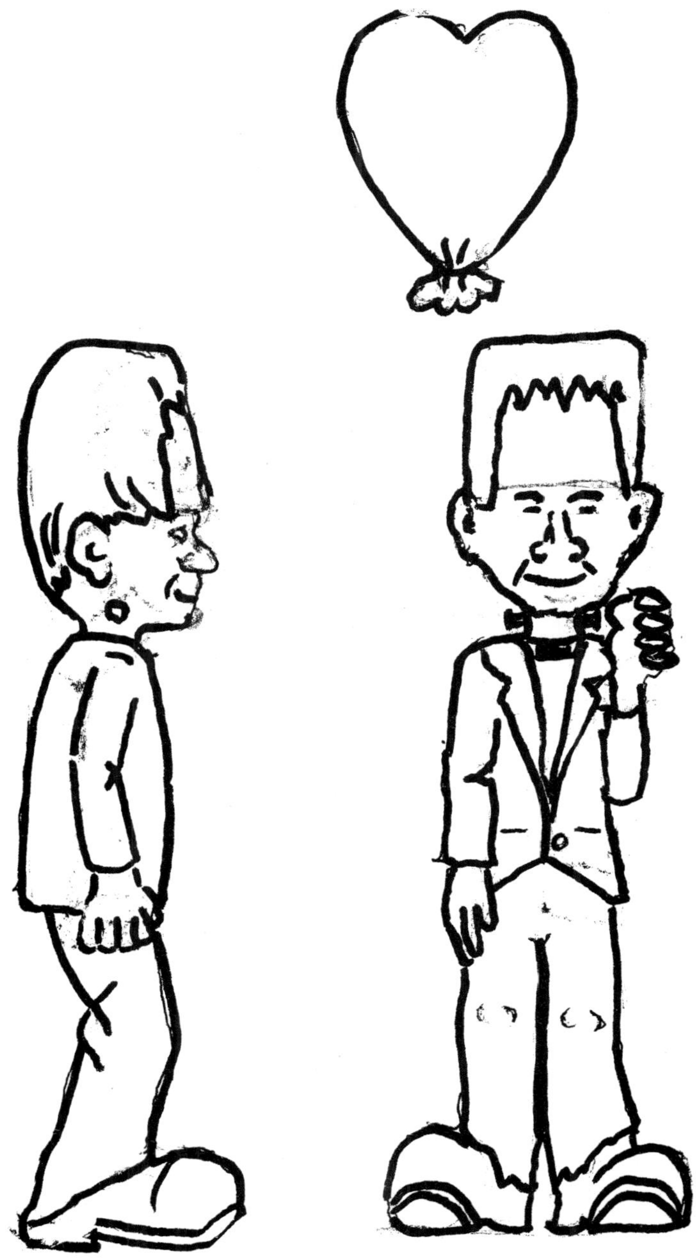

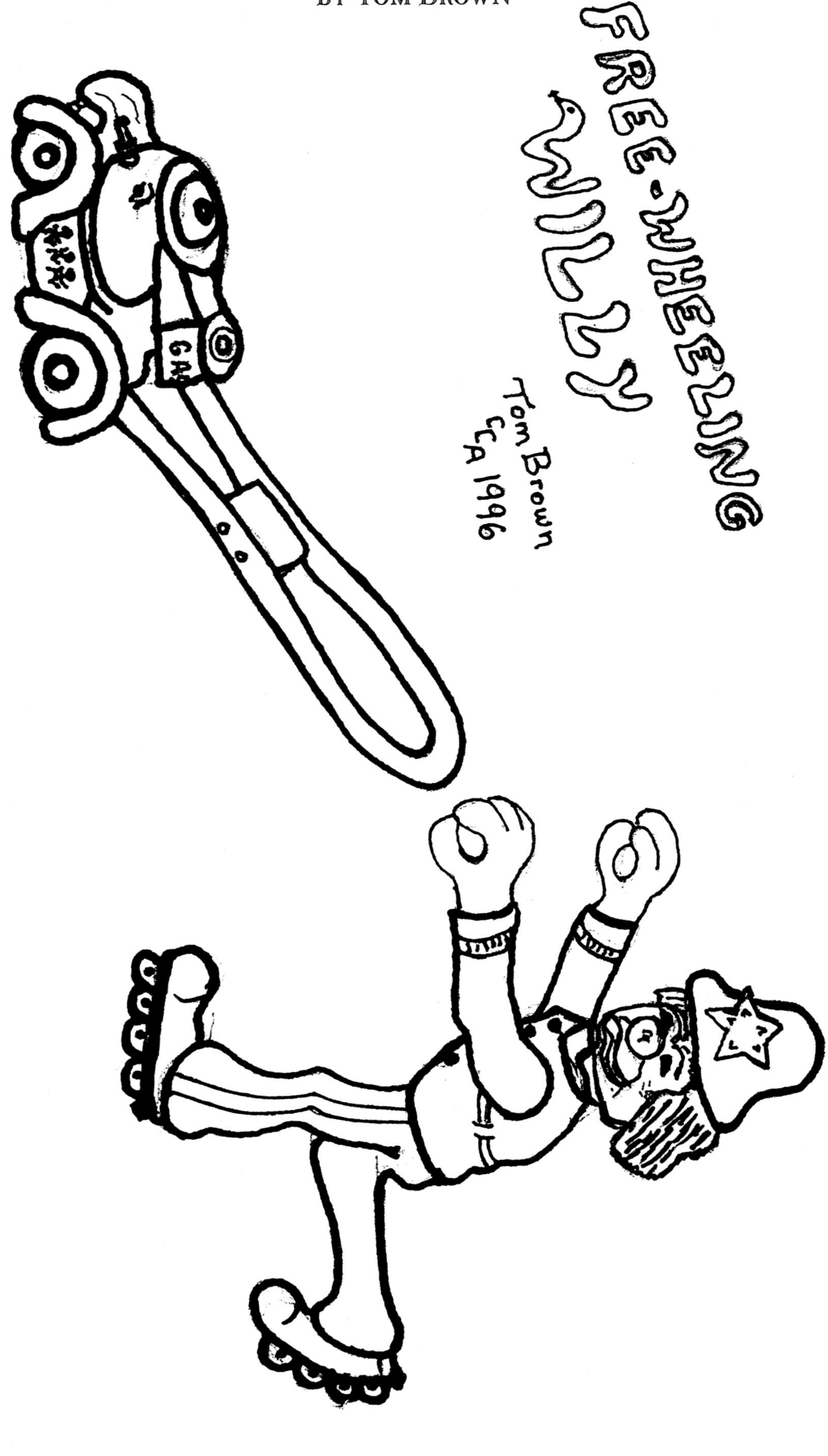
FREE-WHEELING
WILLY
Tom Brown
CA 1996

Hang Tight
by Bob Travis

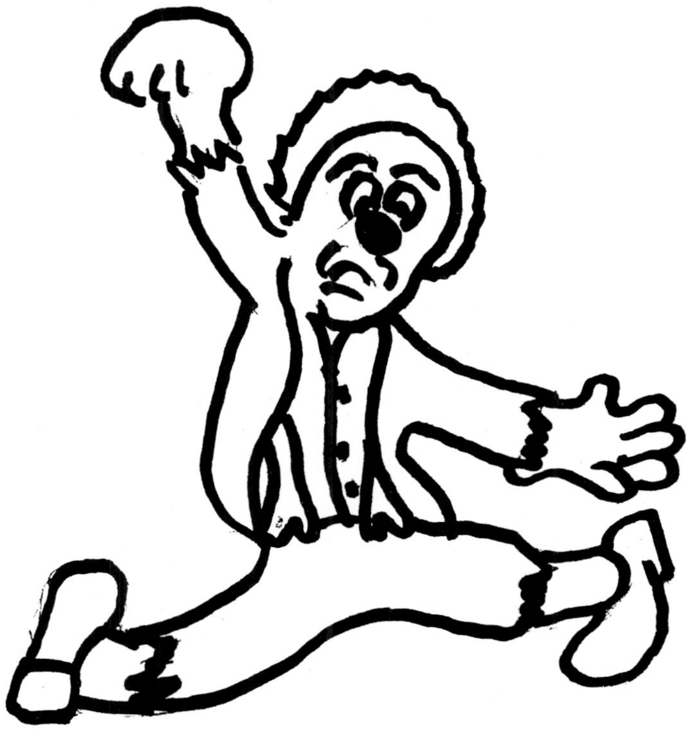

I Scream
by Dave Rasmussen

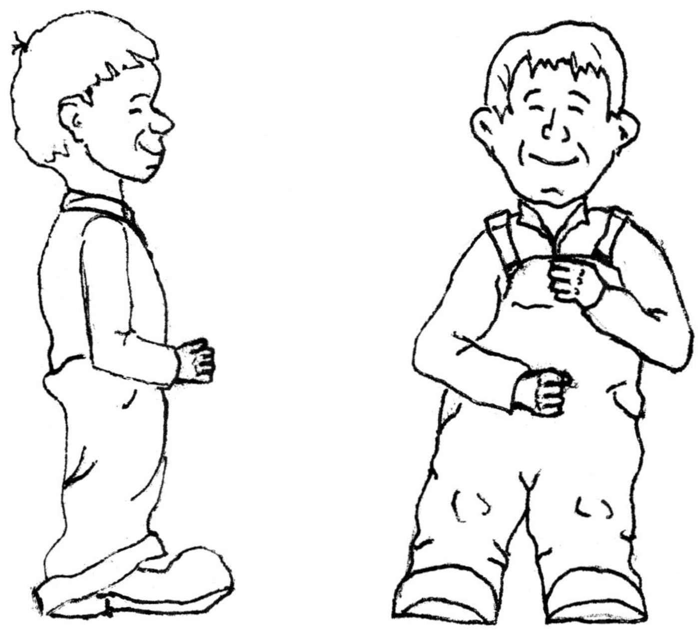

Kernel P. Cobb
by W. "Pete" LeClair

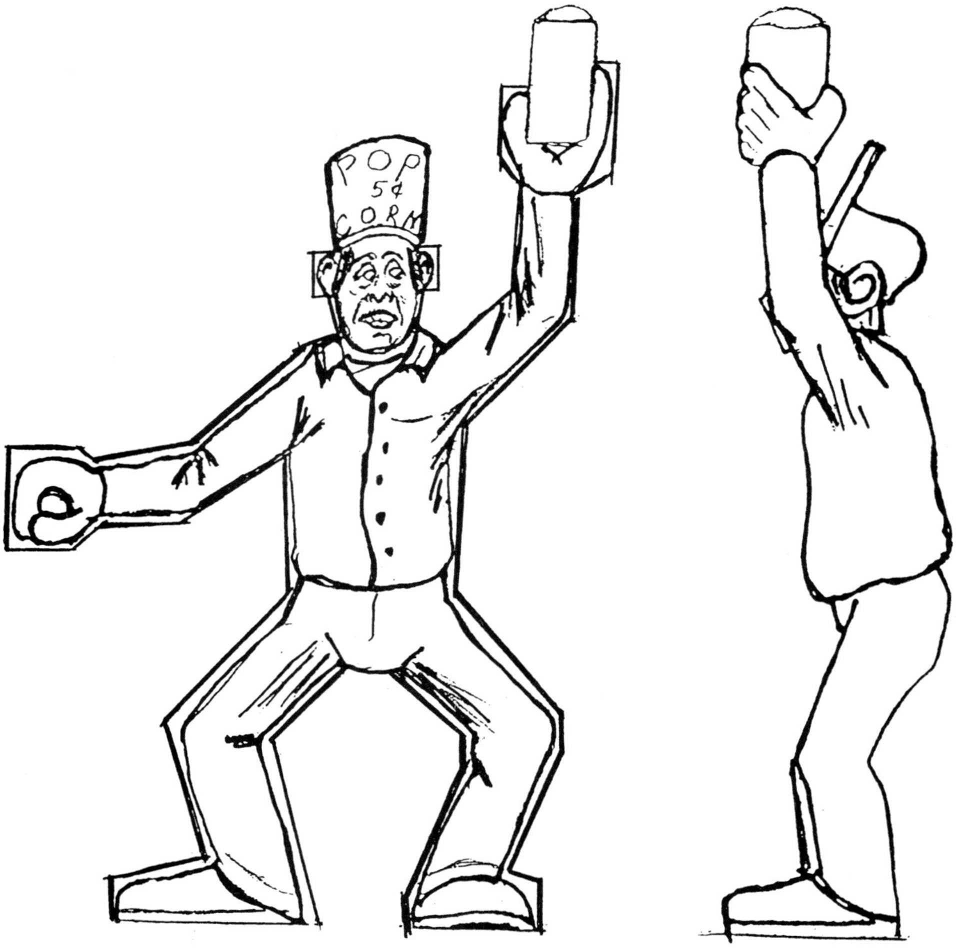

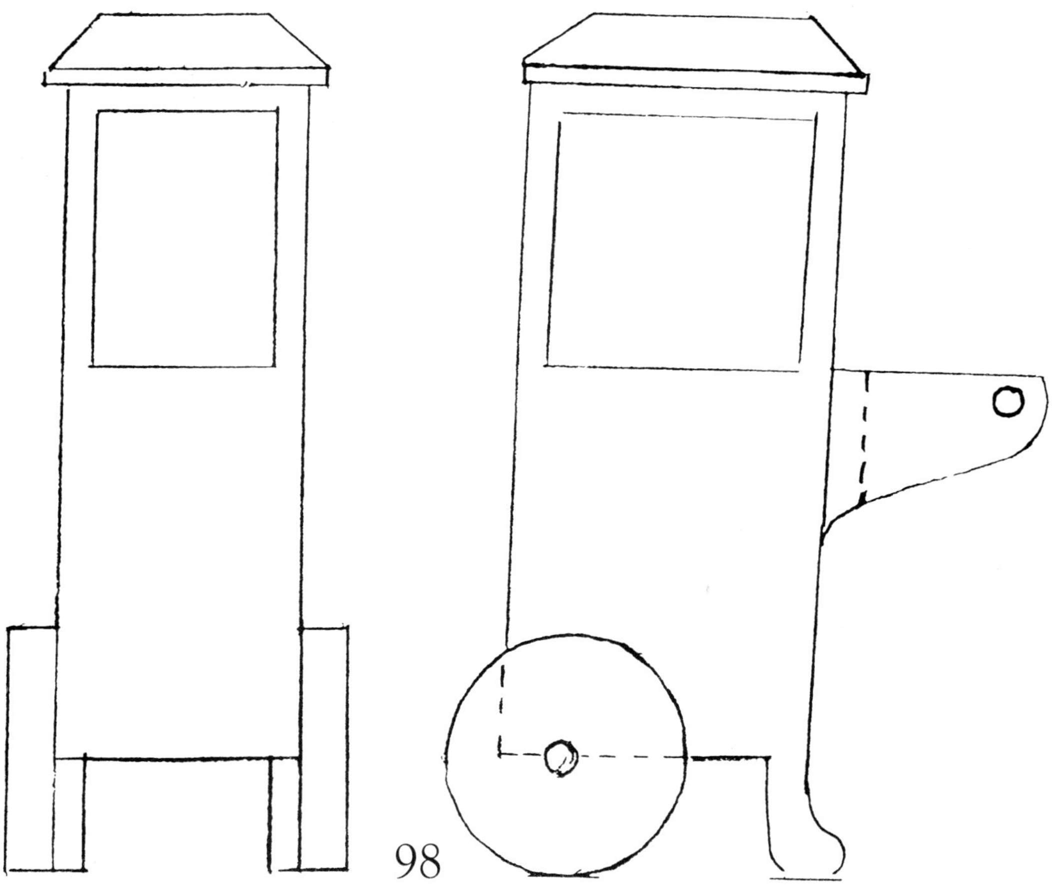

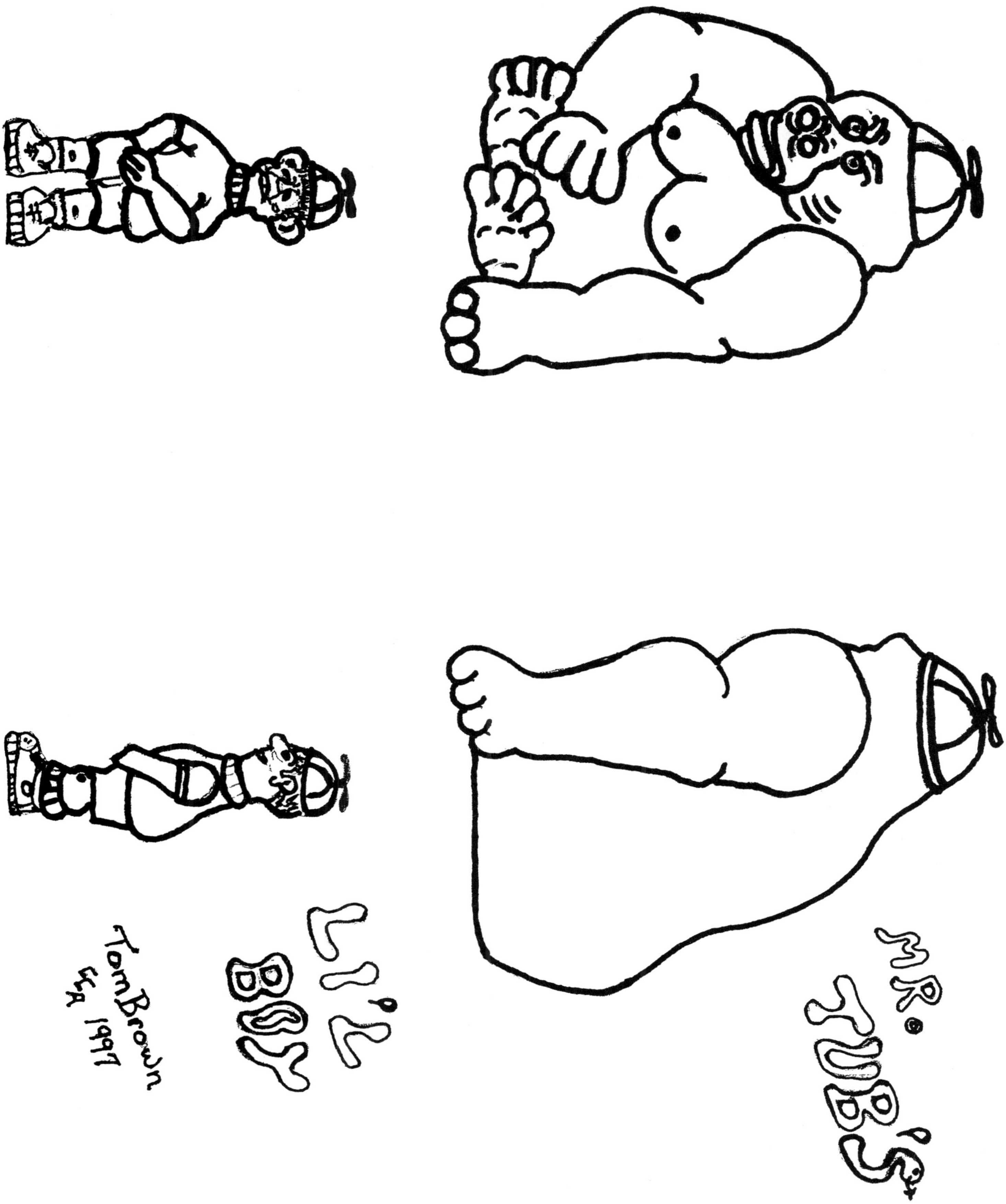
MR.
TUBS
LI'L
BOY
TomBrown

Ronald the Raccoon
by Desiree Hajny

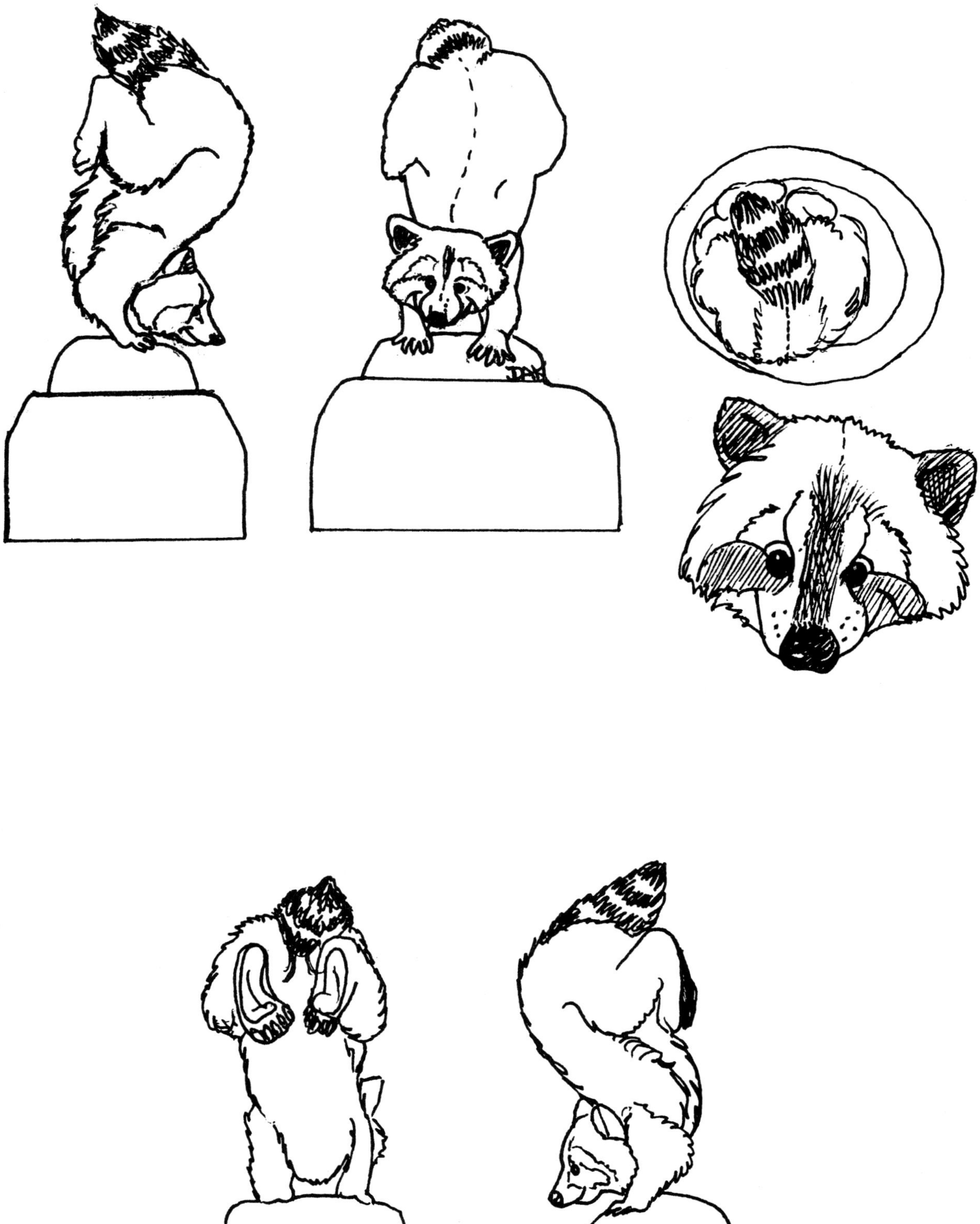

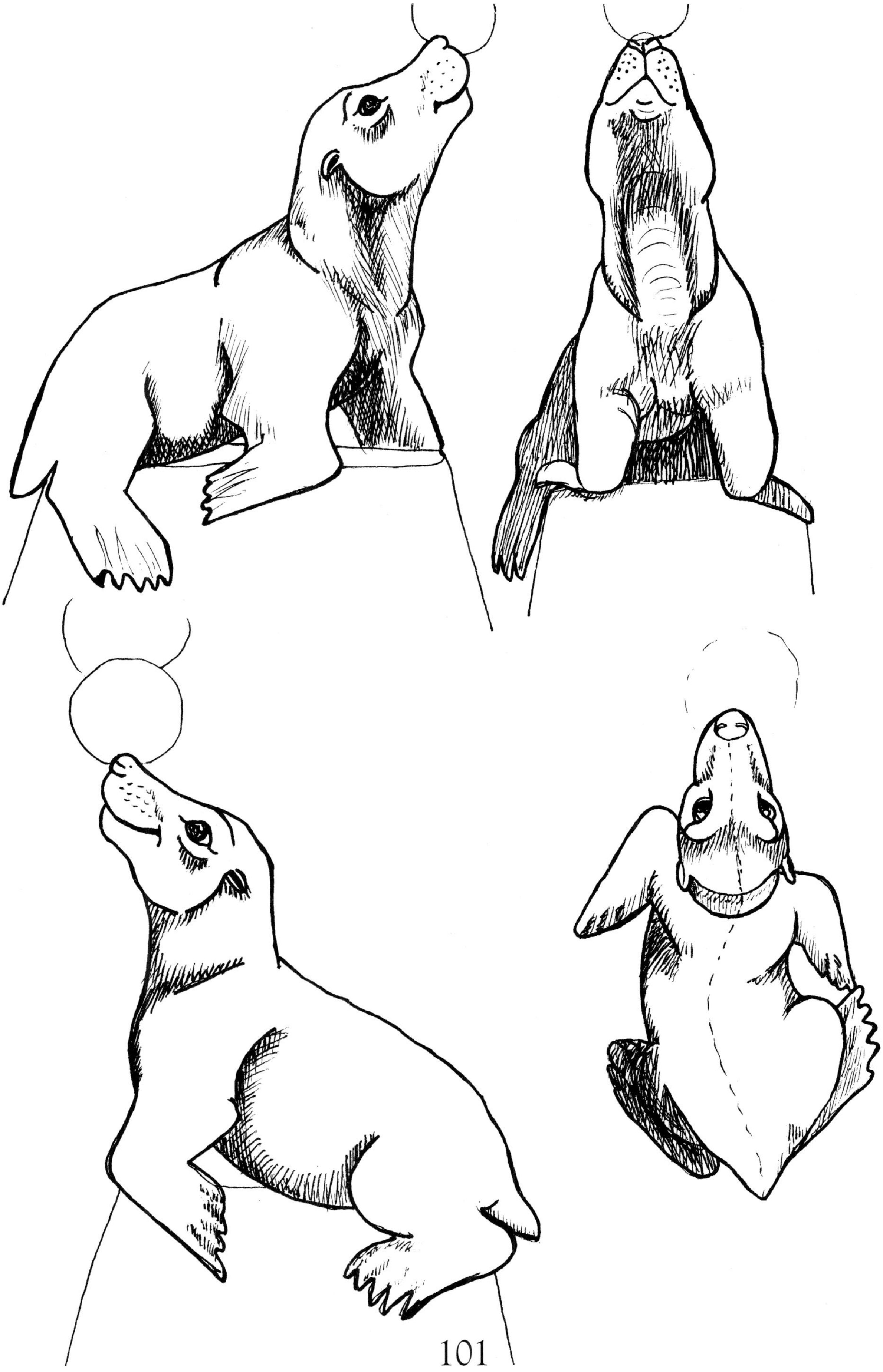

That's Some Zebra
by Gary Batte

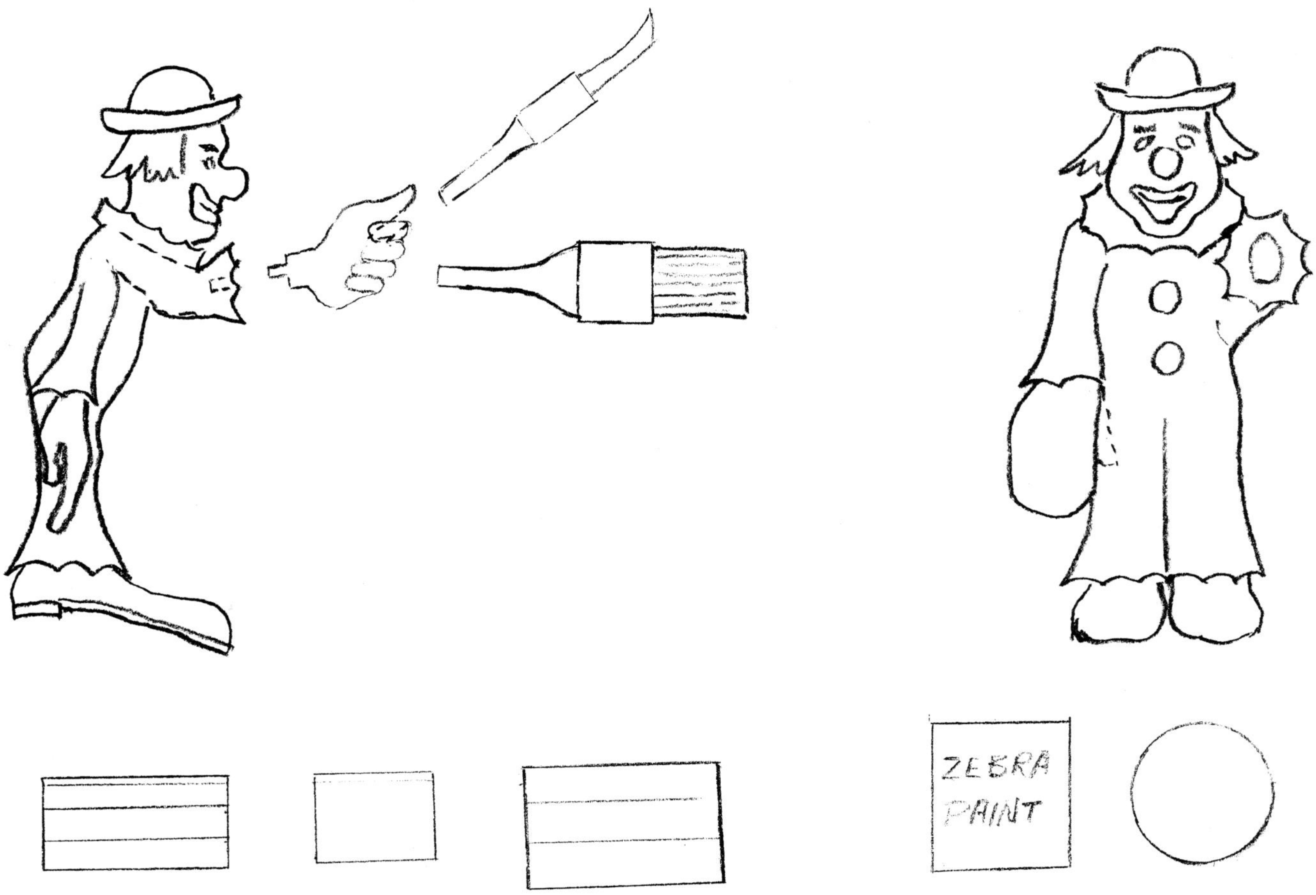

That's Some Zebra
by Gary Batte

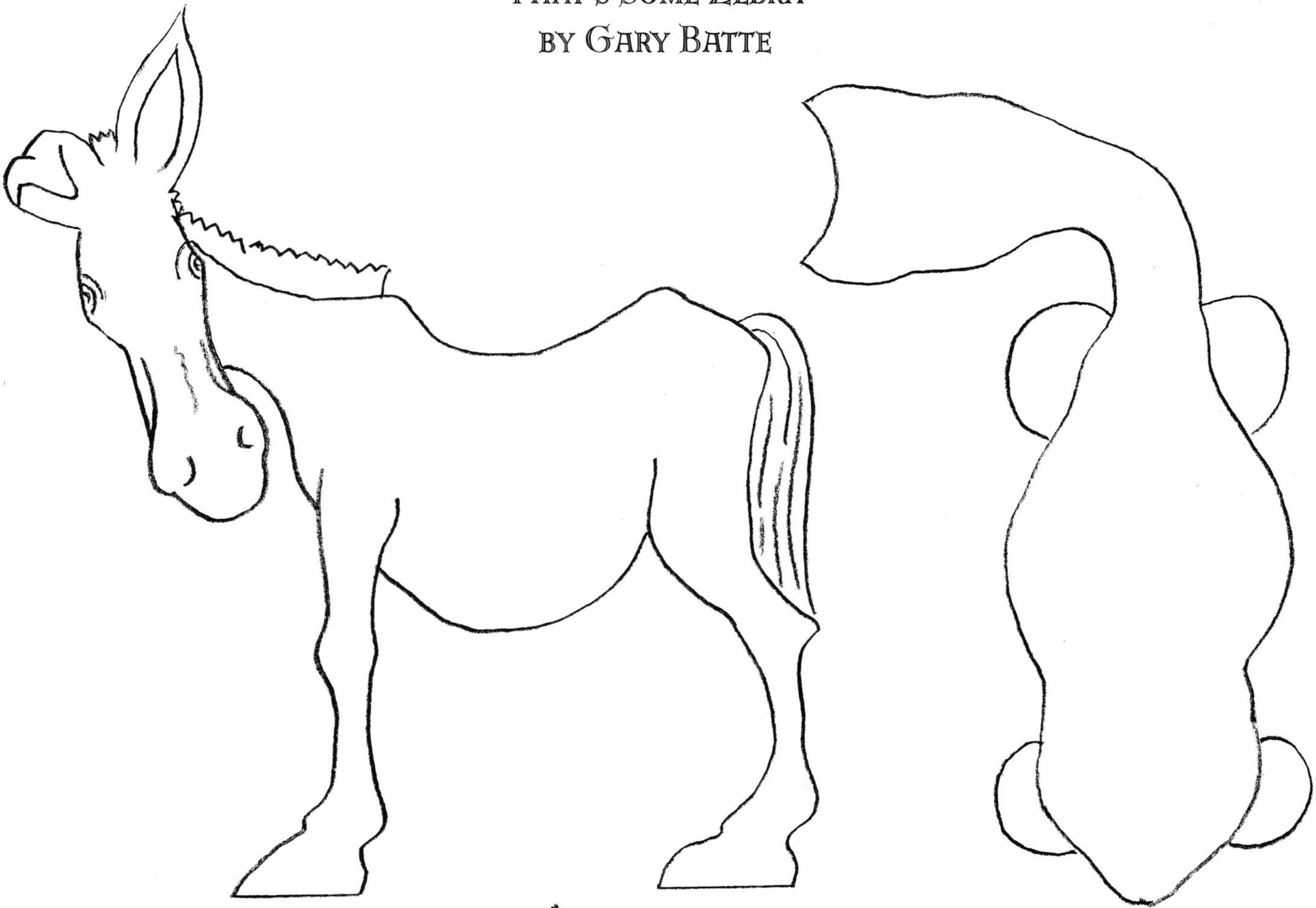

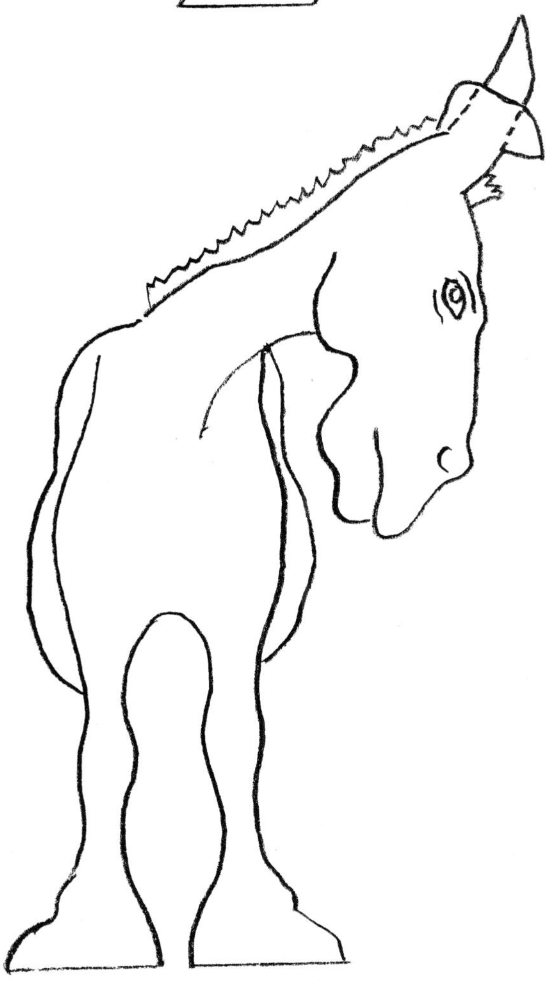

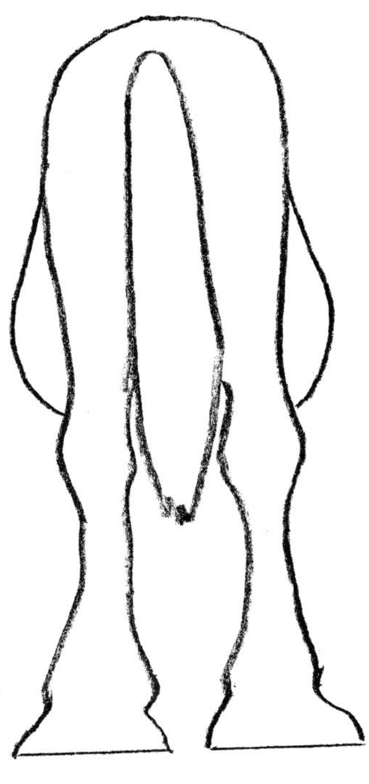

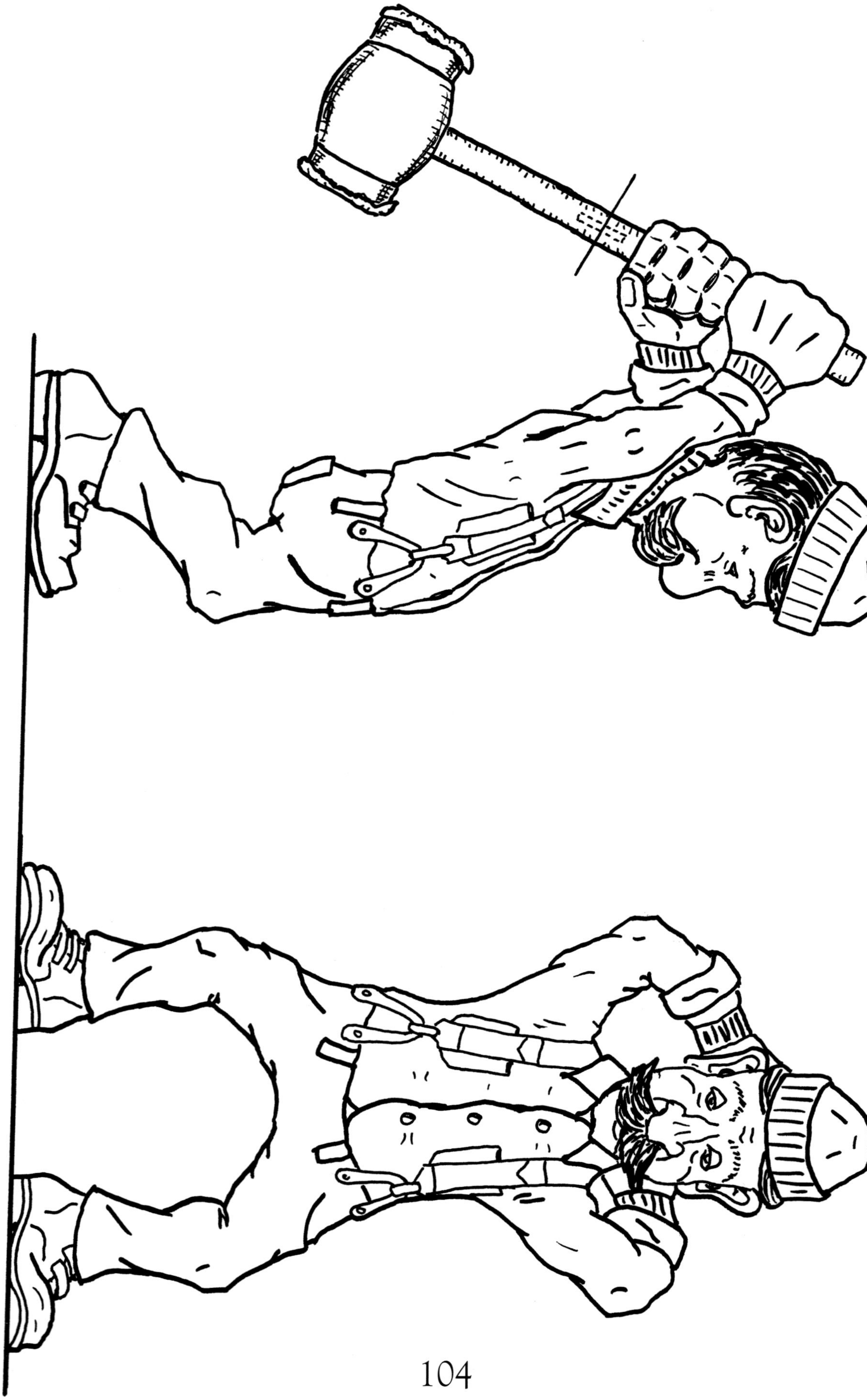

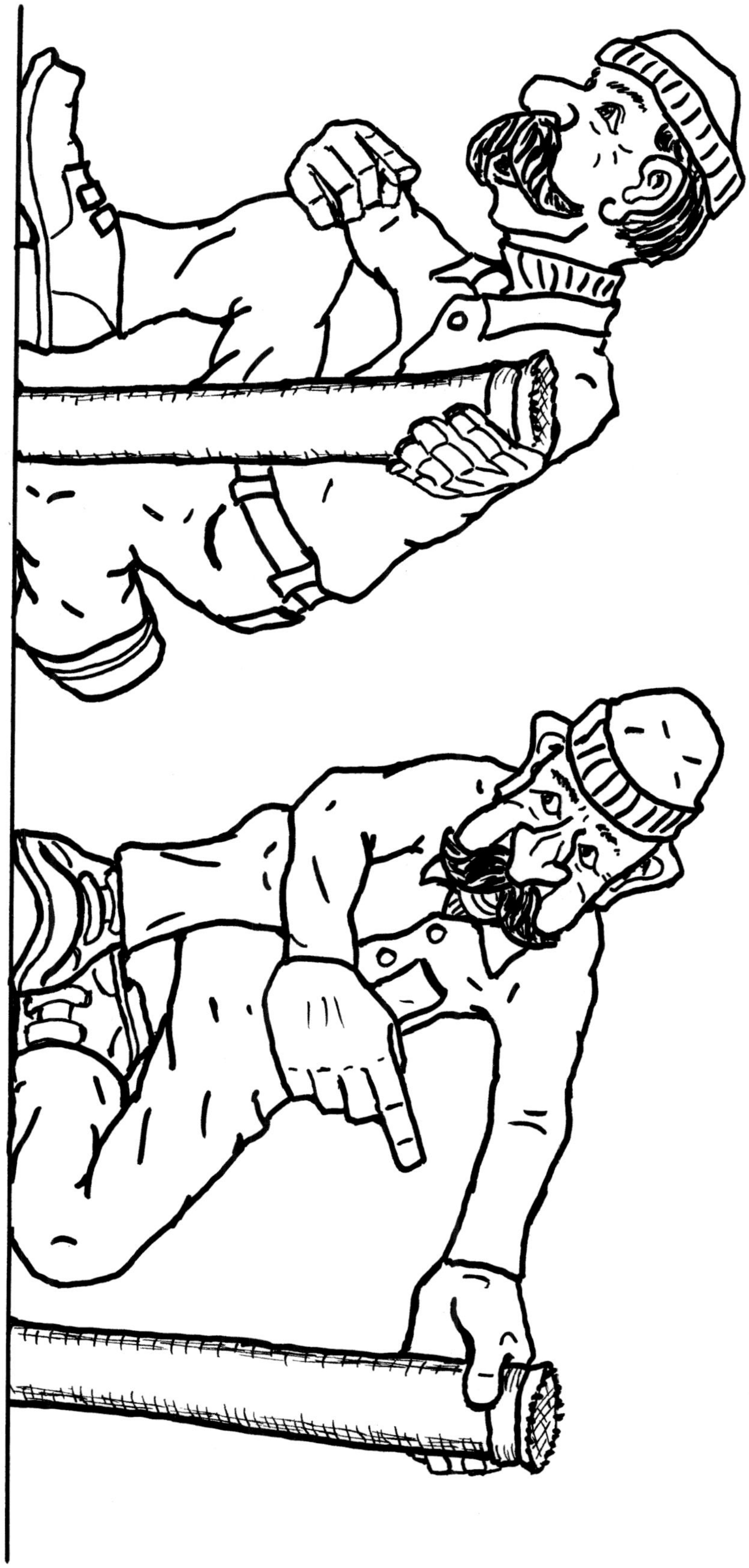

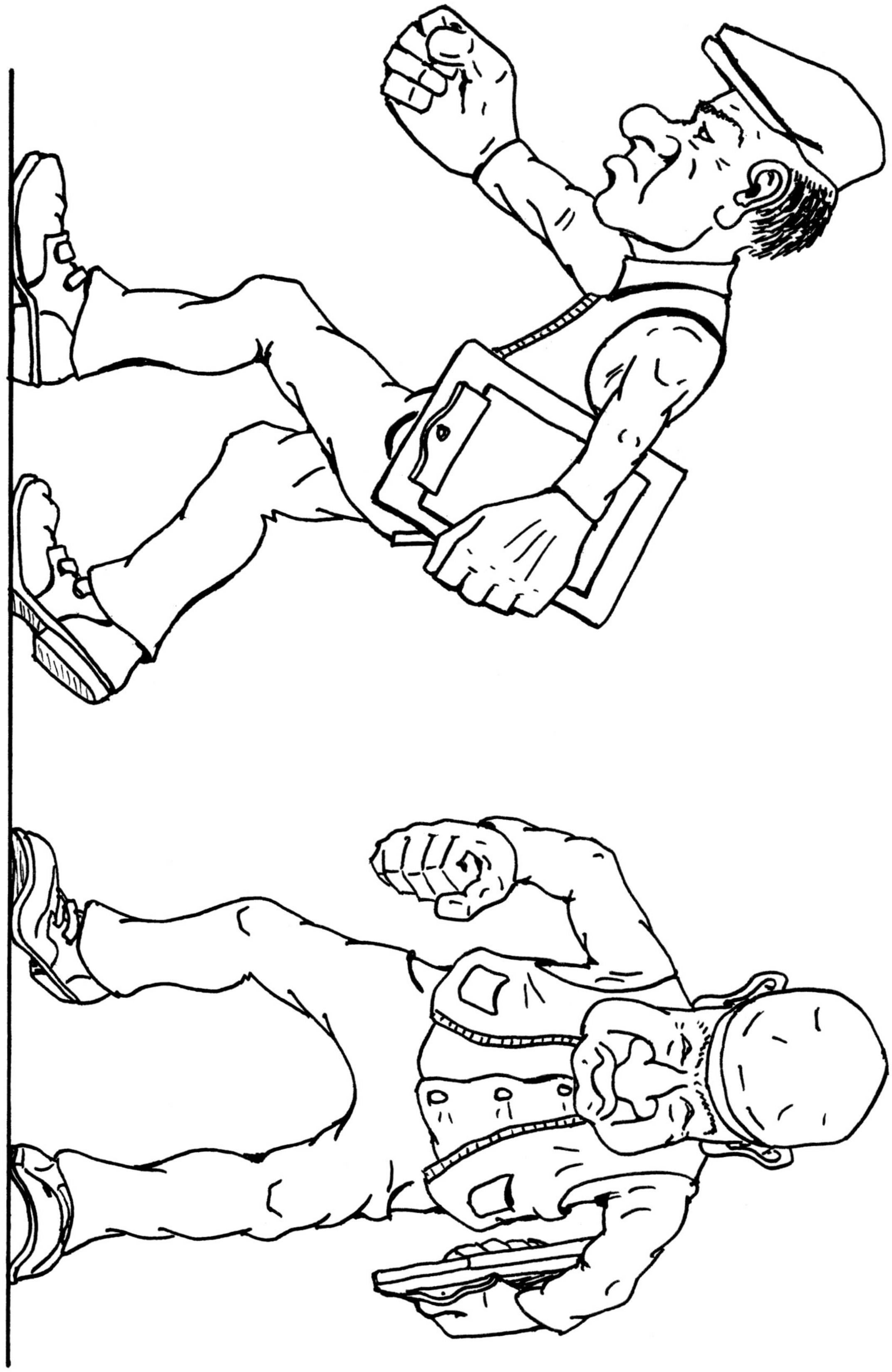

The Buzzard
by Gary Batte

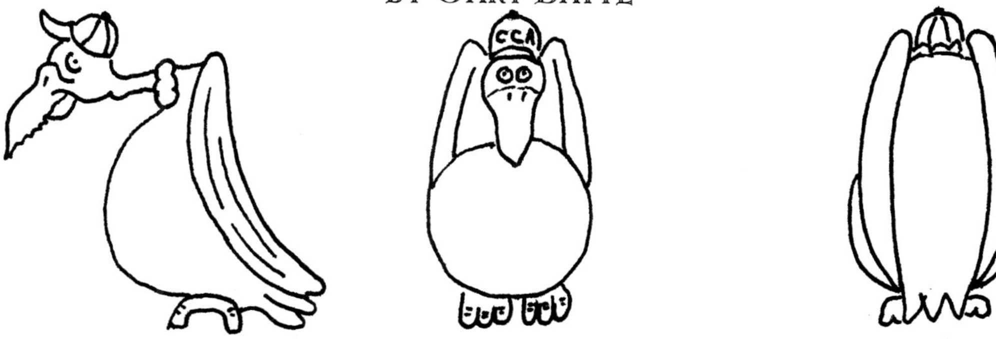

The Ringmaster
by Gary Batte

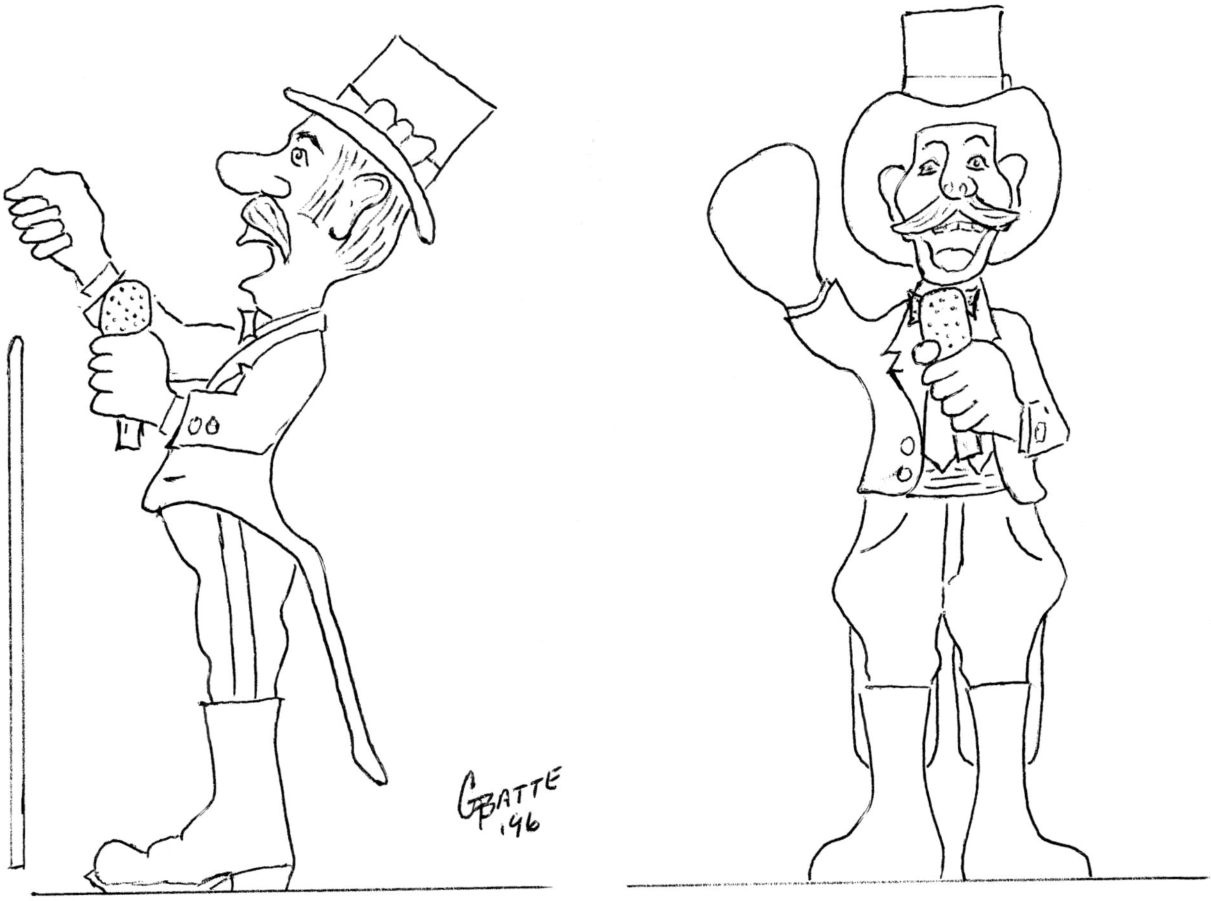

The Con Man

by Marv Kaisersatt

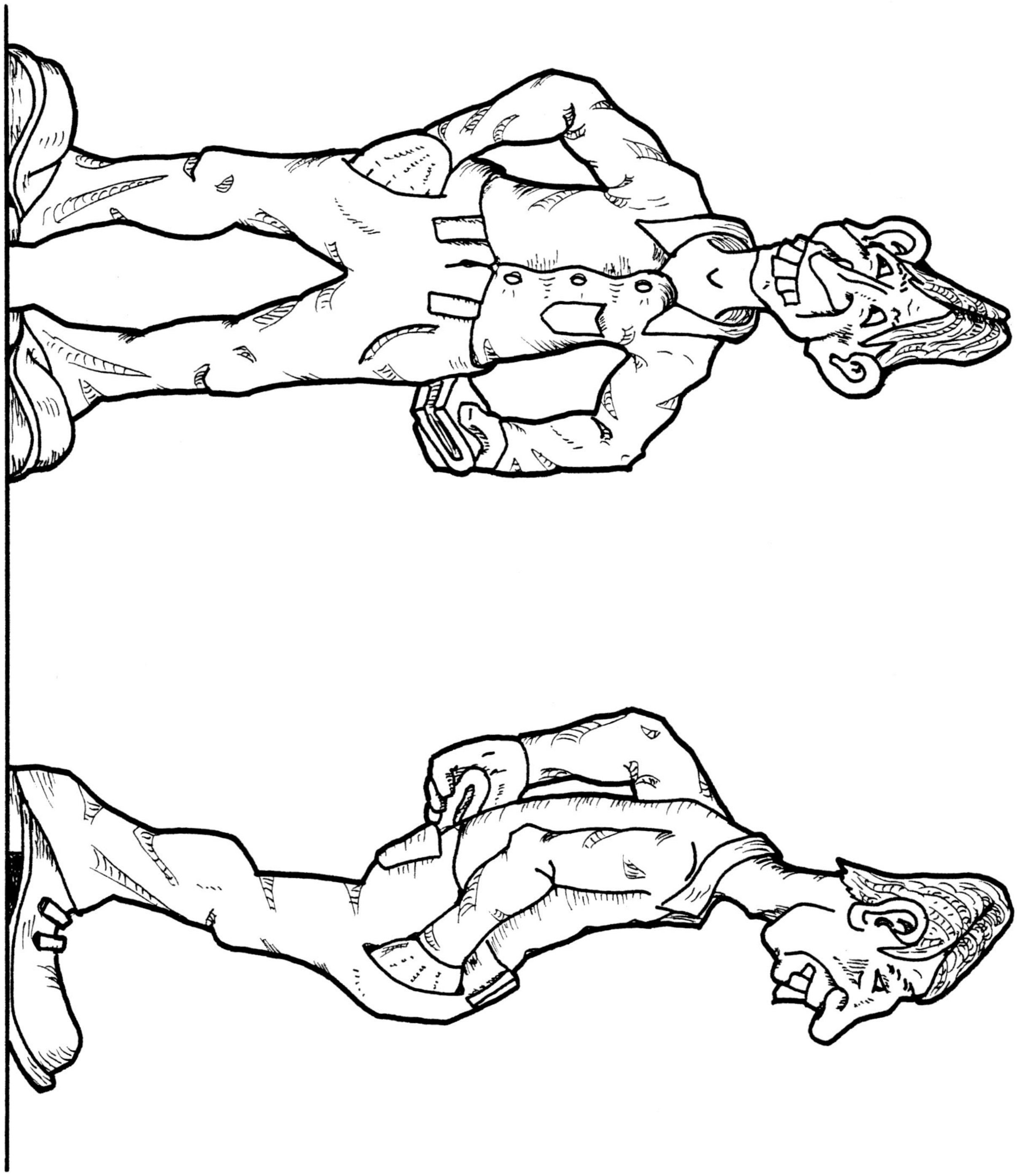

The Con Man

by Marv Kaisersatt

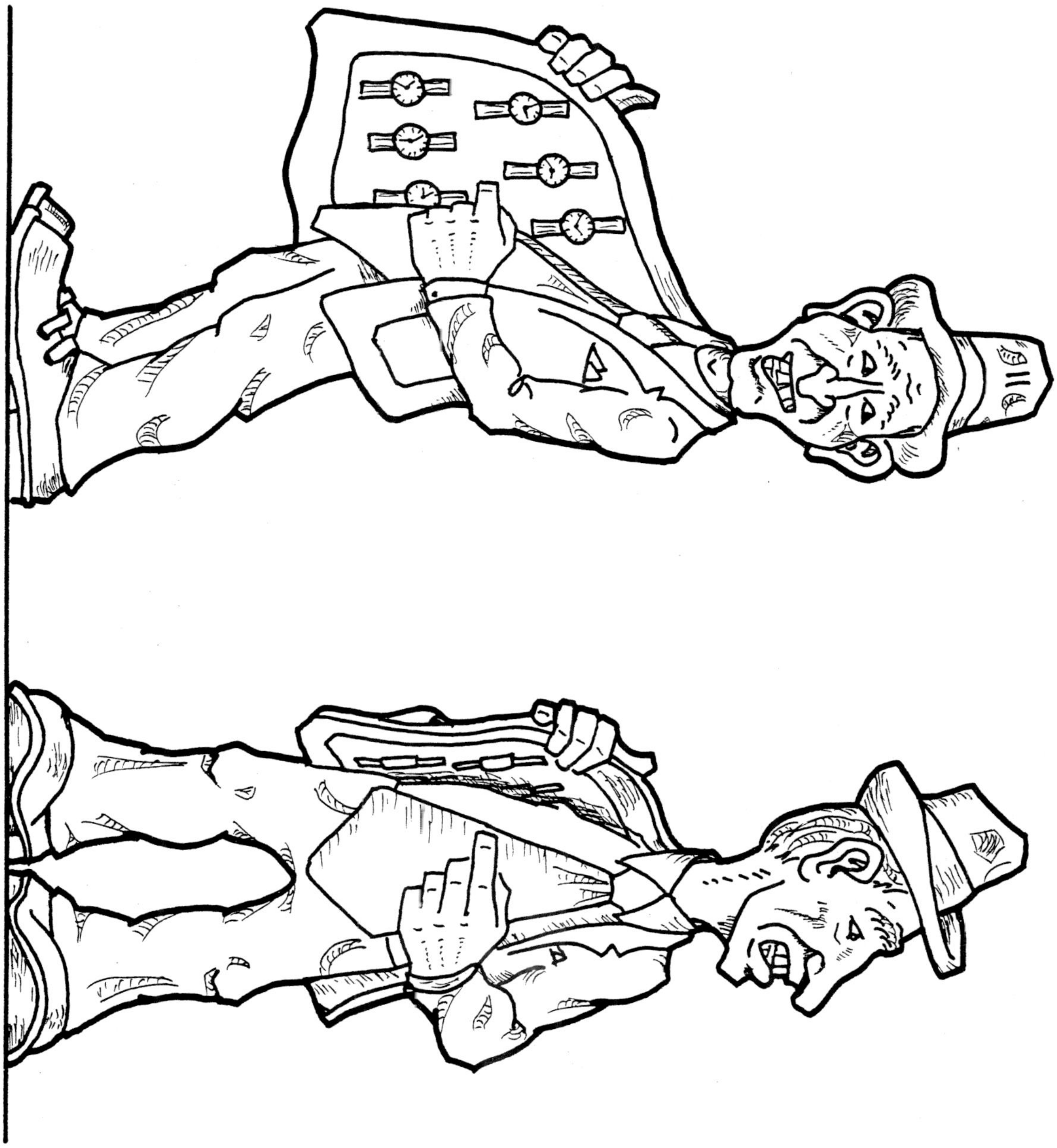

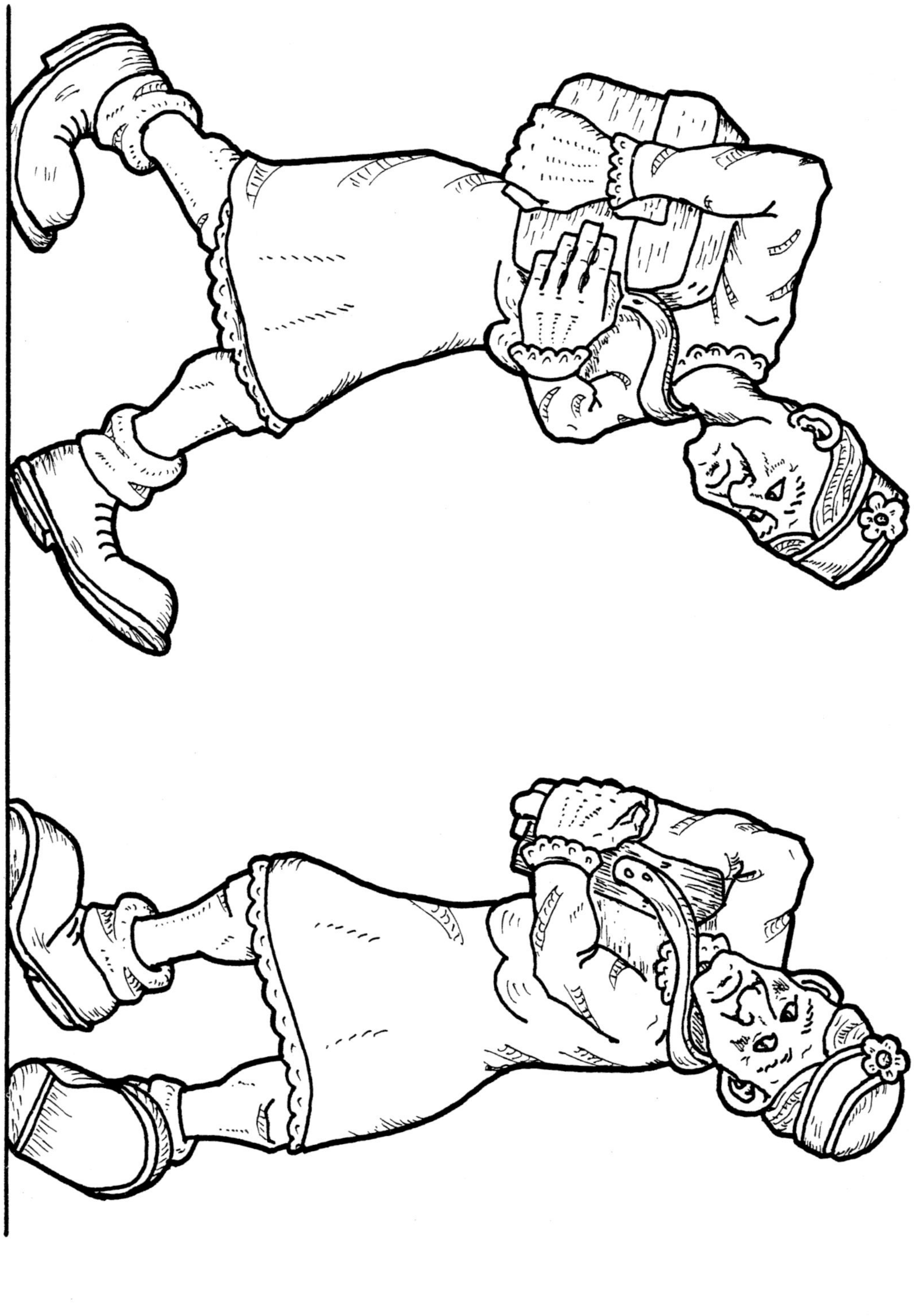

The Juggler
by Claude Bolton

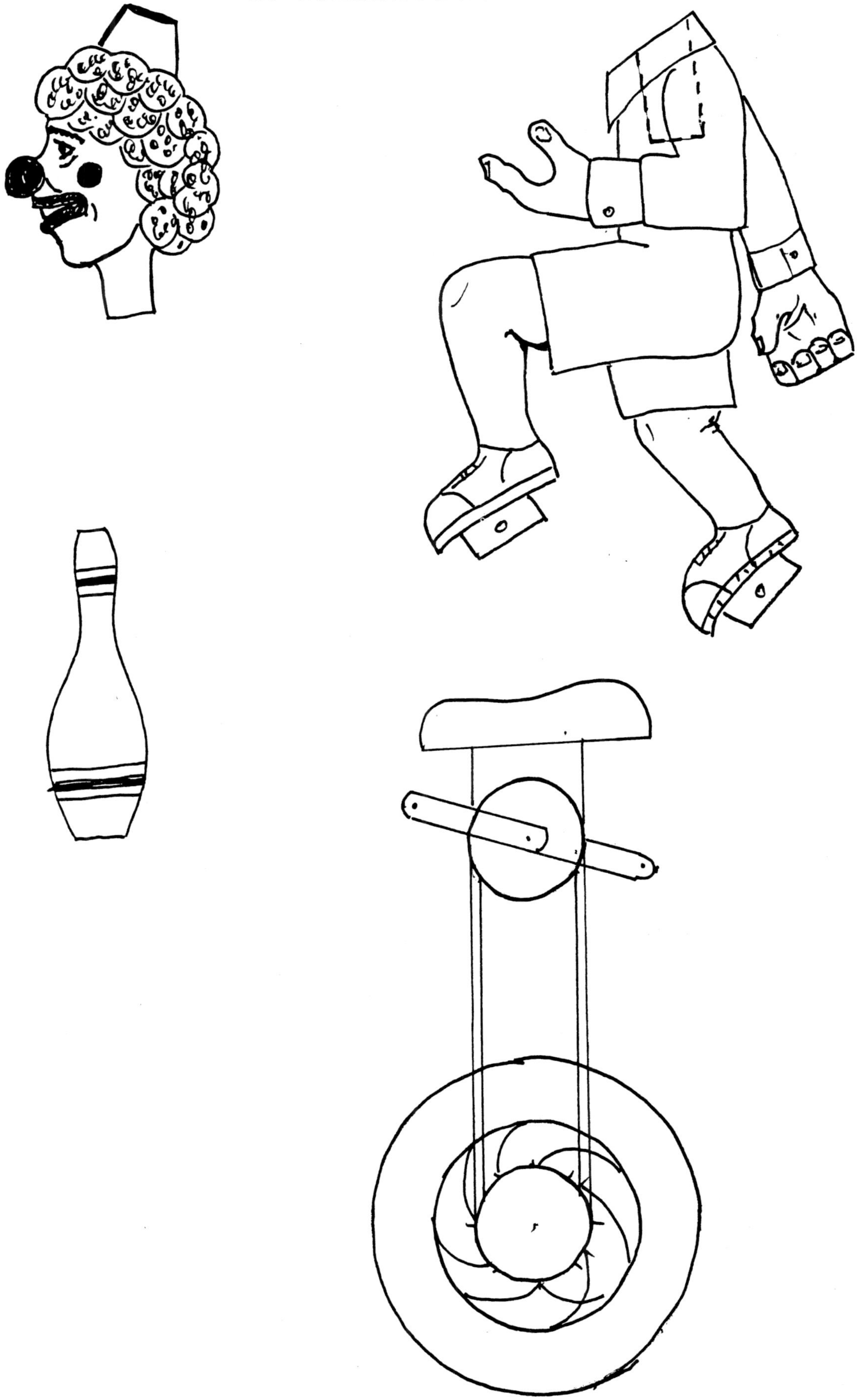

The Human Cannonball
by Keith Morrill

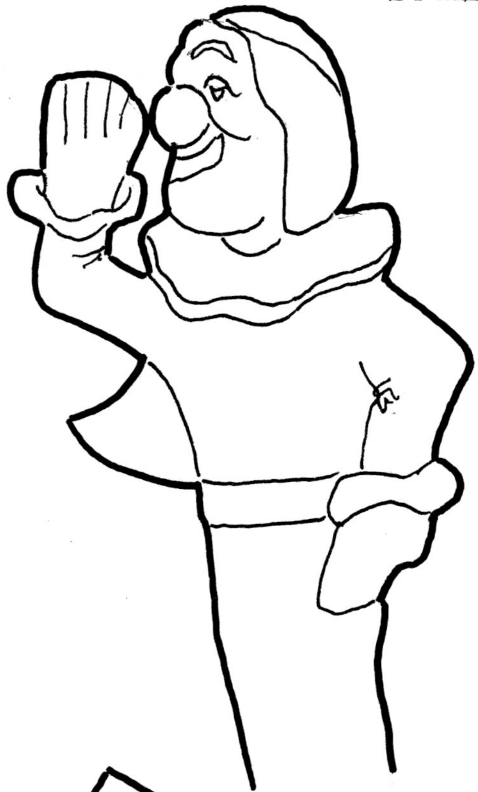

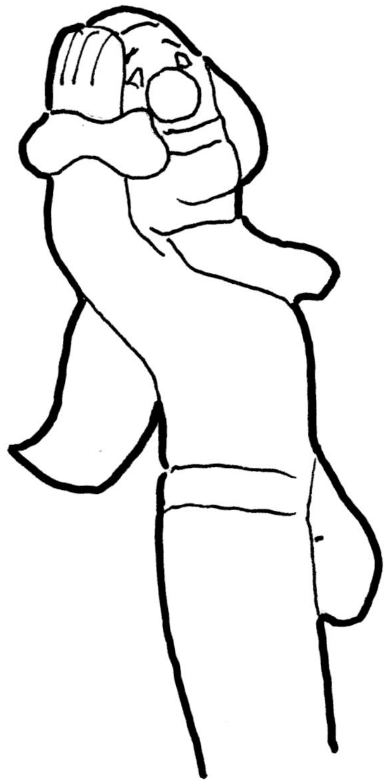

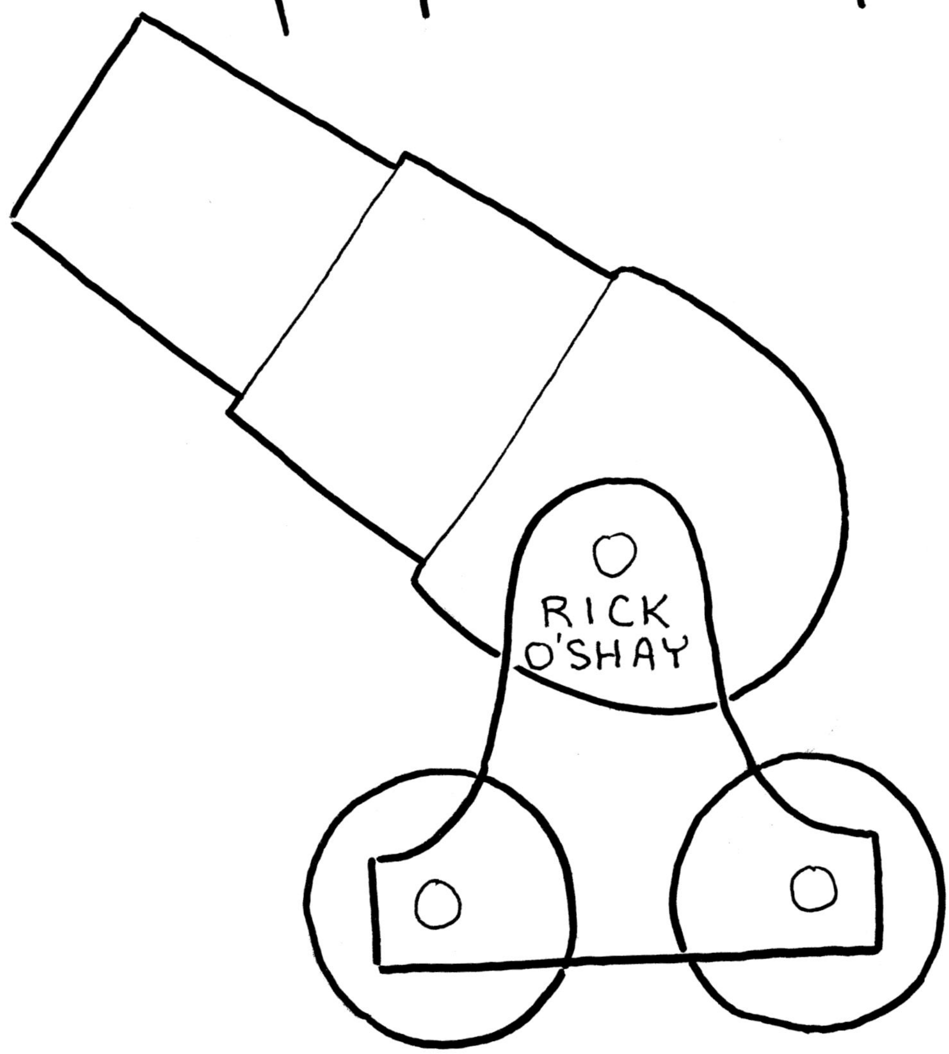

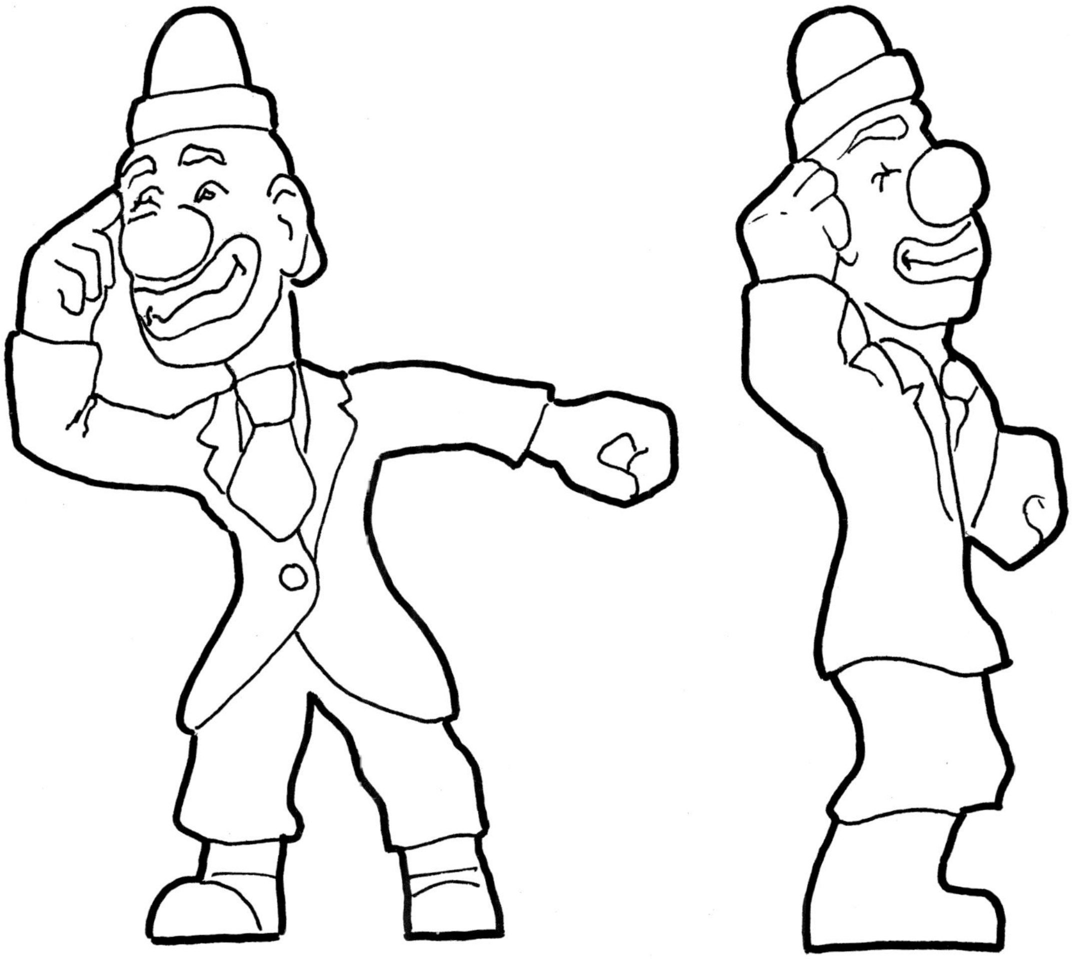

The Knife Thrower
by Keith Morrill

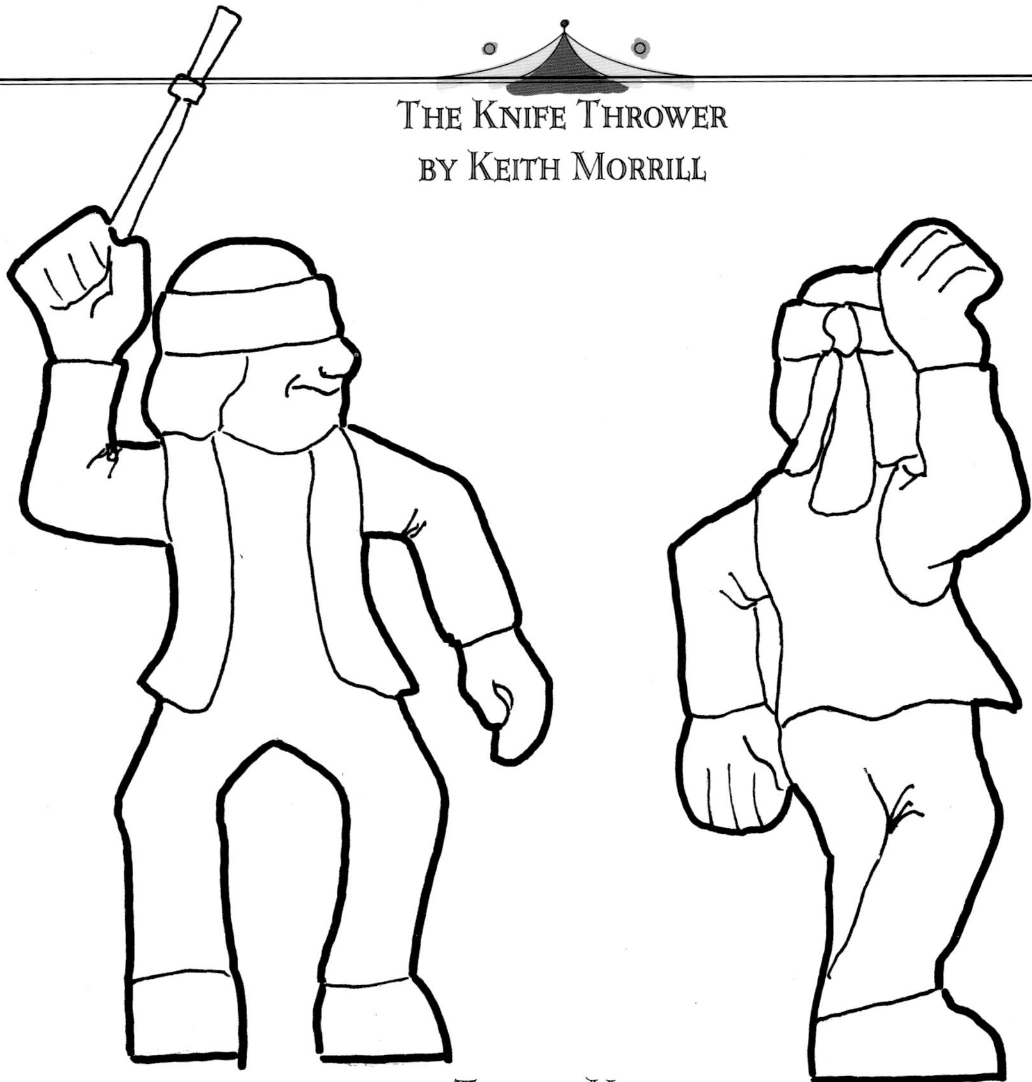

Tickets Here
by Will Hayden

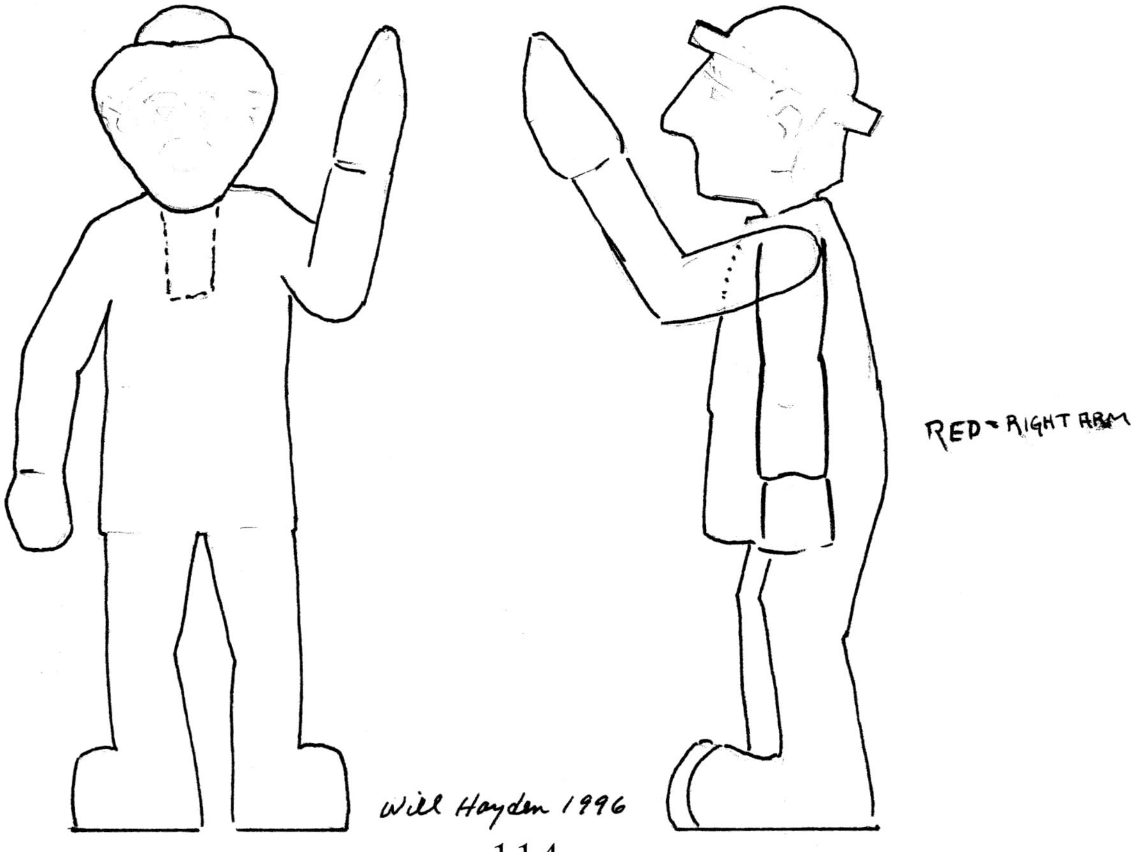

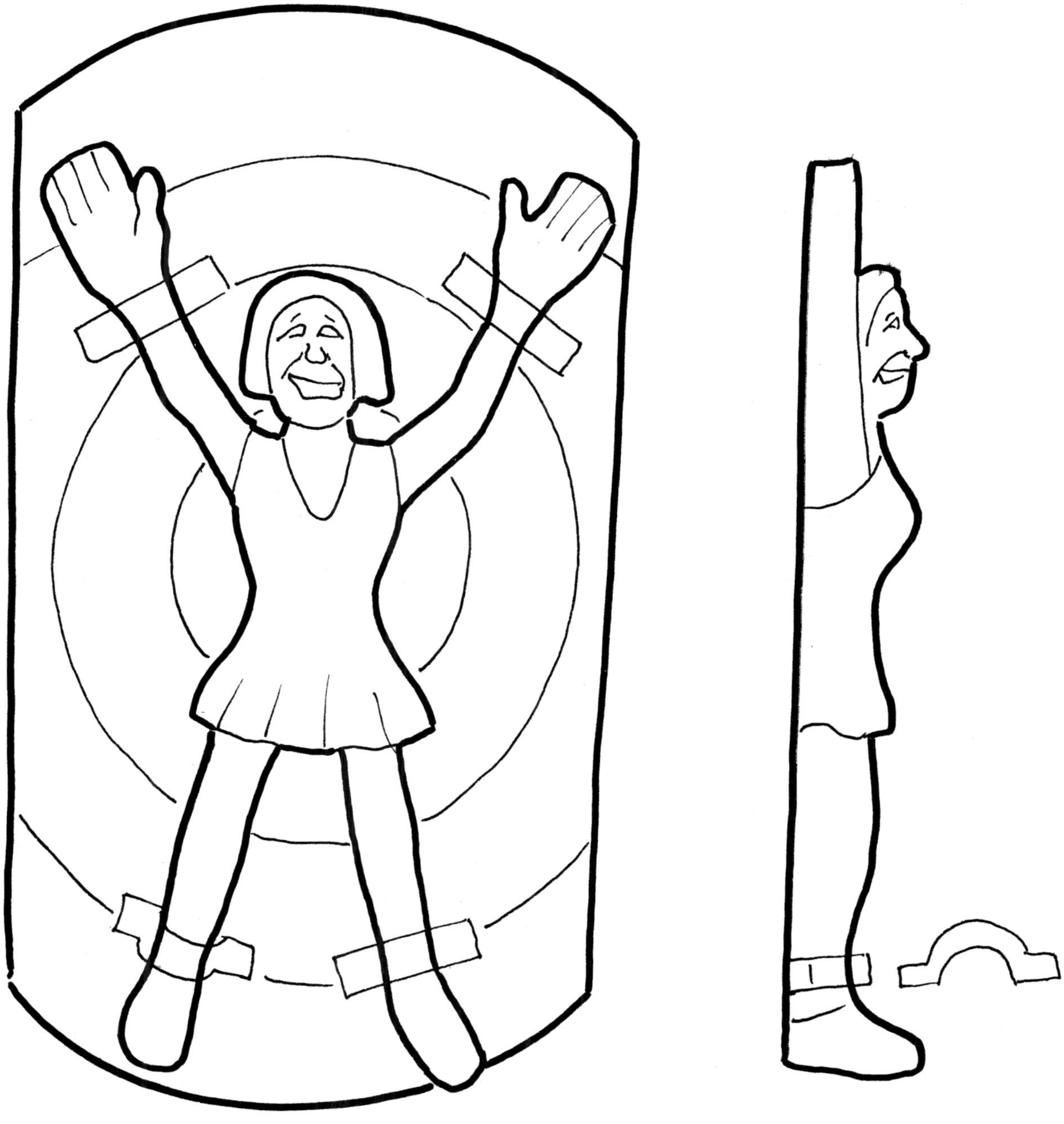

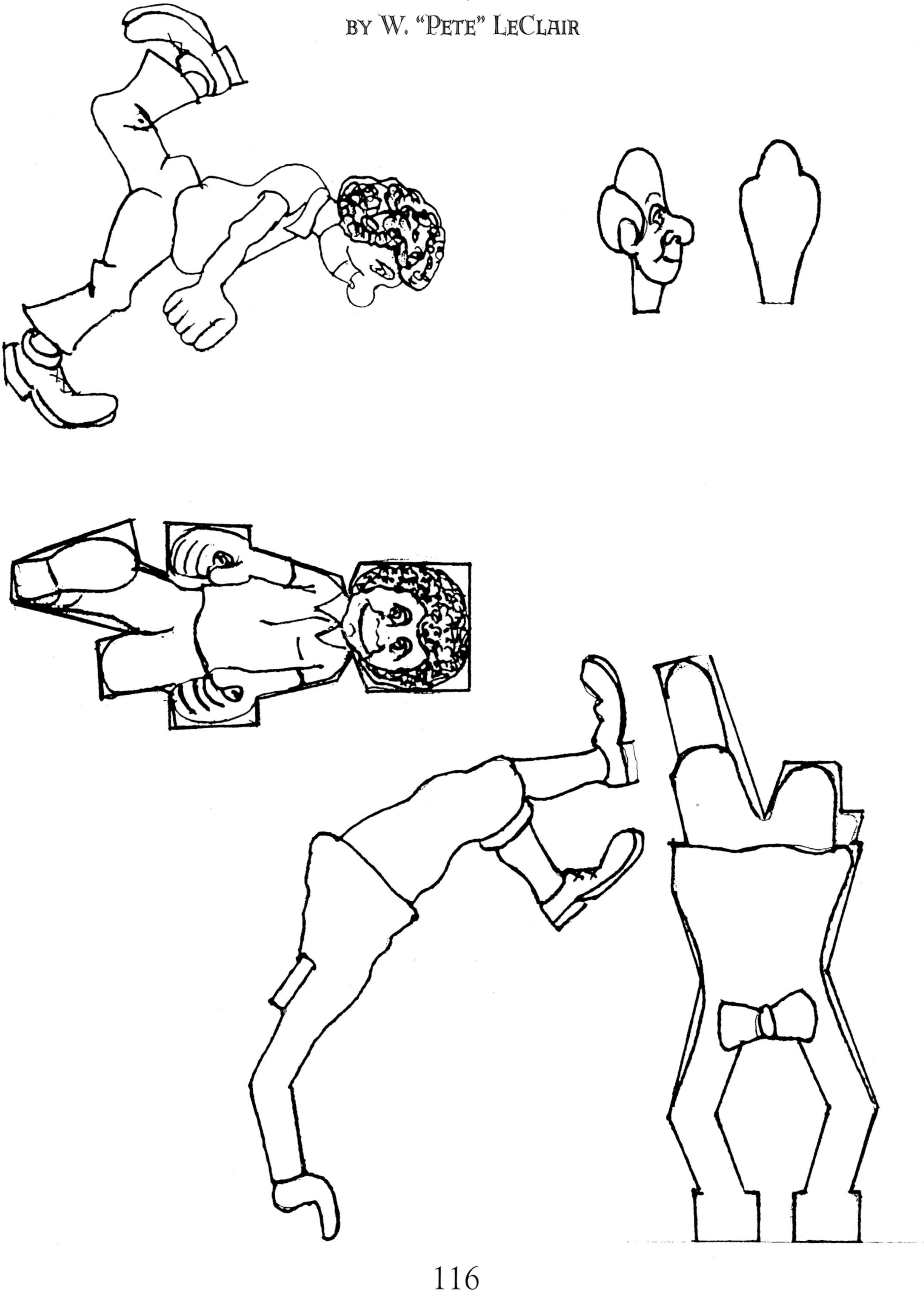

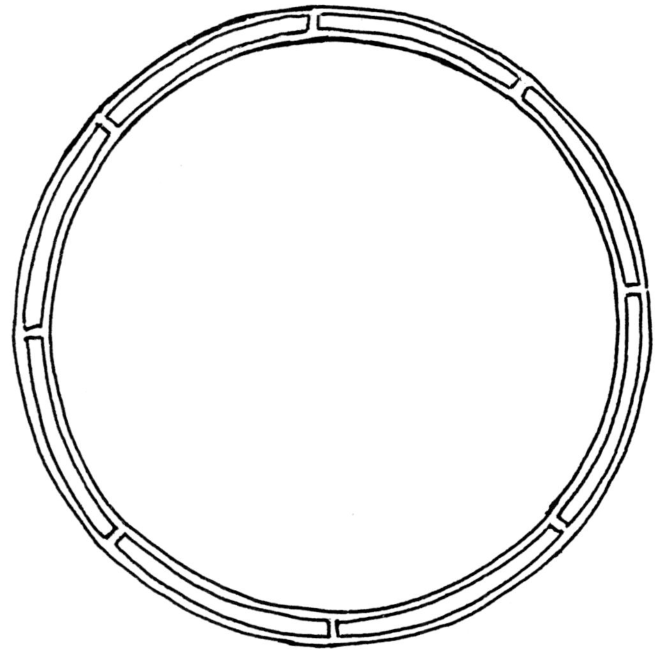

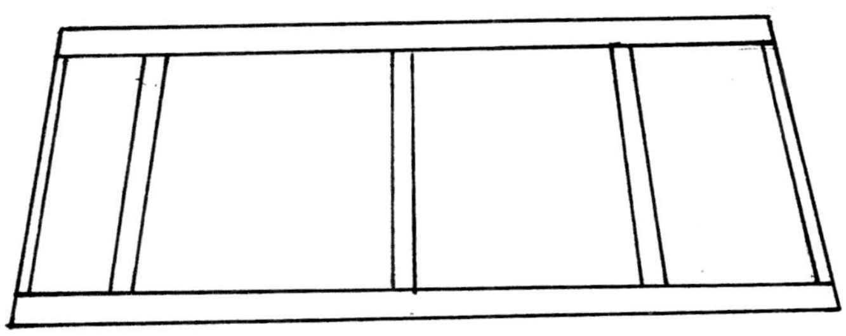

The Three Leopardo Brothers
by Harold Enlow

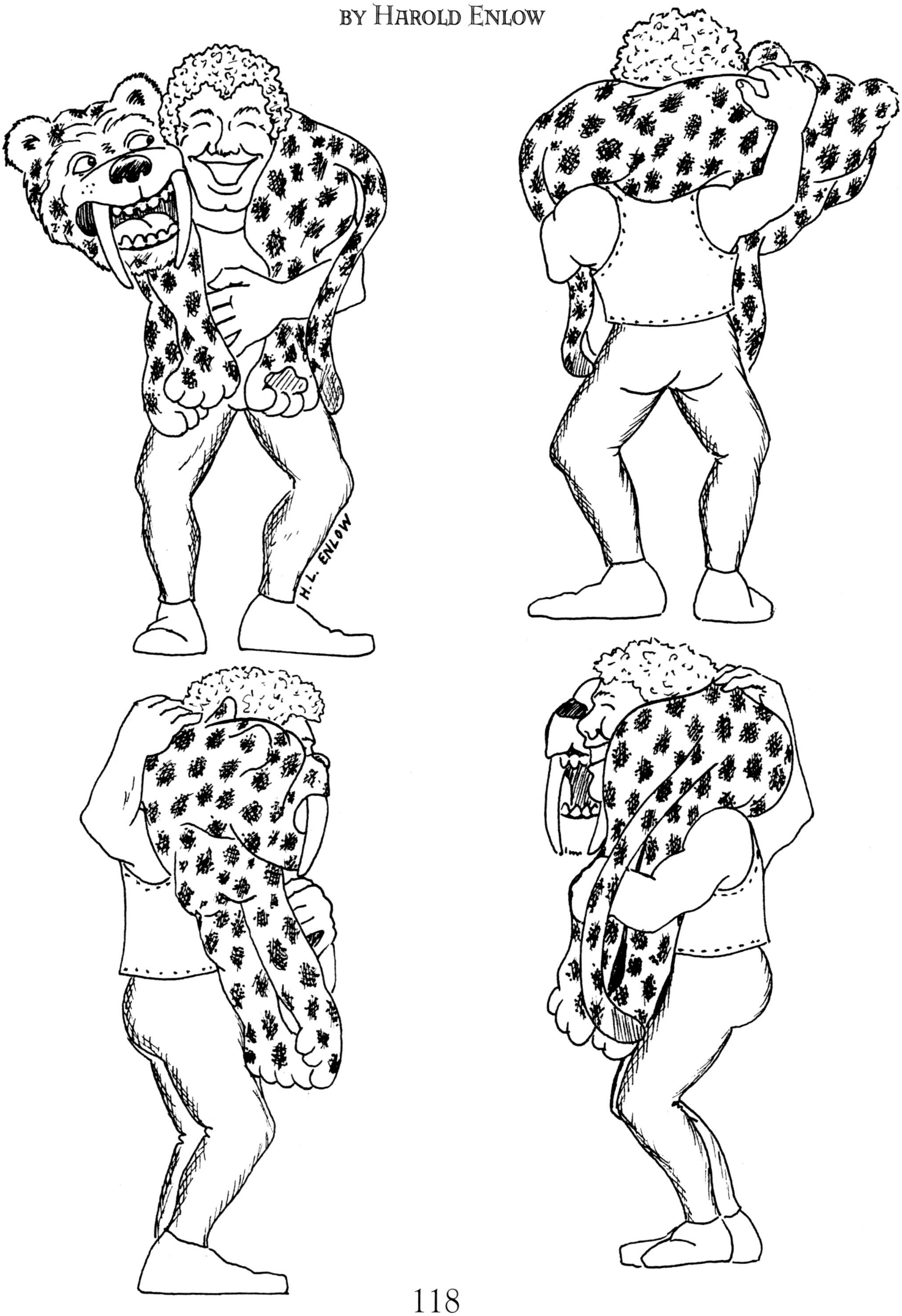

The Three Leopardo Brothers
by Harold Enlow

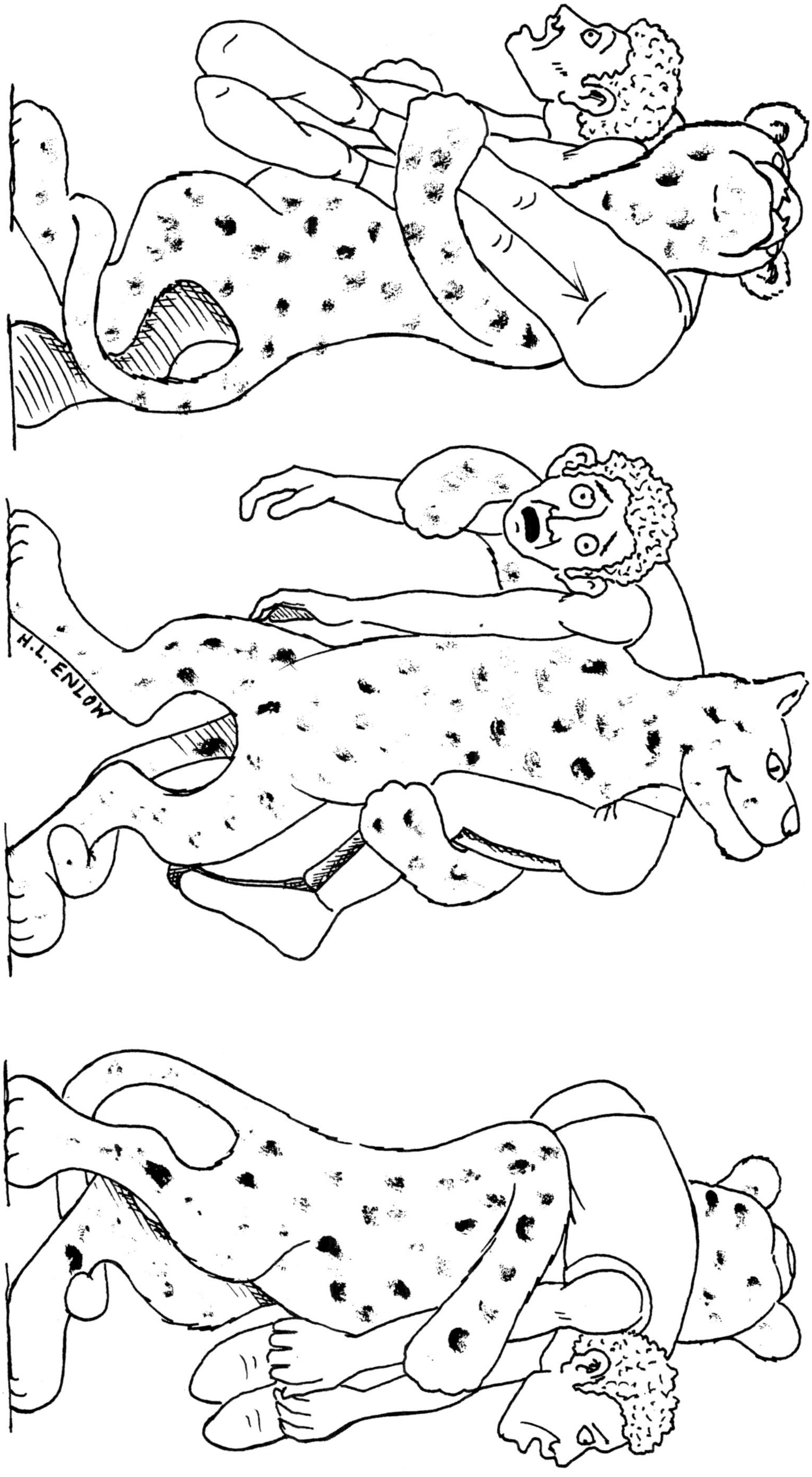

The Three Leopardo Brothers
by Harold Enlow

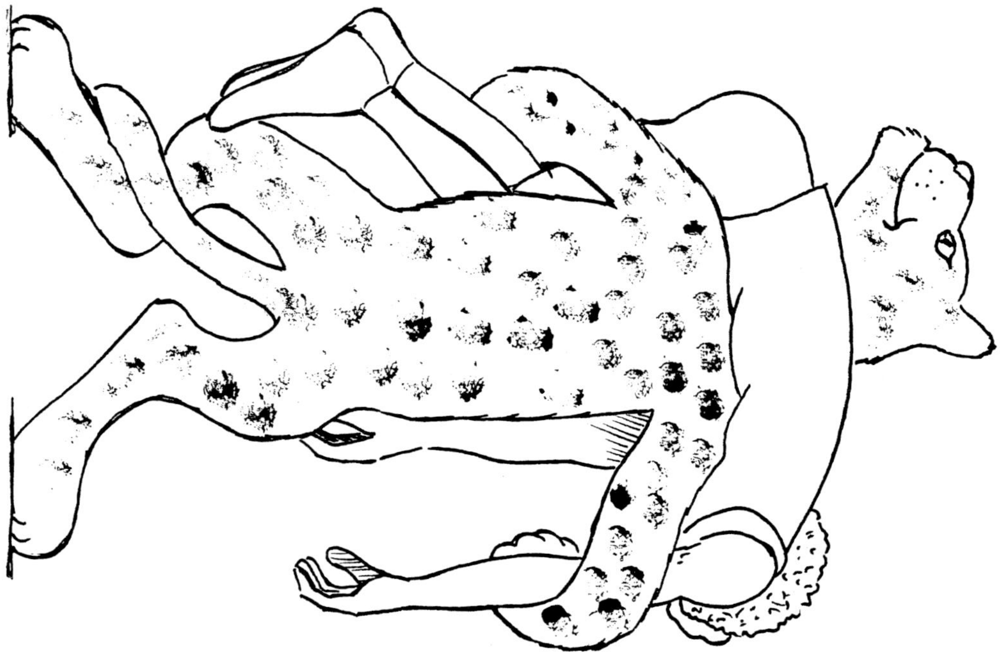

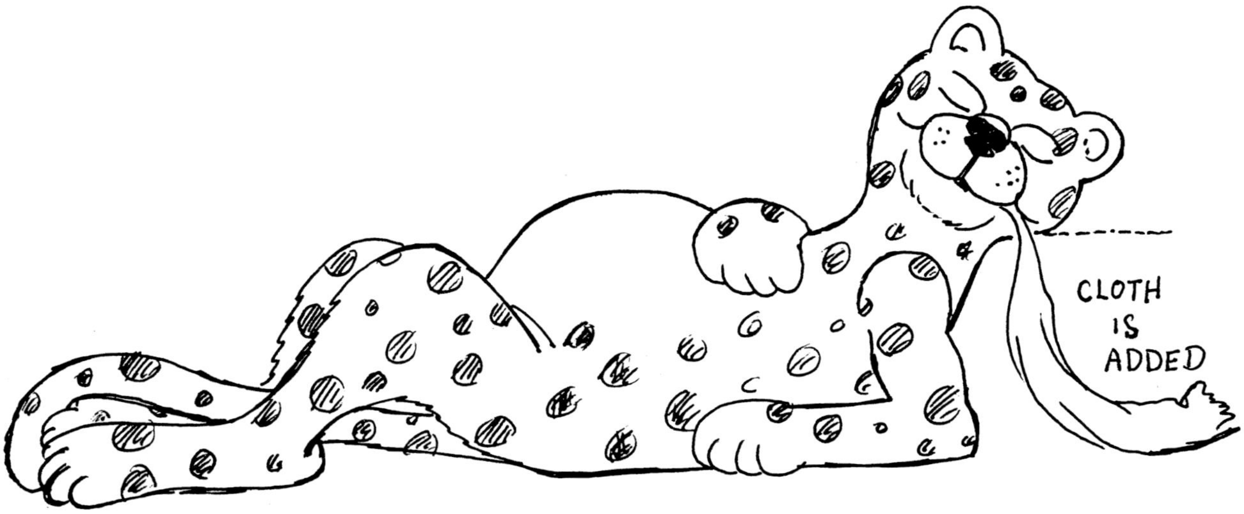

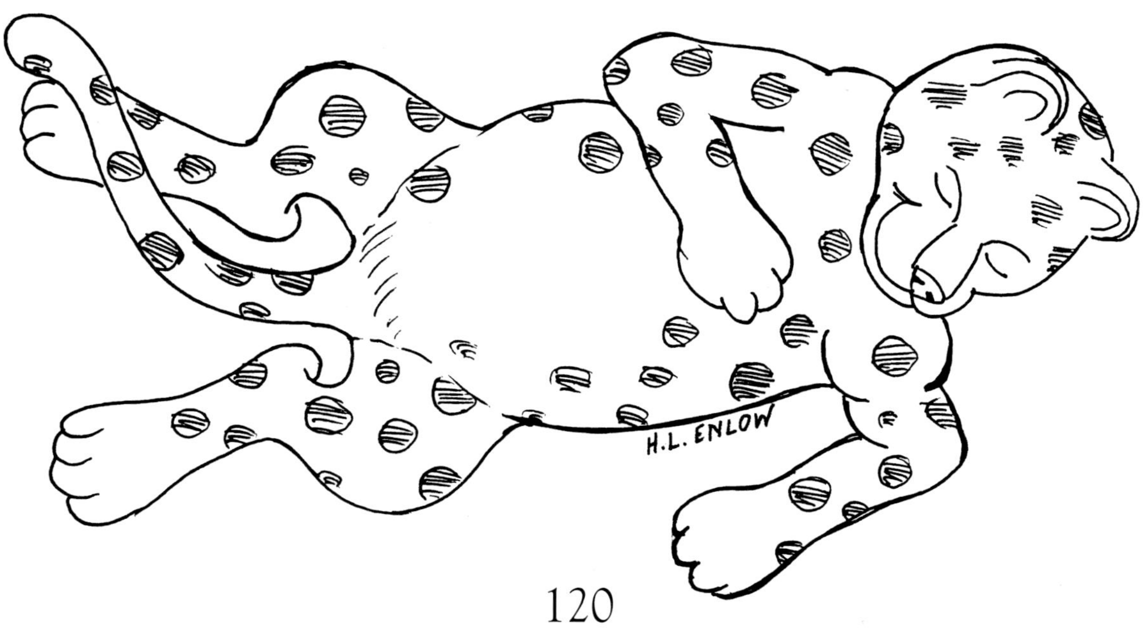

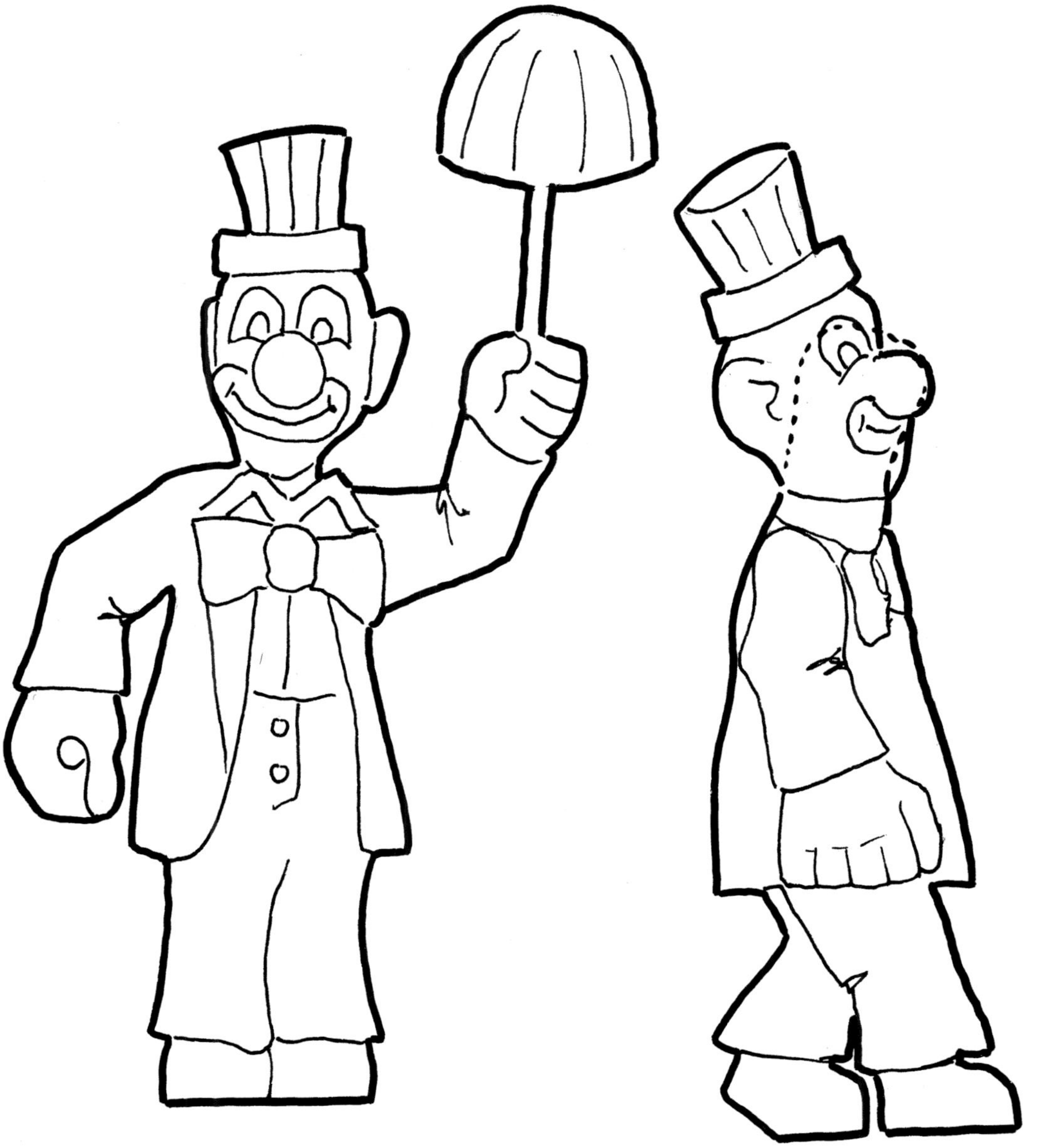

Up, Up and Away
by Randy Landen

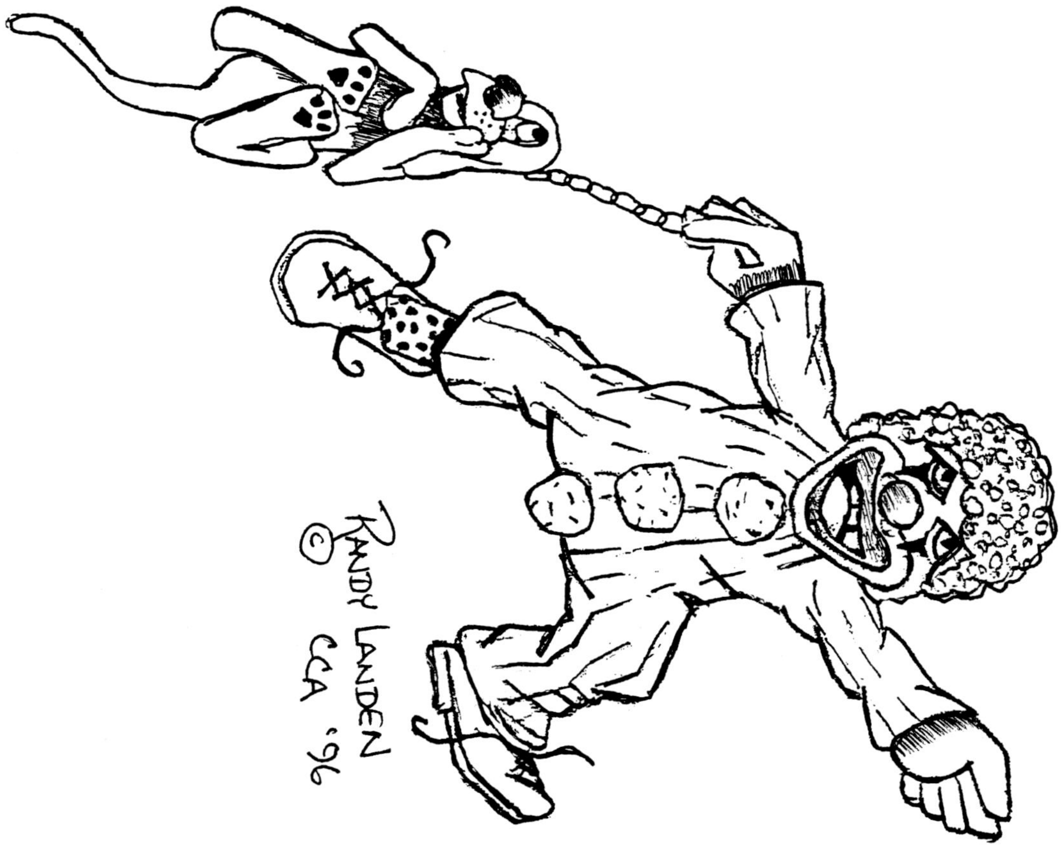

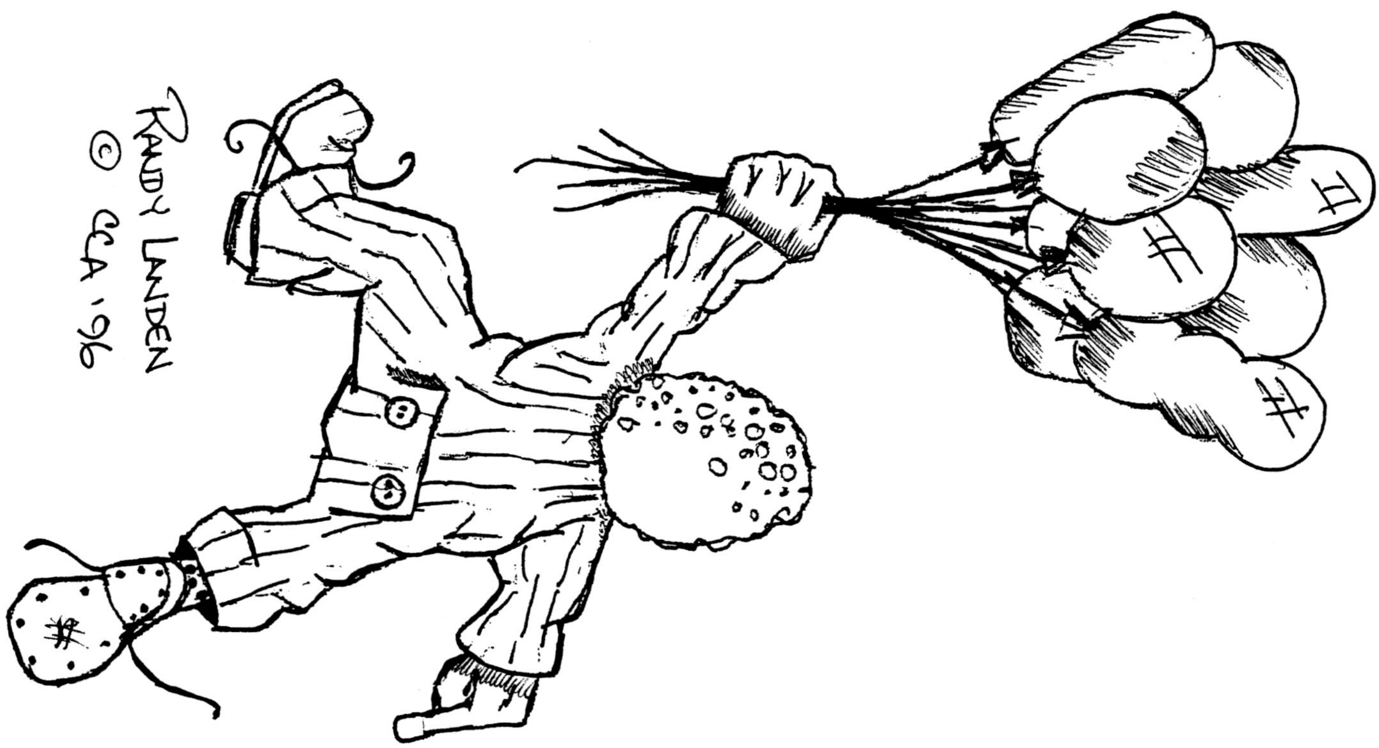

Upside Down
by Keith Morrill

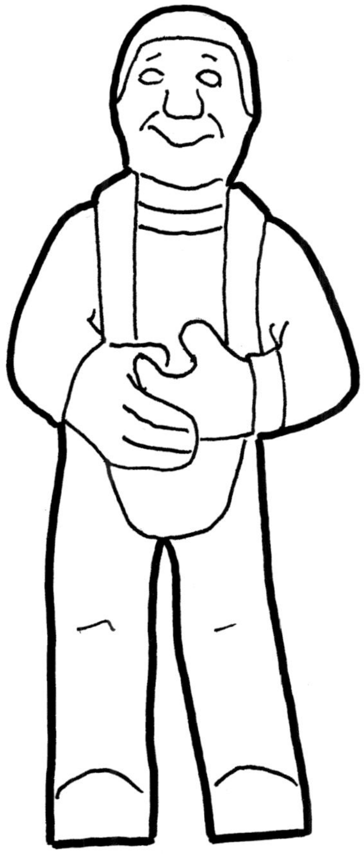

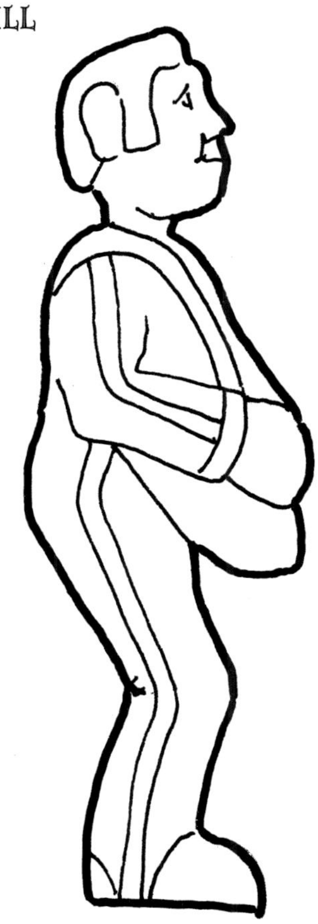

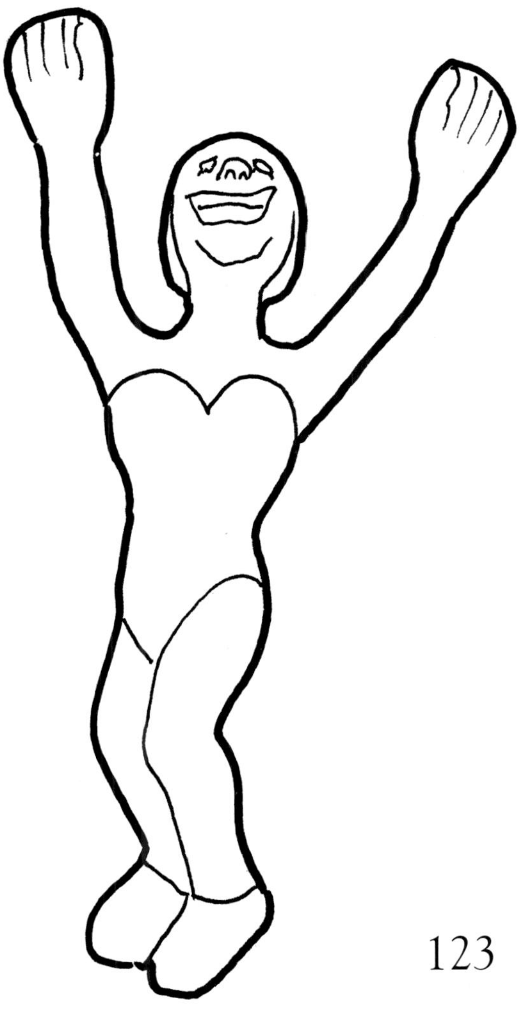

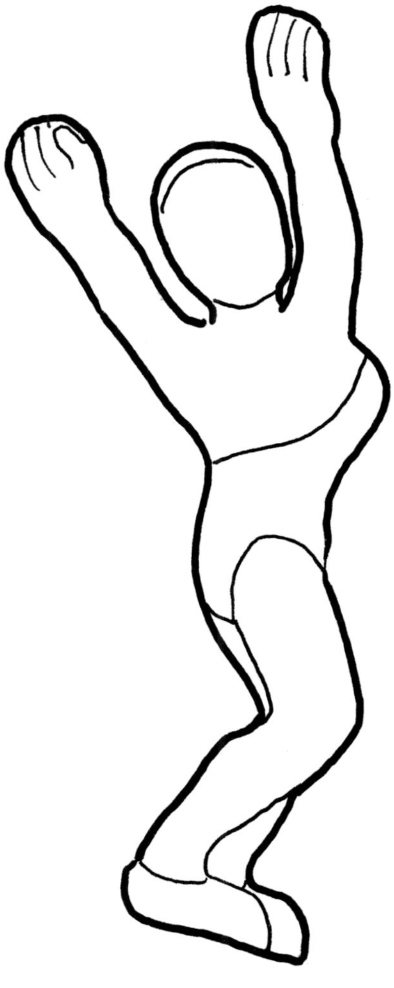